SCIENTIFIC IMAGING WITH PHOTOSHOP

Methods, Measurement, and Output

JERRY SEDGEWICK

New Riders

Scientific Imaging with Photoshop: Methods, Measurement, and Output

Jerry Sedgewick

New Riders

1249 Eighth Street
Berkeley, CA 94710
510/524-2178
510/524-2221 (fax)

Find us on the World Wide Web at: www.newriders.com
To report errors, please send a note to errata@peachpit.com

New Riders is an imprint of Peachpit, a division of Pearson Education

Project Editor: Victor Gavenda
Production Editor: Hilal Sala
Development Editor: Anne Marie Walker
Copyeditor: Anne Marie Walker
Technical Editors: Dr. Marna Ericson and Traci Bernatchy
Proofreader: Liz Welch
Compositor: Kim Scott, Bumpy Design
Indexer: Ann Rogers
Cover design: Mimi Heft
Interior design: Mimi Heft

ISBN-13: 978-0-321-51433-2
ISBN 0-321-51433-5

9 8 7 6 5 4 3 2 1

Printed and bound in the United States of America

Contents at a Glance

Table of Contents

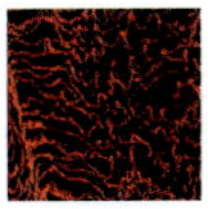

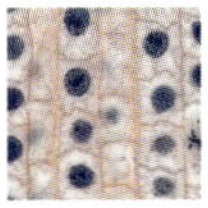

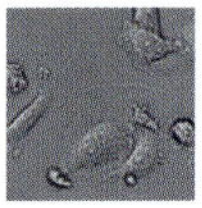

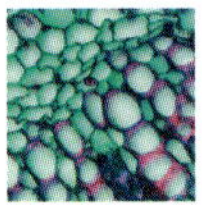

Register this Book!

Purchasing this book entitles you to more than just a couple of pounds of paper.

You're also entitled to peruse and download a good number of electronic documents which are available at the book's companion Web site. To get there, start by following this link:

www.peachpit.com/scientificimaging

This takes you to the book's page at the Peachpit Web site. Once there, click **Register your book** to log in to your account at peachpit.com (if you don't already have an account, it takes just a few seconds to create one, and it's free!). After logging in, you'll need to enter the book's ISBN code, which you'll find on the back cover. Click Submit, and you're in! You'll be taken to a list of your registered books, Find *Scientific Imaging with Photoshop* on the list, and click **Access to protected content** to be taken to the download page.

Here's what you'll find (most documents are in PDF format):

- The supplement "Tools and Functions in Photoshop"
- The bonus chapter "Scale Bars and Options for Input and Output"
- Additional imaging methods of interest to scientists, including methods for eliminating periodic noise (for example, using Fast Fourier Transform procedures to clear dots from published image)
- Sets of Photoshop actions and scripts that can be used as one-button solutions for multi-step methods
- Additional methods and actions for quantization of problem images.
- Templates for stereological probes, symbols, and patterns
- Links to relevant websites, including links to monitor calibration tests
- Complete descriptions of camera calibration and print proofing methods
- Updated colorizing methods used in fluorescence microscopy, along with updates to other methods described in the book
- One-page reference materials for methods, flowcharts and "short lists"

Further information can be found at the author's own Web site:

www.quickphotoshop.com

Acknowledgments

Thanks to all who helped me on my seven-month writing journey. Those in my family bore the brunt of a largely absent husband and father: my wife, Jan and my children, Levi and Luc. I am especially grateful to them for their patience. At the University of Minnesota, my colleagues John Oja and Gregg Amundson put in extra efforts to be available when I wasn't, and for that I am thankful. Those who commented on the text deserve praise, among these Dr. Marna Ericson, Dr. George McNamara, and Traci Bernatchy; along with Esha Bhargava who assisted with the development of material early on and several colleagues who donated images: Dr. Kalpna Gupta, Nicholette Zeliadt, Dr. Betsy Wattenberg, and Marlene Castro. The development editor, Anne Marie Walker, and the extraordinary folks at Peachpit, notably Victor Gavenda, Mimi Heft and Hilal Sala, took what was rough and made it shine.

Kudos to those named and unnamed, to parents who spawn in their children a love of learning, to those things we possess in ourselves that cannot be named or measured but keep us fascinated about the world around us, to a sense that we are held together in a human spirit of understanding that can only be the intent of God.

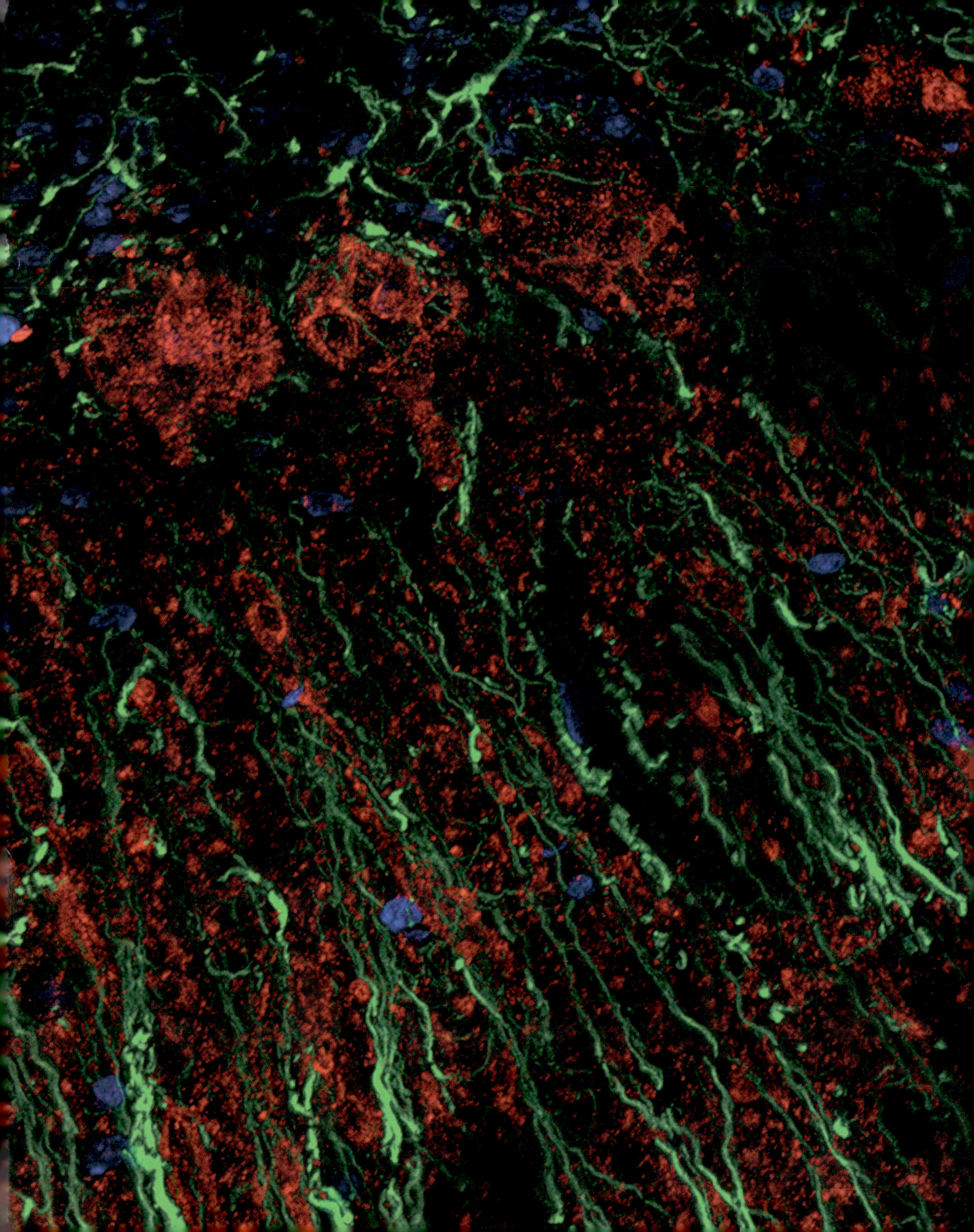

PART 1

Ethics and Background Information

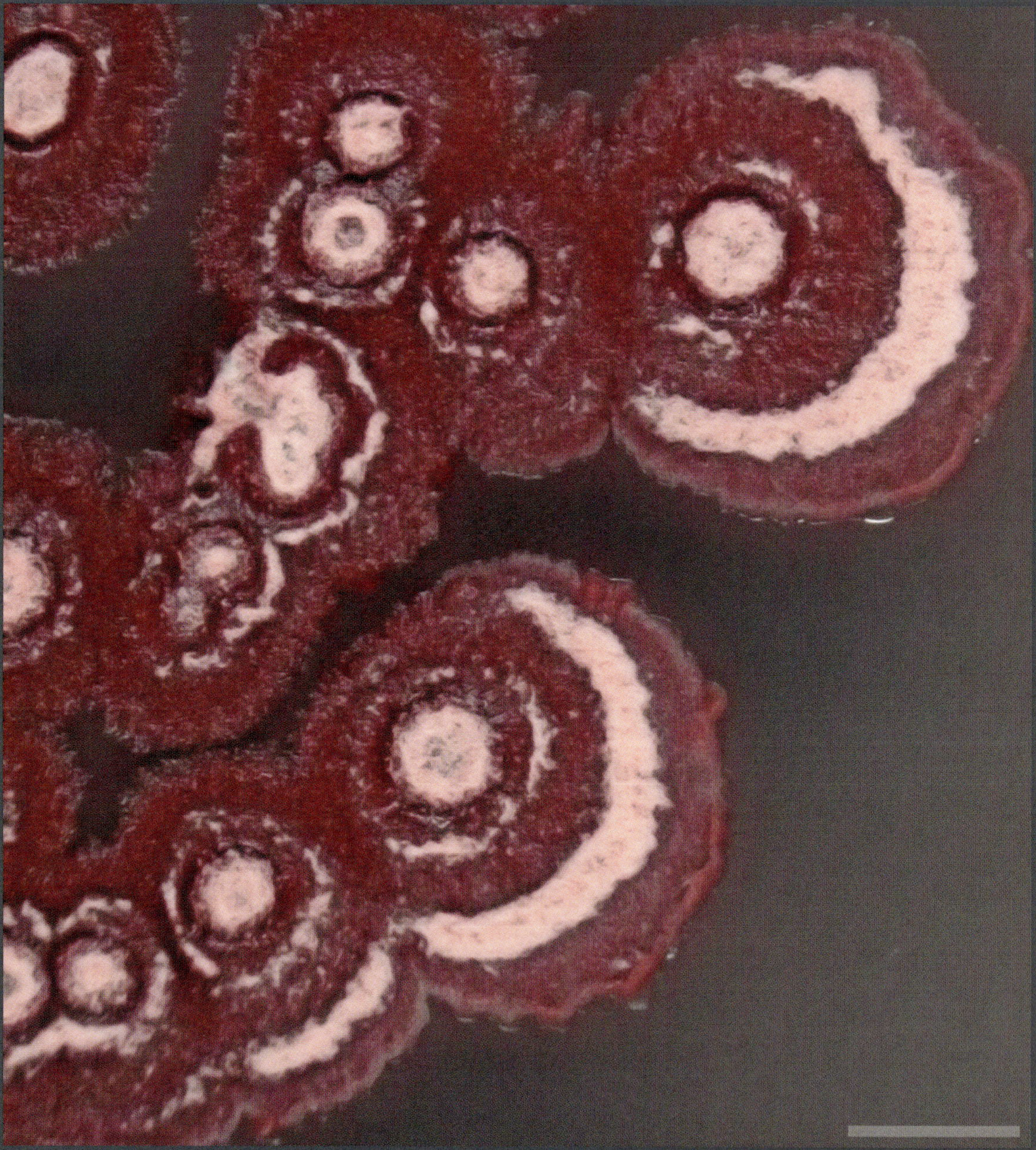

CHAPTER 1

Visual Data and Ethics

IN THE WORLD OF SCIENTIFIC RESEARCH, images fall broadly into two categories: the original image and the corrected image. The original is acquired via an imaging device without any corrections applied in software. The corrected image, often referred to as "enhanced," is often used for presentation and publication.

The distinction is crucial when suspicions arise about content in images. Because images are used as visual proof of experimental evidence, certain alterations to the content *may* be viewed as unethical. Certainly, any additions to the content from other images, or intentional alterations of visual data to accommodate the experimental hypothesis, will always be unethical. The sole means for determining the extent or the existence of alterations or additions lies in looking at the original.

A kind of reasoning can then follow: If the original is the indisputable visual evidence for experimental conclusions, *only* the original should be used. No alterations to visual data should be applied, and no corrections should be made for imaging device inconsistencies or shortcomings.

This view operates along incorrect assumptions. Out of many assumptions, the following two are most often voiced (informally):

- Imaging systems and associated instrumentation can always produce a visual representation identical to what was seen by eye (within limitations inherent to two-dimensional renditions of three-dimensional specimens or scenes) if only those using the instrumentation were more knowledgeable.

Bacteria colonies (*Streptomyces coelicolor*) in agarose, day 1 for a longitudinal, colorimetric study. Image acquired using a Leica NZ FL3 stereo microscope with a 1x lens. A SPOT RT camera and SPOT Advanced acquisition software, version 4.6 (Diagnostic Instruments, Sterling Heights, MI) were used for imaging. Color correction, sharpening, cropping, and resampling were done in Adobe Photoshop CS3 Extended, version 10.1 (Adobe Systems Incorporated, San Jose, CA). Scale bar = 10mm.

- Problems with images are often a result of poorly prepared samples or the use of suboptimal dyes and stains: Bench practices need to be improved.

While both of these assumptions are true in many instances, they are based on a false premise that the instrumentation by itself, even when used correctly, produces accurate representations.

Accurate Representation of Visual Data

Efforts must be taken to present visual data as closely as possible to what was once perceived by eye. In other words, an image offered as proof must be a true *representation* of what was once seen. Any deviation from a correct representation is a *mis*representation, and the images become varying degrees of inaccurate data.

Accurate representation more often requires post-processing than not, except in instances in which optical densities or intensities (OD/I) are measured. Post-processing is required, for the most part, because of limitations in imaging devices and associated instrumentation. These limitations include, among others, the use of anti-aliasing filters in front of light detectors in many cameras, leading to blurring of images; inclusion of noise in images as a result of approaching detection limits for instrumentation; and variability in the energy source. Thus, for any of these reasons, the original image is corrected to create a better representation of visual data.

Additional reasons for inaccurate representation of the original as a result of imaging and display devices follow:

- **Screen calibration.** The screen on which the image is viewed may not display intensities and gradients of colors and grayscale levels appropriately (**Figure 1.1A**). The gradients/intensities displayed on the screen may be inaccurate. When these images are incorrectly displayed and then presented or published, the inaccuracy is either perpetuated or the colors and contrasts change to even greater misrepresentations. Post-processing in color- and contrast-managed programs (Photoshop) will lead to better representations than the original (**Figure 1.1B**).
- **Hue shift.** If a digital camera or scanner is used and the image is in color, the raw image is subject to a phenomenon known as "hue shift" (**Figure 1.1C**) wherein the overall color shifts toward a hue,

such as red or green. This can occur even after white-balancing the camera, and the shift differs among brands of cameras, flatbed scanning devices, and other types of scanners. Post-processing corrects for color shift so that the final images are better representations of the original than the raw scans were (**Figure 1.1D**).

- **Dynamic range.** Some important features in the object or sample may be outside the dynamic range of the image recording device. These features show up as pure white or pure black in the image and contain no details (**Figure 1.1E**). Often, the researcher will amplify (or diminish) these features when acquiring the image to reveal details in other features that are darker or brighter. Without the ability to alter the relationship of grayscale values (e.g., lighten the darker values in relation to the brighter values), the image is a misrepresentation of the specimen. Again, post-processing is required to create a truer representation of the original (**Figure 1.1F**).

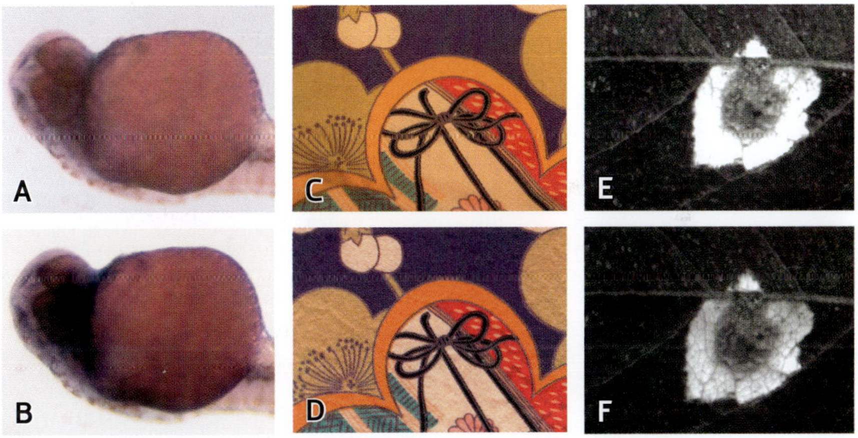

FIGURE 1.1 Specimens showing variability among imaging and viewing conditions.

When and Where Misrepresentation Takes Place

Each example cited previously is an argument for the use of post-processing even when instrumentation is used correctly. Still, this argument is not intended to dismiss the necessity for proper preparation of specimens or the need for greater education in regard to the use of imaging equipment and associated instrumentation. These devices must be used correctly before post-processing.

Also, another factor needs to be considered—how to maintain accurately represented images for various outputs, including hard copy (prints and posters), display on computer screens, inclusion in electronic documents, laptop projection at meetings, and publication. Originals must be conformed to each output, because each associated output device or software will modify the appearance of the image to the degree that the image can become inaccurate.

Thus, the potential for misrepresentation of visual evidence lies in three areas: when taking an image (acquisition), when correcting that image (post-processing), and when conforming that image to the output (conformance).

Much has been written about potential errors for a variety of imaging systems, including digital cameras, video cameras, scanning beam systems with photomultiplier (PMT) tubes, and flatbed scanners. The more frequent mistakes made in acquisition are covered in Chapter 4.

In the area of image processing, attention has been drawn either to instances in which the potential for misrepresenting visual data exists or to specific instances in which a researcher purposefully altered visual data to get a desired result. Of course, the potential to alter visual data is always a possibility, but the system of scientific publication demands repetition of experiments to corroborate results, making the system self-correcting. The use of post-processing programs like Photoshop CS3, when done correctly and when users in all labs are trained in these methods, results in changes that should be made versus those that misrepresent visual data. Thus, in this chapter, references to changes made to an image are often termed as corrections versus more widely used terms like alterations or manipulations.

Conforming images to a specific output is an inevitable part of post-processing. Changes to the image almost always require adjustments to grayscale or color tonal values, correction of the contrast, and possibly a change in both the format and mode of the image.

Note that conformance steps must be taken or images may become misrepresentations of visual data when reproduced to various outputs (**Figure 1.2**, left). While many scientists rely on hardware devices and software to interpret and interpolate visual data or on color correction professionals at printing presses, at some point the visual data *will* be changed. Ultimately, greater control over reproduction can be in the hands of scientists (**Figure 1.2,** right). That kind of control, with the aid of reference material such as the material found in this book, is more likely to prevent perhaps the greatest instance of misrepresentation in research and what has not been publicly addressed: reproduction to outputs.

FIGURE 1.2 Two reproduced images: researcher did not conform color to press output before sending image to the publisher (left); color was corrected before publishing (right). *Science*/NSF Visualization Challenge, 1st place, Photography, 2004: image courtesy of Marna Ericson, PhD.

Further Division of Areas into Categories

Images can be divided further into categories, depending on the intent of the image and the imaging system used for acquisition. Each group demands its own particular acquisition and post-processing treatment.

For example, if the visual data is intended for measurement of OD/I, changes to images acquired from that imaging system must be kept as close to the original image as possible, with only a few "allowable" post-processing methods and only the necessary methods for conformance to outputs (assuming the original was acquired on an imaging system that results in a linear distribution of grayscale or color values).

On the other hand, if the image is intended for visualization (in this sense, a conscious enhancement of visual data to draw attention to experimental phenomena, such as an image destined for a publication's cover or a cartoon model) or any subsequent quantification (except OD/I), many more changes are allowable. In the case of quantification, these changes are absolutely necessary for separating measured features from the surrounding areas, often referred to as "background."

The following categories broadly separate the intent and/or the means for acquiring the image:

- **OD/I from flatbed scanners.** Images made for measurement of brightness/darkness levels. These include electrophoretic samples done in the field of molecular biology (**Figure 1.3A**).
- **OD/I from camera and scanned beam systems.** Images made for measurement of brightness/darkness levels, or for the measurement of color, not acquired from flatbed scanners. These include samples imaged via microscopes, confocal instruments, electron microscopy, x-ray devices, magnetic resonance imaging, and so on.
- **Representation.** Images made from any imaging device for purposes of creating an accurate representation of what was once seen (**Figure 1.3B**).
- **Quantification/Visualization.** Images made through conscious alteration of data using pseudocoloring, binarizing, and other techniques to separate relevant visual information from the background (**Figure 1.3C**).

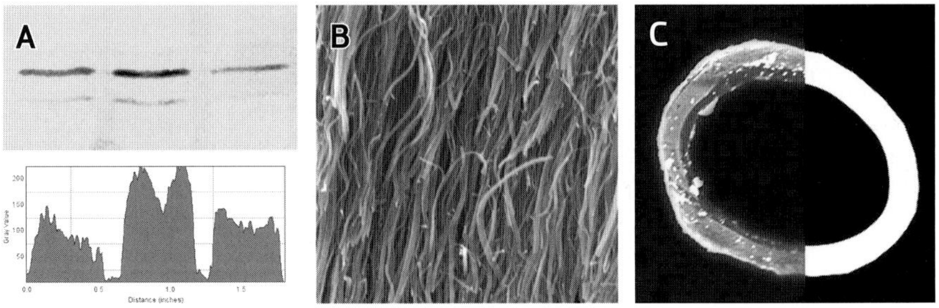

FIGURE 1.3 Three image types: specimen for OD/I (**A**), representative specimen (**B**), and sample intended for quantification with right side binarized (**C**).

Author Guidelines

Following specific guidelines for acquisition, post-processing, and conformance ensures accurate representation of what was once seen by eye. Because part of the aim of research is to report or publish, the "gold standard" for ethical guidelines is found in the author guidelines from major scientific publications.

But the division of visual data into areas and categories will *not* be found in author guidelines from major scientific publications, at least to date. General guidelines are set forth in scientific publications to varying degrees of detail, but often these lack specifics for *when* and *where* potential for misrepresentation may exist. That lack of clarity leads to varying degrees of interpretation from one investigator to another and inconsistent responses from journal reviewers and editors.

The first three chapters of this book, based on author guidelines from major publications, have been written as a first attempt to clarify *when* and *where* visual data can potentially be misrepresented when specific steps are not followed or when changes are made that are not allowed or discouraged.

Using Standards and References

In addition to when and where potential for misrepresentation exists, there is also the question of *how*: How can representative images be made while preserving a consistent approach to imaging?

The answer isn't simple. In the best of situations, grayscale and color values can be objectively determined by fitting the imaging system (or the image, or the data derived from the image) to an *external* standard. Ideally, that standard is a calibrated object with known values. The imaging system can then be calibrated to the standard, and presto, all images from that system are also fitted to the known values. This is typical for situations in which OD/I measurements are derived from images acquired with self-calibrating, scanner systems.

However, other situations present difficulties. A calibrated standard may not be available, as in fluorescence imaging. Calibrated standards may work in an ideal world but not in the real world, such as in colors that can be defined by standards but do not exist with the same purity in a sample. The actual specimen may change in grayscale or color value as a result of preparation techniques and inherent factors, making a calibrated standard useless. Labeling of specimens may vary in intensity, making it more important to calibrate to an internal reference that is part of the specimen versus a calibrated standard. For these reasons and others, the use of an external, calibration standard is not always the answer for a consistent approach to imaging, which is what is desired for reproducibility and correct representations.

A consistent external reference—instead of a standard—may need to be substituted for a calibrated standard to provide a predictable reference value against which colors can be corrected or to which energy source intensities or exposure consistencies can be tracked over time. As in the calibrated standard, the external reference can be included with the specimen or taken at the beginning or end of an imaging session.

The reference can be *internal*: Specimens may have intrinsic values that can be ratioed against each other, or a consistent grayscale or color value may be found within the specimen, eliminating the need for either a calibration standard or external reference.

When no standards or references are available, distributions of grayscale or color values (histograms) can be matched to either a "perfect," reference image, or images can be fit to the dynamic range of the imaging instrument (when acquiring images) or fit to a common histogram (post-processing). In that manner, all images are uniform.

As long as a reasoned approach is chosen for the type of specimen and the intent of the image, representative images can be produced, and imaging procedures can be duplicated. A summary of the approach to consistent imaging through the use of calibrated standards, internal references, or situations in which no standards or references exist is shown in **Table 1.1**.

TABLE 1.1 **Determining Image Grayscale or Color Values by Standards/References**

INTERNAL STANDARDS/ REFERENCES	EXTERNAL STANDARDS/ REFERENCES	NO STANDARDS/ REFERENCES
Consistent reference value is part of specimen	Calibrated standard included with images of specimens or taken by itself at each imaging session	Histogram is matched visually, automatically, or through measurements to most representative image of specimen
Specimen values are ratioed	Consistent reference included with images of specimens or taken by itself at each imaging session	All images are equalized to a common histogram or dynamic range

CHAPTER 2

General Guidelines for All Images

WHILE GUIDELINES WILL VARY depending on the category to which images belong, some overarching ethical methods and procedures apply to all images, with few exceptions. These rules can be classified according to the three areas of acquisition, post-processing, and conformance.

Acquisition is not normally considered in discussions about digital imaging ethics, but following guidelines for acquisition is as critical as it is for post-processing. Using incorrect methods when acquiring images can obscure relevant visual information and place untoward emphasis on the desired outcome, which is often the accusation directed at those who use Photoshop. This obfuscation and emphasis is seen mostly when the brightness range of the image exceeds the dynamic range of the acquisition device, which is all too typical of published images of fluorescently labeled specimens. It is also seen in brightfield images when colors do not match the specimen, often due to incorrect acquisition procedures.

Post-processing depends on correct acquisition procedures. But that does not eliminate the necessity for post-processing. As discussed in Chapter 1, "Visual Data and Ethics," several anomalies of digital imaging *require* correction. When *not* corrected, images may arguably become misrepresentations of visual data. Two corrections that are critical include restoring colors to those that mimic the specimen (color correction) and cropping the image to focus attention on relevant features.

High-magnification image of a feather showing repetition of structures, acquired on a Zeiss Axioplan 2 microscope using a 10x lens (N.A. 0.3) X 2 Zoom. A Spot 1 camera and SPOT Advanced, version 4.1 software (Diagnostic Instruments, Sterling Heights, MI) were used for acquisition. Image was color toned, rescaled, resampled, and conformed to printing press, reproducible colors in Photoshop CS3 Extended (Adobe Systems Incorporated, San Jose, CA). Scale bar = 110 microns.

Conformance of images to outputs is another critical area often overlooked. Again, a potential misrepresentation of images often occurs. Here misrepresentation can occur in the form of pixilated images and incorrect color reproduction, among other problems. Photoshop provides the tools to maintain correct representations when images are reproduced.

Guidelines

The guidelines that are followed for acquisition, post-processing, and conformance are outlined in **Table 2.1**. The rules concerning what *cannot* be done are also included in the table, as well as the most frequently observed instances in which methods and procedures are *not* followed. Each entry in the table is then described in this chapter in the order in which it is listed.

These guidelines, when followed, conform to author guidelines for selected publications. However, no written guidelines for these publications mention acquisition or conformance; only permitted and

TABLE 2.1 General Guidelines for Correct Acquisition/Permitted Alterations of Visual Data

ACQUISITION: REQUIRED	POST-PROCESSING: PERMITTED	CONFORMANCE: REQUIRED	POST-PROCESSING: WHAT CAN'T/ SHOULDN'T BE DONE
Prepare specimen appropriately	Make global changes	Bit depth decrease	Spot changes
Optimize imaging system	Apply same change to related images	Set white/black limits	Transfer of features
Turn off auto-filtering	Crop & Straighten	Image size changes	Intentional manipulation for specific outcome
Use greatest bit depth	Change mode	Color: RGB to CMYK	Subsampling
Avoid clipping of significant features	Bit depth increase	File format changes	Use of Brightness/ Contrast tool
Color: white balance manually	Color correction	Documentation	Copying/pasting
Noisy image: frame average	Color noise		
Save as non-lossy format	Merging and Image Stack functions		
Archive original images	Symbols, lettering, scale bars		
Use controls			

prohibited post-processing methods are mentioned. Thus, in the table, only post-processing steps are shown as permitted (or not). Acquisition and conformance guidelines are shown as "required."

These guidelines apply to all images: Specific guidelines for the kind of image, whether it is intended for optical density/intensity (OD/I) measurement, as a representative image, or for quantification/visualization, are discussed in Chapter 3, "Guidelines for Specific Types of Images."

Acquisition

Guidelines for acquisition ensure the best possible image quality. Shortcuts are taken when users are unaware of proper methods or workgroup requirements demand less than optimal images (most often to save hard disk space) and varying degrees of misrepresentation result. Attention to each of the areas discussed in the following sections will lead to the best specimen representations.

Specimen Preparation

Each imaging modality requires that specimens be prepared in specific ways. It is of utmost importance that scientists and technicians understand the shortcomings and advantages of specimen preparation for correct interpretation of experimental results gained through visual information, even when these preparations are being done by external agencies.

For *in vitro* preparation when using microscopes, not only does the experiment often require that correct staining procedures be followed, but it requires the correct mounting on microscope slides. The coverslip must be a correct thickness (0.17 millimeters for most applications unless an objective with a correction collar is used), and for most applications, the mounting media must match (or exceed) the refractive index of the medium used between the microscope lens and the microscope slide (air, water, or oil).

When in vitro specimens are not prepared correctly, the results are often detected by eye because it is difficult to focus on the specimen or features that are poorly resolved. These features may not be positively identifiable, resulting in misrepresentation.

In vivo imaging requires that living animals and cells be in a state of health (or sickness) that is not compromised by anesthesia, dosing, or phototoxicity. The use of tissue section comparisons and careful monitoring of animal health can contribute to understanding the level of compromise. For cell damage due to phototoxicity, infrared wavelengths are used for imaging. Volumes of books have been written on specimen preparation and understanding what contributes to the visual data. It is up to each person in his or her respective field to understand appropriate specimen preparation methods.

Optimize Imaging System

The instrument to which the imaging device is attached, along with lens elements exposed to the environment, must be kept clean to obtain optimal resolution. Maintenance of moving parts is also important to ensure that optical filters and other devices move in or out of position appropriately. While this procedure may appear obvious, it is sometimes overlooked when problems arise with resolving details, resulting in the misrepresentation or potential misinterpretation of features.

● **More:** *The procedure for Koehler illumination can be found at www.quickphotoshop.com.*

Focusing and alignment of light sources for microscopy, and of beams for electron microscopy and other imaging modalities, provide consistent exposure patterns over time and improved resolution. In the former instance, for brightfield (dark objects against a lighter background) microscopy, Koehler illumination techniques are used, because light scattering at the edges of features can create artificial effects (**Figure 2.1**, left). Proper focusing of light on the specimen, on the other hand, does not introduce effects that could be mistaken for real features (**Figure 2.1**, right).

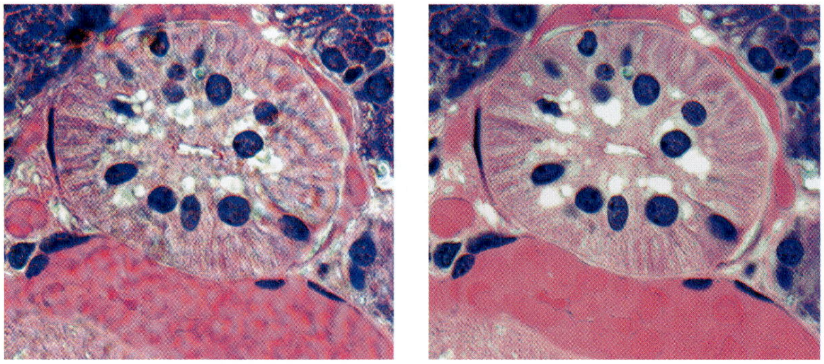

FIGURE 2.1 Brightfield images showing the effect of poorly focused light (left) and light focused through the Koehler illumination procedure (right).

Turn Off Auto-filtering

Especially with imaging devices made for the consumer market (as opposed to the scientific market), the implementation of sharpening, blurring, noise removal, and other filters may be done automatically. In other words, those who use these imaging devices must

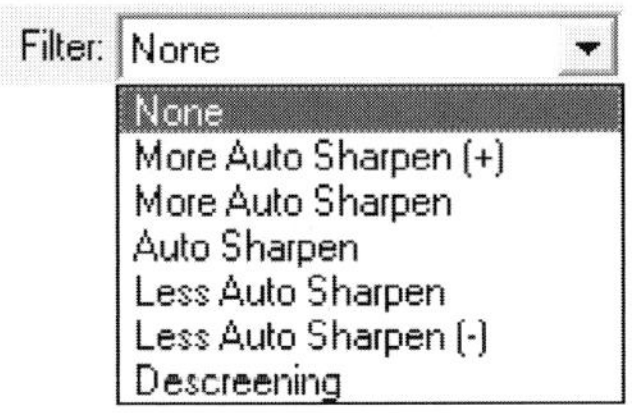

FIGURE 2.2 An example of the filtering options commonly available in flatbed scanner software.

consciously disable auto-filtering to obtain noncorrected visual data. Often, that means the user must investigate the default settings for the imaging device by examining every dialog box in the associated imaging software and assuming that auto-filtering is more likely to occur than not (**Figure 2.2**).

These filters not only alter the representation of visual data, but depending on the category for which the image is destined, may create a misrepresentation of the visual data.

The sharpening filter is a good example. Sharpening filters can alter darkness and lightness levels at the borders of features to varying degrees, which can potentially lead to erroneous readings when images are destined for OD/I.

Bit Depth

Detectors are capable of collecting increasing amounts of photons until a threshold is reached, and then all pixels (picture elements) become clipped (pure white) in a grayscale or color image. The term *bit depth* is a means for describing the upper threshold, or limit (as well as the inferred lower limit, which is zero). The actual number used for bit depth is an exponent of 2. So, an 8-bit camera is capable of producing 2^8 "units," which means that an 8-bit camera has a 256 unit range. Practically speaking, in an 8-bit image, each pixel is assigned a tonal value with 0 as the lower limit and 255 as the upper limit (including 0, the total is 256).

The unit of measurement is confusing. It is not a reference to how many photons the detector can collect, but rather a reference to the resulting levels of black-to-midtone-to-white in the image (**Figure 2.3**). The gray levels are assigned (mapped) pixel by pixel via the camera system. The number of photons striking the detector is not known unless a photon counter is available on the system.

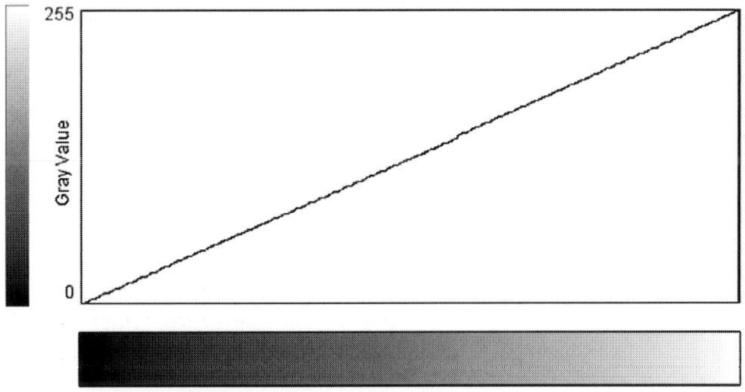

FIGURE 2.3 For an 8-bit image, grayscale levels are assigned to each pixel from 0 to 255 with 0 as black and 255 as white.

■ **Note:** *Physically covering each detector with a filter is not the only means for creating color images. Three images can be taken separately, first with a red filter, then green, and then blue; or a prism can separate the three colors to three chips, a method often used with video cameras.*

DETECTING COLOR

The detectors that make up rows and columns on a chip (the flat substrate for the detector in a digital camera), often numbering in the millions, can have a filter physically placed over each so that only photons at discrete colors pass through. Three filters are used in a pattern—red, green, and blue. Because all colors of light are made from mixing the primaries of red, green, and blue (RGB), RGB values in a scene or specimen can be acquired and then interpreted to produce a means for creating up to millions of colors. Images are saved with the three primary colors as components or channels (**Figure 2.4**).

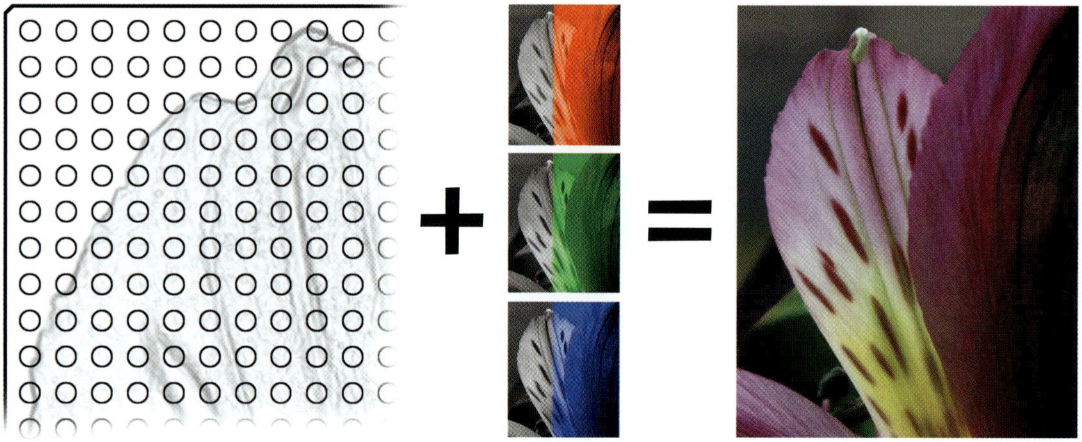

FIGURE 2.4 Red, green, and blue channels are combined to make a color image.

■ **Note:** *Color can also result after acquiring an image in grayscale: A single color, or multiple colors, can be assigned to grayscale tones for one or more channels.*

The channels are in essence grayscale channels that are colorized red, green, and blue before being combined. Each channel represents a grayscale image with intrinsic bit depth. Three channels at a particular bit depth are combined to create three times the bit depth of the image derived from the chip. Thus, three 8-bit channels equal 24-bits, three channels at 16-bit equal 48-bits, and so on.

8-BIT VS. 12- OR 16-BIT

A photodetector can collect more than 8 bits per channel and thus possesses the capacity to collect a wider range of photons. Consequently, the detector's dynamic range is expanded to include brighter whites, and the expanded range intrinsically contains more divisions of gray values. These camera systems are often rated as 12-bit or 16-bit.

The advantages of a greater dynamic range and more discrete divisions of gray values for 12- and 16-bit imaging systems make these devices more desirable to use. The expanded range is especially useful because, in post-processing, every correction to an image leads to a loss of visual data. Mathematical computations involved in changing visual data must round up or down gray and color level values, leading to rounding errors. The rounding errors can be regarded as inconsequential, depending on the accuracy desired. With 8-bit images and a smaller total of gray value numbers, the errors will be greater than with the larger set of numbers available with both 12- and 16-bit detectors. Thus, 12- or 16-bit images are therefore more desirable for this so-called "headroom."

Another advantage to higher bit-depth detectors lies in OD/I, where the increased dynamic range may allow for measurement of a broader range of dark-to-bright within a sample. But perhaps the greater advantage lies in the fact that the differences in gray values are farther apart on a 12- or 16-bit scale, which makes the resulting OD/I data more convincing.

If an option exists for imaging at a bit depth greater than 8 bits or 8 bits/channel, choose the greater bit depth, even though storage for larger file sizes may become a concern. OD/I measurements gain greater acceptance by reviewers, and images are less likely to lose discernable visual data.

Clipping

When insufficient photons from specimens strike the sensor because features are too dark, the resultant pixels appear as pure black. Conversely, when too many photons "fill" a sensor where features are too bright, the resultant pixels appear as pure white. Those pure whites and pure blacks are referred to as clipped.

■ **Note:** *Detritus included with the specimen can be clipped (these extraneous features are more often called "artifacts").*

All dark and bright areas outside the dynamic range of the imaging system can only be measured at the upper and lower threshold values (0 and 255 if an 8-bit detector is used). While some features in a specimen may actually contain darkness or brightness levels at "threshold" values, it is never assured that those values do not also include parts of the specimen that are brighter or darker than threshold values. Thus, images are acquired at values *less* than the upper limit—and *more* than the lower limit—of the dynamic range, which would be 1 and 254 for an 8-bit detector (versus 0 and 255). Otherwise, if visual data is measured for OD/I, incorrect data will likely result. A second result of clipping lies in the irretrievable loss of detail in what can be important features of the image. It is best to retain all the visual information so that these details are not lost.

With scientific camera systems, often an overlay called a LUT (*look up table*: a reference to the method in which colors are assigned to grayscale values) can be activated during the image taking process to reveal areas in the sample in which clipped values exist. Frequently, LUTs are created to show a red color when pixel values are too white and blue when pixel values are too dark (**Figure 2.5**, left). Acquisition settings that control brightness and darkness can be adjusted to "fit" the image within the dynamic range of the instrument, which is easily determined by the disappearance of red or blue (**Figure 2.5**, right).

FIGURE 2.5 The image of collagen fibers on the left is a duplicate of the image on the right. The image on the left includes a color overlay, or LUT.

When significant features are clipped and no details exist to identify structures, the loss of visual features may result in misidentification. If the features are stained, confusion about levels of staining will result because that information is gone. This misrepresentation of visual data can lead to false assumptions when experiments are repeated in other labs.

Color: White Balancing for Brightfield Images

Two ways of imaging specimens can be broadly defined as brightfield imaging and darkfield imaging.

Brightfield imaging, as mentioned earlier, consists of all specimens or imaging methods that result in images of dark features on bright surroundings. These would be standard environmental scenes taken when light illuminates darker objects. In microscopy, these are darker stains taken against lighter backgrounds over a specific dimension in *x*- and *y*-axes—what is called the "field of view," or "field."

■ **Note:** *Darkfield images, especially when using fluorescently labeled specimens, do not typically require white balancing when colors are intense.*

Darkfield imaging is the opposite occurrence: bright features on a dark background, like bright stars against the field of a dark sky. In microscopy, it is becoming increasingly common that specimens are stained with a fluorescing substance that glows against darker tissue,

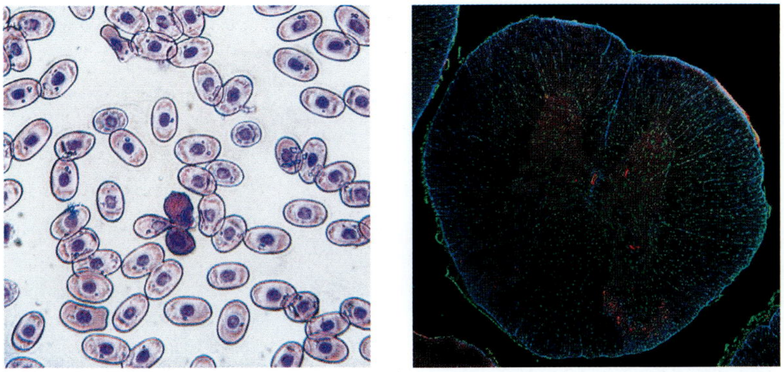

FIGURE 2.6 The image on the left comprises dark and light values against a lighter background, or a brightfield image. The image on the right shows bright features on a dark background, or a darkfield image.

so fluorescence imaging is a significant subset of darkfield imaging (**Figure 2.6**).

COLOR TEMPERATURE

In brightfield imaging, the color of the illumination source affects the colors of the specimen or scene. If, for example, the color of the illumination source is yellowish, the colors of features in the specimen or scene will reflect or transmit the yellower illumination. The result will be a pollution of all the colors in the features, each showing a shift in hue.

The color of an illumination source can be compared to a black pot that is heated by fire. As it heats up, its color turns from red to orange to yellow to white and even to blue—each color relating to the temperature of the heat. This scenario has been translated into the "heat" of the illumination source creating similar colors—called the *color temperature*. Color temperatures in the illumination source can change over time and can depend on the influence on the light from reflective objects in the scene, such as the effect of reddish light at dusk from light reflecting off atmospheric particles. The color temperature can also be influenced by psychologically "cooler" colors like green.

■ **Note:** *A neutral (meaning that equal amounts of red, green, and blue exist) gray color (called 18% gray for its reflectance of light) can also be used as a reference.*

When brightfield specimens and scenes are imaged, the imaging device must take into account the color temperature of the illumination source, or incorrect and polluted colors will result (**Figure 2.7**, left). Imaging devices determine how to interpret colors in the specimen or scene by using a uniformly illuminated white field as a reference. Because white is made up of equal amounts of the three primary colors—red, green, and blue—an interpretation of how far each of these colors needs to be shifted to obtain white is determined against this reference, and then applied to the colors in the entire image. This is called white balancing, a reference to the use of white to correct or balance the spectrum of colors in the specimen or scene (**Figure 2.7**, right).

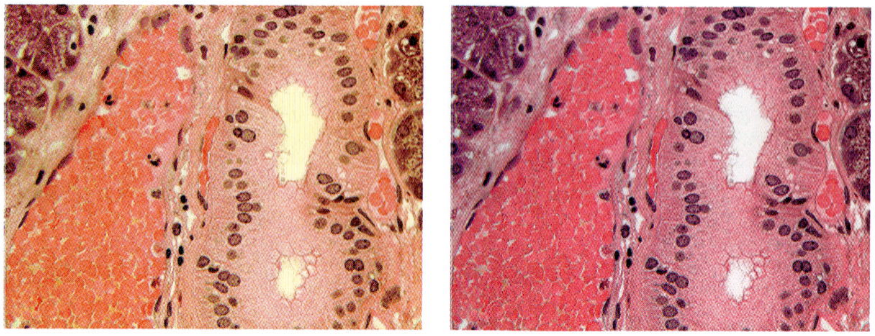

FIGURE 2.7 Color temperature in the left image shows the addition of a yellow cast when white balancing isn't done: On the right is a specimen illuminated at 3200K after white balancing and minimal color correction have been done.

AUTO WHITE BALANCING VS. MANUAL

Cameras can contain automated functions to guess the color temperature of the light source, the light source can be manually identified, or the white balancing can be done manually. The manual method is the most accurate and is preferred for accurate color interpretation. If white balancing is not done or if automated functions are relied on, the color temperature of the light source may be misinterpreted and a misrepresentation of colors will result.

Thus, it is crucial that white balancing be done for each change of lighting conditions. If the power of illumination on a bulb is turned up or down (attenuated), manual white balancing must be done at each power setting.

When white balancing cannot be done for a specimen or scene, white or neutral gray balancing can be done later in post-processing if a white or neutral gray object is part of the field. For a neutral gray object, neutral gray cards and references can be purchased from professional camera stores.

White balancing may not completely eliminate the pollution of colors with a predominant hue. Camera manufacturers decide on the representation of color differently with different algorithms, each leading to overall hue shifts that must be corrected in post-processing. Also, problems with more than one illumination source or with the effect of reflective (mirroring) objects can introduce colors that can only be corrected in post-processing. Thus, the original colors of the raw image cannot be completely relied on as "true" colors until they are further balanced in post-processing.

Noisy Image: Frame Averaging

Detector noise is prevalent when samples are especially dim, a far too common experience when using fluorescently labeled specimens or when acquiring astronomy images. This kind of noise is a result of detectors heating up (for CCD chips) or because applied voltage is excessive (e.g., photomultiplier tubes, often used for detecting at low-light levels).

Noise coming from the detector causes neighboring pixels to be arbitrarily darker or lighter in areas where pixel brightness should be identical (**Figure 2.8**, left). Because luminance values of individual pixels often vary dramatically when polluted by noise, techniques for reducing noise must be implemented to yield readings bereft of high standard deviation, which are essential for OD/I measurements. Noise reduction also reveals more details, which are necessary for an accurate representation of the image (**Figure 2.8**, right).

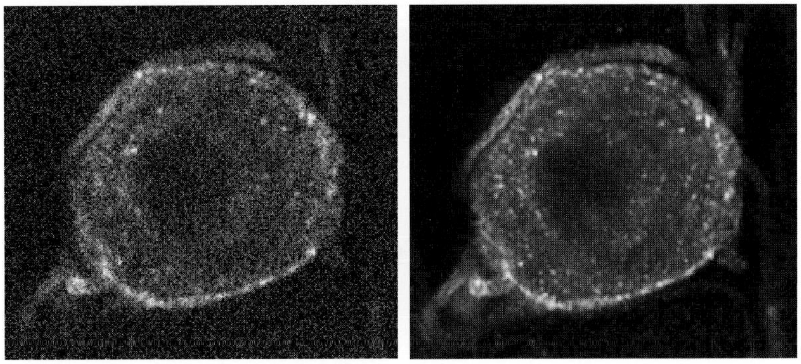

FIGURE 2.8 Frame averaging was used on the image of a cell (left), thus reducing the noise that was originally present (right).

This kind of noise changes rapidly in random patterns over time. Therefore, if images are acquired sequentially of the same specimen, each image (or frame) will contain its own varied pattern of noise. The frames can be averaged together to reduce noise. This is known as frame or Kalman averaging.

The ability to frame average may be available in acquisition software. If not, more than one image can be acquired and then averaged together later in Photoshop CS3 as a part of its image stack statistics feature (see Chapter 6, "Opening Images and Initial Steps"). The efficacy of frame averaging depends exponentially on the number of images used: Four averaged images reduce noise to 1/2, 16 averaged images reduce noise to 1/4, and so on.

NON-LOSSY IMAGES

Once the image is taken, the image must be saved in a format that retains all the visual data. The most common file format is TIFF (Tagged Information File Format). Other formats that retain all the visual data are often proprietary to a particular manufacturer, such as the Canon (CR2) Raw file format. File formats that retain all the visual data are often large files that require plenty of disk space for storage.

To reduce large file sizes, several formats were created that incorporate file compression. These formats are classified as lossy or non-lossy—the former a reference to a file format that relies on the elimination of visual data to reduce file size (like JPEG), and the latter a file format that reduces file size without the loss of data (e.g., a Lempel-Ziv-Welch—LZW—compression of a TIFF image). The most universal lossy format is the JPEG format.

Because files saved as JPEGs result in a loss of visual data, this format could potentially contribute to misrepresentation and therefore should *not* be used. However, the caveat is that images can be compressed as JPEGs at varying strengths. The lowest strength compression removes only the elements of an image that are not visible to the human eye. Higher strength compression can break up images and cause a reduction in detail, which is most noticeable as a reduction in discrete colors (**Figure 2.9**, top). Low strength compression (or no compression) maintains image detail and color integrity (**Figure 2.9**, bottom).

FIGURE 2.9 An image saved using lossy compression at high strength (top) and at low strength (bottom).

If a JPEG is saved from the camera system as the original image, each time it is saved over itself compression will occur again, leading to cumulative loss of visual data. If JPEG-compressed images are a requirement in a workgroup, the original JPEGs should be resaved as TIFFs or in the Photoshop format while they are being edited.

If computer hard disk space is an issue and is the reason for saving as JPEGs, consider DVD or CD storage as options.

Archiving

The use of DVD-ROMs or CD-ROMs—when not rewritable—guarantees the integrity of raw data file archiving. The general rule for workgroups is to save files to at least two DVDs or CDs and to store them in different locations or keep one and give the other to the lab manager/supervisor to ensure the preservation of the raw data.

When reviewers or editors question the visual data, the original file is often requested for confirmation. Also, when original images contain settings for camera systems and instruments (called metadata), archiving the original image can be crucial if the metadata was not recorded in lab books. Additionally, the stored, original settings can be referred to when acquiring images in future experiments.

Archiving these instrument and camera settings is done for retaining evidence, but recording that information also satisfies Good Laboratory Practices (**Figure 2.10**).

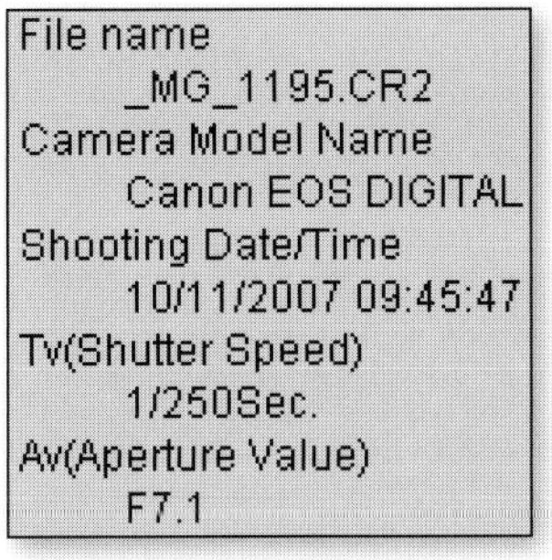

FIGURE 2.10 Example of metadata from a Canon 350D camera, which is recorded when the image is acquired.

Controls

Results gained through scientific imaging require the same rigorous use of controls as those used in experiments. Both positive and negative controls need to be used, especially when embarking on scientific research and new techniques that are unfamiliar. A dye color that is used for labeling must be checked against a different dye color to confirm results. When using contrast agents, two different contrast agents should be checked against each other when possible. Otherwise, visual data can be misinterpreted, leading to erroneous results.

Modern imaging systems are often very sensitive and can amplify the brightness of nonlabeled, or nonspecifically labeled, features in the specimen. When settings on imaging systems are increased to their highest values to amplify weak signal from those features, users must be especially vigilant about determining the source of brighter features.

BLEED THROUGH

In the instance of fluorescent labeling, when more than one dye is used, brightness levels can be affected by the contribution of one dye to another. That phenomenon is referred to as *bleed through*. Thus, a red-emitting dye may contribute brightness to a green-emitting dye, especially when the green signal is overamplified. To prevent misinterpretation of signal in this instance, similar tissues are stained individually (e.g., label one specimen with green-emitting dye only, another with red-emitting dye only). These can serve as controls to confirm specificity of labeling.

Post-processing

The kinds of editing changes that follow are permitted without having to report them. In some instances, a gray area can exist. For example, the distinction between a "global" and a "local" change can be difficult to discern. Changes to specific tonal ranges within an image can be deemed a local or a global change. The change is local because it affects only parts of the tonal range, but it is global because it is applied to the entire image. When that kind of confusion exists, ethics may dictate that the change be reported.

Other changes are necessary and expected, such as cropping, changing mode, increasing bit depth, performing color correction, and adding symbols. The removal of color noise and image stack functions can be done excessively—or incorrectly—leading to a loss of visual information, but these changes are also expected. Note that the use of filters in post-processing may have to be reported, depending on the publication.

The following sections review each kind of alteration to visual data.

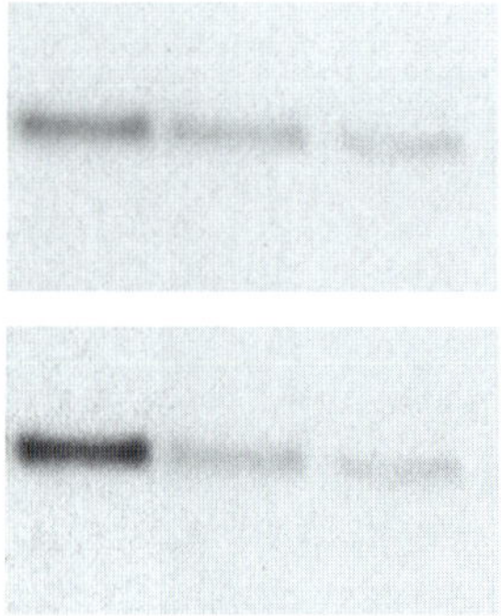

FIGURE 2.11 The electrophoretic specimen on the top shows a global change compared to one lane that was isolated and darkened (bottom).

Global Changes and Application

Global corrections and alterations to an image are made to the entire image (**Figure 2.11**, top), not just parts of it (**Figure 2.11**, bottom). Editors and reviewers are circumspect when changes are detected in only a part of an image because of the possibility that pertinent visual data has been removed or diminished, thus creating a misrepresentation. When global changes are made, pertinent data, for the most part, *can't* be removed or diminished.

Global changes must also be applied to all images in the same experimental set. In so doing, all images can be evaluated under the same conditions, which is critical for scientific accuracy.

▶ **Warning:** *Any change to a part of the image not only risks rejection by reviewers at publications, but can ruin credibility and careers. If a change to a part of an image is deemed necessary, the change must be documented, and the documentation must accompany the image.*

Cropping and Straightening

Cropping occurs when only a part of an image is selected for presentation rather than the whole image. So only pertinent visual data is presented. This is permissible, but for electrophoretic samples, author guidelines for specific publications must be read to determine the degree to which cropping can be done. Removal of visual data by overzealous cropping can be a misrepresentation when surrounding data is pertinent.

Note that cropping does not change the *sampling resolution*: The density of pixels within the area of interest does not increase or decrease. Cropping does not change magnification, and scale bars used for the whole image can be used for parts of the image after cropping.

When cropping tools are used in Photoshop, they can be oriented along the vertical or horizontal axis of features to "straighten" the image. Images can also be straightened using other alignment tools to align image borders with the *x* or *y* axis (or both).

Color Mode Changes

Changing the color mode of the image is a legitimate—and often necessary—procedure. The color mode is a reference to the method used to create the components of an image. Only three modes are considered in this discussion because the three are commonly used in image acquisition. In Photoshop, an image's color mode is indicated at the top of the image window (**Figure 2.12**).

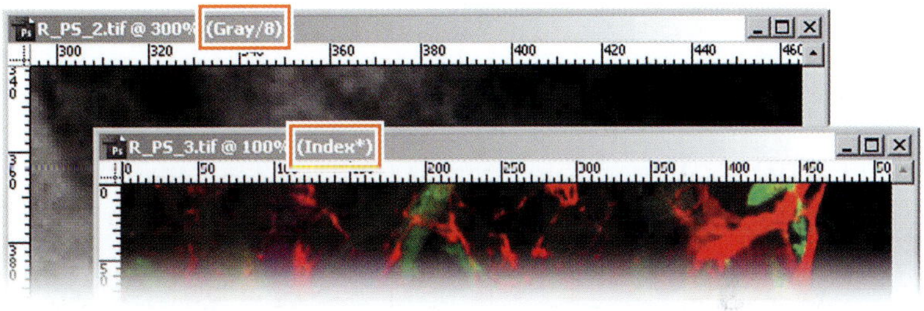

FIGURE 2.12 The top of the image window in Photoshop shows the image mode.

GRAYSCALE, INDEXED COLOR, RGB COLOR MODES

Grayscale images are composed of white to gray to black tones. (In silver-based photography this is referred to as a black and white picture.)

For an indexed-color image, the grayscale component is assigned a single color or multiple colors from a table with predefined colors (a LUT) by the acquisition software. The resulting darkness or brightness of the color(s) depends on the darkness or brightness of pixels that comprise the image. An indexed-color image is limited to 256 discrete colors (8-bit).

A second method can also be used to create indexed-color images after the images are acquired as grayscale. Colors can be assigned through color tables in Photoshop or scientific software programs. These 256 component colors can be made into the Indexed Color mode.

RGB Color, as mentioned earlier, is composed of the three primary components of light: red, green, and blue. It is composed of three channels, each, in essence, a colorized grayscale image. To name the color mode by its components—RGB—differentiates it from other ways in which color is separated into components. Separating the color into Hue, Saturation, and Lightness (HSL), for example, is a different way of dividing color components.

An image in any of these color modes—Grayscale, Indexed Color, or RGB Color—can be converted to another mode if done appropriately. The following sections, "Color to Grayscale," "Pseudocoloring," and "Colorizing," explore mode changes often used in scientific imaging.

COLOR TO GRAYSCALE

Whether the color is assigned or interpolated, color images can be made into grayscale. This is often a requirement for publication. The procedure for converting to grayscale must be done correctly (see Chapter 7, "Color Corrections and Final Steps"). If it is not done correctly, brightness levels will become dimmed overall, and a compression of grayscale values will result.

The elimination of color provides what is arguably a more representative image. The use of certain colors can impede perception, especially when the viewer is color blind.

PSEUDOCOLORING

Images can be colorized to show differences in grayscale levels, often along the visual spectrum. Violet colorizes the darkest grayscale values and red the brightest, with blue, cyan, green, yellow, and orange progressively colorizing the remaining values. These images can be generated in post-processing to aid in visualizing differences (**Figure 2.13**).

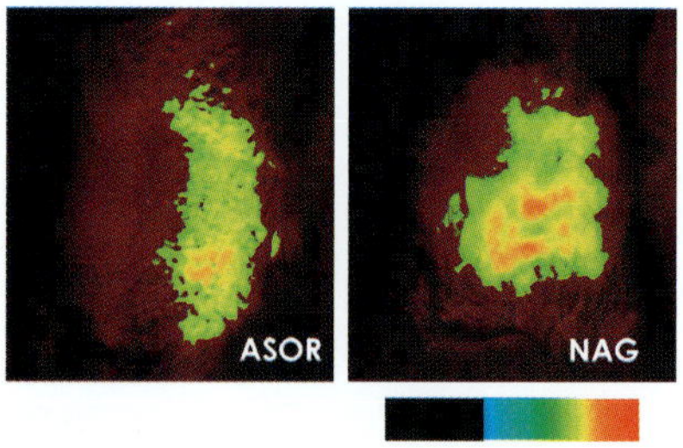

FIGURE 2.13 Images of dim fluorescent labeling on two specimens undergoing different experimental conditions.

A pseudocolor gradient representing black to midtone to white is required as a reference with pseudocolored images to show where each color begins and ends along ranges of grayscale values. It is an essential reference when colors are reassigned to ranges of grayscale values to make visualization of important features more apparent or when the full 8-, 12- or 16-bit scale is not used. In the latter instance, the uppermost grayscale value is purposely lowered to amplify *relative* differences in grayscale values (e.g., in luciferase imaging where a brightest grayscale value of 65,535 [16 bits] is theoretically possible, pseudocolored images are often created with variable upper limits, depending on the brightness of luciferase). It is assumed that all images compared with each other contain the same range of pseudocolored grayscale values. If not, comparisons are invalid.

COLORIZING

■ **Note:** *While the hue used to colorize an image helps differentiate and characterize the dye used, the choice of the hue is moot: In fluorescence and luminescence imaging, the visual data is a product of the number of photons that were emitted by that dye at respective wavelengths and where it localized.*

Grayscale images can also be colorized to differentiate emissions wavelengths, which is often done in darkfield imaging. A red-emitting dye, for example, can be colorized red in post-processing when the image was obtained in grayscale values.

Colorizing does not affect the relationship of grayscale values, so it is considered a legitimate alteration. However, as mentioned earlier, a change from grayscale to color can affect perception. For that reason, grayscale images are often recommended for evaluation purposes instead of colorized images (**Figure 2.14**).

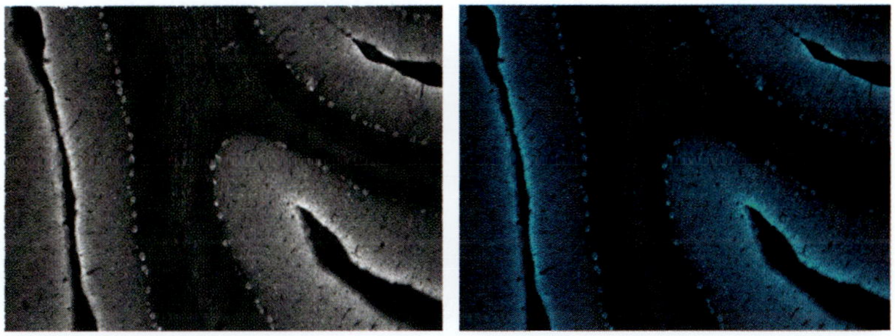

FIGURE 2.14 The image on the left shows grayscale values: On the right, a cyan-blue hue is used to colorize the same image.

Changing Bit Depth

If you are using 12-bit images, they will automatically open as 16-bit images in Photoshop and in some other software programs, such as Image J. The original 12-bit values are retained in Photoshop only under certain circumstances (discussed in "Dark or All Black Images" in Chapter 6). Otherwise, the 12-bit values in the original image are rescaled (increased through multiplication) to 16-bit values. Even though the original values are reassigned, this does not create a misrepresentation of the visual data.

Color Correction

When images are *not* colorized to create color from grayscale (such as what is done in photomultiplier tube systems), color balancing is not only acceptable, but necessary. Because each model of each imaging device contains a slight shift in hue and because each imaging session introduces the possibility that lighting conditions are not identical, color balancing is essential. While white balancing vastly improves color rendition, white balancing alone will not always create a match of colors to what was once seen in the specimen.

Color correction also has to be done for images that were acquired incorrectly without the use of white balancing or with poor automatic white balancing. Some of these images may be so far off in color from the original that they may not be fit for correction and will need to be reimaged.

A reduction in the intensity of a color (desaturation) may also need to be performed as part of the color correction procedure. Digital cameras can produce images with colors that are too pure (saturated). The relevant colors may need to be desaturated, thus restoring colors to those that are representative of the specimen.

Color Noise: Digital Cameras

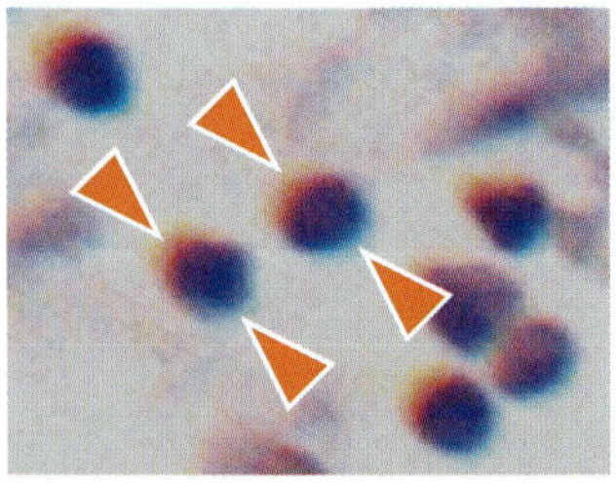

FIGURE 2.15 A zoomed image shows color fringing along the sides of individual cells.

Chromatic aberration (different wavelengths of light not focused on the same plane) creates incorrect colors from the specimen. These colors appear at the edges of features when backlit, where the greatest contrast between dark and bright occurs (**Figure 2.15**). The edging color is often purplish, but it can be other colors. "Color fringing" is the term used to reference color shifts at the edges of features. Here it is considered as "noise" because it introduces an artifact.

Colors at the edges of features are misrepresentations of what was once seen by eye. So it is reasonable to reduce the intensity of the colors so that they blend with neighboring hues, which is done when a correction filter is applied.

Another kind of noise may also occur in the form of introduced colors that should not be present, often a result of using digital cameras with long exposures and high ISO (International Standards Organization) speed settings. These colors can be ameliorated or removed with filtering in Photoshop, which is a reasonable correction because the colors are misrepresentations of the specimen.

Because color noise corrections require software filters in post-processing, this may have to be reported in publication, depending on the author guidelines.

Merging and Image Stack Functions

When more than one image that is labeled with a specific fluorophore is used, when RGB channels are taken separately, or when a number of images create an image "stack," the images can be combined (merged). Merging involves blending more than one image using different methods: They can be averaged, maximum or minimum values can be used, or other parameters can be applied. These choices are available in Photoshop and in other scientific software programs.

■ **Note:** *More rigorous methods for determining coexistence may be required by reviewers, such as the use of FRET (Forstner Resonance Energy Transfer).*

Merged images can reveal areas in which two or more differently colored labels coexist. Those areas of coexistence (or multiexistence if more than two labels are used) become colored differently because two or more colors combine. Red and green are popular combinations of colors because they combine to create the readily identifiable color yellow. Labeling indicates which specimen structures are present and where these structures coexist (**Figure 2.16**).

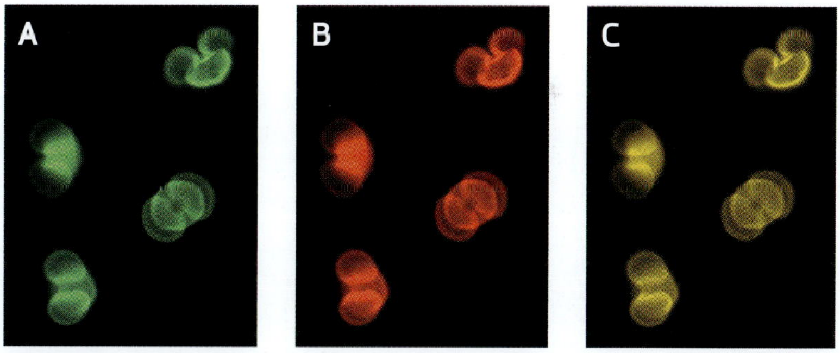

FIGURE 2.16 Image **A** shows auto-fluorescence at green emission wavelengths and image **B** at red emission wavelengths. Image **C** shows the combination of A and B, yielding the color yellow.

In an attempt to better reveal the color that results from coexistence (called colocalization in biology, though the term can have different connotations), it is possible to brighten color values to the point at which these values are clipped. The labeled areas are then pure "pools" of color, resulting in images that are misrepresented: Conclusions drawn from visualizing these images can be suspect.

That said, the clipping of values can be justified, although the image is no longer a representation but a means for visualization. The justification comes from the contributions of noise and the contributions of variable brightness levels and optical properties at different wavelengths when acquiring images. In these conditions even perfectly coexisting colors will not reveal a combined color that is pure, so clipped values are used.

While this practice is not specifically targeted as unethical in author guidelines, the clipping of values to show coexistence should be mentioned in the methods portion of the manuscript. Otherwise, those who repeat the experiments will be at a loss to replicate results.

WARPING, SPATIAL REPOSITIONING

When images that make up a stack are taken from separate specimens (versus a stack of sections taken from a single specimen), some procedure must be used to align images to each other. That can be done manually if fiduciary marks were embedded in the specimen or if marks on the actual specimen can be used as landmarks. The alignment can also be done automatically through the use of software, such as Photoshop CS3 Extended. Automated functions use edges of features and borders to align images from specimen to specimen.

As a consequence of sectioning specimens or of creating specimens on different substrates (as in 2D gels), changes in spatial location and in specimen shape are inevitable (**Figure 2.17**). These modifications are seen visually in a repositioning of the specimen and in feature borders not only changing in dimension, but also in shape. In one specimen, for example, the shape can be round and in the next oval.

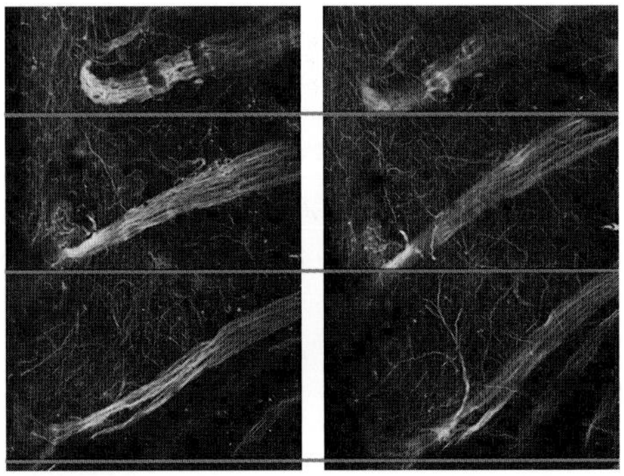

FIGURE 2.17 Two images of nerve fibers in a retina; the image on the right is misaligned with the adjacent section on the left; an inevitability when specimens are sectioned and mounted.

The alignment of specimens in an image stack requires repositioning of each specimen and some adjustment to the specimen shape through a function called "warping." A reference specimen must be identified, and then subsequent specimens are spatially aligned and warped to "fit" the reference.

This procedure is a legitimate and necessary means for creating an accurate representation of a three-dimensional specimen, as long as the alignment appears correct. Misalignment is easily detected by eye.

Symbols, Lettering, Scale Bars

The addition of symbols, lettering, numbering, and scale bars is an obvious post-processing step that need not be described. These additions are expected and easily seen.

It is important that the additions be easily read. Choosing Arial or Helvetica as the font for the lettering is often not just recommended, but is required for many publications. Lines (including the scale bar) also need to be at required widths, which are found in author guidelines.

As an added note, the inclusion of scale bars is accurate: Magnification values described in captions under images generally are not (e.g., "Images are at 200X"). Because magnification depends in part on the physical dimensions of the reproduced image when published, magnification values must take those dimensions into account, and that is rarely done. Magnification values are often misrepresentations.

Conformance

Conformance changes are necessary for adapting images to respective outputs. Some of these changes may be perceived as those done by experts (e.g., RGB Color to CMYK conversion), but in this book, scientists are encouraged to make these changes. Though experts have been trained in these procedures, they may not be familiar with the visual data. As a result, the images can be altered to the degree that images are misrepresentations.

The changes that follow are critical for accurate reproduction, and each conformance step—when applicable—is a necessary part of the post-processing procedures.

Bit Depth Decrease

After all the discussion about the value of using images derived from 12- and 16-bit imaging systems, when images are reproduced, the images must conform to 8- or 24-bit outputs.

If the final output is a computer screen, and the 16-bit image displays so that all grays or colors are easily discriminated, viewers may be misled into believing that the 16-bit image is within the dynamic range of human vision. As a result, it may seem unnecessary to convert to a lower bit depth. This is not always true. Most likely, adjustments have been made to the way a 12- or 16-bit image is displayed. The "real" dark to light values are not shown; instead, the "adaptation to human vision" values are displayed. So there is a difference between the intrinsic values and the display.

To conform images to outputs, images with 8- or 24-bit levels (or less) must be generated. While the elimination of visual data (maybe seen in a loss of detail and gradients) may misrepresent original visual data, ultimately that data needs to be reproduced to an output, so this step is justified. As long as 16-bit grayscale and 48-bit color images have been used in the post-processing steps, the loss of visual data as a result of conformance will be minimized.

White/Black Limits

Limitations in the output prevent reproduction of the lightest and darkest grayscale and color values along the 8-bit range. When important features lie in the darkest and lightest areas of the image, they may not be visible in reproduction (**Figure 2.18**). The image then becomes a misrepresentation of the original.

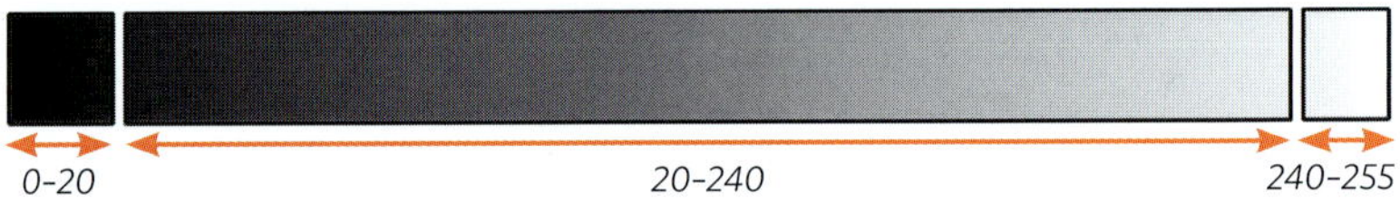

FIGURE 2.18 A grayscale gradient shows pixel values of 0–255. Smaller boxes show values that cannot be differentiated by most outputs.

To preserve details in the lightest and darkest areas, limits must be set for the darkest black and the brightest white. In other words, the dynamic range of the image that appears on the computer screen must be augmented to fit the dynamic range of the output. This is done by reducing or increasing the maximum and minimum grayscale/color value for all pixels that make up the image. The net effect is a lightening of the dark values and a darkening of white values of only those pixels that exceed the limit.

For example, an image may contain grayscale pixel values that make up a range from a min of 2 and a max of 245. The output device has a dynamic range from a min of 20 to a max of 240. In Photoshop, the min and max values need to be changed so that the lowest value in the corrected image is 20 and the max value is 240. Photoshop recalculates values to "fit" the greater dynamic range to the limited output.

■ **Note:** *Setting these limits is especially critical for printing press output, but other outputs also benefit: laptop projectors retain values in brighter features; printers of all kinds resolve details, especially in the darker regions; and images for video or the Web are not so dark that features are obscured.*

Image Size Changes

The Image Size dialog box in Photoshop can be used to change the number of pixels that make up an image and the dimensions of images when outputted to hard copy (**Figure 2.19**). One or both of these modifications may need to be made when conforming to outputs.

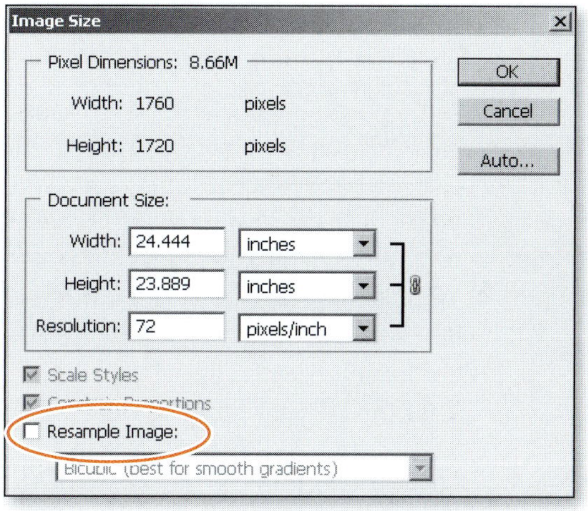

FIGURE 2.19 The Image Size dialog box in Photoshop.

■ **Note:** *For nonpublication resolutions, the merits of perceived quality differences from images that exceed maximum output resolutions must be weighed against efficiency: Higher resolutions equal larger file sizes. The larger files can slow down or freeze the computer. Especially when these images are destined for laptop presentations, the merits of predictable displays of images outweigh the importance of preserving subtle details often only seen by the person most invested in the images.*

PIXEL RESOLUTION

The number of pixels across and down in an image will very likely need to be changed to conform to the output. Each type of output has a maximum number of pixels it can use for images. That maximum defines the resolution in terms of the number of pixels it uses in x and y to divide up the image: The more pixels (the more the pixel density), the greater the divisions (or samples) of the image, and the greater the resolution. When the number of pixels that make up an image are changed to a greater or smaller total number, the image is *resampled*.

Resampling can occur consciously, when purposely resampling using the Image Size dialog box in Photoshop. Or it can occur without user knowledge, such as when resampling occurs in PowerPoint when enlarging or shrinking images to fit the slide template. The point is that resampling often occurs when images are produced on output devices with or without user intervention

Resampling to lower resolutions (subsampling or downsampling), as a general rule, should not be performed during the post-processing steps (see "What Can't Be Done in Post-Processing" later in this chapter), but it is a necessary part of conformance when producing outputs. To preserve as many details as possible—thus avoiding potential misrepresentation of visual data—images are generally resampled to twice the resolution of the output for publication. In so doing, each image preserves the greatest amount of detail that is possible for the maximum pixel resolution of the the printing press. For other outputs, resolutions can be set to the maximum resolution of the device.

■ **Note:** *The unit of measurement for image dimensions for the image file does not correspond at all to the physical size of what was photographed (except in the instance of a flatbed scanner where the physical size of the platen is known).*

▶ **Warning:** *A common mistake is to increase the Resolution (in pixels/inch or pixels/cm) in the Image Size dialog box in Photoshop and reduce the output dimensions (dots/inch or centimeter). That can lead to a downsampling of pixels in the image, which results in fewer pixels that make up the image in x and y and a smaller file size. This reduces the sampling resolution and can result in pixilation and loss of detail . This mistake is made because of a common superstition: 72 dots per inch equals poor resolution. The designation of 72 dpi (or 96 dpi) is based on an outdated practice of correlating image dimensions to an Apple 13-inch screen. Only the number of pixels that make up the image in x and y define the resolution, not the dots or pixels per inch.*

OUTPUT DIMENSIONS

Image size also refers to the dimensions of the image. The dimensions refer to the physical *x* and *y* width and length in a spatial unit of measurement, such as centimeters.

The spatial dimensions apply to the image to be printed by an output device. Thus, the size or dimensions are more appropriately called the output dimensions.

In many instances, only the output dimensions need to be changed, not the pixel resolution (indicated by pixels/inch or centimeter); for example, when printing to an office printer. Users must ensure that the number of pixels that make up an image remain the same after changing the image dimensions (remedied by deselecting the Resample box in the Image Size dialog box in Photoshop).

When the pixel resolution and the dimensions need to be changed, resampling may be necessary, which can affect the image. When the image is upsampled (images are interpolated to fit on more pixels) blurring can result; when the image is downsampled (images end up on fewer pixels), a loss of detail and noticable stairstepping effects (aliasing) at slanted or rounded edges can occur (**Figure 2.20**, left). In Photoshop edges are ghosted, or antialiased, to make edges appear smooth at lower magnifications (**Figure 2.20**, right).

Upsampled images can be corrected by sharpening, if mentioned in the Methods section of a manuscript (sharpening is generally discouraged). Downsampled images, on the other hand, are more difficult to correct, but methods can be used to varying degrees of success (see "Problem Images" in Chapter 6).

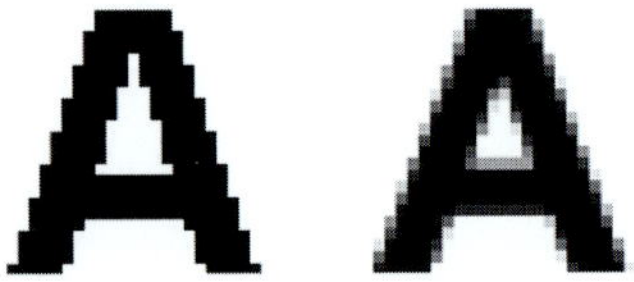

FIGURE 2.20 The image on the left shows the aliasing effect along a slanted edge: On the right the aliasing effect is mitigated by ghosting.

Color Changes: RGB to CMYK

For publication and for some specialized printers, the primary colors that make up the image must be changed from those that make up the colors of light (Red, Green, Blue [RGB]) to those that make up the colors of pigments plus black (Cyan, Magenta, Yellow, black [CMYK]). The conversion is necessary because printing presses use cyan, magenta, yellow, and black inks to create colors, and the amount of each ink deposited on the paper must be indicated for every pixel in the image. Thus, grayscale or color levels assigned to each pixel along a dark to light range change to a unit of measurement based on ink levels.

CMYK images are increasingly requested by publications, so this conversion is a necessary and legitimate change in visual data. However, the conversion from RGB to CMYK is fraught with the capacity

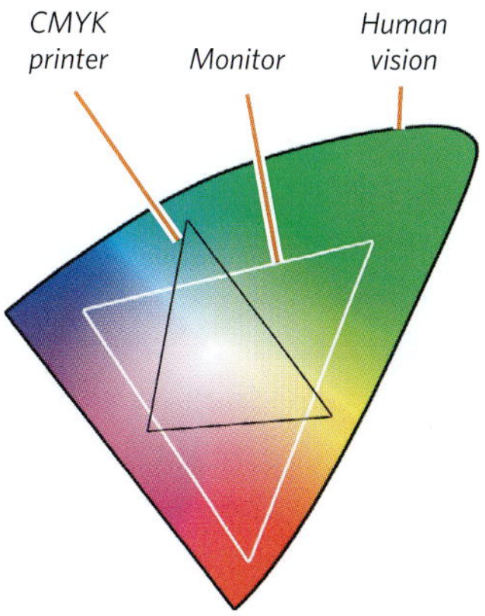

FIGURE 2.21 This image shows the approximate range of colors seen by human vision compared with those reproduced by computer monitors and by CMYK printers (including printing presses).

■ **Note:** *The saturated hues and intensities of colors used in science often create confusion for color correction specialists at publications. Saturated hues lie outside the range of colors routinely corrected by specialists. Also, these specialists are not in a position to decide on the hue, and they are obliged to desaturate hues as a solution when a slight color shift can solve the problem while maintaining the more important relationship of dark to bright levels. Because researchers are familiar with their images, often a far better representation is obtained when they perform the conversion.*

for image misrepresentation, especially because of shifts in hue and brightness values.

The causes for color and brightness shifts are twofold:

- The range of colors that can be reproduced by RGB imaging devices does not overlap with those reproduced by CMYK devices.
- The colors used in science are often saturated (pure colors) and most can be readily reproduced using RGB primaries (e.g., computer displays), but few of these saturated colors can be reproduced in CMYK.

The millions of colors that can be made from the primaries of light are greater in variety and different than the colors that can be made from pigments (**Figure 2.21**). In many instances, similar colors can be made from both; in other instances, especially with saturated colors, colors cannot be matched, most likely because of a limitation in the CMYK palette. Add to that the back-projected illumination of a computer screen (an RGB device), and RGB colors will always appear more brilliant and intense than what is reflected from paper in CMYK.

While the RGB to CMYK conversion process may take some practice, this book provides conversion methods that maintain the relationship of brightness values, though for darkfield images the hue may be slightly shifted to accommodate gamut. In so doing, the final reproduction in publication is more likely to be an accurate representation.

File Format

Often, the file format must be changed to conform to the various outputs. TIFF files are arguably the most universal and are most often required by publications. However, for grants, Word documents, PowerPoint, and Acrobat, conversion to JPEG may be necessary to create smaller file sizes and to prevent software from “hanging up.”

While much has been said about loss of visual data with the JPEG format, some outputs and destinations demand its use. As long as saving in the JPEG format occurs at the end of the post-processing steps and saving occurs where the level of compression can be chosen (as in Photoshop), the loss of visual data can be visually imperceptible.

Documentation

Documentation is a conformance to Good Laboratory Practices and to regulations within industries. Frequently, digital imaging procedures and settings are not regarded as important for documentation as laboratory procedures and protocol. Yet, increasingly, documentation is requested as a means for understanding conditions leading to the data that is seen.

● **More:** *To download the free supplement "Tools and Functions in Photoshop" please visit www.peachpit.com/scientificimaging and register your book.*

As stated earlier, often annotations known as metadata are saved with the image file. These may or may not include both camera and instrument settings: Be aware of these limitations. Post-processing and conformance protocol can be saved by using specific tools in Photoshop (see "History Log" in "Tools and Functions in Photoshop") (**Figure 2.22**).

FIGURE 2.22 Text of changes made in Photoshop CS editions can be exported automatically to a History Log.

```
Levels
        Levels
                Adjustment: levels adjustment list
                levels adjustment
                Channel: composite channel
                With Auto
Hue/Saturation
        Hue/Saturation
                Without Colorize
                Adjustment: hue/saturation adjustment list
                hue/saturation adjustment
                Local Range: 1
                Begin Ramp: 315
                Begin Sustain: 345
                End Sustain: 15
                End Ramp: 45
                Hue: 0
                Saturation: -22
                Lightness: 0
Lab Color
        Convert Mode
                To: Lab color mode
                With Flatten
                Without Rasterize
        Select a channel
Gaussian Blur
        Gaussian Blur
                Radius: 3.2 pixels
        Select b channel
```

If these means are not available for documentation, or if they are not used, documentation will need to be done manually. Description of methods used in Photoshop are important as well. Some of these methods must be described either in the Methods portion of manuscripts or as additional information.

What Can't Be Done in Post Processing

Some changes to images are not allowed when using Photoshop. These include spot changes, transfer of features from one image to another, and intentional manipulation of visual data to prove the hypothesis.

Other changes *can* be made, but they have the effect of removing or obscuring visual data. These include unintentionally subsampling; using the Brightness or Contrast tool while evaluating its effects visually; and using Copy/Paste methods for transferring images between different software programs made by different companies.

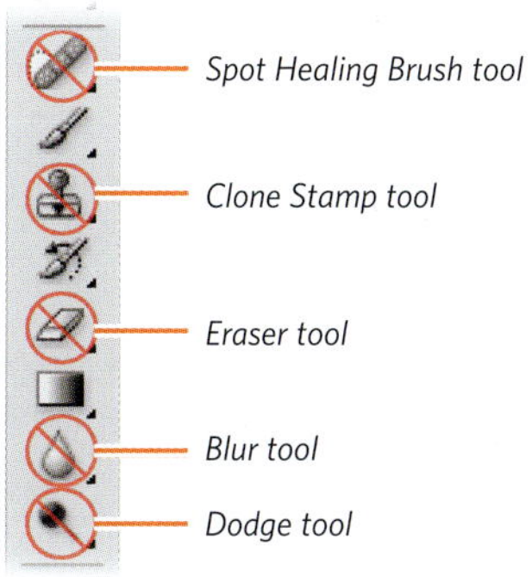

FIGURE 2.23 Tools in Photoshop that make spot changes to an image are indicated by the "Prohibited" symbol.

Spot Changes

Spot changes include any alteration done to a small area or portion of images. In Photoshop, these would include any use of the retouching tools: the Spot Healing Brush, Clone Stamp, Dodge, and Burn tools (**Figure 2.23**). Generally, the Spot Healing Brush and Clone Stamp tools are used for detritus removal, but that removal can be accomplished through the use of noise removal filters, which must be described when publishing. Dodge and Burn tools are often used to make illumination even across the sample, but that can be accomplished using flatfield correction techniques applied to the entire image.

Spot changes can potentially remove relevant information. So, a greater degree of caution has been implemented at publications, leading to a universal ruling.

Outlining a feature of an image for quantification would, of course, be an exception to this rule. As a part of both quantification and visualization (as defined later in this chapter), some isolated details may also need to be removed. In any instance, a detailed description of the procedure must be provided.

Transfer of Features from One Image to Another

Transferring isolated features, such as cells, from one image to another is not allowed. If these features could not be found in one field when photographing the sample, it is fair to believe that they simply do not represent the visual data in the experiment. Rather than transfer features, reimage samples.

Intentional Manipulation of Visual Data

Intentional manipulation includes any transfer of features, alteration of position of features, inclusion of falsified features, gross amplification of some features relative to others, and so on. In all instances, the intent is to mislead those who view the visual data into believing false data. Eventually, the false data will be discovered when experiments are replicated, so not only is this a bad idea, but also a sure means for ending careers.

Image Size Changes (Subsampling)

The most common change that shouldn't be done is to resample images, usually to lower pixel densities. Often, resampling occurs when changing the output dimensions in the Image Size dialog box with the thought that only the dimensions are affected, not the sampling resolution. The default setting in the Image Size dialog box includes a selected Resample box. When that check box is selected, the output resolution shown in the dialog box is often at a low resolution (such as 72 dpi), and the inches across and down are set higher than desired. When the dimensions are set to lower values and the image is resampled (because the Resample box is left selected), the net effect is a reduction of pixel density along with the change in image dimensions.

When image dimensions need to be scaled to match the dimensions of other images in a figure or plate, use the Scale option in Photoshop (Edit > Transform > Scale). Be sure to hold down the Shift key when scaling to proportionally increase both the width and the height (preserve the aspect ratio).

Space saving is another reason image size changes are made. Image files by their nature take up lots of room on hard disks, but the increasingly lower prices for hard disks and storage media make the desire to save space a poor argument. Also, saving space by reducing the number of pixels that make up the image eliminates data and could potentially lead to loss of detail and misrepresentation (**Figure 2.24**, left). Once that data is eliminated, no amount of upsampling to greater pixel densities will restore it. Images kept at their original resolution retain their full resolution (**Figure 2.24**, right).

FIGURE 2.24 Two sets of lines: The image on the left has been subsampled and then restored to its original resolution; on the right, the image at its original resolution.

Brightness/Contrast Tool

The Brightness/Contrast tool in image processing software, especially when used in programs other than Photoshop and in pre-CS3 versions, is a tool that *should not* be used unless the consequence of using the tool is understood. When the Brightness slider is increased or decreased, the tool adds or subtracts the approximate or exact indicated value to all pixels. When the Contrast slider is increased or decreased, the tonal range is expanded or contracted. By using the two in tandem, entire ranges of pixel values can be mistakenly eliminated.

This doesn't necessarily occur when the user is familiar with the tool, but most users are inexperienced. Users gravitate to this tool and struggle with the outcome, often repeatedly using the tool while consequently degrading the image. The Levels or Curves commands in Photoshop work only by expanding or contracting the tonal range so that all pixels are more likely to be preserved.

Copying and Pasting

Copying and pasting to transfer graphics and images from one application to another shouldn't be done unless it is between applications made by the same company and the procedure is done correctly. When a graphic or image is copied, it is placed in an area of computer memory called the Clipboard, possibly at computer screen resolutions and likely with a small range of colors. The screen resolution is often lower than the original resolution of the image, so the image is subsampled and visual data is lost. The narrower range of colors eliminates visual data as well.

Copying and pasting can work for graphics when Paste Special (as Windows Metadata) is used between Microsoft products. As a general rule, however, the use of copying and pasting is discouraged because of the near certainty of data loss.

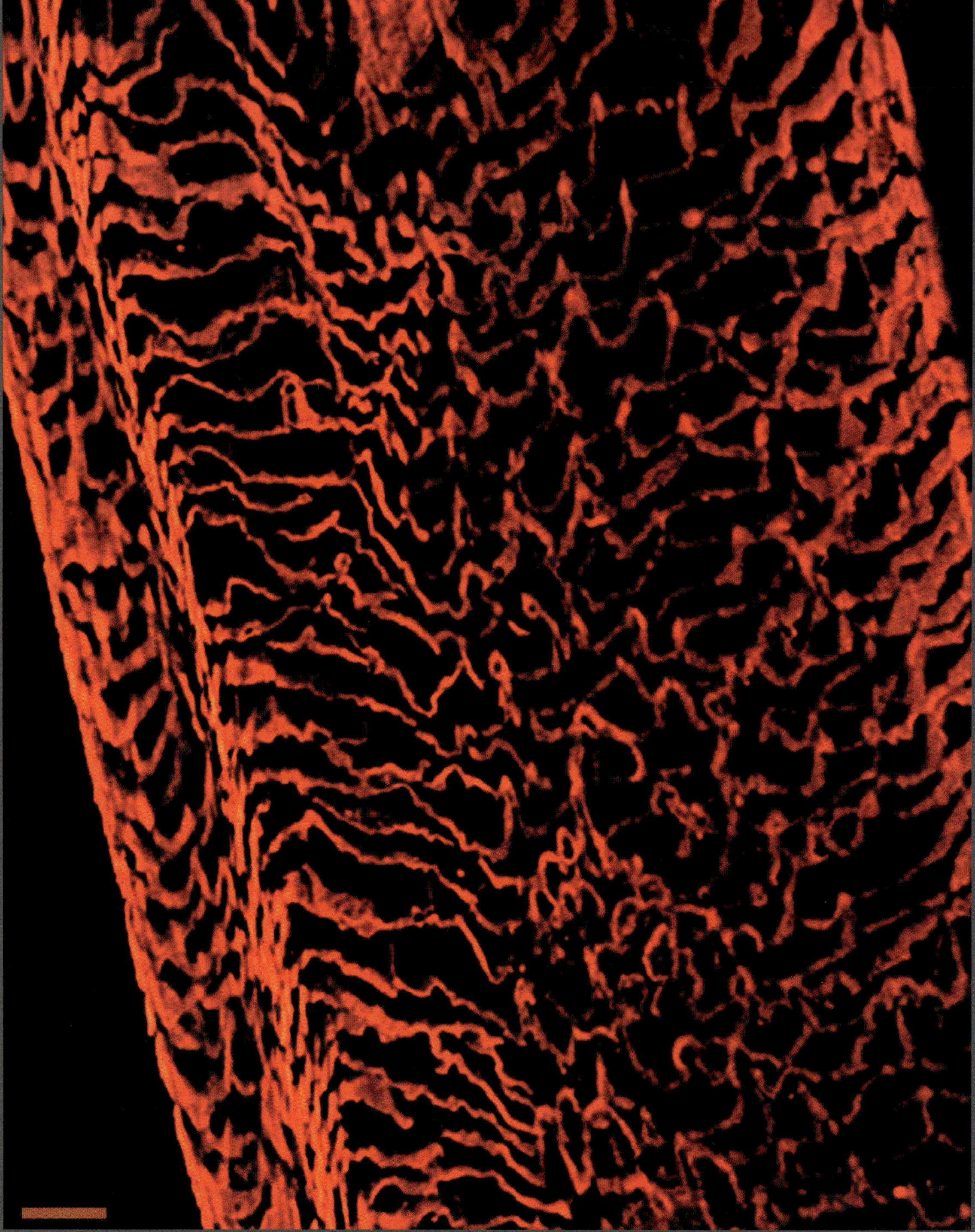

CHAPTER 3

Guidelines for Specific Types of Images

WHILE SOME CHANGES to images are universally applicable, other changes are specific to the intent. Based on intent, the most limited number of changes (or none at all) is applied to those images intended for optical density/intensity measurement (OD/I), and the greatest to those images intended for modeling (such as three-dimensional reconstructions). The latter intent is called "visualization" in this book, because the definition covers a broader scope: It includes any conscious or deliberate enhancement of visual data to draw attention to experimental phenomena. The kind of image that is created—often a cartoon—by its nature suggests that the image is for visualization purposes.

As mentioned earlier, this categorization of image intents is not clearly spelled out in author guidelines for major scientific publications.

The categories for the intent of images are as follows:

- Images intended for OD/I measurements acquired by flatbed scanners and camera/scanned beam systems.
- Representative images, which are the greatest number of images produced for science, medicine, and industry.
- Images intended for quantification and visualization.

Human beard hair stained with CY3 and acquired on a BioRad 1024 confocal microscope system with LaserSharp 3.1 software (Bio-Rad Corporation, Hercules, CA). Image was colorized in and color conformed to CMYK publication in Photoshop CS3 Extended (Adobe Systems Incorporated, San Jose, CA). Scale bar = 10 microns. *Image courtesy of Marna Ericson, Ph.D.*

Images Intended for OD/I Measurements

Images destined for OD/I are divided broadly into those images acquired by a scanner (primarily electrophoretic samples) and those acquired by a camera or a scanned beam system (such as a confocal microscope system). In some instances, there is overlap (e.g., setting the gamma to 1), but in other instances the nature of the hardware used determines the guidelines, especially when it comes to acquisition. Flatbed scanners (and associated software) intended for OD/I self-calibrate, generally produce images without the effects of noise or uneven illumination, and give the user choices for pixel resolution and bit depth. Camera and scanned beam systems, on the other hand, do not typically self-calibrate; nor do these systems produce noise-free images, even illumination, or options for selecting pixel resolutions.

Because of the differences between flatbed scanners and camera/scanned beam systems, different guidelines apply when acquiring images (**Table 3.1**).

TABLE 3.1 Guidelines for Images Destined for OD/I Measurement

	ACQUISITION	POST-PROCESSING: PERMITTED
Flatbed scanner	Use standards in specimens	Eliminate dust and scratches (report use of a filter)
	Include a calibration standard or reference*	
	Choose adequate pixel resolution	
	Keep gamma at 1	
	Use consistent imaging system settings	
	Use a higher bit depth	
	Measure areas within the dynamic range of the substrate	
Camera/ Scanned beam	Use calibration and consistent imaging system settings	Flatfield correct (if not done at acquisition)
	Use adequate pixel resolution and magnification	Use masking
	Keep gamma at 1	Use deconvolution
	Flatfield correct image	Use color and histogram matching (report use of a function)
	Use background subtraction	Use noise reduction filters (report use of a filter)
	Do not measure when label fades (bleaches)	

* Unless scanner is self-calibrating

Each guideline listed in the table is discussed in detail in the following sections.

Electrophoretic Specimens on Flatbed Scanners

Specimens made in the field of molecular biology, which include SDS-PAGE gels, blots, films, phosphor screens, and other flat materials, are often scanned on flatbed scanners. The advantage of this kind of imaging system lies in its ability to evenly illuminate the sample. On many scientific-grade flatbed scanners, a second advantage also lies in the means often incorporated for measuring luminance of light from the light source, and then correcting the exposure time to adapt to changes in the intensity of the light over time as the light source dims. These scanners self-calibrate to ensure consistent exposures over time, so that a sample with a particular brightness will provide the same OD/I over the lifetime of the scanner.

Acquisition

Whether or not scanners self-calibrate, it is useful—and sometimes critical—for an accurate measurement to test against calibrated standards, especially when using consumer-grade, flatbed scanners. Adequate pixel resolution, a gamma value of 1, consistent settings, a higher bit depth, and the dynamic range limitations of the substrate are of equal importance. A discussion concerning each of these areas follows.

USE INTERNAL STANDARDS IN SPECIMENS

Molecular weight ladders and internal standards correct for potential misreadings of visual data, as mentioned in Chapter 1. The use of standards should be a given for scientific experiments involving electrophoretic specimens (and others as well, such as genomics gene standards), but surprisingly, these standards are sometimes excluded.

INCLUDE AN EXTERNAL CALIBRATION STANDARD OR A REFERENCE

When internal standards are not used—or cannot be used—such as when absolute (versus relative) values are sought or when samples from day to day are compared to each other, calibration standards are critical for accuracy (**Figure 3.1**).

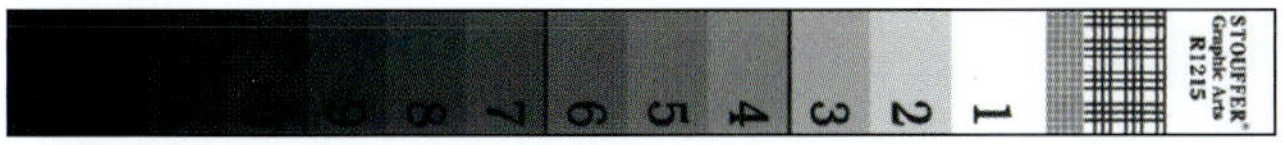

FIGURE 3.1 A reflective Stouffer step wedge (left) and a fluorescent reference slide (right).

External calibration for brightfield images. Calibration standards for dark bands on lighter substrates come in the form of narrow strips with light to dark steps of increasing density. The steps are divided into darkness levels along a logarithmic scale with luminance measurements (which are obtained through the use of a densitometer at the factory) shown for each step. These step wedges, available from the Stouffer company (Stouffer step wedges), are useful as a means for determining day-to-day variations in light source levels and as a means for fitting measurements made in software programs to a consistent optical density scale.

Fluorescent specimens. For specimens labeled with fluorophores, fluorescent reference slides and beads can be purchased from various suppliers. They do not come with known values as of this writing: Instead, they provide *consistent* fluorescent intensities (when used according to the directions). They are useful to determine variations in the brightness of the light source over time.

When calibration standards and fluorescent references are not used from session to session and scanners do not self-calibrate, a misrepresentation of the specimen OD/I is likely and erroneous measurements will result.

CHOOSE ADEQUATE PIXEL RESOLUTION

Pixel coverage refers to the number of pixels used across and down (in *x* and *y*) to compose either the entire image or a single feature: The greater the number of pixels used to compose a feature, the higher the pixel coverage (also called the *sampling rate*: here it is called *sampling resolution*).

For OD/I measurement, a high enough pixel resolution must be used to obtain statistically valid results. The minimum pixel resolution can be found by scanning specimens at several different pixel resolutions, plotting the results, and then determining which pixel resolutions fall outside the acceptable results. In instances in which the specimen is labeled with a dim, fluorescent or chemiluminescent dye, more pixel coverage is necessary to account for increased standard deviation of pixel values as a result of noise.

■ **Note:** *Even though higher pixel resolutions are not always necessary, to avoid resampling, electrophoretic specimens are scanned at publication resolutions. This is typically at 600 ppi for text included with an image, which is typical with electrophoretic specimens.*

For a flatbed scanner, the sampling resolution is shown in microns/pixel, ppi (pixels per inch), or dpi (dots per inch) units: *Decreasing* microns/pixel and *increasing* ppi or dpi will increase pixel coverage. For more information about dpi and pixel resolutions for scanners, see Chapter 4, "Getting the Best Input."

KEEP GAMMA AT 1

Gamma refers to the mathematical operation typically used to convert a linear set of brightness levels into the non-linear response of the human eye to brightness. Dark areas need to be lightened logarithmically to fit within human vision while keeping bright values at the same levels. The following formula is used:

$$\text{output value} = \text{input value}^{\gamma}$$

The gamma value, when available in acquisition software or hardware, is chosen by the user. Any gamma other than 1 will change the tonal values. Because it is a power function, the values will not be changed in a linear way but will instead change in a nonlinear way: A gamma value greater than 1 will increase darkness primarily in the middle tones and incrementally less so as tonal values get brighter or darker; a gamma value of less than 1 will brighten primarily in the middle tones and incrementally less so as tonal values get brighter or darker.

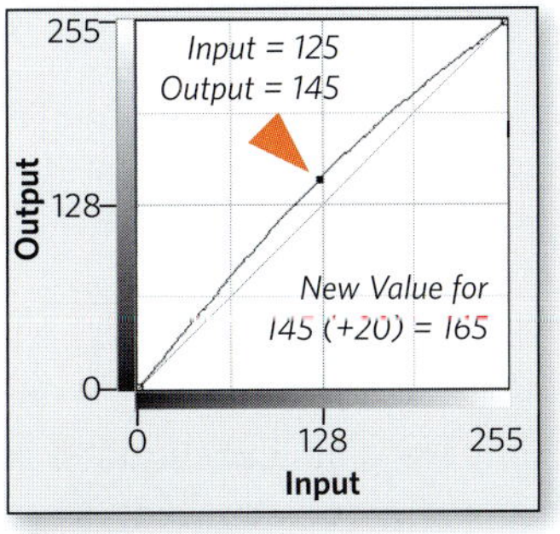

FIGURE 3.2 An example of the reassignment of tonal values by bending a line away from the existing tonal values.

The relationship of the grayscale values can also be changed by using a dialog box similar to the Curves dialog box in Photoshop (see Chapter 5). In this dialog box a straight line (indicating a 1:1 relationship of input and output values along a 45 degree baseline) is bent by the user so that all grayscale or color values along the bend are reassigned (remapped)—added to or subtracted from existing values—based on any discrete tone's deviation from the origin. In general usage, this kind of change is also called a gamma adjustment, though, in the strict sense, a gamma change is a power function, not a straight addition or subtraction formula (**Figure 3.2**).

On a scanner intended for scientific use, the gamma is automatically set to 1, so that tonal values are identical to the scanned specimen. For scanners that are intended for the consumer market, however, the gamma setting can be changed in scanner software, or the value may be automatically changed without the knowledge of the user. In those instances, the relationship of grayscale values becomes nonlinear, resulting in flawed measurements.

Check all the scanner software dialog boxes to ensure that the gamma remains at 1. Also, scan a calibrated step wedge to use for measurements. Compare the optical density measurements of the step wedge made in Photoshop or other scientific software to known densitometric values of steps on the wedge. If they correlate, the gamma is at 1: If they don't correlate, a gamma correction was automatically made, and the scanner cannot be used for making OD/I measurements.

USE CONSISTENT IMAGING SYSTEM SETTINGS

When using scanners that are *not* self-calibrating, scanning images from imaging session to imaging session using identical settings ensures consistent and repeatable results. To ensure that consistent settings are used, a step-by-step guide can be created and should be posted near the scanner for all users.

The potential for inconsistent settings being used on a scanner that is *not* self-calibrating can be great, especially with multiple users. Inconsistent settings that do not conform to posted guidelines will likely result in a misreading of OD/I and a misrepresentation of data. Workgroups must take care to make an exhaustive guide and post it.

USE A HIGHER BIT DEPTH

Scanners either scan at fixed bit depths or bit depth settings can be chosen in software. The highest bit depth setting provides the maximum dynamic range and finest division of grayscale values, so it is often chosen as the default.

But the highest bit depth value may not always be the most reasonable choice. The dynamic range of the substrate may be limited, such as the limitation that exists with autoradiographs on film. Films are limited to a maximum of approximately 256 gray values, so measuring for OD/I at greater dynamic ranges is unreasonable. However, because many scanners are multiple-use devices on which a multitude of substrates are used, a higher bit depth may be chosen as a default. When too many choices must be made for mundane tasks, the possibility of overlooking appropriate settings for the particular sample that is scanned increases. It is best to simply choose the setting that works for *every* sample.

FIGURE 3.3 Darker lanes in this rotated image exceed the dynamic range of the film, which can be visually determined by attempting to read the text through the lanes.

MEASURE AREAS WITHIN THE DYNAMIC RANGE OF THE SUBSTRATE

Especially in the case of films, the dynamic range of the substrate can be exceeded. In films, these areas appear as pure black.

A level of black that exceeds the dynamic range can be difficult to determine visually: How black is too black? A simple method is to attempt to read text through the dark areas in room light (**Figure 3.3**): If that is impossible, very likely that area has clipped the dynamic range. More exposure, loading, or development of that film, if possible, would not make the area darker. Instead, the area would simply expand outward at nonlinear rates. Often, these lanes are not measured, but when included, the films must be exposed again using shorter exposures.

SDS-PAGE gels can also contain dark lanes outside the dynamic range of the substrate. Tests need to be made to ensure a linear response between progressive loading amounts and measurements.

Measurement from areas that are too black or white include clipped values. As a result, these measurements misrepresent true specimen densities/intensities.

Post-processing

The only permissible change to electrophoretic specimens, aside from those taken to conform images to outputs, is to eliminate dust and scratches, but only by a global application of a filter. Be sure to check with the author guidelines to be sure that this change can be made without having to report it.

ELIMINATE DUST AND SCRATCHES

Electrophoretic specimens are prone to dust, and films may contain scratches. These are generally referred to as artifacts. Scanners accentuate artifacts as a result of inherent resolutions and good focus (**Figure 3.4**).

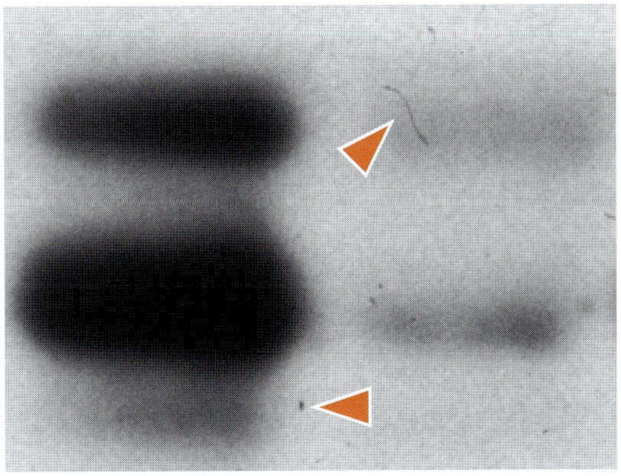

FIGURE 3.4 Small artifacts in the form of dust and specks distract attention from visual data in this scanned image.

Small artifacts can be removed by adding a slight blurring effect on large features. This is done with a noise removal filter.

But using any noise removal filter in post-processing is either discouraged or rejected in the author guidelines for many publications. Check with the desired publication before using a filter to remove artifacts. Noise removal filters remove or minimize unnecessary and distracting visual data, but at the same time may obscure lighter bands. Excessive use of a noise removal filter can also lead to banding, a condition in which similar gray values pool together to form what can look like a topographical map.

Because noise removal can lead to a misrepresentation of visual data to varying degrees, using noise removal filters for electrophoretic gels is not widely accepted.

OD/I Measurements Using Camera and Scanned Beam Systems

Incorrect camera system settings and image-capture procedures will create a misrepresentation of visual data for images from which OD/I measurements will be made. Strict adherence to procedures is absolutely crucial when these measurements are needed.

Be aware that correct settings and procedures must be followed *before* obtaining OD/I measurements: If images have been taken from a past session and correct settings were not used, nothing can be done to correct the images. Samples must be imaged again.

Especially for measurements of fluorescence intensities from cells, it is important to consider all the possible pitfalls. Besides changes in luminance that are not a result of fluorescent dye uptake, noise, camera settings, nature of the substrate, calibration of equipment, sampling resolution, gamma, and consistent exposure are important considerations. Biological anomalies that may variably affect the uptake of fluorescent dyes, consistent focusing across many samples, and other phenomena may pose additional experimental problems that cannot be overcome. Further education about how these potential pitfalls can affect OD/I measurement is strongly encouraged.

Acquisition

When using camera or scanned beam systems, some acquisition procedures are similar to those of scanners (calibration, pixel resolution, and gamma); but other steps are taken to correct for anomalies introduced as a result of uneven illumination and potential fading because of longer exposure times at higher light intensities. Noise from the camera system can also be introduced when exposure times are too long, and this too is corrected during acquisition, if possible. For accurate OD/I measurement, adhere to the procedures outlined in the sections that follow.

● **More:** *For more information on measuring out-of-range specimens with in-range specimens, visit www.peachpit.com/scientificimaging.*

▶ **Warning:** *Imaging systems must not be set to automatically determine their settings, because the settings will change from specimen to specimen.*

USE CALIBRATION AND CONSISTENT IMAGING SYSTEM SETTINGS

When using a camera or beam scanning system, all images must be taken with the same settings, which include gain, exposure time, offset, aperture, and so on. Settings must be entered manually, and the same settings must be used from one imaging session to the next, with one caveat: Because of potential specimen to specimen differences in brightness or darkness levels, when the brightness or darkness of any specimen exceeds the dynamic range of the camera, settings must be changed. Otherwise, the brightness or darkness values will be clipped. Exposure settings or energy-source attenuation can be changed at a discreet increment for a specimen that exceeds the dynamic range, and the percentage of that change would be calculated against the OD/I measurement as a correction. As a result, the out-of-range specimen can be measured along with in-range specimens.

Note that day-to-day variations in the instrument's energy source must also be calculated against a calibrated standard or reference when taking images over time. Again, the percentage change in energy-source intensities must be applied to all OD/I measurements for each session. Note as well that energy sources can change in the course of a single session: Do not rely on an imaging system without exhaustive tests to verify the consistency of its energy source.

As mentioned earlier, Stouffer step wedges and fluorescent reference slides can be used to determine light source variation. Neutral gray cards can also be purchased to obtain a consistent gray color and reflection.

Some camera imaging systems self-calibrate to maintain their consistency. These systems are best to use, though even they should be subjected to measurements against known calibrations to ensure their accuracy.

Correcting for energy-source intensity changes and using consistent camera settings (insofar as exposure does not exceed the dynamic range) is not necessary when standards exist in the same image as the experimental data, such as when two fluorophores at two emissions/excitation wavelengths are used in calcium imaging. In that instance, experimental data is ratioed against an internal standard.

USE ADEQUATE PIXEL RESOLUTION AND MAGNIFICATION

For OD/I measurement, a certain number of pixels must make up a feature for subsequent measurement. To find the minimum number of pixels to use for a feature that will be measured, use the procedure described earlier in the section "Choose Adequate Pixel Resolution."

■ **Note:** *Several adjacent images can be acquired at high magnification, and then stitched (montaged) together to obtain Nyquist sampling rates.*

If a higher sampling resolution is not available, a higher magnification must be used to enlarge features. In so doing, features will be sampled at a higher pixel resolution. Adequate sampling resolution is required not only to have enough pixels for measurement, but to positively identify features in images. When sampling resolution is inadequate, incorrect identification of features is possible. To avoid potential mistakes in identifying features, particularly when the spatial areas of significant features are close to the resolution limits of an instrument, a sampling resolution can be chosen according to the Nyquist theorem. The Nyquist theorem requires at least two times the pixel sampling rate than what is necessary to resolve a feature. These rates, called Nyquist rates, ensure a high enough frequency of sampling so that pixels do not "miss" small features. If the system detector does not have the pixel sampling rate to match the Nyquist rates, a greater magnification can be used.

KEEP GAMMA AT 1

When a numeric value for gamma can be input, set the gamma to 1 to retain a linear relationship of grayscale values.

Unless you are certain about the gamma settings of the imaging equipment, check the measured settings against a calibrated standard (such as a Stouffer step wedge) to be sure that the gamma from the imaging system produces images that are indeed at a gamma of 1. Consumer imaging systems will likely introduce gamma corrections to change the relationship of tonal values. When opening images from consumer cameras saved in a Raw format, for example, gamma is very likely changed from a gamma of 1 to a nonlinear setting.

If the gamma is unavoidably set to a value that is greater or less than 1, and is therefore nonlinear, alternative means must be found to maintain a gamma of 1. Otherwise, the nonlinear relationship of grayscale and color values will render OD/I values incorrect, and visual data in images will be misrepresented.

FLATFIELD CORRECT THE IMAGE

Aligning and focusing techniques do not always provide even illumination across the entire sample, even when the energy source is scanned across the specimen (**Figure 3.5A**). Often, an area such as the center of the specimen may be more brightly illuminated than the edges, which is referred to as "vignetting." It is painfully present on light microscopes and some types of electron microscopes. Vignetting can be corrected in image acquisition software, in hardware that is provided with the camera, or in post-processing.

When the correction is done in image acquisition software, an image that reveals the unevenness is numerically divided into the image of a sample (along with other possible calculations). This unevenly illuminated image is called the flatfield, blank field, or shading image.

The flatfield image (**Figure 3.5B**) is created by removing the sample and taking an image of the light that strikes the detector when using backlit illumination (e.g., brightfield microscopy). When using epi-illumination (e.g., fluorescence imaging) and other methods in which light must strike a sample before a signal is collected, a reference sample with a constant illumination across the entire sample is used. For fluorescence imaging, a fluorescent reference slide (as mentioned earlier) provides constant illumination across the field.

In situations in which a flatfield image was *not* taken, the acquired image can be defocused in post-processing to create the uneven illumination pattern. This method of correction can be done in Photoshop. Excessive correction will, however, introduce a loss of image contrast. See "Uneven Illumination Correction" in Chapter 6.

If OD/I readings are done from several *x*, *y* locations on a sample, illumination must be made even from edge to edge (across the "field" of view); otherwise, inaccurate readings will result. Flatfield correction is essential for OD/I measurement (**Figure 3.5C**).

FIGURE 3.5 An image with uneven illumination across the field (**A**), the flatfield image (**B**), and the flatfield corrected image (**C**).

USE BACKGROUND SUBTRACTION

Both ambient light and defects in light detectors contribute to OD/I readings, along with other possible ambient sources (such as gamma rays, in the case of long exposures). To correct for the addition of defects and ambient sources, an image referred to as the "background image" is acquired.

The energy source is turned off and the specimen is removed when the background image is taken. Also, the room lighting conditions are the same as they will be for measured images. The resultant, all-black, background image is then subtracted from images intended for measurement. Subtraction can be included in the acquisition steps (if possible) or subtracted during post-processing steps in Photoshop.

■ **Note:** *With fluorescent labels, resistance to bleaching can be improved with the addition of a chemical that inhibits bleaching to the mounting medium by using a nonaqueous clearing agent and a mounting medium.*

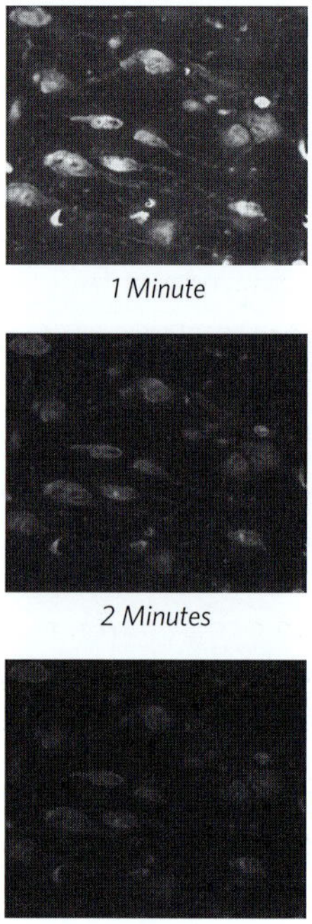

1 Minute

2 Minutes

3 Minutes

FIGURE 3.6 The images show the fading of fluorescence over a period of five minutes with continuous excitation (photobleaching) with light.

DO NOT MEASURE WHEN LABELING FADES

When fluorescently labeled cells and materials are struck by light, a fading in brightness can result. This phenomenon is known as bleaching (**Figure 3.6**).

All fluorescently labeled specimens, as well as other types of specimens that fade when exposed to respective energy sources, must be measured for OD/I against time of exposure to the energy source to determine the degree of fading. If the fading continues over time—without reaching a point at which the label stops fading or fades more slowly—a more stable dye, a lower power of the energy source, or another mounting protocol can be tried.

Post-processing

In general, images destined for OD/I measurements should not be altered in any way. Exceptions to that rule are discussed in the following sections and are acceptable as long as the procedures are documented and described in the publication.

FLATFIELD CORRECTION

As described earlier, flatfield correction can be done through camera control software when that function is available. In instances when that function is not available, flatfield correction must be done in imaging software before measurements are made. This is necessary to correct for uneven illumination and consequent incorrect OD/I measurements where unevenness results in brighter and darker areas. Flatfield correction is not necessary in evenly illuminated specimens (rare on a microscope) or in measurements always taken in the same *x*, *y* position in every image.

MASKING

To aid in the automation of OD/I measurements, it is useful to create solid black, white, or colorized overlays on parts of the image that will *not* be measured. In other words, cover up (mask) the unimportant areas of the image and leave only the relevant features visible. The masked portion of the image can be ignored by measurement software by using simple scripting (by using software tools) and only important features will automatically be measured.

DECONVOLUTION

When stacks of images are made, such as taking sequential images along the *z* axis and then saving all images from each plane to a single file, out of focus visual data will very likely be included. Out of focus visual data often intrudes from one or more *z* planes above and below the captured optical section. As a result, features on each *z* plane can potentially be made brighter by out of focus, additional illumination above and below the plane of interest. The intensity of the additional illumination will vary depending on the shape and size of each feature within a single plane. OD/I measurements from these features would then result in variable measurements and erroneous results.

Out of focus information from adjacent planes can be determined by using several different algorithms, each with varying degrees of accuracy. These algorithms reverse (deconvolve) the overlap (convolution) of out of focus visual data from planes above and below the plane of interest. These algorithms can also deconvolve from estimates of out of focus visual data, depending on several parameters (e.g., numeric aperture of the lens, the medium used for imaging the specimen, pixel dimensions, etc.).

The most accurate deconvolution algorithm depends on a reference stack of images in which subresolution fluorescent beads are used. The fluorescing beads cast single pixels representing out of focus visual data. These single pixels, or points, spread out from the in-focus bead to a defined distance. From several of these images averaged together, a "point spread" function can be derived as a reference.

■ **Note:** *The point spread function depends on specific wavelengths used, indices of refraction (based on the medium and materials between the objective and the microscope slide), magnification, and pixel resolution. If any of these elements change, a new point spread function needs to be generated.*

Because of varying effects from out of focus visual data when using image stacks, deconvolution is required when measuring OD/I to avoid misrepresentation (**Figure 3.7**).

Deconvolution is also increasingly being used on single images to eliminate out of focus information or to remove colors (color deconvolution). These algorithms rely on specific parameters so that predetermined out of focus information can be used for deconvolution.

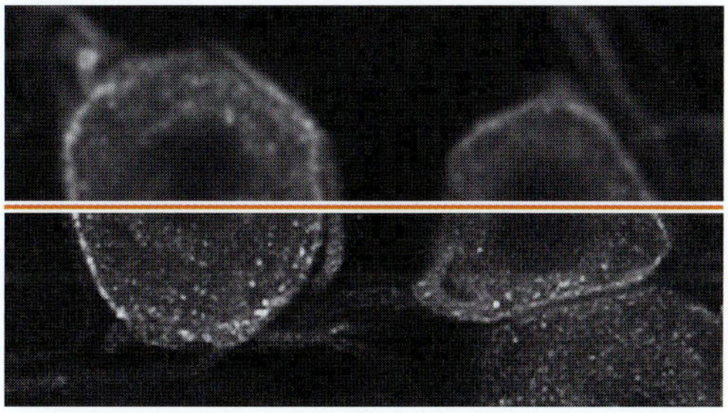

FIGURE 3.7 The original image (top) and a deconvolved and much more focused image (bottom).

BRIGHTFIELD (INCLUDING ENVIRONMENTAL SCENES): COLOR AND HISTOGRAM MATCHING

As mentioned in Chapter 2, white balancing is best done by turning off the auto white balancing (AWB), and then white balancing manually against a white or gray standard. When manual white balancing is consistently used, the likelihood of maintaining consistent and closely matched colors of the specimen or scene increases.

What hasn't been mentioned is the effect of inherent biological differences from specimen to specimen, variation in the preparation of specimens, and in staining differences depending on the specimen and disease states. Even with carefully controlled color balancing and consistent exposure settings, specimen to specimen differences in color brightness levels can result in inconsistent measurements. Comparing specimens on the basis of color composition and OD/I will end up being comparisons between apples and oranges. Variable visual data will result in a misrepresentation of data.

When colors or OD/I values can be changed according to an internal reference on the actual specimen, accurate measurements can be obtained. When no internal references exist, the distribution of pixels from dark to bright (represented by the histogram) are matched. One reference image is chosen and overall brightness levels of related images are matched to it (see "Histogram and Linear Histogram Matching" in Chapter 9).

USE FILTERS TO REDUCE NOISE

Sometimes noise is inevitable when acquiring images. When specimens bleach rapidly and when specimens move, multiple images cannot be obtained for frame averaging to reduce noise.

In these instances, only a filter applied in post-processing will minimize noise. These include blurring (Gaussian) and noise (Median and Reduce Noise) filters (**Figure 3.8**).

Noise in a measured feature would contain standard deviations that are very likely outside acceptable limits. Pixels containing erratic values could be determined as outliers by using statistical methods, and then be eliminated from the measurements.

Or, to avoid statistical methods, those pixels can be averaged with neighboring pixels in the actual image by using noise reduction filters. As a result, outliers would no longer affect the final measurements and standard deviations would be reduced. This method can avoid misrepresentations of data by including outliers that arbitrarily weight data, especially when a small number of pixels

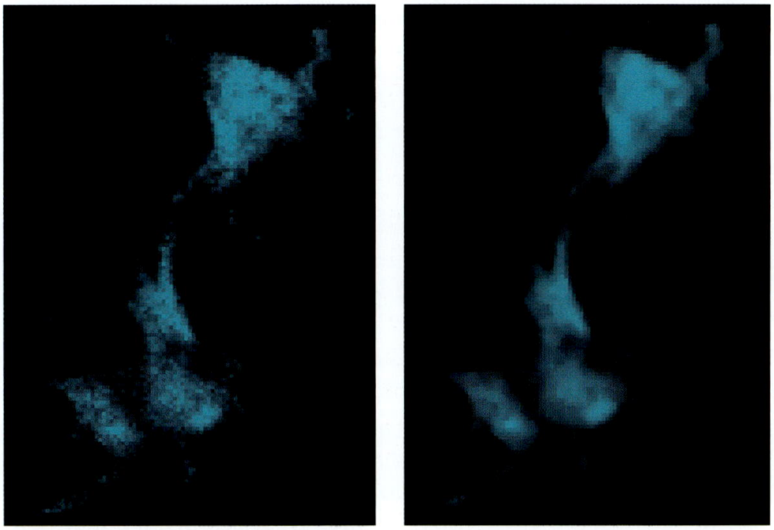

FIGURE 3.8 Widely varying pixel values from a noisy image (left); a median filtered image applied to average together neighboring pixels (right).

covers the features of interest. Using noise reduction filters in this instance would be legitimate. Because filters can be applied at varying strengths based on the number of neighboring pixels used for averaging, the strength of the filters will have to be determined. Noise filters would logically be applied to the degree to which the resulting measurements' standard deviation falls within acceptable limits, and no further. Filtering to a stronger degree could weigh together too many neighboring pixels and could potentially make the median measurements for each feature closer to identical.

While noise reduction filters alter visual data, filtering can be justified for noisy images.

Representative Images

Images taken as representations of a specimen are acquired and post-processed in a different way than those intended for OD/I measurements. Representative images are taken to match what was once seen by the human eye. Images taken for OD/I measurements, on the other hand, match what was once seen by the detector. For representative images, all details in the image—whether light or dark—are expected to be visible. For OD/I measurements, the brightest and darkest details must be outside the range of human vision and are not expected to be changed to conform to human vision (grayscale values can be pseudocolored to aid in visualization).

TABLE 3.2 Guidelines for Representative Images

ACQUISITION	POST-PROCESSING: MAY BE ALLOWED	CONFORMANCE
Consistent imaging system methods	Contrast and Brightness changes	Hue changes for colorized images
Gamma can be nonlinear	Color toning	
Use a reference image	Sharpening	
Use a higher bit depth, if available	Gamma changes	
Flatfield correct, if desired	Desaturation of offending colors	
Use controls		

Representative images are acquired and corrected to conform the images to human perception. In so doing, images are corrected to reveal obscured details, often in dark regions of the image or in regions that are subtly different than the surrounding features. To modify the images to comply with human perception, follow the guidelines in **Table 3.2**. Each guideline is explored in more detail in the following sections.

Acquisition

Representative images are acquired within the dynamic range of the camera. When specimen details are obscured, gamma can be changed, though it may have to be reported in the publication. In any case, a reference image can provide a tonal range reference to which related images can be matched. Representative images can be acquired with low bit depth settings, and flatfield correction can be applied. As an additional precaution, controls to verify the appearance of specimens in images must also be used to confirm that the visual data is not a result of overamplifying the brightness of the stain or dye. See the following sections for more information about acquisition procedures.

CONSISTENT IMAGING SYSTEM METHODS

Representative images are taken so that all resultant pixel values from the specimen encompass the full dynamic range of the imaging instrument. Those settings can change from image to image and are related to specimen-to-specimen differences (though changes to the settings are more often done on a session-to-session basis). The brightest significant level in the specimen would be brightened until it was near maximum levels for the dynamic range of the instrument. The darkest value would be darkened until it was near the minimum level.

Settings may also vary within a specimen for different dyes or markers. For fluorescent dyes, when images are taken at different wavelength ranges, settings often do not match. For example, an image of a green-emitting dye often requires different settings than a red-emitting dye.

Thus, camera and instrument settings are *in*consistent, depending on the specimen and possibly the dye. But the approach to image acquisition is consistent: Adjust the settings on the basis of fitting the tonal range of the specimen within the dynamic range of the imaging device. This approach guarantees the greatest breadth of pixel values, which is crucial for rendering all the visual data.

GAMMA CAN BE NONLINEAR

Images destined for OD/I measurements must maintain a gamma of 1. But images meant for representation may need to be changed from a linear relationship of grayscale and color values to the nonlinear range that is constrained within human vision—conventionally, a gamma of greater than 1. A nonlinear range in which dark values are lightened and bright values remain the same mimics both human vision and photographic films. Representative images, in many instances, often *require* an increase in gamma, or a misrepresentation occurs because dark features are obscured (**Figure 3.9**).

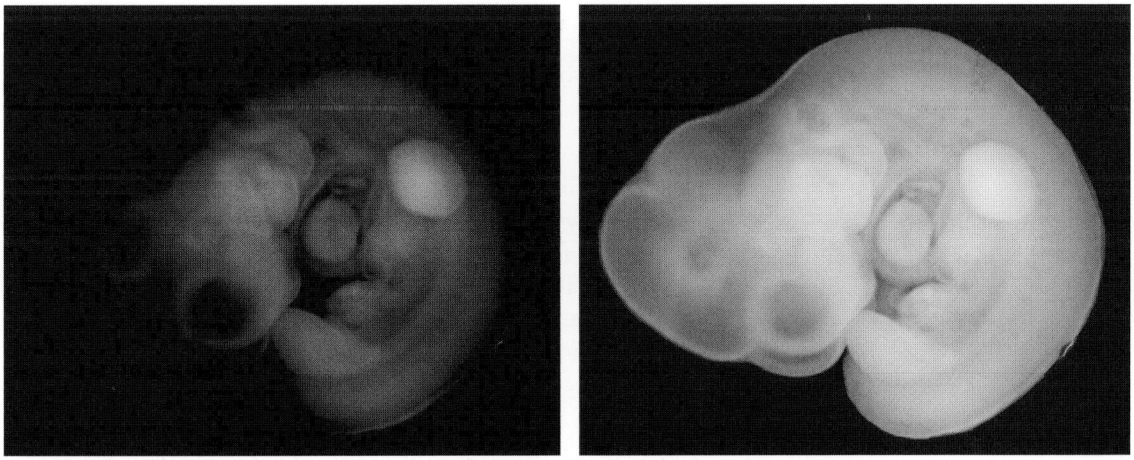

FIGURE 3.9 An image acquired with a gamma of 1 (left); the same image at a gamma of 3 (right).

Gamma correction can also be done to decrease the value of dark pixels. Thus, greater contrast is gained through darker blacks against which the whiter features stand out, but with little change in the values of the white features in relation to the darker features.

Changing the gamma is more likely to create a misrepresentation when darkening images to obscure details for the sake of the aesthetic appeal of greater contrast. Generally, contrast changes are made by expanding the histogram to include darker values (making the addition of contrast a linear function) versus a gamma change.

Some specimens may contain a limited range of values in which details cannot be adequately separated unless both contrast and gamma changes are made. When that type of specimen is imaged, gamma changes can be justified as the only means for creating a representation of the specimen.

USE A REFERENCE IMAGE

Imaging system settings for representative images can also be determined by using a reference image. This image is taken from a specimen in which pixel values fill the dynamic range, and colors (if in color) appear representative. This "perfect" image of the specimen can be saved to backup media or to a hard disk. The image can be opened in later imaging sessions and used to visually match contrast, color, brightness, and gamma in images taken at later sessions.

As a more exacting method, the specimen can be rephotographed at each imaging session to obtain a match to the reference image. The same location can be found on the specimen by visually locating landmarks or boundaries in the specimen or by marking the specimen in some way. As a result, instrument and camera settings are changed consistently and objectively from session to session, allowances are made for power loss (or gain) from the energy source, and potential problems with incorrect instrument settings can be determined.

Using a reference image ensures that a consistent, objective method is used to acquire images of similar specimens. A reference image prevents having to perform major image corrections in post-processing, where a loss of visual data would inevitably result to varying degrees. This method works best for stable specimens, such as those labeled with brightfield stains, versus specimens labeled with markers that fade.

USE A HIGHER BIT DEPTH

As stated in Chapter 2, a greater bit depth will result in less visual data loss due to rounding errors when post-processing. Thus, a 12- or 16-bit image is desirable.

However, that doesn't mean that an 8-bit depth should *not* be used. Human vision is limited to a dynamic range of less than 8 bits, so it follows that the use of 8-bit imaging is reasonable, especially when few post-processing corrections are made.

Also, when OD/I measurements are *not* made, the finer divisions of gray levels and greater dynamic range are relatively unimportant. Representative images can be perfectly adequate for viewing and reproduction in 8 bits.

FLATFIELD/BACKGROUND CORRECT

Flatfield correction and background subtraction are unnecessary when images are meant for representation. Because OD/I measurements are not being made, and the contribution of uneven illumination and background do not have to be eliminated for accurate measurements, corrections do not have to be done.

Note: *Flatfield correction is also crucial for separating features of interest from surrounding, background areas. It must be done when images are destined for quantification, whether flatfield correction is done in acquisition or post-processing.*

But for both aesthetic and professional reasons, flatfield correction provides a truer rendition of images. For that reason, flatfield correction is done, along with background subtraction.

USE CONTROLS

Data misrepresentation can occur when markers used to label features in the specimen are almost the same grayscale or color level as the specimen. These color values will be overamplified if settings are changed to better separate the label and the specimen. When colors are amplified to fill the dynamic range of the imaging system, the relationship of these color values are overemphasized, resulting in a misrepresentation of the original specimen.

As stated earlier, using positive and negative controls is of utmost importance. By using controls, the presence of a label, even if it is weak, can be verified. Camera and instrument settings can then be used to amplify weak signals to create an image that is a true representation. If the degree of amplification is excessive, mention it in the methods section of the publication.

Post-processing

Representative images can be sharpened, colorized, and adjusted for brightness, contrast, and gamma. Colors can be desaturated to match the specimen. Each of these actions is performed according to specific guidelines so that excessive changes are not made. When images are sharpened—which should be required for all images—the post-processing step may have to be reported. Consult with the author guidelines for the exact procedures for sharpening images.

SHARPENING

Sharpening images is generally discouraged in publications. For brightfield images, sharpening can increase the contrast of small, nearly transparent features, or artifacts, creating an effect that simulates light scattering at the edges. These features could potentially be confused as real details.

Sharpening reduces the gradients between the edges of two contrasting features. The gradients occur when edges are not well defined, which happens when features are out of focus. When the edges between features, especially those that are bright against dark, have reduced or absent gradients and appear defined, the image looks focused. Except in instances in which visual artifacts appear, sharpening is justifiable. In instances where a digital camera is used, sharpening may be necessary to return images to the focus seen when using the camera. In all but specialized cameras, filters are placed in front of the detector to serve two purposes: to eliminate near infrared signals (typically greater than 650 to 700 nanometers) and to slightly blur incoming visual data as a way to anti-alias edges. Aliasing refers to a stair-stepping effect in an image that occurs along defined edges, such as diagonal lines. That effect can be mollified by slightly blurring the edge, or anti-aliasing. Blurring helps eliminate aliasing and is often very noticeable and objectionable because it doesn't match what the eye sees.

Sharpening can also be used for aesthetic purposes to match what was once seen by eye or for conforming images to printing presses to preserve sharpness. Generally, sharpening is a post-processing step that is reported.

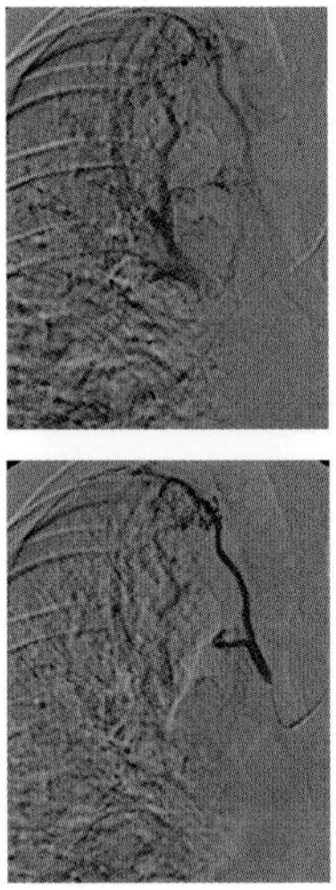

FIGURE 3.10 The image on the top is in grayscale; on the bottom, the image retains its original blue-shifted color from the film.

COLOR TONING

The introduction of a tone into a grayscale image affects the perception of contrast among and within features. A blue-toned image, for example, appears to have a greater contrast. The viewer's perception of that greater contrast results in an improved differentiation of the features (**Figure 3.10**).

But the perception of contrast and detail is only part of the rationale for toning. The other part includes the memory of how an image is best viewed, and that memory often includes all professionals within a field of study: a collective memory. This memory is called "color memory," which is a reference to a color that you know is correctly represented.

Within fields of study, color memory is developed over years of viewing images from stained samples or from past experience with grayscale films and black and white photographs. In the latter instance, with grayscale films and images, each profession determined the ideal manufacturers of films and photographic paper. These films and paper stocks contained a subtle hue that might have made the paper or film bluish, brownish, or greenish, and so on. The subtle hues then became the color memory of how the specimen should be viewed in each profession.

Color toning introduces the same shift in color to not only satisfy the color memory of each profession, but to provide a view that contains a contrast to better reveal important details. While not a widely used method, the addition of a bluish or brownish tone to grayscale images can be done to improve representation.

■ **Note:** *Gamma changes may need to be done when images are not acquired properly as a way to "rescue" the image. Poor acquisition practices invariably lead to post-processing correction. If changes are made, the same changes must be applied equally to all images from that experiment.*

■ **Note:** *It is far preferable to use only contrast changes with fluorescent images to lighten the darkest blacks, which often has the effect of revealing details in darker regions. When these details in darker regions do not become visible, a gamma correction can be made.*

▶ **Warning:** *When a change to gamma is made, references in a manuscript to lighter or darker features cannot reasonably be made because the linear relationship of grayscale or color values has been replaced with a logarithmic one.*

CONTRAST, BRIGHTNESS, AND GAMMA

For representative images, contrast, brightness, and gamma may be altered. Generally, these changes should only be done as a means to conform the image to the specific output (**Figure 3.11**).

It can be argued that gamma correction is necessary for a correct representation of an image when OD/I values are not measured. The linear range of grayscale values obscures details that cannot be seen by eye, especially in darker areas of the image. These darker areas need to be lightened without significantly affecting brighter values to see visual data that may have a bearing on reported findings.

Too often the opposite occurs in research: Darker areas are intentionally left outside the range of human vision to avoid introducing visual data that might have to be explained in a publication. The prevailing thought is to "leave the original as is" rather than change the gamma. Interestingly, for much of the last century, the change in gamma from a linear relationship of grayscale values to one that is logarithmic was inherent in most photographic films used as visual data in science.

Reporting gamma changes is often required by publications. Be sure to check with the author guidelines before considering changes to gamma.

FIGURE 3.11 No gamma changes were made to the image on the left, leading to a misrepresentation of the extent of fungal spread (right) where the gamma was changed.

DESATURATION: DIGITAL CAMERAS

The sensitivity to red-colored features tends to be stronger in digital cameras when compared to the sensitivity of conventional films. Depending on the manufacturer, the red sensitivity is repressed through the use of algorithms or additional filtration, or extended red sensitivity is allowed. On the whole, cameras made for scientific research allow for extended red sensitivity. For that reason, some dyes in the red region (e.g., eosin) appear so bright on computer screens the color appears to have a neon glow (**Figure 3.12**).

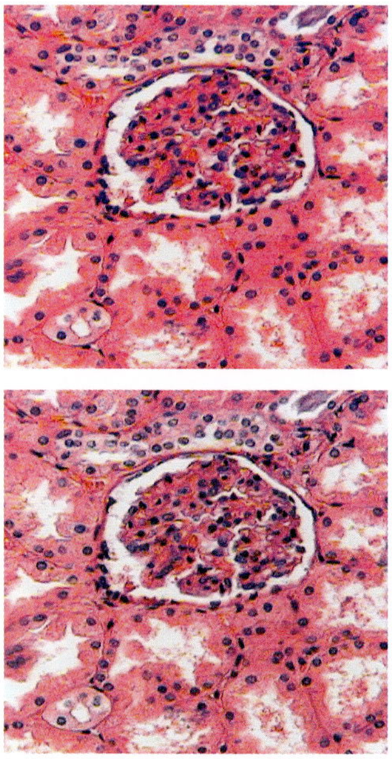

FIGURE 3.12 The image on the top appears as it was acquired; on the bottom, the red areas were desaturated.

When unaware of the red sensitivity in digital cameras, users often believe that the color is incorrect, and then either change the settings of the camera or attempt to color balance in Photoshop.

Red region colors are in fact correct. The problem is not the hue but the saturation of the color. Saturation is a reference to the purity of a color: If the color is 100 percent pure, the color is said to be saturated.

To show the saturated colors as they appear to the eye, the colors require desaturation, which introduces equal amounts of all three colors (gray). Otherwise, saturated colors are misrepresented. Color desaturation is a necessary post-processing change to return the original colors to the specimen.

Conformance

The only conformance step used with representative images that differs from other kinds of images is to make color changes. Color changes are more frequent with representative images, though these changes may sometimes be necessary for other kinds of images.

COLOR CHANGES FROM COLORIZED IMAGES

■ **Note:** *The computer screen always shows colors more brilliantly than paper, simply because the colors are illuminated by transmitted light. Paper is lit by reflection, so it does not have the same brilliance.*

Many dyes and stains used in science, medicine, and industry create pure, saturated colors in images (not only in red, as mentioned earlier). The saturated colors simply do not reproduce in publications as they appear on the computer screen. Images displayed on a computer monitor use the RGB color space, which has a wider range of available colors, or gamut, than does the CMYK color space. The gamut of the CMYK space is limited by the fact that its colors are produced by mixing opaque inks on paper. RGB colors include a far greater number of hues than CMYK. Saturated colors in particular are mostly within the gamut of RGB, but not CMYK.

To preserve bright colors with shadow and highlight details after images are converted to CMYK colors, many of the colors need to be changed in hue (**Figure 3.13**). For fluorescently labeled specimens,

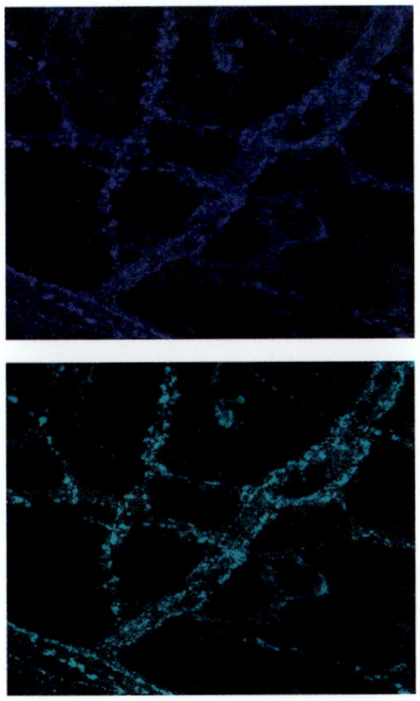

FIGURE 3.13 The image on the top is the original, colorized image using the conventional color of saturated blue; on the bottom, the hue was changed to include more green, shifting it toward cyan.

colors are often assigned the same color as their emissions wavelengths, but that isn't a requirement: Researchers can arbitrarily assign colors. When colors are changed to CMYK-friendly colors, the overall bright color and relationship of brightness levels are retained when images are published.

Colors can also be desaturated to fit within the CMYK gamut. This method of conformance to the CMYK gamut reduces the brightness value to a dullness that is not representative of the original image. So, it's often best to change hues when possible.

Some publications ask that the gamut be reduced even further to those colors visible to the color blind. In this instance, a limited table of colors must be used. Author guidelines provide specific information about appropriate colors to use, and some colors will need to be changed.

When images are colorized, it is legitimate to change the colors to the CMYK gamut to accurately reproduce them in publications. Otherwise, features do not appear like the original specimen. Of all misrepresentations of visual data in publications, poor reproduction of saturated colors arguably provides the most frequent source of misrepresentation.

Images Intended for Quantification and Visualization

Images meant for quantification include all measurements *except* OD/I. This includes images from which data such as counts, lengths, areas, orientation, clustering, and so on are derived from computer-aided image analysis or quantification. These images are often made into purely black-and-white (binarized) images to accommodate computer-aided measurement.

Binarized images are created by setting a threshold at a specific grayscale or color value: All values above or below the threshold are included and are made entirely black, and the surrounding areas are left entirely white (or vice versa). The threshold value is determined by how completely features of interest (also called Regions of Interest [ROI]) separate (segment) from surrounding areas. In this case, the black features of interest are then measured by computer computations. Features of interest can also be segmented by making selections around features.

In either case, the intent of the images meant for quantification is to clearly separate the features of interest from surrounding areas (the background), which is normally done by taking advantage of grayscale or color differences: Either the color or the darkness/lightness of the features of interest can be different than the background. Any method that can enhance the differences is acceptable for this purpose, as long as the method does not erode or change a feature's borders (or other characteristics).

Visualization

Images intended for visualization are different from representative images insofar as they are clearly models of the original data, such as 3D models. To make these models, features of interest need to be clearly separated from the background (just as with computer-aided quantification). When images are poorly separated because color or gray values are similar to the surrounding features (background) or noise interferes, extensive post-processing may be necessary. Filters may need to be applied, along with adjustments to brightness, gamma, and contrast. Sometimes features will need to be manually outlined to select them, and artifacts will need to be removed. What separates OD/I measured images and representative images from those meant for quantification/visualization lies in more extensive post-processing. Post-processing options for OD/I measured images are almost nonexistent. For representative images, post-processing is used only to match the appearance of the original by correcting optical and digital anomalies. Post-processing for images intended for quantification and visualization removes or minimizes visual data to isolate relevant features. Images are not always meant to appear like they were once seen.

The exhaustive reporting of post-processing steps in publications is critical for these images so that experiments can be repeated by other labs. **Table 3.3** contains the acquisition methods and an overview of the post-processing steps that are allowed for images intended for quantification and visualization.

TABLE 3.3 Guidelines for Images Destined for Quantization/Visualization

ACQUISITION	POST-PROCESSING: ALLOWED
Use thick sections for volume data	Filtering for noise and edge finding
Use a reference image	Artifact removal
Flatfield correct and background subtract	Grouping of visual data
Choose adequate resolution and magnification	Isolating features manually
Bit depth can be lowered	Contrast, brightness, and gamma changes
	Thresholding and clipping

Acquisition

Acquisition methods for images destined for quantification and visualization are similar to those used for reference images. Though the use of thick samples is not necessarily an *acquisition* category—rather, it is part of specimen preparation—it is included because the resultant images can be misleading when they come from the topmost or bottommost parts of a tissue section. Using a reference image ensures consistency, just as it does for representative images. Flatfield correction for images meant for quantification and visualization is critical and not always optional. So that features can be positively identified, adequate resolution and magnification are chosen. As with representative images, bit depth isn't always critical. The acquisition methods and post-processing steps in Table 3.3 are discussed in the following sections.

USE THICK SECTIONS FOR VOLUME DATA

When features that are part of a three-dimensional volume (versus a monolayer) are measured and sectioned samples are used for measurement and visualization, some forethought must go into sectioning. The inevitability of features being removed or cut into partial sections during the process of sectioning must be considered. In critical applications where estimates of total numbers, lengths, and volumes of variably sized features are required, sections should be thick enough to contain more than one of the largest feature in depth (z). This provides enough depth for complete features to be assessed, and it provides space at the top and bottom of the section that can be ignored (because it will never be known how many features really exist at the surface as a result of the unknown number of removed features).

Measuring complete and intact features ensures positive identification. Also, the added depth ensures that features removed from the knife's scraping of the cut surface will not affect results. A thick specimen becomes the best representation of the original volume. Sections thinner than the height of the measured features may be misrepresentations, requiring a cogent rationale for using shallow sectioning.

USE A REFERENCE IMAGE

Image acquisition for quantification/visualization follows the same rules as those intended for representation. The exception to that rule lies in the importance of a reference image, control, or calibration standard. Especially when images are taken over time, the need for a consistent reference is critical so that the reference can be tested against known values.

The reference does not *have* to be a precalibrated standard unless the standard is used to determine the parameters of the system, such as what is done to determine scale bars. The reference can instead be an internal reference, a reference from a specimen imaged at the first session, a reference image, or an object included with the specimen (such as a bead of known dimensions).

In many fields of science the aim is not to obtain absolute values but values that are relative, such as when experimental specimens are compared with controls or to other specimens at different time points (longitudinal studies). It is the relative difference between one set of specimens and the controls or the specimens at time points further along that provide the required data.

Matching images to a reference is an objective means for determining image systems settings and for tracking changes in the energy source over time. This approach provides representational images and accurate data.

FLATFIELD CORRECT AND BACKGROUND SUBTRACT

Unevenly illuminated fields are the greatest obstacle to segmentation and separating features from the background, so it is crucial that flatfield correction be used, if possible, during acquisition. When fields are uneven, thresholds will unevenly include features of interest, depending on their *x*, *y* locations: Some features may be included and others only partially included.

For example, the border of a cell in a bright center may be readily apparent, and when thresholding is used, a cutoff value can be selected to binarize the cell all the way to its border. On the other hand, a cell in a dark area at the selected cutoff value will binarize at some extent shy of the border. That extent depends on the level of uneven illumination.

Note that the specimen may also create uneven illumination. When a group of tightly gathered fluorescent cells occur with cells that are isolated in a single image, the brightness of gathered cells may create a cumulative brightness that "lights" the surrounding area, whereas cells that occur alone do not brighten surroundings to the same degree.

Therefore, it is essential that flatfield correction techniques be used. When thresholding is used to separate measured features from surrounding areas or when values need to be amplified to separate features from the background, incorrect measurements and models will result when specimens are unevenly illuminated.

CHOOSE ADEQUATE RESOLUTION AND MAGNIFICATION

The pixel sampling rate must match the spatial separation of details in the specimen, as mentioned earlier when describing Nyquist rates. Too few pixels can result in too few pixels to sample.

The magnification setting follows a rule: Nothing can be measured that cannot be positively identified. That rule is balanced against efficiency. When more features are included in a field of view, more data can be generated per field. As a result, efficiency dictates that the lowest magnification be used at which specimens can be positively identified.

When choosing magnification, be sure to test your ability to positively identify features. At the same time, the pixel coverage of features must be adequate, and at times a higher magnification than desired may have to be used to obtain adequate coverage.

Misidentification of features leads to incorrect data, and efforts must be made to avoid collecting additional data when features cannot be positively identified.

BIT DEPTH

Images destined for visualization and quantification do not absolutely require bit depths higher than 8 bits. For most purposes, 8-bit images can be used. These may be required for use in 3D software or may be used to speed up processing.

Post-processing

Post-processing steps for quantification/visualization images require any post-processing that is necessary for consistency from image to image, and whatever is necessary to aid in segmentation. The following sections provide procedures that can be used.

HISTOGRAM MATCHING

Histogram equalization and histogram matching can introduce consistency into variable distributions of grayscale and color values in images of specimens. These techniques are required in instances where specimen-to-specimen differences exist to correctly represent the visual data.

USING FILTERS

What differentiates images destined for quantification and visualization from representative images and those intended for OD/I measurement lies in the intentional use of post-processing filters, such as those used for blur, noise reduction, smoothing, edge enhancement,

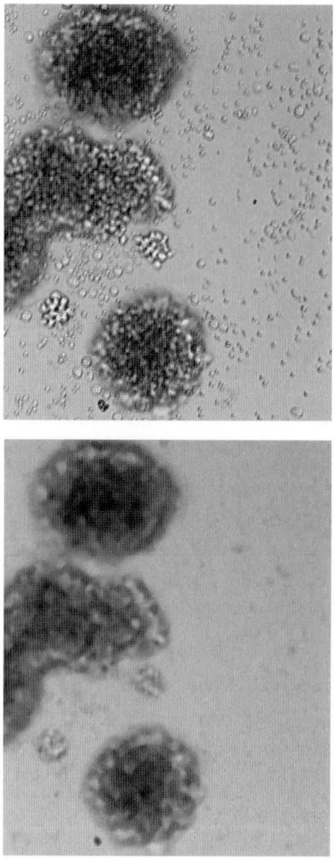

FIGURE 3.14 The image on the top shows individual cells: on the bottom, the individual cells are removed through blurring to reveal agglomeration.

edge detection, and more. These filters, described extensively in publications about image processing, are used to aid in segmentation or provide a means to average grayscale values of pixels when noise is present.

The use of filters must be described in methods for two reasons: each filter adds a level of misrepresentation from the original image and other labs must be able to repeat the method. When segmenting, misrepresentation is essential for subsequent measurement and visualization: It is necessary for separating features of interest from surrounding areas.

ARTIFACT REMOVAL AND GROUPING OF VISUAL DATA

The removal of small specks and debris is expected in post-processing. When images are segmented, single pixels and artifacts might be included with pertinent features, so it is legitimate to remove them (**Figure 3.14**).

Caution must be taken to accurately identify small features as artifacts versus the real visual data. As an example, when looking at fluorescence in situ hybridization (FISH) of DNA, it must be presumed that every small, labeled feature within the cell wall boundaries is a DNA sequence because these features are not well resolved by conventional optics.

Conversely, it is often appropriate to remove fragments of legitimate data simply because they cannot be absolutely identified. Cells are often cut into fractions when slicing specimens. The smallest fractions, though labeled, cannot be absolutely identified, so it is necessary to remove them from measurements.

When it comes to counting, the removal or inclusion of small features can make computer-aided measurement far more accurate than manual methods, with the exception of stereologic methods (see "Segment Images with Photoshop or Use Stereology?" in Chapter 9). When scientists do the counting manually, variability exists from one person to the next in making decisions on exactly how small a feature needs to be before it is included or excluded. A cutoff size can be decided on by using quantification programs (like Photoshop CS3).

Several closely spaced features can be grouped together in instances where it is important to identify clumping or when features should be connected but other segmentation methods cannot accomplish that end. Features' edges may be smoothed as well to average the visual data.

All of these methods are best done globally rather than by using manual selections, so that subjective biases do not enter into the identification of an artifact. However, at times it is unavoidable. As long as human intervention to eliminate or include data is mentioned in the methods, along with a convincing rationale (e.g., an artifact is at varying dimensions, thus human intervention is necessary), its use is legitimate.

Methods for eliminating artifacts and for grouping visual data are acceptable misrepresentations of original data, as long as the methods are used to more accurately obtain numeric data. These methods may also be used to aid in visualization as a means to remove unimportant and visually distracting artifacts.

ISOLATING FEATURES OF INTEREST MANUALLY

Just as artifacts can be removed manually, so too can features of interest be outlined manually to isolate them from surrounding areas (**Figure 3.15**). This needs to be done when methods for segmenting don't work and stereology isn't used.

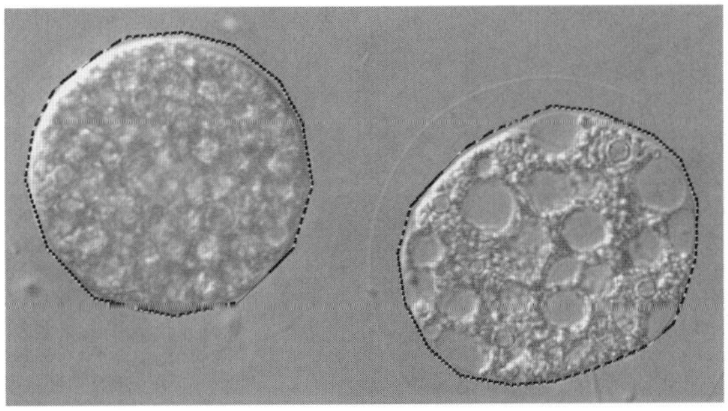

FIGURE 3.15 Differential Interference Contrast (DIC) images often require manual outlining of features, shown as a black line around each cell.

Manually outlining is a local change, not a global change to the image, and is a violation of a rule in the typical author guidelines for publications. Breaking this rule is allowed for quantification and visualization, but it comes with a risk: Publications must agree that manual outlining is a reasonable and repeatable method.

CONTRAST, BRIGHTNESS, AND GAMMA

The relationship of grayscale and color values can be altered to better achieve segmentation.

The adjustment of these values can be especially important for visualization. 3D models demand a clean separation of the significant features from the surrounding areas. The adjustments are applied equally to all images from the same set, which is often more than one channel.

Again, these changes should not be made to the degree that feature borders are altered or to subdue or eliminate valid features. As long as these changes are not destructive and the changes lead to improved segmentation, segmented images will be a representation of the original features.

THRESHOLDING AND CLIPPING

As mentioned at the beginning of this chapter, thresholding isolates features of interest for quantification. This can also be done by adjusting the brightness so that values clip, a phenomenon often seen when visualizing colocalization of two different features on the same cellular structure.

Thresholded, and consequently, binarized images can also be used to automate measurement without user intervention. When more than one feature type needs to be separated, discrete shades of gray can be included in binarized images. As a result, one feature type can be binarized black, and another feature type in a separate step can be binarized black and then colorized gray.

Features that are binarized are easily selected using the selection tools (e.g., using the Color Range command) in Photoshop. The selection tools can be used to automate the post-processing steps without user intervention. Entire directories of multiple images can then be automatically measured.

Binarized images are an expected image mode for measurement. Though these misrepresent the original in terms of its continuous tone, as long as features consistently retain the essential image information, thresholding is appropriate (**Figure 3.16**).

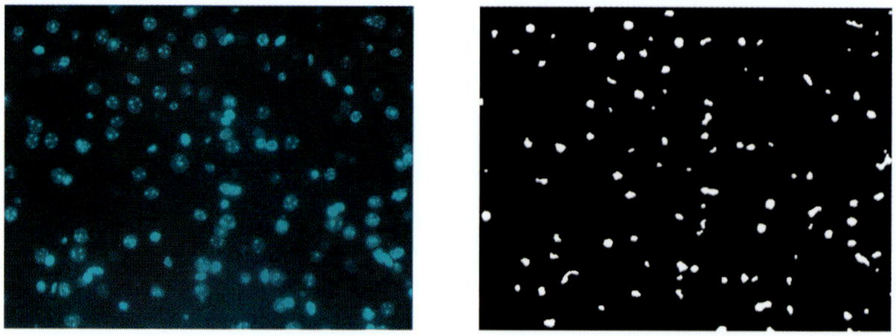

FIGURE 3.16 The original, blue colorized image of nuclei (left): brighter nuclei have been binarized into discrete "blobs" (right).

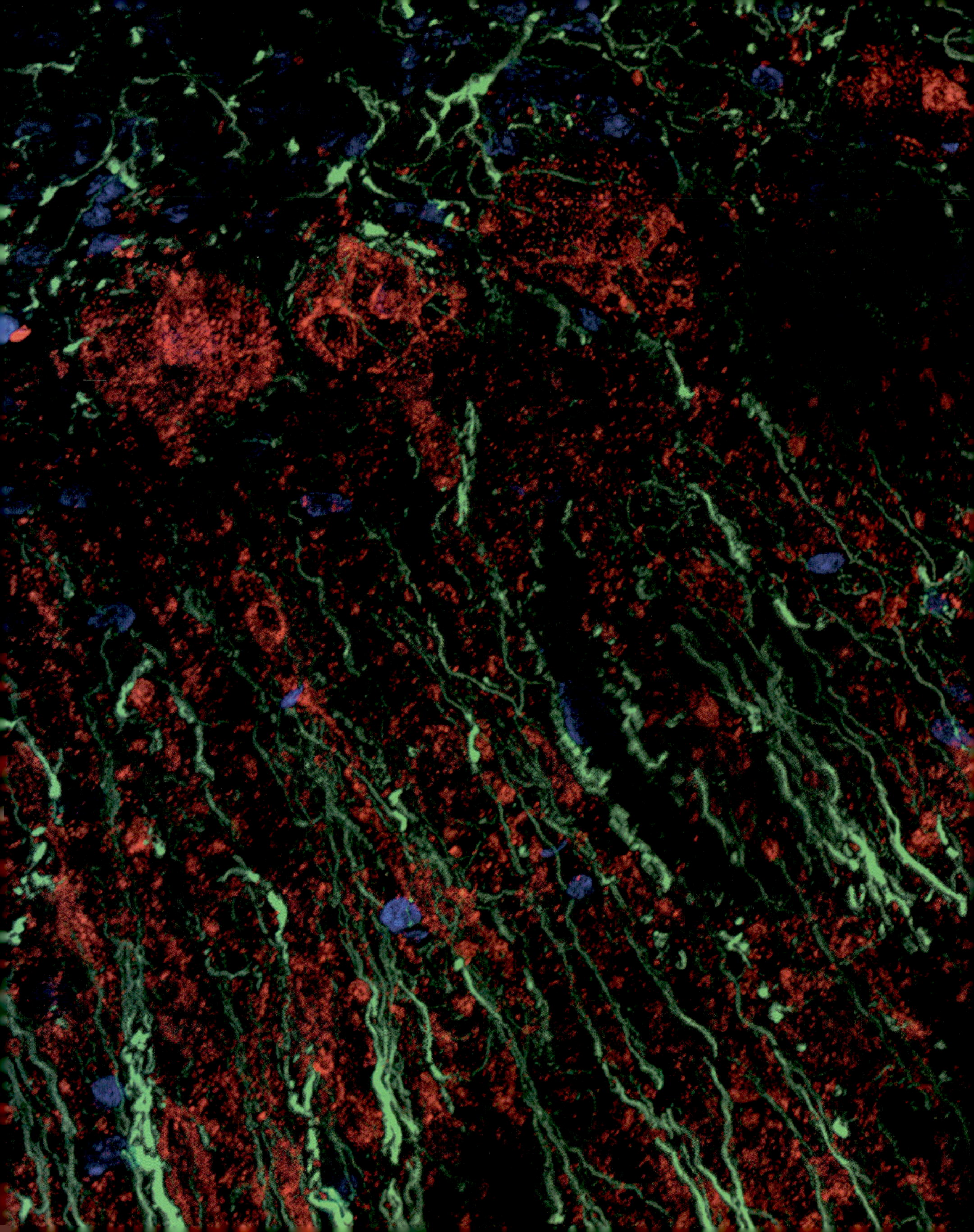

PART 2

Input, Corrections, and Output

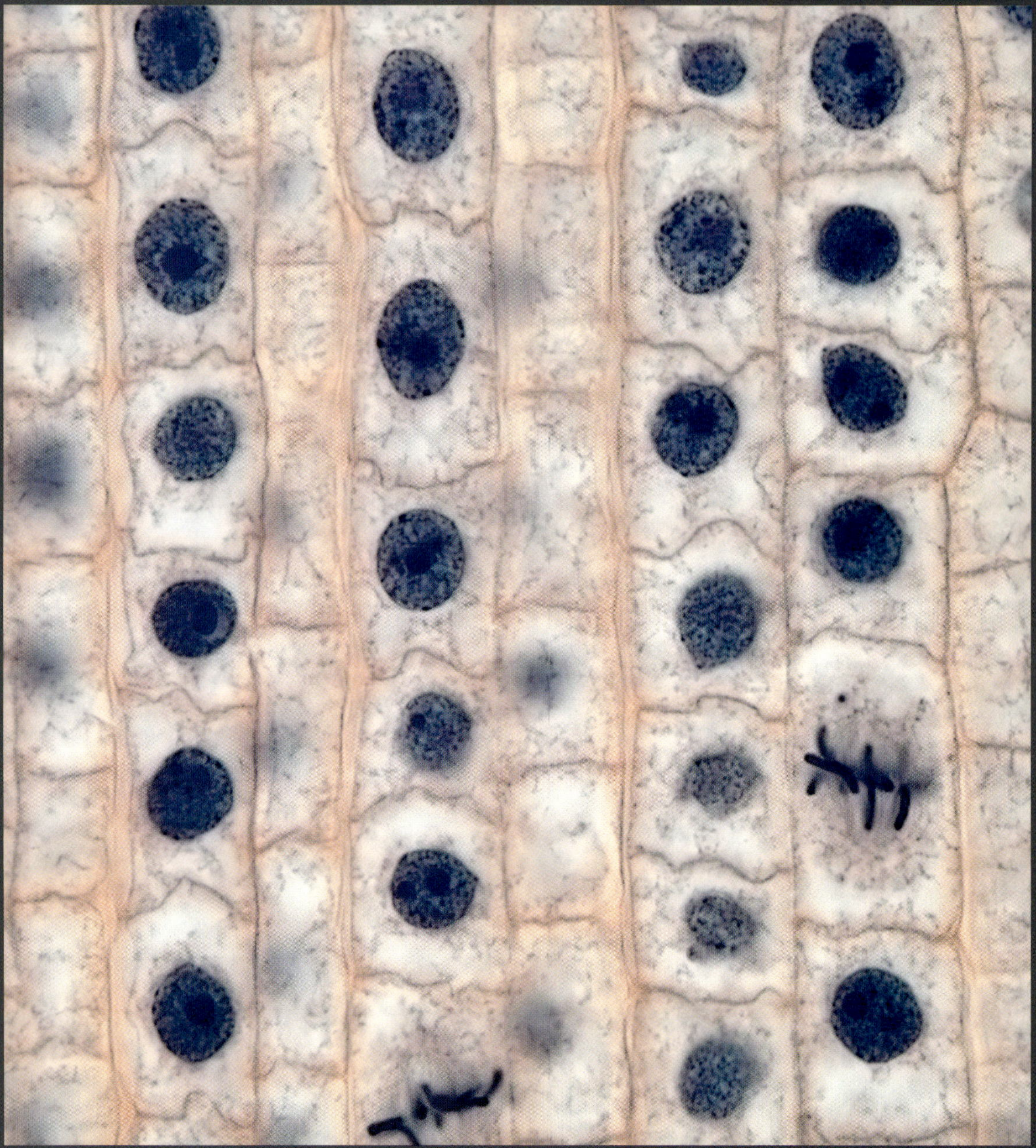

CHAPTER 4

Getting the Best Input

VISUAL DATA INTENDED for any output contains as much detail as possible within the limits of the acquisition device and the kind of energy used (light, electrons, x-ray, etc.). To achieve the resolving of details, the specimen needs to be prepared to optimize the quality of the images, and the medium, if any, between the specimen and the imaging device needs to be appropriate for optimal imaging. As far as controls for the imaging device, the following conditions are met:

- Apertures are set (when appropriate) to optimize resolution of detail.
- The energy source is focused, if possible, so that all parts of the specimen are struck at equal intensities.
- Correct procedures are followed to minimize damage to the specimen and to create conditions for matching what is seen by eye to the visual data through attenuation of the energy source and filters.
- Methods are used to improve signal to noise.
- Dark to bright specimen features are kept within the dynamic range of the imaging device; otherwise, details are lost in areas that are too bright or too dark.

When visual data is derived from specific software applications (versus imaging devices), details are preserved under the conditions that pixel resolutions are either maintained (when images are transferred from one application to another), or dense enough to avoid seeing discrete pixels (when lower resolution images and graphics are destined for outputs).

Image of stained section (Carolina Biological Supply, Burlington, NC) from an onion using a 63x, 1.4 N.A. objective on a Zeiss Axiovert 2. Image was acquired with a Spot 1 camera using Spot 2.1 software (Diagnostic Instruments, Sterling Heights, MI). Photoshop CS3 Extended, version 10.1 (Adobe Systems Incorporated, San Jose, CA), was used to conform image to publication by sharpening and minimally correcting color; and corrected for chromatic aberration with the Reduce Noise filter. Scale bar = 20 microns.

● **More:** *For information on dealing with images derived from low-resolution sources, including Web pages, download "Scale Bars and Options for Input and Output" from www.peachpit.com/scientificimaging.*

Ways to meet imaging conditions in the preceding list using five different devices are covered in this chapter. They include compound microscopes, confocal systems, flatbed scanners, stereo microscopes, and SLR (Single Lens Reflex) cameras. For meeting pixel resolution conditions when images are derived from various digital sources, specific software applications are described, including PowerPoint).

Acquiring Images from Standard (Compound) Microscopes

While various software acquisition programs exist for each brand of camera, the hope is to find certain software components to aid in achieving three end results:

- Accurate representations of a specimen in terms of color rendition and tonal range, and optimal rendition of contrasting features (contrast)
- Evenly illuminated specimens (unlikely on microscopes)
- Images of specimens devoid of electronic noise (visible noise is more likely with dim specimens)

Accurate Representations

Optimal representation of specimens is achieved by setting up the microscope correctly and by adjusting camera settings. Specimens prepared for brightfield imaging (darker specimens on a bright background) require specific set up procedures for focusing the illumination beam (Koehler illumination). Darkfield imaging (brighter specimen on a darker background), when it is of fluorescently labeled specimens, may also require focusing of the illumination beam. Setup of the microscope for darkfield and other microscopy techniques are outside the scope of this book, but the information can be found at http://micro.magnet.fsu.edu.

Adjustment of camera settings include white balancing for brightfield, color images; determination of method for determining exposure (automatic or manual); adjusting exposure and possibly attenuating the light level so that the tonal range of the image is within the dynamic range of the camera; choosing appropriate camera settings depending on the sample; and acquiring the image to evaluate. Filters may be put in the illumination path to improve contrast within the specimen.

Even Illumination

Especially with lower magnifications, uneven illumination across the field of view is likely to be seen when evaluating the image. Illumination is evened out by applying a flatfield correction through the use of image acquisition software, if that component is available. When software components for achieving flatfield correction cannot be found in image acquisition programs, uneven illumination can be corrected later in post-processing. These methods are described in the "Flatfield Correction" section.

Noise Reduction

The presence of noise can be ameliorated or removed by using components found in acquisition software. They include background subtraction for removing hot pixels and frame averaging. But when these components don't exist, additional images can be taken to correct for noise and uneven illumination in post-processing. Corrections for uneven illumination can also be made in post-processing without additional images, but they are likely to result in a loss of image information to varying degrees.

The step-by-step procedure for acquiring images on a microscope depends on the mode of the resultant image (grayscale or color) and the technique used for illuminating the specimen (brightfield or darkfield). A flowchart that includes relevant steps is shown in **Table 4.1**.

TABLE 4.1 **Microscope Imaging**

DARKFIELD, FLUORESCENCE	BRIGHTFIELD, COLOR	BRIGHTFIELD, GRAYSCALE
Allow equipment to warm up	Allow equipment to warm up	Allow equipment to warm up
Set Exposure/Gain and Contrast	Set Koehler illumination	Set Koehler illumination
Bin for more sensitivity, if necessary	Set light source to 3200K	Use filters, if necessary
Frame Average, if noisy	Set Exposure/Gain and Contrast	Set Exposure/Gain and Contrast
Flatfield correct	White balance	Flatfield correct
Background subtract	Flatfield correct	Background subtract
	Background subtract	

Setting Up the Microscope

For color images, brightfield, use the following settings:

- **Brightfield, color: Set color temperature.** The color temperature of the light on the microscope is best set to 3200 degrees Kelvin for consistency. It provides a discrete color temperature for the detector at which parameters for interpretation of color are well defined along a common standard. Often, markings exist for setting this color temperature. When the markings don't exist, it is likely that turning the power all the way up will create a color temperature of 3200K.

  However, the light may be too bright at this setting. Look for a means to place neutral density filters in the light path. These filters block visible wavelengths equally (thus, the word "neutral") at gradients (densities) along a logarithmic scale.

- **Brightfield: Set Koehler illumination.** The light passing through the specimen needs to be collimated to varying degrees, depending on the lens (objective) that is used. Go through methods for setting up Koehler illumination. This method is described in detail at http://micro.magnet.fsu.edu.

Capturing Images on Camera or in Acquisition Software

The first decision that has to be made (or is instituted by the workgroup already) concerns the method for acquiring images: whether to use camera software/controls for automatic or manual exposure settings.

AUTOMATIC EXPOSURE

Automatic determination of exposure can be used for all images except those destined for optical density/intensity (OD/I) measurements.

When this feature is chosen, cameras must read (meter) brightness or darkness levels from the specimen to determine the length of time the detector requires to collect photons to fill the dynamic range. The camera meters in several ways.

Darkest/lightest feature on specimen to avoid clipping. For many scientific cameras, the brightest or darkest value in the specimen is used to determine exposure. The exposure is determined based on having enough photons to fill detectors for values above the bottom limit for the darkest value, and not too many photons to overfill detectors at the top limit.

The net result of this method for metering is that bright or dark artifacts can skew the exposure so that images are overall darker or lighter, respectively. In **Figure 4.1** the image on the left demonstrates overall lightening as a result of the meter exposing to keep dark spots (artifacts) within the dynamic range—shown most dramatically in the loss of black borders around the features and gain in overall contrast. Exposure is correct on the image on the right where no dark spots confuse the meter reading.

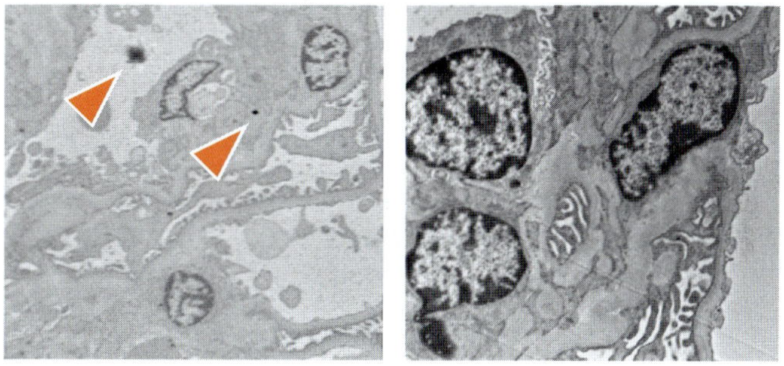

FIGURE 4.1 An image showing mistaken exposure reading as a result of artifacts (left); a correct reading is on the right.

When the exposure is misread, the following approaches can be taken:

- Find a different location on the specimen.
- Find a way to override the Automatic Setting by adjusting exposure time. **Figure 4.2** shows an Adjustment Factor to decrease overall exposure, thus compensating for the misreading of exposure.
- Use the Manual feature.

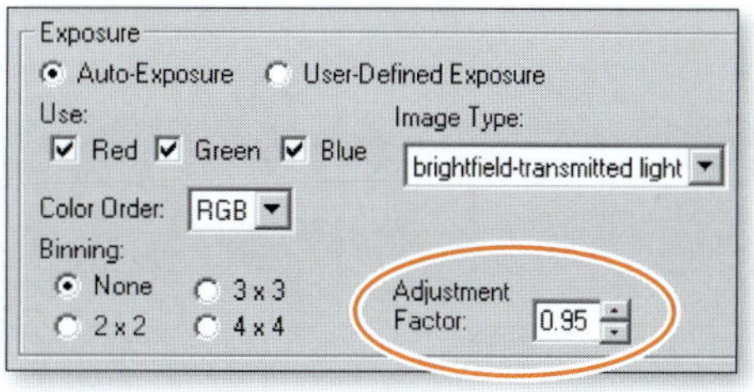

FIGURE 4.2 Exposure dialog box showing a 5% reduction in the Adjustment Factor.

Weighted average or spot metering. Consumer cameras often provide different options based on an average. These can be set (often the default setting) to find an average of brightness and darkness values to determine exposure, generally metering from the lower part of the specimen, because this method is often most reliable for landscapes with a bright sky. Or varying patterns for metering down to a narrow, circular pattern (spot metering) can be chosen and used.

Depending on the specimen, these options can be effective, but significant gray or color values can be clipped!

MANUAL EXPOSURE: SETTING DYNAMIC RANGE LIMITS

Manual determination of exposure is used when subsequently measuring OD/I values. It is also used when correcting for noise and uneven illumination. Certain workgroups may also use manual features for consistent imaging of specimens. In a workgroup scenario, the exposure is set once and then stays at that setting over time, or for each imaging session.

Automatic exposure or auto gain features must be turned off to use manual settings; alternatively, a manual setting is chosen. When determining exposure, any one of three situations—or a combination—arises:

- Exposure is set interactively when the image is live on the screen.
- Specimen exposures are calculated through a software feature as a starting point, after which exposures may have to be iteratively determined.
- Exposures are determined by trial and error only.

■ **Note:** *When specimens contain a range of tonal values that exceed the dynamic range of a camera, three or more separate images can be taken at an ideal exposure, twice that exposure and half. These images can be used to build a High Dynamic Range image in Photoshop CS2 and CS3 only (see "Creating an HDR image [CS2 and CS3 only] in Chapter 6, "Opening Images and Initial Steps").*

The brightest and darkest significant values in the image can be measured to determine whether they remain within the dynamic range of the detector. Most acquisition software includes an interactive way to place a cursor over the brightest/darkest area and then to read grayscale or color values. If a means is not available, these images can be saved, and then opened in Photoshop to obtain measurements. A means may also be available for placing a color overlay on the image to show specimen areas that are clipped while the image is live.

For imaging a set of specimens in which OD/I will be measured, the manual setting is determined by finding the brightest labeled specimen (darkfield) or the darkest labeling (brightfield) from a set of specimens. That setting then remains the same for all subsequent specimens with adjustments only for fluctuations in the light source or when new specimens from a different experimental set exceed the dynamic range of the detector (see Chapter 3, "Guidelines for Specific Types of Images").

▶ **Warning:** *On some detectors, noise levels become excessive at higher values. Determine the highest limit for detectors by contacting the salespeople or the manufacturer. Confirm by determining the value at which additional exposure renders the same reading of a grayscale value.*

Darkest significant values are set above 0. Brightest significant values depend on the bit depth of the camera, as shown in **Table 4.2**.

TABLE 4.2 Grayscale/Color Limits for Significant Bright Areas on Specimen

8-BIT	12-BIT	16-BIT
254	4094	65,534

COLOR, BRIGHTFIELD: WHITE BALANCE

To correctly compensate for the color temperature of the light source, a calibration step is done. The calibration is to the color white. Once this color is correctly interpreted and displayed, all other colors should then be displayed correctly. This step can be done automatically or manually. The manual method is preferred, because it is more precise.

Automatic. Some cameras can be set to auto white balance, which appears in some acquisition software as AWB. When this setting is used, the camera attempts to read from the specimen to interpret colors, or the color balance is obtained via a predetermined setting when the white balance feature is set to incandescent light (3200K light).

If auto white balance does not correctly interpret colors, use manual white balance. Note that cameras may auto white balance after using a mouse to outline a region of your specimen that is white, as in **Figure 4.3** where the image on the left contains greenish background values: When corrected by outlining the white balancing area with a mouse (shown by a rectangular outline) and then clicking the AWB button, the image on the right is the result.

Manual. Other cameras white balance after the specimen is removed from the light path. In that instance, the light source is used as the white reference.

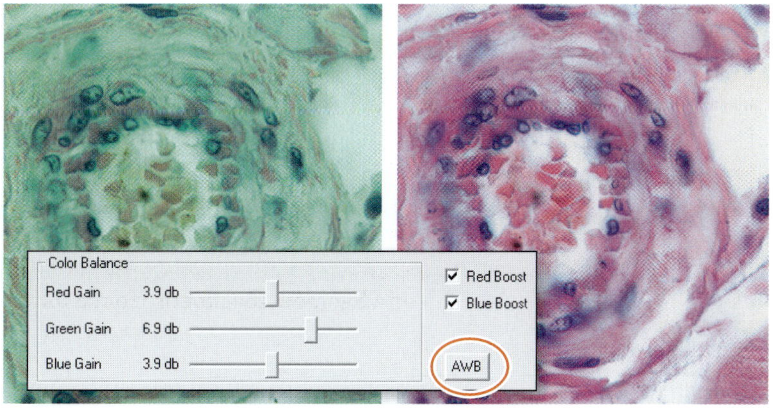

FIGURE 4.3 Images showing the result (right) when using auto white balance.

CAMERA SETTINGS

Additional camera settings may or may not be available in acquisition software for cameras (**Figure 4.4**). A list of settings that may be available follows:

- **Gain.** Gain might be available in image acquisition software instead of, or in addition to, exposure. Increases in gain result in images that are brighter overall. Because gain is an electronic amplification of signal, noise levels accompany higher gain settings. Determine the highest gain setting possible without the introduction of noise and stay beneath that setting if possible. Use exposure, gain, or both to increase brightness of a specimen with the least possible addition of noise when the specimen is dim.

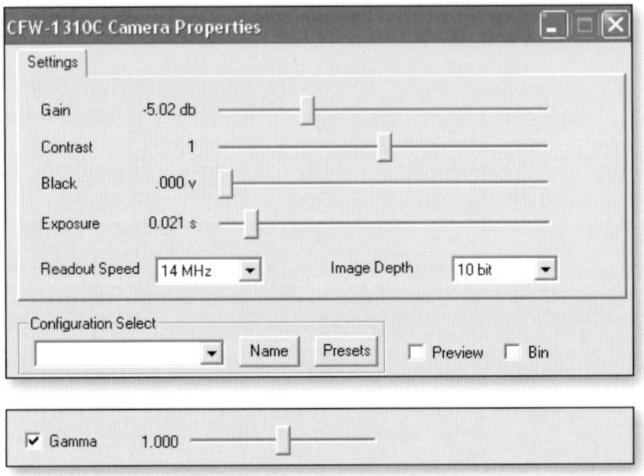

FIGURE 4.4 A settings dialog box in acquisition software showing camera settings.

- **Contrast.** Contrast works like a Brightness/Contrast setting in many image processing programs by increasing the brighter pixels (making them brighter) above the midpoint and decreasing darker pixels (making them darker) below the midpoint. Alternatively, the acquisition program can increase contrast by incrementally darkening from the darkest black to the brightest white in the image with the greatest change occurring in the darker regions and little change to the brightest regions. This can be done with greater precision in Photoshop.
- **Black.** This setting is an electronic function that is used as a means to set the darkest black value. This option is set so that no value in the image reads zero, because that would clip the darkest values. Set the darkest values so that they are slightly above zero.
- **Exposure (or Integration; sometimes named Brightness).** The brightest values are changed by adjusting Exposure. This option attenuates the amount of time the detector is exposed to light from the specimen. Attenuate Exposure while measuring the brightest significant values so that values do not exceed the dynamic range of the instrument (clip).
- **Readout Speed.** This setting adapts the camera to the capabilities of the computer to show live images. A slower readout allows the

computer more time to display new images (refresh) when viewing images live. Higher speeds may increase the noise level of the image, depending on the capabilities of the electronics in the camera, so lower speeds are advised.

- **Image Depth.** This setting is the same as bit depth and should be set to higher values.
- **Preview.** This option allows for a smaller display of the image in the event that the size of the image overfills screen resolutions. For example, if the screen resolution is set at 1024 × 768 and the live image is at 1380 × 1035, the image will be larger in dimension than the screen, and the outer parts of the image will not be visible.
- **Bin.** To increase sensitivity, discrete fractions of the image can be specified with a resulting increase in the number of sensors used for each pixel. For example, if a Bin of 2 is used, each resultant pixel would then be the sum of the photons from four sensors (two horizontal, two vertical). The image size would then be one fourth the total number of pixels (half horizontally and vertically), leading to less pixel resolution but a consequent increase in the sensitivity to light from the specimen. Bin the image when specimens are dim and the image is noisy.
- **Gamma.** The Gamma setting is typically kept at 1 to maintain a linear relationship of tonal values, which is absolutely required for OD/I destined images. When the linear relationship is not required or is not as important as being able to see visual information in darker or brighter areas, gamma can be altered (for publication, the Gamma setting is reported). A gamma adjustment alters midtones while maintaining detail in brighter and darker areas. Gamma is a reference to the Greek symbol used in a math formula in which the numeric value chosen becomes a power function. The gamma formula is applied after tonal values have been assigned to the pixels (after the electronics have read out the brightness values for each pixel), which can be done in post-processing with more precision in Photoshop.

■ **Note:** *Consumer and SLR (Single Lens Reflex) cameras are likely to automatically set the image gamma to the monitor's Gamma setting. For a Macintosh computer, the Gamma setting is often at 1.8. For a Windows computer, the typical setting is 2.2. To preserve a gamma of 1, these images must be taken in the Raw format (available on SLR cameras), and then opened in Photoshop with correct settings in the Color Settings dialog box (see "Color Settings" in Chapter 5, "Photoshop Setup and Standard Procedure").*

ACQUIRE THE IMAGE

Once settings are determined, acquire the image. Once the image is acquired, it can be evaluated visually and then other steps can be taken to improve the quality of the image. Chief among these steps is a correction of uneven illumination (flatfield correction) across the length and width of the image, which is difficult to see by eye. This correction is recommended for all images from microscopes.

Images and additional steps that can be taken to improve image quality follow (**Figure 4.5**):

- **Accurate image.** If the image appears to be an accurate representation of the specimen, consider producing a flatfield image, which is crucial for quantification and image stitching. See the "Flatfield Correction" section to produce evenly illuminated specimen.
- **Dim and noisy image.** If the specimen is dim and the resultant image contains visible noise levels, see the "Noise Reduction" section.
- **Binning.** If the specimen is so dim that gain and exposure create unacceptable noise levels, consider binning.
- **Uneven illumination.** If the specimen is unevenly illuminated, see the "Flatfield Correction" section.
- **OD/I image.** If the image is measured for OD/I, remove or reduce noise and flatfield correct.
- **Incorrect colors.** If the specimen is in color and colors are not correct, white balance again. If coloring changes across the width of the image, the illumination bulb may not be centered (ask your microscope representative for assistance).
- **Contrast.** If stains do not contrast with background information or if the specimen is lacking in contrast (or the contrast is too high so that details are obscured in darker or brighter areas), adjust gamma or contrast in the camera acquisition software or in Photoshop. If the image is in Grayscale mode, consider using filters. See the "Grayscale: Filters" section.

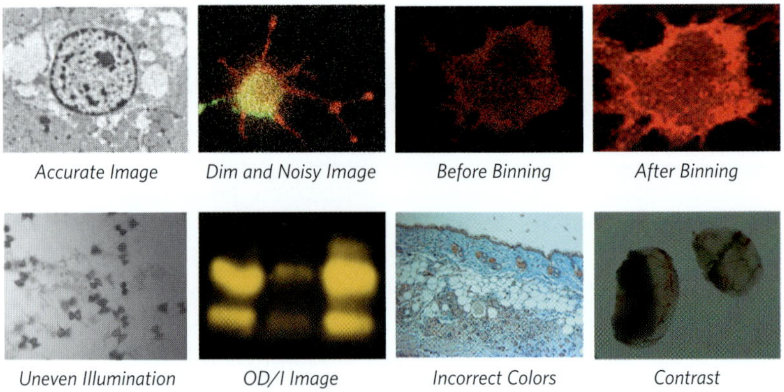

FIGURE 4.5 Examples of problematic images and techniques that can be used to fix them.

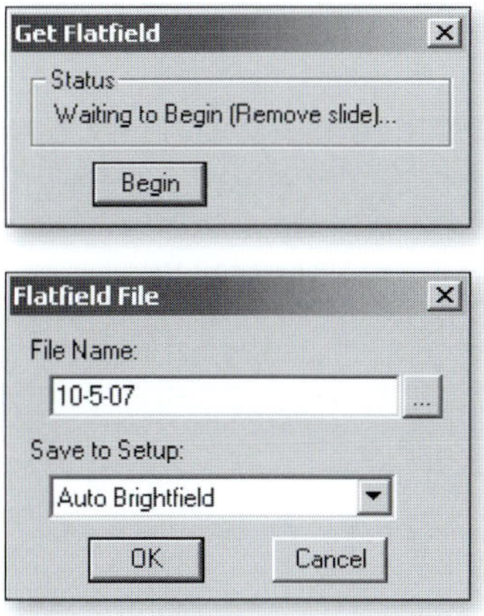

FIGURE 4.6 Examples of Flatfield capture dialog boxes in image acquisition software.

FLATFIELD CORRECTION

Light sources often produce uneven illumination across the field of view. This is rarely observed by eye and is not often seen in the image. After the unevenness is corrected—variously called flatfield, shading, or blank field correction—the appearance of the image is not only improved but made ready for quantification and image stitching (also called montaging). To correct for uneven illumination, the flatfield image is divided into the specimen image, and then multiplied by a constant. Often, this is done after subtracting a background image.

Flatfield correct in image acquisition software. Check for the ability to specify a flatfield image for subsequent use in correcting uneven illumination in acquisition software (**Figure 4.6**). If flatfield correction can be done in software, for brightfield specimens, acquire the flatfield image by moving to an empty area of the slide sans debris. Defocus slightly, if necessary.

For fluorescently labeled specimens, remove the microscope slide, and then insert a fluorescent reference slide either consistent with the wavelength range of the labels for the specimen (when neutral density filters can be placed in the light path because the emissions light is often too bright for the detector) or inconsistent so that only bleed-through emission light is collected (not as bright). Focus below the surface of the slide so that detritus and scratches on the surface are defocused.

■ **Note:** *Flatfield images need to be made for every lens magnification. They also need to be made at each imaging session because uneven illumination may change patterns from day to day, especially with multiple user microscopes.*

Saving flatfield image for subsequent correction. If the camera software does not have flatfield correction, save and date the flatfield image. Make sure that no pixel value exceeds the dynamic range of the instrument (e.g., values at 254 for an 8-bit camera system): Values can often be found in image acquisition software. Flatfield images can be used for correction of uneven illumination later in Photoshop (see "Uneven Illumination Correction" in Chapter 6).

NOISE REDUCTION

Several sources of noise are present in images, but two more common sources are mentioned here. Random noise is due to fluctuations of a finite number of photons and electrons from one moment to the next when that number is low, such as when specimens are dim. Fixed pattern noise appears when certain pixels become bright. These pixels are called "hot pixels" and are most apparent at long exposure times.

Darkfield, frame averaging to correct for random noise. To correct for random noise, more than one image is taken and they are averaged together. If the frame averaging option is available in camera software, the number of images (frames) are specified and the images are automatically taken and then averaged (**Figure 4.7**). If not, several images must be taken for subsequent averaging (see "Frame Averaging to Reduce Noise" in Chapter 6). Brightfield specimens are generally well illuminated, and images are more likely to be devoid of random noise. Noise reduction is more often necessary for fluorescently labeled specimens.

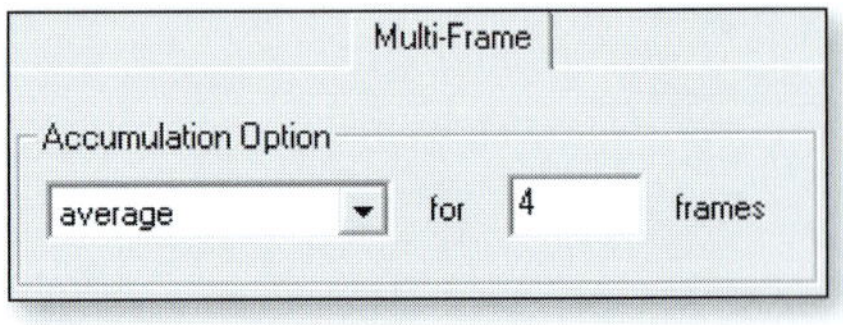

FIGURE 4.7 An example of a Multi-Frame dialog box that shows averaging of four frames to reduce random noise.

■ **Note:** *Background and specimen images can be used for all specimens in a single imaging session as long as the light source power remains constant and is not changed. Changes to magnification do not require reimaging the background.*

Fixed pattern noise: background subtraction. To remove hot pixels, an image is taken in ambient light with the light source blocked. The image is taken at the same setting as the time required for imaging the specimen, which was determined earlier. It may be difficult if not impossible to see hot pixels, but when the dark image is brightened, these pixels become visible. The dark image is subtracted from the specimen image. The common reference to this procedure is "background subtraction" (**Figure 4.8**).

If the ability to background subtract is not available in image acquisition software, save and date the dark image for both darkfield and brightfield specimens for background subtraction in Photoshop (see "Hot Pixels Removal Methods" in Chapter 6).

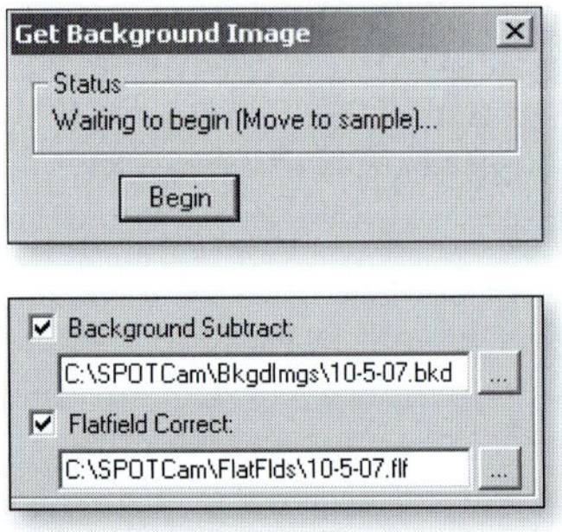

FIGURE 4.8 Examples of dialog boxes for acquiring a background subtraction image and for naming background and flatfield images.

GRAYSCALE: FILTERS

Filters can be placed in the light path to darken or lighten colors of interest. Colors that are complements (opposites) of staining colors will make the staining colors darker. Colors that are similar to the staining color will lighten stained colors (**Figure 4.9**).

Strong filters are required, especially when staining is weak. A reference chart is included with recommended Wratten filters, which are available from professional photography stores.

If a color camera is used for image acquisition and filters are used, ignore the resulting, strong color cast: Use the Channel Mixer dialog box (Image > Adjustments > Channel Mixer) in Photoshop to isolate the ideal grayscale image based on color that is meant to be darkened or lightened (see "Brightfield: Color to Grayscale" and "Single Color, Darkfield Images" in Chapter 7).

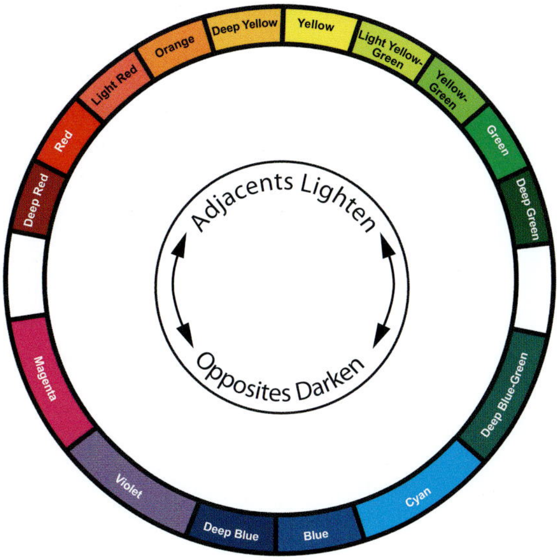

FIGURE 4.9 The color wheel showing color relationships.

Laser Scanning Confocal Systems

The major difference between a camera and a scanning system that moves a point of light (rasterizes) across the specimen is in the use of a single detector rather than an array of microdetectors on a chip. That single detector is generally a photomultiplier tube (PMT), which is used for its extraordinary sensitivity to finite numbers of photons. The PMT is used in concert with electronic amplification (gain) to further brighten signal from fluorescently labeled specimens.

The difference between a confocal and a standard microscope is the use of an aperture or pinhole (also called an iris). The pinhole restricts the angle of photon collection so that mostly in-focus photons incident to lens elements are included, and off-axis photons are rejected. Thus, fluorescence above and below what is in focus (the focal plane) will be out of focus and therefore not included.

In theory, an instrument set up with an aperture at the correct position along the light path will provide a perfectly in-focus plane (called a *z* plane) without contribution of out-of-focus light above or below, but in practice the *z* plane will include some out-of-focus light. The degree of *z* plane optical resolution depends almost entirely on a second aperture in the system: the rated aperture of the objective that is used. That aperture is called the Numeric Aperture (N.A.). The higher this aperture is rated the less out-of-focus light and the greater the *z* plane resolution.

Yet even with the highest numeric apertures and the smallest, functional pinholes, *z* resolution can still include out-of-focus light. To eliminate that, software programs that deconvolve image stacks can be used. These eliminate out-of-focus light based on mathematical models and system parameters.

A second solution involves the use of a laser that can be modified to strike fluorescent dyes with two photons (or more) at once instead of only one. The possibility of two photons striking simultaneously is rare, and it can only occur at the focal plane (as long as the projected laser light fills the back aperture of the objective). These are called two-photon, or multiphoton confocals.

Because of these components for confocal and like instruments, some of the parameters change for digital imaging:

- **Exposure** becomes the amount of time a laser excites a single spot, which is called dwell time. The speed of the scan will affect the dwell time and so will pixel resolution.
- **Pixel resolutions** can be set on confocal instruments. The greater the resolution, the longer it takes to scan the image. When bleaching (loss of fluorescence intensity due to being struck by light) interferes with acquisition of labels or when specimens move, smaller pixel resolutions can be chosen. Ideal pixel resolutions can be set according to Nyquist rates: ideal rates for the number of times elements of an image are captured for subsequent pixels to obtain the best resolution.
- **Focus** becomes dependent on two parts: physically focusing the microscope to find the brightest *z* plane of the specimen (to find its centermost position in depth) and the aperture or iris setting. Confocal systems mated with microscopes set apertures automatically based on the N.A. of the objective that is used. Ideal apertures can also be determined based on Nyquist rates.
- **Gain** is achieved in two ways: electronically through attenuation of voltages to the PMT (called High Voltage [HV]; can also be called by other references) and to a post-PMT amplifier (often called Gain). Instructions on setting both differ from lab to lab. As a general rule, when High Voltage amounts create visible noise, Gain is increased for additional amplification of signal and high voltage is decreased.
- **Laser power** is at 100% on confocal instruments, and neutral density filters are placed in the light path to attenuate the power. “Laser power” is a reference to the percentage reduction of light

through the use of neutral density filters or other means for reducing light levels. The confusion is in nomenclature: "Laser power" is often the denotation versus "neutral density filter."

- **Black Level** achieves the same end as Contrast: Both are used for setting the black limit or the deepest significant black in the image.
- **Additional magnification** (also called Zoom) can be chosen in confocal acquisition software. Up to a cutoff, the magnification is optical, not simply additional pixels. Contact the manufacturer to determine the cutoff.
- ***Z* plane selection** is available on confocal systems. The *z* step is set automatically on systems mated with microscopes, or ideal *z* steps can be calculated according to Nyquist rates. Here Nyquist rates determine the *z*-step increment necessary for the best resolution.

Confocal Imaging Depending on Intent

The settings used in the "Steps for Imaging on a Confocal System" section that follows depend on the intent and are briefly provided in **Table 4.3**.

TABLE 4.3 Confocal Imaging Depending on Intent

	GREATER DEFINITION IN IMAGES*	COLOCALIZATION AND THIN OPTICAL SECTIONS	3-DIMENSIONAL MODELS	GREATER RESOLUTION	THICK SECTION IMAGING
Single plane?	Yes	Yes**	No	No	No
Multiple planes?	No	No	Yes: > 50 sections	Yes	Yes
High pixel resolution? High > 640X640 Low < 512X512	High	High or Low: depends on feature dimensions	Low: to accommodate 3D software	High: Nyquist rates	High or Low (depends on features)
Kalman averaging? High: 8–32 Low: 2–4	High or Low***	High, or noise will obscure measurements	Low, or bleaching may result	High or Low, depending on noise levels	High
Confocal aperture at nonoptimal dimensions?	Yes	No	No	No	Possibly

*This is not meant to be interpreted as a desire for greater optical resolution, especially at or near resolution limits for confocal instruments.

**Deconvolution can be done on single planes, but more accurate deconvolution formulas require three or more planes. Deconvolution may be necessary for eliminating out-of-focus information.

***Higher rates of Kalman averaging can introduce blurring at the borders, so the amount of averaging is a trade-off between noise levels and blurring, and is visually determined.

There may be some exceptions to the recommendations given in the table, and it is up to each researcher to carefully investigate previous publications in his or her respective fields of study for additional information about methods.

Note that images intended for optical intensity measurements are not included. Laser fluctuations over time preclude measurement unless an internal standard exists. Those who are not dissuaded can still pursue optical intensity measurements as long as laser fluctuations are measured, bleaching rates are determined, and linear uptake of fluorescent dye into cells is proven. Be sure to Kalman average so that noise is reduced to minimal levels.

Steps for Imaging on a Confocal System

To better understand the steps involved when using a confocal system, steps are categorized into four phases. Phase 1 involves finding the brightest *z* plane on the microscope and the setup steps involved in seeing the image in the acquisition software. Phase 2 concerns setting the tonal values for the brightest significant features and black background within the dynamic range of the detector. Phase 3 includes the final steps, such as setting the *z* plane parameters, Kalman averaging, and saving. Phase 4 reviews documentation procedures.

PHASE 1: FIND BRIGHTEST PLANE AND SET UP

Start by finding the specimen on the microscope:

1. Find the brightest *z* plane of the specimen by focusing up and down.
2. Find the area of interest on the microscope and choose a field adjacent to the field of interest (to prevent bleaching of significant field during setup).
3. Switch the instrument settings to allow light to travel to the confocal head.

On confocal acquisition software:

1. Choose appropriate dyes from the DyeList dialog box.

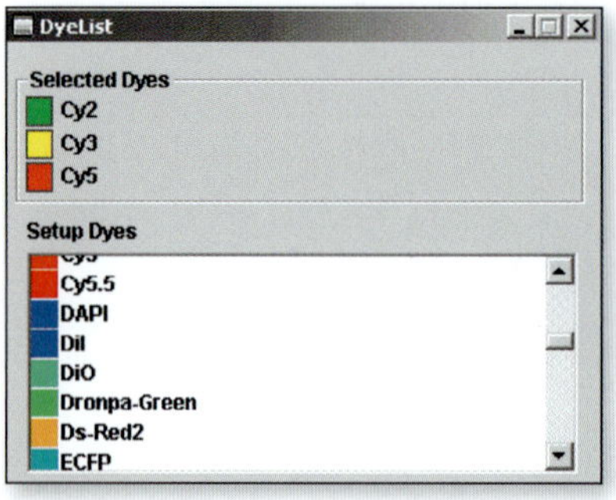

2. Set to Sequential (if available) and choose the brightest and most stable dye wavelengths only (DAPI is often used for its brightness and stability).

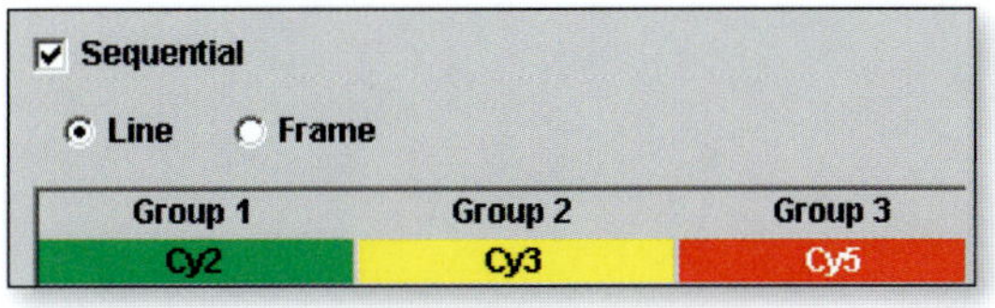

3. Choose the fastest scan speed for the initial scans. Note that Focus settings may scan so that every other line is used along the *y* axis. This may bleach the labels of the specimen, leading to a patterned bright/dark appearance. A smaller "box" size, or pixel resolution in width and height, can be chosen for initial imaging to locate the specimen and reduce bleaching.

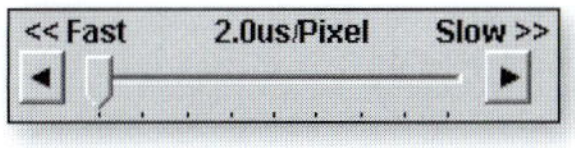

4. Scan the image, and while scanning either physically rotate the focus knob on the microscope or adjust the *z* steps to find the brightest plane (in the event that the focus to the eye through the microscope is different from the confocal head).

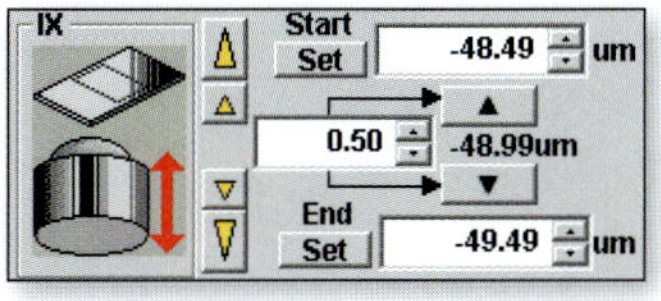

5. If the plane cannot be found because the sample is dim, increase High Voltage and Gain to higher values and attempt to image again. Increase laser power and the confocal aperture until the plane can be found.

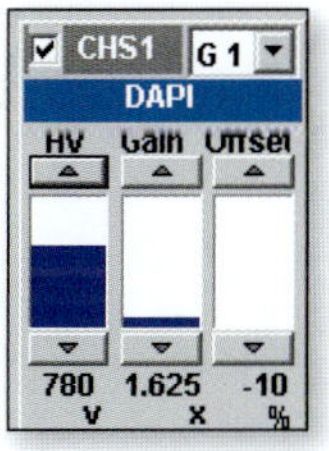

6. If the image appears all black, a setting is incorrect, the laser is off, or the instrument isn't communicating with its components, get help.

PHASE 2: SET DYNAMIC RANGE

1. Adjust the settings to fit the image within the dynamic range of the instrument.

2. Set the panel to a Look Up Table (LUT) overlay to indicate levels at which the deepest black and brightest significant whites "clip" (exceed the dynamic range). Typically, when areas of the image clip in the brightest region, a red color is overlaid on the bright areas. When areas of the image clip in the darkest regions, a blue or green overlay appears. Adjust settings depending on whether the dye is bright or dim:
3. For bright dyes:
   - Keep the laser power low to minimize bleaching.
   - Decrease Gain to 0 and increase High Voltage values until the whitest significant parts of the image show up as red (unless the whites in the image are already red colorized). Back off from High Voltage until no red appears in the significant white areas.
   - Increase or decrease the Black Level to create a blue overlay in the shadow areas of the image, and then back off until the blue or green disappears.
4. For dim dyes:
   - Increase both High Voltage and Gain until the whitest significant parts of the image show up as red.
   - If white values are still too dim or if the presence of noise is too significant (it will be reduced by frame or Kalman averaging later on), the choices are as follows:
     - If the sample readily bleaches, the alternative is to decrease the pixel resolution or open the aperture to a larger diameter. Each presents its own challenge: Decreased pixel resolutions and larger apertures negatively affect resolution. Depending on the intent of the image, however, this may be an acceptable solution.
     - If bleaching occurs to a point and then plateaus, the alternatives are to decrease the scan speed (which increases dwell time) or increase magnification by zooming in or choosing a higher numeric aperture objective. Magnification changes will more likely increase resolution (depending on the specimen) but may not include a large enough field of view.
     - Adjust the settings individually for other dyes using the same methods.

PHASE 3: SET *Z* PLANES AND FRAME AVERAGING

A few final steps and saving your settings are required:

1. Set the remaining parameters for all dyes and collect the images.
2. Set the LUT overlay relevant to each dye used in the specimen. Using a gray LUT is preferred, because levels of brightness and darkness are easier to see and compare in grayscale.
3. Set the upper and lower positions for *z* sectioning. This can also be done by selecting a single dye when bleaching is a concern. The caveat, however, is that one dye alone may not label features in all *z* planes.
4. Set the increment of the *z* step. The Op setting for this acquisition software sets the optimal *z* step based on Nyquist rates. The number of slices from the top to the bottom of the specimen is shown.

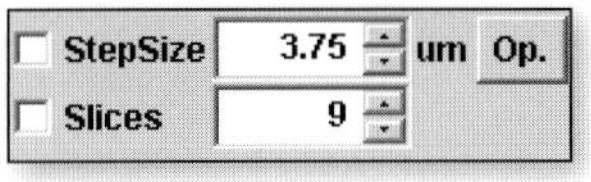

5. Rotate the section, if necessary, and if the tool is available.
6. Set the Frame or Kalman value. In newer confocal systems, a scan line by scan line average can be done, or *z* frame by *z* frame. Typically, line scans are preferred.

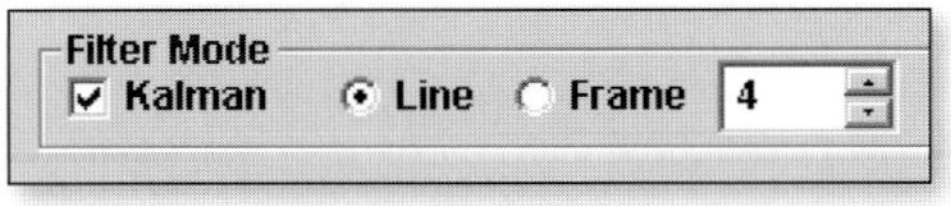

7. Set the pixel resolution, if necessary.
8. Scan the specimen and save.

PHASE 4: DOCUMENTATION

Make certain that all parameters are written down or saved with the file as metadata. The most important settings are excitation and emissions wavelengths for the dyes used, numeric aperture of the lens, power of the lens, medium between the lens and the specimen (e.g., oil), confocal aperture, step size, pixel size (found in readouts), and zoom.

Save the image in the proprietary format of the manufacturer. The image may also be saved as a TIFF file (if available): Beware, however, that TIFF files are not "screen saves" at computer screen resolutions; the images may be at subsampled resolutions. Archive images to two CDs or DVDs.

Flatbed Scanners

Flatbed scanners are often overlooked when capturing digital images for a number of specimens in science and industry. With their high resolutions, even lighting, and expanded dynamic range, they are ideal for specimens often photographed with great difficulty on stereo microscopes. Scanners have the additional benefit of freedom from glare off reflective surfaces, which can contribute to a loss of visual data.

The better flatbed scanners are high in resolution and high in dynamic range. The resolution is reported incorrectly at two times the true, optical resolution, with the vertical resolution lower than the horizontal, because the vertical is controlled by a stepper motor (not as fine) and the horizontal by a row of microdetectors (much finer).

The dynamic range is determined by the lower (black) limit of the dynamic range using optical density units of measurement from 0.0 (white) to 4.0 (black). This limit is referred to as Density Maximum or Dmax. The best scanners have a Dmax of 4.0 and are preferred.

Flatbed scanners can be purchased with light sources in the top and bottom of the scanner so that transmissive (light going through the specimen) or reflective (light reflecting off the specimen) modes can be used.

Scanners often calibrate off the first 25 mm (~1 inch) of one end of the glass. Do not cover that area with the specimen or grayscale/color values will be dramatically altered. The calibration does not mean that a consumer flatbed scanner (versus a scanner intended for densitometry) can be used for imaging specimens destined for optical density measurements. Consumer scanners do not, as a rule, produce images with a gamma of 1: Such scanners may automatically apply a gamma of greater or less than 1, and the user has no control over the gamma settings. A calibration strip, such as a Stouffer step wedge, should be scanned and measured to determine whether or not gammas greater or less than 1 are applied before using the scanner for images from which optical densities will subsequently be measured.

Flatbed scanners meant for densitometric measurement, on the other hand, produce an image with a gamma of 1. These scanners do not include many of the settings described in the following section.

Prescan Settings for Flatbed Scanners

Before scanning a specimen or material, set the preferences in the scanning software according to the characteristics of your sample. Some possible settings are listed here (and shown in **Figure 4.10** on next page):

- **Scan Mode: Normal.** The scan mode contains presets for different kinds of materials. These presets can be chosen if desired to eliminate further choices except to prescan and scan. Note, however, that these settings may not provide adequate resolutions (**Figure 4.10A**).
- **Original.** This setting concerns whether the original is transmissive (transparency) or reflective (**Figure 4.10B**).
- **Pos/Neg.** The scanned material is positive unless the material is film; the film can be positive or negative. Even when the film is a negative (inverse image of a positive), it can be more desirable to scan the negative as a positive (retain the negative) and invert the image colors in Photoshop to produce a positive image (**Figure 4.10C**).
- **Scan Type.** Choices are provided for binary (black or white, such as text or line art), grayscale, or color (**Figure 4.10D**).
- **Filter.** None is the most desirable setting, because filters can be subsequently used in Photoshop with greater precision conforming to specific intents. The only exception might be the use of Descreening for eliminating or reducing dot patterns from published images and illustrations (**Figure 4.10E**).
- **Image Type.** Generally, this option can be set to Standard. Color interpretation can be done in Photoshop (**Figure 4.10F**).
- **Scaling functions.** These settings can be determined later when the output dimensions are known, so scaling would remain at 100%. If the output dimensions are known prior to scanning and they represent the only output for the image, set scaling before scanning (**Figure 4.10G**).
- **Microns per pixel.** Settings may be available for microns per pixel on calibrated systems. When scanning features smaller than about 2 mm, less microns per pixel are desired (check with the manufacturer for specifics). Other specimens will likely contain enough pixel resolution at the greater microns/pixel settings (**Figure 4.10H**).
- **Bit Depth.** Choose higher bit depth (Pixel Depth) even though it creates a larger file size (**Figure 4.10I**).

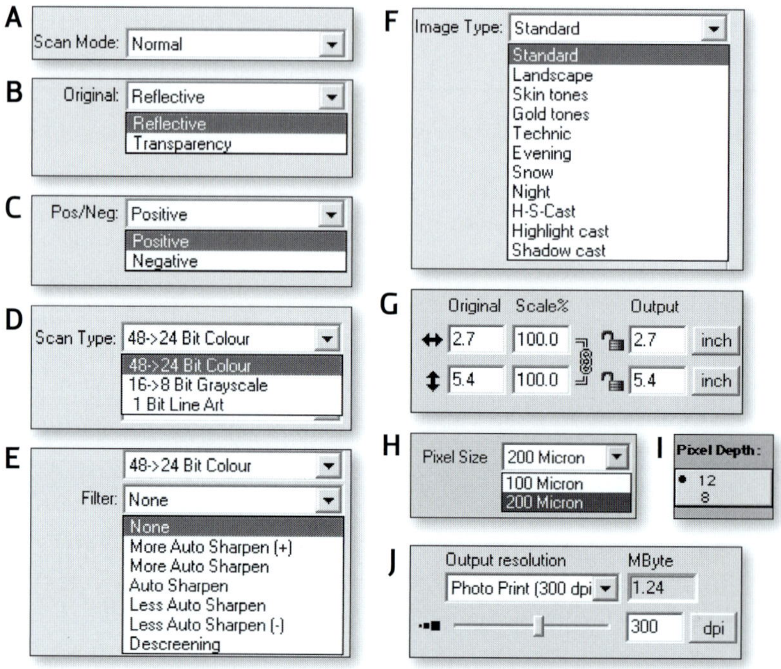

FIGURE 4.10 Several dialog boxes commonly found in software accompanying flatbed scanners.

■ **Note:** *The synonymous use of pixels or dots can be misleading. Images are set at more than twice the resolution used for printing presses, and in the end, more than one pixel is used for every printed dot.*

- **Output resolution.** This is the resolution of the image that will be produced by the scanner in dots per inch (dpi). The net effect of this setting will be a resolution that matches pixels per inch (ppi) to dots per inch (dpi), though the two are not synonymous in practice (see note to the left). Laser printers and printing presses create dots, so this is a useful unit of measurement for those who print to pages for a living. To print at 1:1 to a printed page, 300 dpi is a large enough resolution setting. But when the specimen is small and will likely be enlarged to greater dimensions, 300 dpi will be inadequate. Because the final dimensions are often unknown or variable, depending on the output, this option can be set according to the size of the file or by the number of dots per inch (see next section). Set the output resolution after prescanning and outlining the area of interest (**Figure 4.10J**).

General Procedure for Scanning

Once settings are determined for the specimen or material, the remaining steps involve prescanning—outlining the desired scan area and setting the output pixel resolution (**Figure 4.11**).

FIGURE 4.11 The image is prescanned (left), outlined (center), and Output resolution is then set (right).

1. **Click Prescan.** The prescan image can be lower in resolution. It is only meant to provide enough resolution to make out the location of the specimen on the scanning bed. Colors and contrast may be way off as well: These will be corrected in later steps.
2. **Outline desired scan area.** If the scanner is set to auto or if an auto setting is the default, colors and contrast may change at this point. The more closely the outline surrounds the specimen, the better the contrast and color settings. Alternatively, an Auto button can be clicked.
3. **Set Output resolution.** Set the Output resolution of the specimen according to the file size when the final output is unknown. File size settings according to bit depth are suggested (**Table 4.4**) when desiring to preserve a target output resolution for publication. Maximum optical resolutions for the scanner are used when

TABLE 4.4 General Guidelines for File Size or DPI Setting

	8-BIT	8-BIT	24-BIT	12-BIT	36-BIT	16-BIT	48-BIT
	Grayscale	Graphs, Line Drawings	Color	Grayscale	Color	Grayscale	Color
For easily resolved features by eye	> 1 MB*	1200 DPI	>3 MB	> 1.5 MB	> 4.5 MB	> 2 MB	> 8 MB
For Publication at 1:1 (dpi)	300/400**	1200	300/400	N/A	N/A	N/A	N/A

* Megabyte
** Depends on publication requirements

desiring the highest resolutions for small features, such as those found in 35 mm films or microscope slides. Note that text and line drawings for publication require 1200 dpi resolutions.

4. **Accept scanned image.** If the contrast and color of the image are close to that of the specimen, click Scan to perform a final scan. When these do not appear correct, continue with remaining steps or correct by following post-processing steps in Photoshop.
5. **Levels/Curves buttons.** If a consistent means is desired for scanning, both the Histogram (distribution of grayscale or color values) and the tonal Curve can be set manually (**Figure 4.12**). Return these functions to their original values to retain nonadjusted values or set them appropriately to the specimen. Record these values for scanning future specimens. More information on setting Levels and Curves can be found in Chapters 6 and 7.

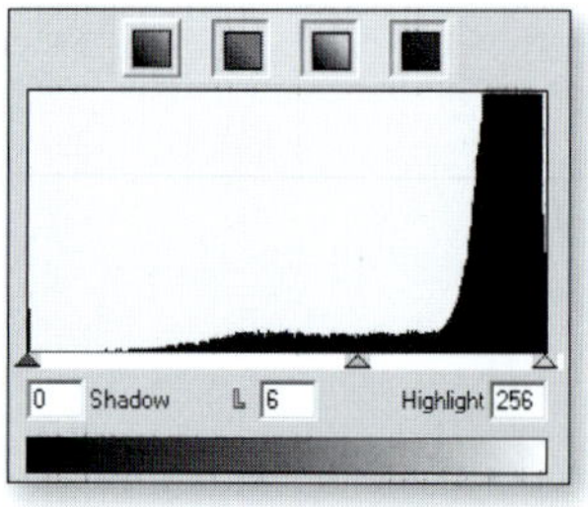

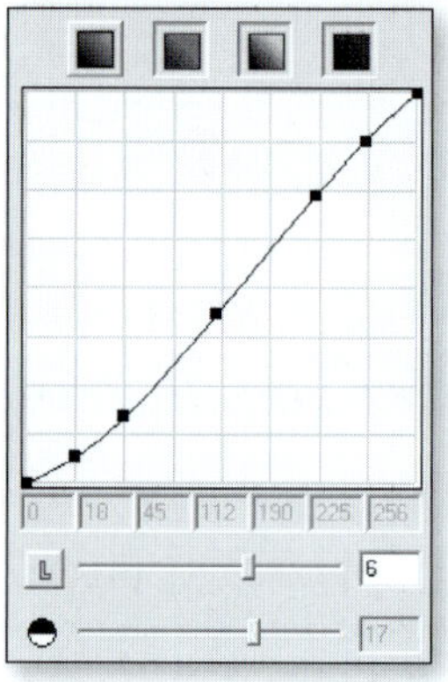

FIGURE 4.12 Levels (top) and Curves (bottom) dialog boxes.

After slight adjustments to Levels (also shown in Curves), the final image is captured (**Figure 4.13**). Note the sharpness of the black end caps: They are not resting on the glass platen of the flatbed scanner; instead, they are raised 12 mm (0.5 inch) off the surface.

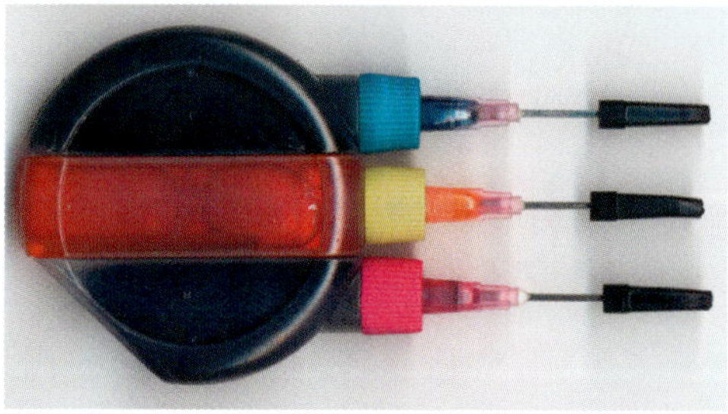

FIGURE 4.13 Final scan of a three-dimensional inking device.

TIPS FOR SCANNING

Additional information about films and documents is presented here for higher-quality results:

- **35 mm slides, negatives, x-ray films, and microscope slides.** Negatives and microscope slides require maximum optical resolution to retain visual information (**Figure 4.14A**). The inset in Figure 4.14A shows the level of detail from a specimen mounted on a microscope slide. Microscope slides and films may have to be lifted off the surface of the glass to prevent the formation of Newton's rings from moisture at the glass surface (**Figure 4.14B**). Films can be scanned at resolutions greater than 1500 dpi to retain resolution for most films. Lettering, line drawings, and symbols that are part of the slide image will never contain crisp edges

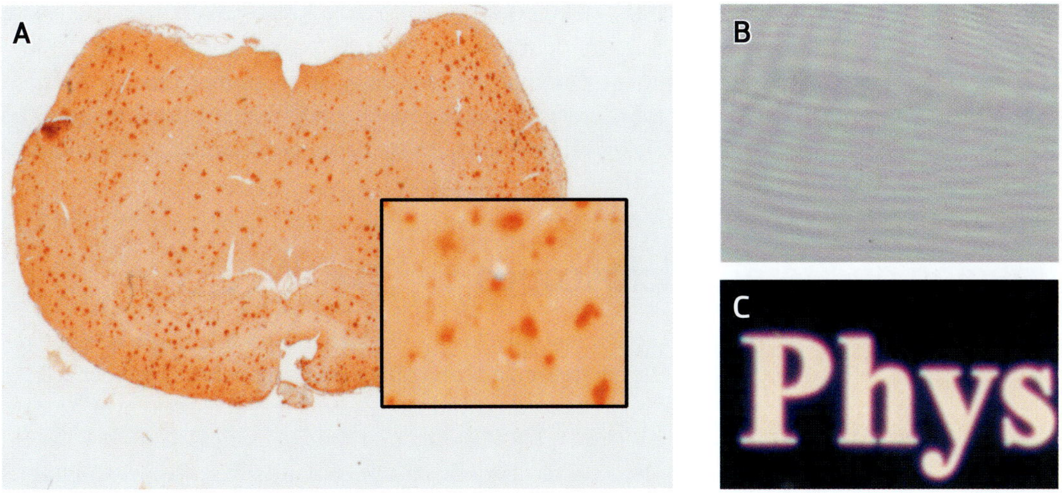

FIGURE 4.14 Examples of scanned specimens.

and will have to be relettered and redrawn (**Figure 4.14C**). X-ray films can be lower in resolution and may not need to be scanned at resolutions higher than is required for print publication.

- **Pages from publications.** Once copyright approval is given, printed pages from publications can be scanned. Images in print publications contain a dot pattern that can cross with the dot pattern of the computer screen to create a moiré pattern (and look somewhat like Newton's rings in Figure 4.14B), which is visible except when the image is zoomed in. The dot pattern can be ameliorated by descreening via scanner software or eliminated in post-processing by removing periodic noise in Fourier space (which is outside the scope of this book). Pages from books are scanned with black paper behind pages so that inks from the reverse side are not detected.
- **Eliminating colored lines or grids.** Colored lines that are part of a printed page can be removed after scanning in color. If the lines contain red, green, or blue, channels can be split in Photoshop to find a grayscale image sans the lines (see "Grayscale Channel with Highest Contrast" in Chapter 9, "Separating Relevant Features from the Background").
- **Line drawings, graphs, and poorly printed text.** Scan these items as grayscale or color, and be sure that the background is not pure white. Often lines become faint along their lengths: To retain

that information, gray values are necessary. Increase contrast and brightness in Photoshop using Levels or Curves (see "Graphic Images" in the "Problem Images" section of Chapter 6). If, however, text is being scanned for text recognition (Optical Character Recognition [OCR]), these pages are scanned as black and white with no shades of gray.

Imaging on Stereo Microscopes

Stereo microscopes (also called dissection microscopes) provide an intermediate range of magnification somewhere between a 1:1 macro lens on a consumer camera and a microscope (with overlap). Depending on lenses that are used on the stereo microscope and the projection lens on the camera, specimen widths from approximately 8 cm (3 inches) to 1 mm (~1/16 inch) can be imaged.

The denotation of "stereo" refers to separate and angled optical paths used for the right and left eyepiece to provide depth perception. For that reason, stereo microscopes are also used as a magnification tool for working with small objects.

For specimens with dimensions that exceed the field of view for a stereo microscope but are still small objects at less than 30 cm (~12 inches) or so, a copystand is often used. With additional diopters or a bellows, a copystand can duplicate magnifications of stereo microscopes, but the working distance between the object and lens can present problems with handling objects and with lighting.

Digital imaging choices when using image acquisition software is identical to what was covered earlier. Differences lie in the creation of flatfield images for front-illuminated specimens, where a white card is used as a reflective surface. The white card is put in place and imaged either before the specimen is put into place, or the specimen is removed (if practical) once the lighting decisions have been finalized.

On three-dimensional surfaces, flatfield images may be useless, depending on how the object is lit. Test the efficacy by comparing a flatfield corrected image of a specimen and an uncorrected image. If the lighting is focused more like a spotlight and the position of the lighting changes depending on the position of the specimen, or when uneven illumination is the objective of lighting, flatfield correction is counterproductive.

Controlling Glare and Lighting

The major disadvantage of macroscopy (small object photography) is that glare can be produced by specimens no matter what kind of lighting is used. For that reason, no stereo scope or copystand should be sold without a means to control glare. Often the thought is to place a polarizing filter in front of the lens, but that only controls glare when lighting is at a specific angle.

For effective control of glare, polarizing filters must be placed in front of lights *and* the lens (**Figure 4.15**). The polarizer in front of the lens turns so that the level of polarization can be controlled. The polarizers on the lights need to be fixed at a single angle of polarization (sometimes marked on filters). If the angle of polarization is not marked, a reflective object, such as crumpled tin foil, can be placed under the lens and the polarizer in front of one light can be turned until the glare disappears (or diminishes as much as possible). The disappearance of glare indicates "cross polarization." Then the same can be done for another light, one at a time. Do not turn the polarizer in front of the lens when going through this process, because the polarizers on the lights are being cross-polarized with the (stationary) polarizer on the lens.

Once the polarizers on the lights are set at the same angle of polarization, the polarizer on the lens can be turned to vary the level of polarizaton.

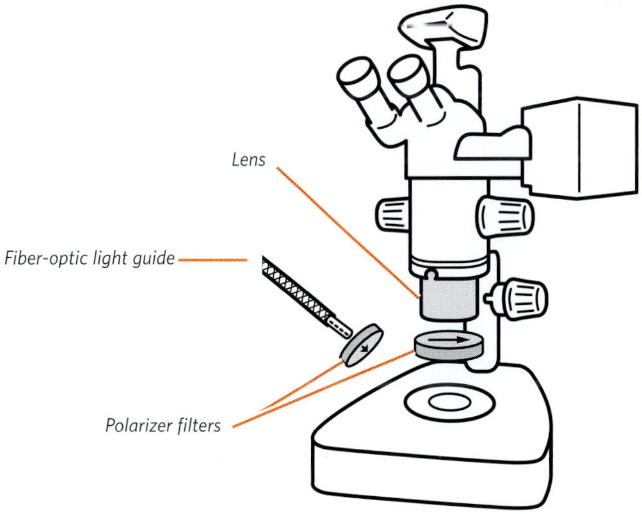

FIGURE 4.15 Illustration showing polarizing filters in front of lens and light source (fiber-optic light guide).

The advantage of stereo microscopes and copystands is in the multitude of ways to light specimens (when the lights are not fixed). Typically, lighting is done by using a fiber-optic lamp. Several ways of viewing a quartz rock with flecks of crystalline mica and a mouse embryo follow (**Figures 4.16** through **4.18**).

- **One fiber-optic light at 45 degrees, no polarization.** This lighting shows both topographical information on the surface of the rock and specks of glare from the mica (**Figure 4.16A**). The bright specks help identify the mica as a crystalline structure.
- **One fiber-optic light at 45 degrees, polarized.** This lighting shows topographical information without glare from the mica by turning the polarizer in front of the lens to cross-polarize it with the polarizer at the end of the fiber optic (**Figure 4.16B**).
- **Two line (or comb) lights pointed across the surface.** Comb lights enhance the surface topography of the rock (**Figure 4.16C**). These lights are also effectively used to create darkfield images from unstained and near-transparent samples.

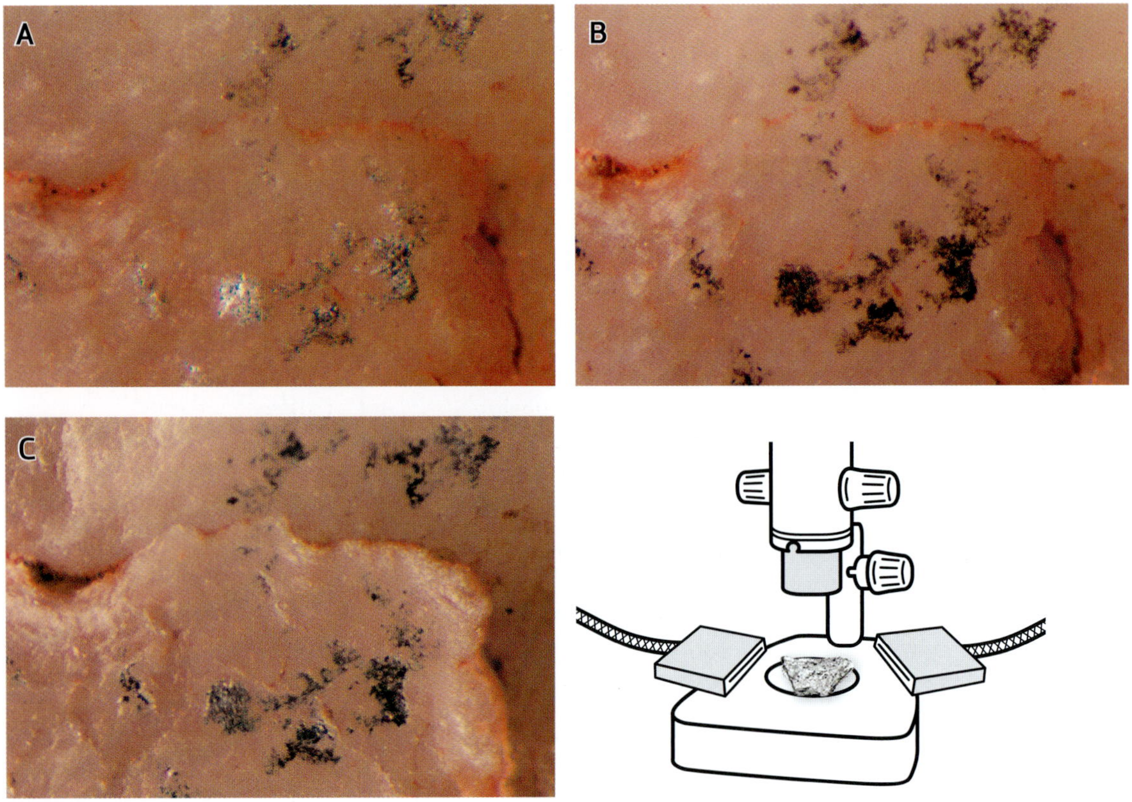

FIGURE 4.16 Three methods for lighting a specimen.

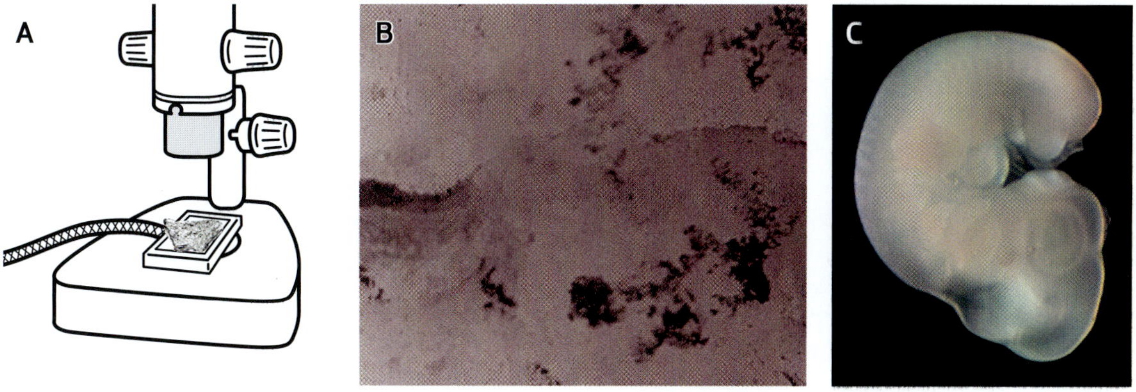

FIGURE 4.17 Backlit rock and mouse embryo.

- **Backlit by a single fiber-optic light.** This method of lighting eliminates surface features to reveal only veins and mica (**Figure 4.17A** and **B**). A specimen of a mouse embryo is also shown (**Figure 4.17C**): This image is backlit off-axis by a single fiber optic.
- **On-axis lighting.** Light can penetrate into crevices when using a 45-degree mirror in front of the lens (**Figure 4.18**). This mirror can be half-silvered (one half of the light is reflected, one half transmits through the mirror) or coated so that particular wavelengths are reflected (on the way to the specimen) and others pass through (emitted or reflected by the specimen to the camera). Ring lights can also be used for this purpose, but they are yet slightly off-axis from the lens, and some shadowing can result.

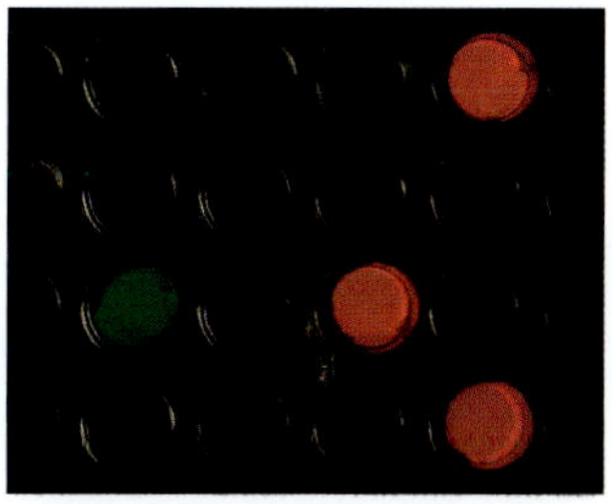

FIGURE 4.18 Portion of 96-well plate showing on-axis lighting and penetration of light into wells.

Tips for Imaging Challenging Specimens

Depending on materials or composition of specimens, some can be very challenging to position and light in order to produce accurate images. Their appearance can be visually confusing because of reflections or because textures and roundness do not translate well in images. Here are some suggestions:

- **Specimens that reflect surrounding objects.** A white tent can be created to surround highly reflective objects, such as highly polished metals. White paper can be made into a funnel. The camera is then focused through the opening in the funnel. Another alternative is to rub a thin layer of soft wax on reflective surfaces.
- **Removing glare via setting specimen underwater.** Glare can also be removed by setting the specimen underwater. Some elongation of the specimen will result because of the difference in the refractive index of air and water.

- **Polymers and glass.** Polymers and glass present difficult challenges for creating good representations of a specimen. Lighting is often pointed on the glass or the polymer itself. The better means for lighting may be to point a narrow beam of light on a part of the specimen that is not visible to the camera, and then to allow the light to "pipe" through the glass or polymer, or back light off-axis with a black background (as shown in Figure 4.18 with the embryo).

Environmental Imaging

Digital imaging in the real world with an SLR digital camera requires consistency in approach. It's most important when real colors and contrasts are meant to be exact representations of the scene and when the representations are compared over time.

Several steps need to be taken to ensure consistency and accuracy. Of immediate importance is to acquire images of the scene with the correct exposure and aperture setting so that grayscale and color values remain within the dynamic range of the camera.

Exposure Time and Aperture

Exposure refers to the total amount of light that falls on the detector when taking a photograph, and is determined by the size of the lens opening through which the light passes (aperture) and the length of time that the shutter is open (exposure time, or shutter speed). Exposure time is measured in fractions of a second. Aperture values are expressed as the ratio of the focal length of the lens to the diameter of the aperture opening. Thus, a setting of *f*/16 means that the diameter of the aperture will be 1/16 the focal length. Larger values result in smaller apertures and greater depth of focus.

Exposure and aperture values can be determined by using a light metering system in the camera. The method for choosing a metering pattern should be reviewed by reading the accompanying manual. A metering pattern can be chosen according to the appropriate scene or specimen.

Metering systems can call for exposures that lead to the clipping of white values. Determine if the camera tends to overexpose when metering indicates correct values by photographing scenes in which small areas of white are present. Measure the whites in Photoshop and determine if these values are clipped. If so, a feature on many professional cameras can be set to consistently underexpose by a chosen value.

Lighting

Consistency and accuracy of results require conditions in which the lighting is consistent. The ideal setting is when a single camera is used under controlled conditions with a light source such as strobe or flash that is consistent over time and that can overpower other light sources. Flash units are very consistent as long as they are fired several times for stabilization before important images are acquired (**Figure 4.19**). Flash-on-camera units are effective when multiple objects being photographed are in the same plane: They are not effective when objects are nearer and farther away because the difference in brightness alters the lightness of colors.

FIGURE 4.19 Parasitic mushrooms growing on a stump photographed over time with a strobe (flash) unit. Note the consistency in color and contrast.

Most settings involve lights that fade over time or conditions in which lighting changes, such as outdoor photography. Consequent shifts in color temperature create inconsistent color interpretation of scenes.

Three methods can aid in consistent color interpretation:

- Manual white balancing
- Reference standards
- Saving in the Raw format (if available)—not in the JPEG or TIFF format—and then using the Adobe Camera Raw plug-in for Photoshop for color interpretation

MANUAL WHITE BALANCING FOR CONSISTENT RESULTS

Professional (and some consumer) cameras will have options to manually white balance. This is preferred over generic settings for various conditions (e.g., Outdoor, Cloudy, Incandescent, etc.) because manual white balancing provides greater accuracy at determining the color temperature of the light source. A white or gray card, or a card with increments of gray, can be purchased from a professional photography store. Alternatively, a white disk—available at professional photography stores—can be mounted in front of the lens for the same purpose. The nonreflective, flat white or gray cards (or disk) provide surfaces that are uniform, which is best for determining average reflectance. Find out how to white balance manually by referring to the camera's manual. The difference between using generic camera settings for white balancing and manual white balancing can be dramatic (**Figure 4.20**).

FIGURE 4.20 The image on the top shows color interpretation from a camera when a generic setting (in this instance, Cloudy) is used versus the image on the bottom when manual white balancing against a reference is used.

For manual white balancing to work with white and gray cards, reflect from the main light source. Hold the card so that it contains the reflection of the light source. When multiple light sources are used, hold the reference card close to the scene, aiming the card mostly toward the most important light source. Another way to use a white or gray card is to include it in the scene or with the specimen when practical. Later, in Photoshop, these images can be used for correcting color (see "Manual Match Color to Reference Method" in Chapter 7, "Color Corrections and Final Steps").

White balancing against a reference card or disk can produce consistent colors and contrasts, even when images are taken over time *as long as the same light source is used*. Consistency is far more difficult when light sources change; for example, when a specimen is photographed under tungsten light and then under daylight.

■ **Note:** *Daylight color temperatures can change dramatically, depending on several conditions: time of day, clouds in front of the sun, under shade, and whether nearby objects or surfaces reflect onto the objects photographed. If manual white balancing can be done, consistency can be achieved. Including a gray card in the picture, and, when applicable, using a flash to overpower daylight, will aid in obtaining consistent colors and contrasts.*

FIGURE 4.21 A 24-patch Macbeth color chart is included with the scene as a reference against which to create consistent color and contrast readings.

REFERENCE STANDARDS

A Macbeth color chart can be included for critical applications in which colors need to remain consistent (**Figure 4.21**). The 24-square card, available in credit card size to larger dimensions, is adequate for most imaging applications. It can be used for calibrating or as a reference from the first session. When used as a reference, changes to colors in subsequent sessions can be used to adjust colors and brightness to the scene or specimen in the first session.

JPEG, TIFF, AND RAW

Images that are saved as JPEGs and TIFFs will be color balanced, and contrast and color corrected in camera acquisition software. While that automatic process saves time, it can lead to inconsistent results (**Figure 4.22**).

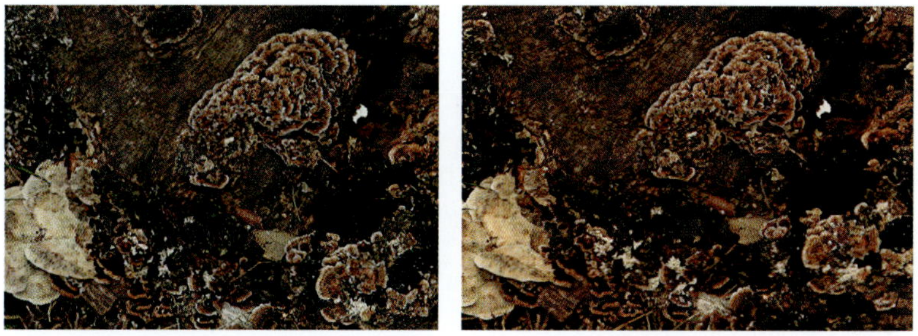

FIGURE 4.22 Two images saved as JPEG on different days after manual white balancing show different interpretations of color.

Raw files, on the other hand, contain only the original values of red, green, and blue at each sensor position. Remember that each sensor in a mosaic chip (the kind of chip used for professional consumer cameras and many scientific cameras as well) is filtered by a single red or green or blue filter. The estimate of color at each position is based on information gathered about neighboring sensor values, and then an estimate of the true color is made (called demosaicing). Allowing software to demosaic while providing user adjustments gives users not only more flexibility, but a way to record values for settings. These values can then be applied to all images.

● **More:** *More information about Adobe Camera Raw can be found at www.peachpit.com/scientificimaging.*

▶ **Warning:** *ACR will auto-adjust gamma to the RGB working space gamma. If a gamma of 1 is desired, the RGB working space with a gamma of 1 must be chosen in the Color Settings dialog box in Photoshop (see Chapter 5).*

Photoshop includes demosaicing software in the form of a plug-in called Adobe Camera Raw (ACR). This plug-in opens automatically when opening Raw files (though ACR can be used when opening TIFF or JPEG files: see "Opening Images in Adobe Camera Raw" in Chapter 6). The ACR plug-in includes settings for color and contrast corrections, and is often cited as a superior means for editing Raw images.

Though off-camera, demosaicing programs are more robust, color interpretation still occurs, and some automated functions need to be reset. ACR may interpret the color temperature of the scene incorrectly and add a tint if an overall color shift is detected. If the camera has been manually white balanced, the color temperature and tint may need to be reset. To use ACR, follow these steps:

■ **Note:** *Photoshop's ACR may change attributes of the image more so than image acquisition programs that come with the camera. Compare images that are opened through Photoshop's ACR program against image acquisition programs provided by camera manufacturers. If the images are more consistent in proprietary programs, convert RAW formats to TIFF formats in these programs before opening them in Photoshop.*

1. In the main window of ACR, make sure the Basic tab is active. From the White Balance menu, choose As Shot.
2. Using the Tint slider, adjust so that the tint is set to zero (0).

Images taken on different days under the same lighting source, when following these steps, can be compared for similarity or differences in color (**Figure 4.23**). Color accuracy in longitudinal studies can be ensured when including an external reference with the specimen.

FIGURE 4.23 Images of the same scene taken on two separate days in outdoor conditions.

Calibrating Cameras

The advantage of ACR is in its capability to work with a number of RAW formats from various manufacturers and to calibrate each to a standard interpretation of color and brightness levels. In so doing, workgroups with several different cameras can each produce similar interpretation of colors and contrasts.

■ **Note:** *The Macbeth color chart is not the only calibration target. The Kodak Q60 target is a transparent film that can be used as well as other targets from various manufacturers. The advantages of the Macbeth chart are in its nonreflective, flat colors and fewer colors to balance.*

● **More:** *The steps for color calibration can be found at www.peachpit.com/scientificimaging.*

To create a calibration, first white balance manually. Then photograph a Macbeth color chart in daylight, tungsten, or flash (strobe) lighting, depending on typical conditions for scenes or specimens. The colors and brightness level values are subsequently matched from the image of the Macbeth chart to known values. The known values are taken from the gamut of colors used to view images on computer screens, which is mentioned in more detail at www.creativepro.com.

This calibration can be saved and then applied to images in ACR.

Images from PowerPoint and Other Applications

Many modern applications whose principal purpose is not image editing can now save images at higher resolutions than they could in the past. Also, it is increasingly common that software programs that use vector graphics (for text, line drawings, and symbols) can export those graphics as bitmapped images. If an application can export images in TIFF or EPS format at the desired resolutions, it may be possible to use these images for publication. Publication images are typically desired at 300 or 400 ppi or dpi at width and height dimensions determined by the author according to the number of columns the image will span. Line drawings, graphs, and artwork are required at 1200 pixels or dpi.

Yet many of these programs save only in the JPEG format, and then only at relatively high levels of compression, resulting in a significant loss of visual data. The resolutions that result from saving as TIFF from these programs may also be *less* than what can be obtained

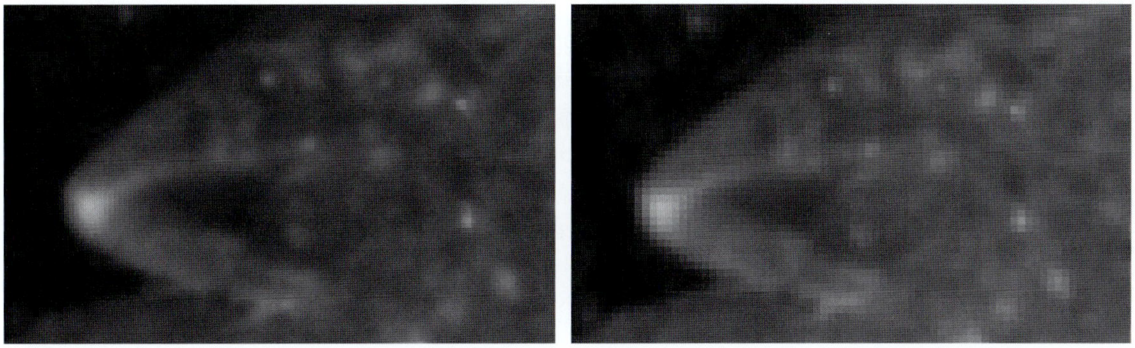

FIGURE 4.24 A zoomed image of a leaf printed to Adobe PDF (left) and as a TIFF file saved in PowerPoint (right).

through means discussed in this section. In **Figure 4.24**, for example, a zoomed image of a leaf shows that better resolution was achieved (on the left) when printing to Adobe PDF (Portable Document Format) using the Press Quality preset, versus saving a 300 ppi TIFF file from PowerPoint (right image). Note the coarser pixilation of the PowerPoint derived image.

Also, many specialized graphing programs, older scientific programs, legacy QuickDraw programs, and programs on SGI (Silicon Graphics, Inc.)/SUN units do not provide any options for saving as TIFF or EPS through the Save As or Export commands. When documents from these sources are made into TIFF files, lettering and edges of drawings can be aliased.

Copy and Paste as a (Poor) Solution

Whenever possible, copying and pasting images from one application to another should be avoided. This is especially true when copying images and graphics from one software manufacturer (e.g., Microsoft) to another (e.g., Adobe). Copied graphics and images are saved at computer screen resolutions in memory (the Clipboard) at resolutions that are generally lower than the original.

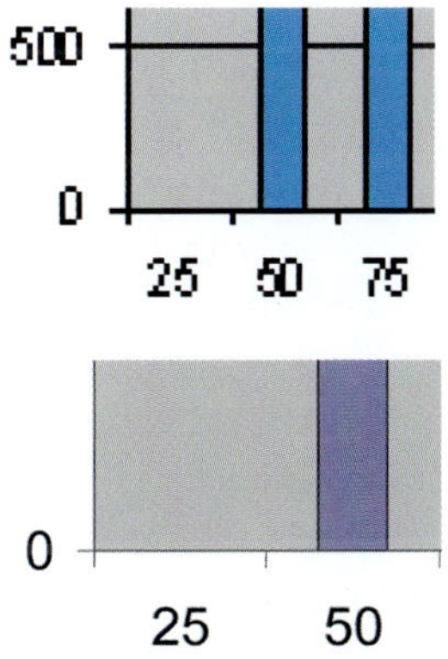

FIGURE 4.25 On the top is a copied and pasted image of the graph; on the bottom is the graph printed to Adobe PDF and saved as an EPS file.

For example, in **Figure 4.25** a small portion of a graph is zoomed in to inspect the quality of lettering. A copied and pasted image of the graph is shown on the top; the same graph printed to Adobe PDF and saved as an EPS file is on the bottom. Note the change in colors of the bars in the copied and pasted image, along with the pixilation of the graphic indicated by the 5 and 0 in the number 50. Colors also shifted in the PDF derived EPS file: The graph was created in a Microsoft program in which color management is not used, resulting in interpretation of the colors by the Adobe PDF driver.

Best Methods for Retention of Resolution

To retain as much visual data as possible without aliased lettering, the following approaches can be used for graphic (vector) line drawings, graphs, text, and so on:

- **Low-tech solution 1.** Enlarge the graphic to eight times its size and save or export it in bitmap format (e.g., TIFF, JPEG, BMP, PICT). When the file is opened in Photoshop, in the Image Size dialog box, change the dimensions and resolution to the desired settings (see "Resample for Output [Image Size]" in Chapter 8).

  Choose this method when graphics are easily enlarged and an option exists to save in a bitmap format.

- **Low-tech solution 2.** Print the graphic to an inkjet printer or a deskjet printer (but *only* if it is a vector graphic), scan the page at 1200 dpi in the grayscale or color mode, save it as a TIFF file, and then optimize the image in Photoshop. If the image is a graphic (text, line drawings, graphs), make the grayish paper background white and the lines/text dark (see "Problem Images" in Chapter 6).

  Use this option when no other options exist for saving as a bitmap or when other solutions don't work.

- **Print to Adobe PDF.** Rather than saving a file in PDF format, which is likely to produce a low-resolution file, instead use the Print command and choose the Adobe PDF driver (**Figure 4.26**). This generates an image file in Adobe PDF format that retains the full resolution and detail of the original image or graphic. This method requires the purchase of one of the versions of Adobe Acrobat.

In Properties (or Options), be sure to indicate the intent. In the Default Settings drop-down list, choose either of the following:

- For images, choose High Quality Print. An image no greater than 450 ppi (pixels per inch) will result (Figure 4.26).
- For graphics, choose Press Quality. A 2400 ppi document will result.

Open the document in Adobe Acrobat and check to see if the entire image or graphic fits into the page. If the document does not fit, any of the following actions can be taken:

- If the image or graphic is rotated to the wrong orientation but it fits within the page, in Acrobat choose Document > Rotate Pages to return the graphic or image to the correct orientation.

▶ **Warning:** *Several free sources for Acrobat conversion software are available, and they can be used as well, but results are not always satisfactory, especially when high-resolution files are desired. For example, many users of Mac OS X will be aware that they can output a PDF version of any document by means of the standard Print dialog box. Simply click the PDF button in the lower-left corner of the dialog and choose Save As PDF from the menu that appears. Be aware, however, that this method of creating a PDF is less desirable than using Acrobat. For one thing, you have no control over the parameters of the PDF being created. For another, each application handles the conversion to PDF differently, and unwanted changes may be introduced into your image data. The image might be converted to the CMYK color space, and bitmapped images may be downsampled to lower resolutions.*

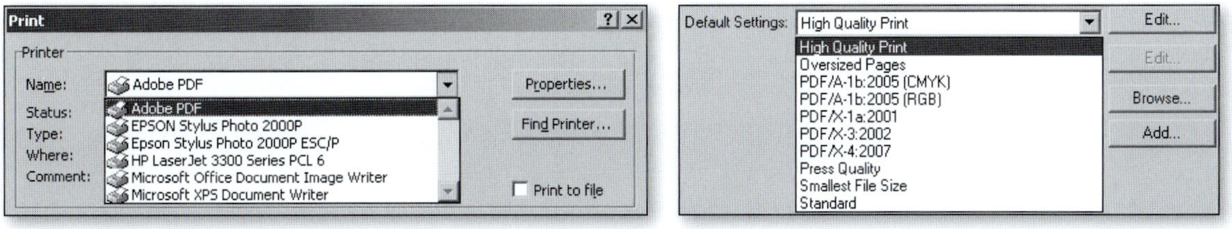

FIGURE 4.26 On the left, the Windows Print dialog box, showing the Adobe PDF driver selected. Clicking the Properties button opens the Adobe PDF Document Properties dialog box, seen at right.

- If the image or graphic doesn't fit within the page because it is at the wrong orientation, change it before printing the PDF again. To do this, choose Landscape or Portrait (whichever is appropriate) in the Layout tab of the Print dialog box in Acrobat 7 for Windows, or in the Page Setup dialog box (File > Page Setup) in Acrobat 7 for Macintosh or Acrobat 8 for either platform.
- If the image or graphic doesn't fit within the page and it is at the correct orientation, rescale the image to the page size or increase the page size, whichever is appropriate. Click the Advanced button to access these options (**Figure 4.27**).

Once you've created a satisfactory PDF file, convert it to the appropriate final format by opening it in Acrobat and choosing File > Save As. The encapsulated PostScript (EPS) format is preferred for publications because it retains details in graphics and produces compact files. Also, EPS files are scalable, meaning that they can be scaled to any dimensions and still retain their inherent resolution, provided that the graphics are in vector format and the original contains no bitmapped images. The TIFF format is preferred for bitmapped images, although JPEG files can be used in word processing documents.

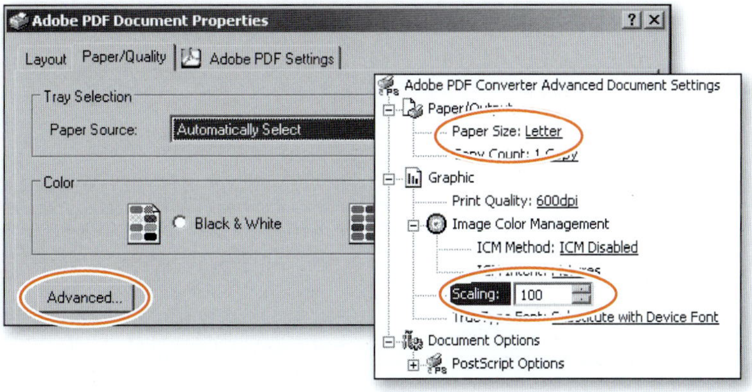

FIGURE 4.27 The Paper Size or Scaling options can be changed to fit the image or graphic within the page size.

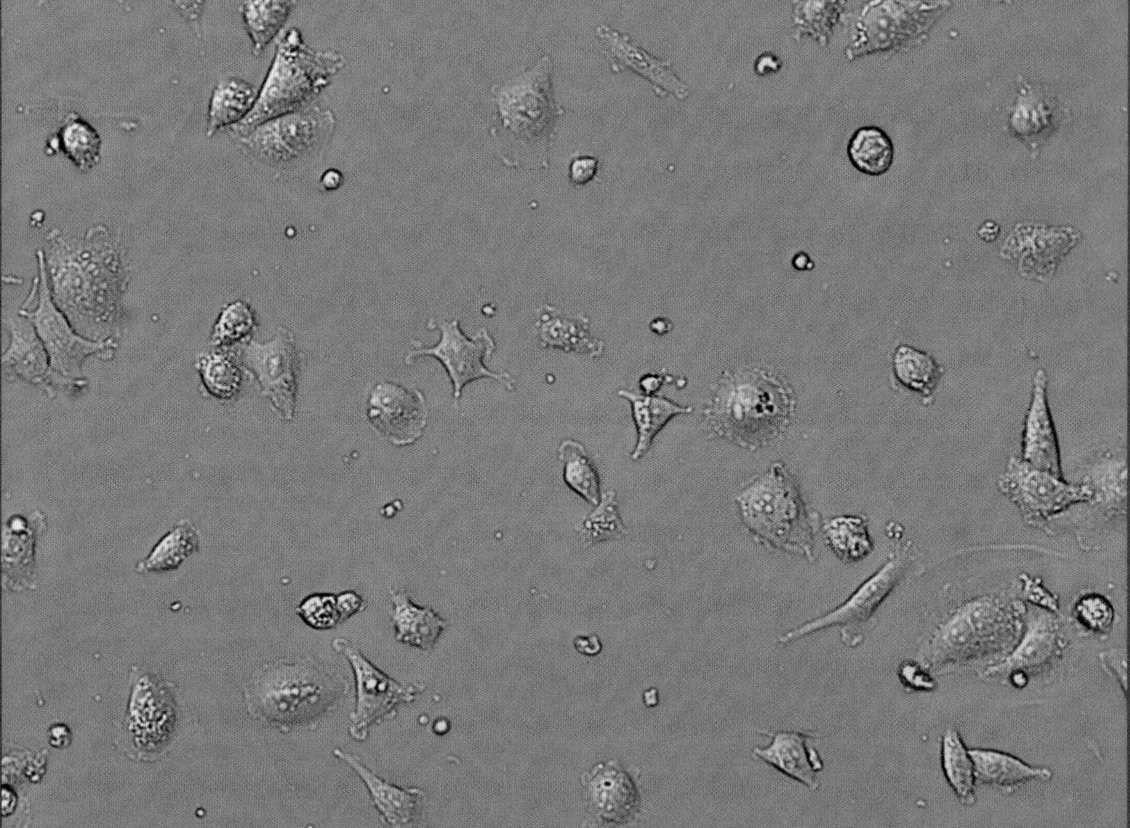

CHAPTER 5

Photoshop Setup and Standard Procedure

BEFORE USING PHOTOSHOP for post-processing, certain viewing conditions need to be in place. These viewing conditions include the following:

- **Computer display setup.** The display should be calibrated for a more accurate display of colors and contrasts.
- **Ambient conditions.** Rooms in which computer displays are located should be dark and devoid of window light.
- **Fine-tuning displayed colors.** Choices should be made to more accurately fine-tune colors to match the colors of the intended output.

Once viewing conditions are met, it's essential to understand the function and location of Photoshop tools relevant to research. These include the toolbox and options bar.

To further optimize the use of Photoshop, user preferences can be reset to increase Photoshop's use of memory. Other preferences can be set to change units of measurement, how images are resampled, and grid sizes, and to record post-processing steps for documentation (History Log).

Image of a monolayer of suspended epithelial cells with DIC (Differential Interference Contrast) illumination, taken on an Olympus IX 70 with a DVC 1310M camera (DVC Company, Austin, TX). Post-processing steps included correction of uneven illumination, color toning, and sharpening using Photoshop CS3 Extended (Adobe Systems Incorporated, San Jose, CA). Scale bar = 100 microns.

● **More:** *For an overview of the commonly used elements of the Photoshop interface (palettes, dialog boxes, and the like), as well as information on setting preferences and troubleshooting, download the supplement "Tools and Functions in Photoshop" from www.peachpit.com/scientificimaging. Familiarity with these tools and functions is critical to the understanding of the methods shown in the remainder of this book.*

Central to the use of Photoshop is a good understanding of relevant palettes and dialog boxes. Palettes are opened so they can be viewed and referred to at all times. The most relevant palettes include:

- **Info and Histogram palettes.** Each shows numeric readouts.
- **Layers palette.** Shows the stacking of images and text in layers.
- **Actions palette.** Provides a means to automate post-processing steps.

These palettes are essential for providing information so that reference numbers can be used when altering images and as a means to document changes. The most frequently used dialog boxes—Levels, Curves, and Hue and Saturation—provide the means to color and contrast correct.

Viewing conditions are described in detail in this chapter, and a standard procedure for setting brightness and contrast in any image is outlined.

Approaches to Color and Contrast Matching

The ultimate aim when viewing images on a monitor is to see colors as an accurate representation of the original scene or specimen. As mentioned earlier, this cannot be a reasonable expectation when some colors are saturated. Saturated blues and violets display darker overall at values similar to other colors, most notably green; saturated yellows and oranges display lighter. Extremes of these colors lie near or outside the gamut of computer displays.

However, it is reasonable to expect that most nonsaturated colors of brightfield stains, objects, and scenes display at brightness and color levels closely approximating what was once seen by eye. That expectation can be met when some allowance is made for viewing conditions, because a specimen viewed by eye with reflective illumination will appear differently than the specimen image backlit by a monitor (though eyes do adjust rapidly to different lighting conditions and color temperatures). It is also reasonable to expect that more than one monitor can display colors similarly within a workgroup.

How colors appear becomes complicated from one monitor to another because each uses hardware and software to interpret how colors should look, which is determined by the manufacturer for each brand of monitor. Manufacturers also determine how colors will appear depending on how they believe consumers will use computers. Most

FIGURE 5.1 Two monitors displaying the same color values but using different profiles. On the left, a monitor using the sRGB color space. On the right, the same color displayed on a monitor using a color space with a wider gamut.

computers are set by default to display a relatively limited set of colors (or gamut), taking a sort of "least common denominator" approach. This is done partly to attempt to ensure that photos displayed on Web sites appear similar on a wide variety of computers running different software. This is accomplished by converting the original color values to a narrow "color space" called sRGB according to a *profile* (**Figure 5.1**).

To create a situation in which colors can be displayed accurately and in which the greatest range of colors and tones can be viewed, several conditions must be met in a workflow. The workflow starts with the input device, and then the colors from that device are converted to colors that make up the display. Colors and contrasts on a display are viewed according to an editing color space and are then printed using the printer's color profile. Users can decide on default or supplied color interpretations and views at each step, or users can knowledgeably choose and generate their own color spaces. The latter is preferable for greater color accuracy (**Table 5.1**).

The following list provides more in-depth information about each table entry:

- **Input profile.** The input from detectors is characterized to a set of profiled colors, whether it is to a large set of colors (a digital camera) or a small subset (colors assigned to grayscale tones according to a LUT). The profile can be included with the image from an imaging device (tagged), or it can be more typical of scientific cameras in which a profile is not included (untagged). The image can be saved in the TIFF or JPEG formats in which color

TABLE 5.1 Viewing Color Along the Imaging Workflow

	INPUT	MONITOR			EDITING SPACE		PRINTER	
Workflow	Input profile	Monitor color temperature	Monitor environment	Monitor profiles	Editing space profile conversion	Monitor editing spaces	Printer profile	Evaluation color temperatures
Default or supplied	Profiles from manufacturer	Manufacturer color temperature	Room lighting	Manufacturer profile	Operating system (Mac ColorSync, Microsoft ICM)	sRGB (default, limited gamut)	Supplied by manufacturer	Available light
User generated or chosen	Calibrate to known standards: create profile	Color temperature: 6500K	Darkened room, neutral gray surroundings	Custom profile through calibration	Adobe Conversion Engine (ACE)	Adobe 1998 or ProPhoto RGB (expanded gamut)	User profiled	5000K, 6500K

interpretation has been performed in camera (when a professional single lens reflex camera is used); or the image can be saved in the Raw format so that color interpretation at each microsensor position can be done in manufacturer-supplied programs or in the Adobe Camera Raw (ACR) plug-in.

- **Monitor color temperature.** The monitor is set to a color temperature (and gamma) that influences the hue of the viewed colors. The color temperature of 6500K is often recommended for optimal display.
- **Monitor environment.** The interpretation of color on a computer screen is influenced by surrounding colors in the room environment. A completely dark room with gray walls and a computer screen enclosed in gray surrounds provide an ideal setting. A dimly lit room with a consistent light source can be used as well. The user's clothing can influence the perception of color, so black clothing can be worn to eliminate this contribution.
- **Monitor profiles.** The monitor displays colors and brightness levels that by default do not display appropriately for viewing images. These levels need to be set by using relatively inexpensive calibration devices. Alternatively, for a less exacting method to set up the monitor display, Adobe Gamma (Windows) or Display Calibrator Assistant (Macintosh) can be used. LCD (liquid crystal display) monitors will not display blacks as dark as CRT (cathode ray tube) monitors.
- **Editing space profile conversion.** Some kind of software interpretation needs to be done to convert from the input color space to the monitor. The preferred interpreter (engine) for Photoshop is the Adobe Conversion Engine (ACE) unless a compelling reason exists for choosing ColorSync (Apple) or Microsoft ICM.
- **Monitor editing spaces.** The appearance of colors is further refined into color spaces that can include most of the colors a monitor can display or a subset. The default setting is usually sRGB. A wider range of colors that is more appropriate for images destined for multiple outputs can be displayed with Adobe 1998 or ProPhoto color spaces (the ProPhoto color space is wider than Adobe 1998).

  Adobe 1998 and ProPhoto are the preferred color spaces for making changes to images. The notion that color conversion is complicated by yet another decision to choose an editing color space (rather than simply allowing the monitor to display all the colors possible) is true. But it's the same decision made by editors of books who must choose language appropriate to their audiences, or audio engineers who must edit according to whether the music will be played on a CD, FM radio, the Web, and so on. In both situations the original has to be output to the respective audience or medium.

Note: *If the print is used only to provide the publisher with an example of how the image should appear, it isn't a proof: It is an example the publisher can strive to reproduce.*

- **Printer profile.** When images are destined for CMYK devices (e.g., printing presses), proofs are often made to indicate how images will reproduce. A printer profile is necessary for accuracy when matching the colors and brightness levels of the image on the monitor to that of the print. The printer profile can be supplied by the manufacturer or a third party based on the paper stock that is used, because colors will change depending on the characteristics of the paper. Printer profiles are also essential for output to RGB devices, like desktop inkjet printers.

  The display of the image on the monitor can be used as a "soft" proof, and the printer can be used to provide an example. But the workflow with the greatest degree of predictability is one in which a proof on the monitor and on the printed page is used. It is also more expensive, because a densitometer specific to reading reflective objects must be purchased.

More: *See www.quickphotoshop.com for a listing of third-party sources of custom calibrations of specific paper and printer combinations. These can be had for a fee.*

- **Evaluation color temperatures.** The color on the print is partly a result of a combination of the color temperature of light sources and reflections off nearby objects. Under available light, especially when it is fluorescent or when lit by a changing sky through a window, the color temperature is not "standard." Under fluorescence, the light has a green color temperature when standard bulbs are used, and window light provides a changing color temperature. At the printing press, a consistent light source is used to evaluate the printed page at a color temperature of 5000K. Color correction professionals either use the printing industry standard of 5000K, or they use a color temperature of 6500K.

Color Settings

The settings in the Color Settings dialog box in Photoshop are of particular importance, because they control the appearance of colors and contrasts. When several individuals are working within a group, these settings are essential for the consistent appearance of colors and contrasts across computer displays.

The settings shown in **Figure 5.2** are generic settings for the CMYK and Grayscale working spaces. If authors contact printing presses, specific settings may be available from each press and can be used instead of the generic settings specified in Figure 5.2.

Select Edit > Color Settings to access the Color Settings dialog box.

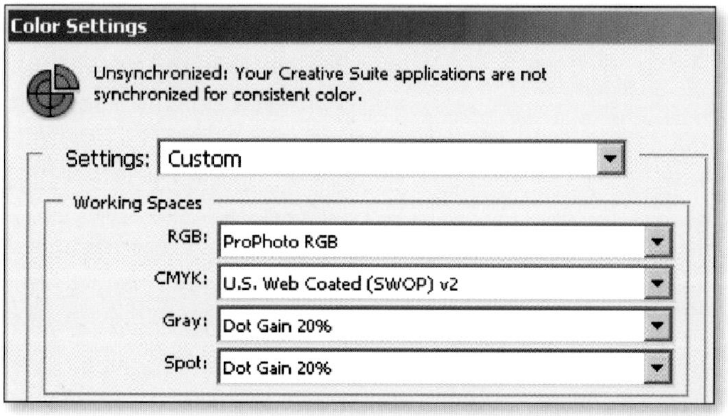

FIGURE 5.2 The Working Spaces area of the Color Settings dialog box.

Unsynchronized

The unsynchronized color settings alert means that other applications from the Adobe Creative Suite that you have installed use different color settings. If you are not using the same images with other programs such as Illustrator or InDesign, you can ignore this warning. If any of the other programs is used, be sure to copy the same settings in the Color Settings dialog box to that program.

Working Spaces

The Working Spaces area in the Color Settings dialog box refers to editing spaces, which were described earlier as a part of the imaging workflow. The following editing spaces can be chosen:

- **RGB.** For RGB (red, green, and blue primary colors of the monitor) the working space is changed from sRGB IEC61966-2.1 to either ProPhoto RGB or Adobe RGB (1998) when working with brightfield or environmental images. ProPhoto is currently preferred for its wider gamut of colors. The sRGB color editing space is limited to a narrower range of colors and should be changed unless the intent of the image is only for the Web or when editing images in which saturated colors exist. This includes darkfield images of fluorescently labeled specimens.

- **CMYK.** For CMYK (cyan, magenta, yellow, and black [or Key] inks used by printing presses) the gamut of colors should be in accordance with common standards of the country where the printing press is located and the kind of paper used for printing. In the United States, for the kind of press used for printing journals (Web press) and a coated paper (a chemical coating to enhance brightness and ink adherence characteristics), the generic choice is U.S. Web Coated (SWOP) v2. SWOP (Specifications for Web Offset Printing) is set every few years by a committee of representatives from the printing industry (www.swop.org).
- **Gray.** For grayscale images, the typical setting is for a dot gain of 20%. Dot gain refers to the enlargement of the dots used for composing an image (much like pixels) on the printed paper due to the absorption of ink into the paper or the spreading of a drop of ink when applied to the paper. The spreading of dots is not equal at all grayscale levels and is variable depending on the dot pattern used, the size of the dots, and the kind of paper. This setting provides a generic target for the dot gain.
- **Spot.** Spot refers to color or grayscale values matched to specific inks. The spatial locations of these colors can be specified on images, and then these colors can be matched to designated inks. Generally, spot colors aren't used in science, and this setting is left at the default.

Color Management Policies

The Color Management Policies area in the Color Settings dialog box offers choices for instituting working spaces and receiving reminders when image profiles do not match the working space (**Figure 5.3**).

FIGURE 5.3 The Color Management Policies area in the Color Settings dialog box.

- **Off.** This selection is misleading because color management cannot be turned off: Colors are automatically converted to some profile, whether it is the working (editing) space or the profile for the monitor. Colors are not left managed in the same way as in Microsoft programs on the Windows platform, which is often the user's objective when choosing this setting (although the sRGB working space can be a close match).
- **Preserve Embedded Profiles.** When it is important to view the color of the image using the profile of the imaging device used to take the picture (not generally supplied with scientific cameras), this is a useful selection because the colors can be viewed in their original state. Using this policy assumes user familiarity with the color working spaces.
- **Convert to Working (Editing) Space (RGB, CMYK, Gray).** When it is more important to view and change color appearance to the editing space that is chosen, this policy is best. Because most imaging done in science occurs with imaging devices in which working color spaces are not assigned (referred to as untagged), this policy allows the user to choose. Given that consistency is most important in research, this setting is suggested.
- **Profile Mismatches.** If Convert to Working RGB, CMYK, and Gray is chosen, color appearances automatically convert to those editing spaces. If users want to be notified when colors are converted, check boxes can be selected.

  When selected, the Ask When Opening option ensures that the Color Settings remain consistent: If another user has changed these settings, the current user will be alerted. An example of that alert is shown (**Figure 5.4**).

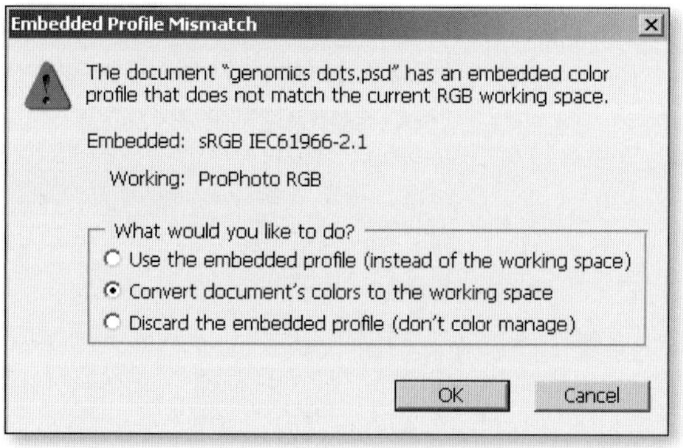

FIGURE 5.4 A warning is displayed when color profiles don't match.

Conversion Options

The Conversion Options (**Figure 5.5**) area in the Color Settings dialog box provides a number of settings related to how images are changed in Photoshop. These settings are described as follows:

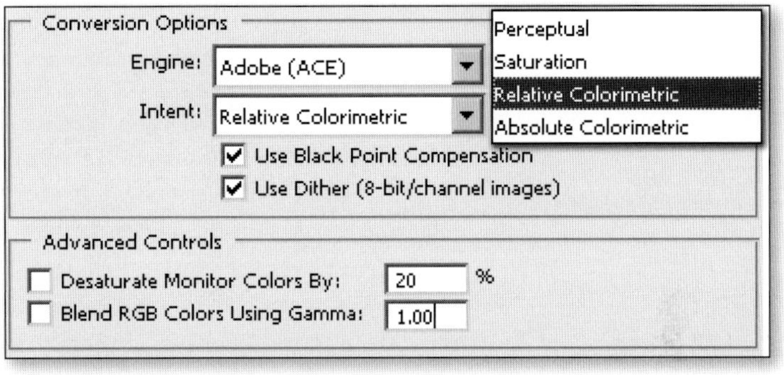

FIGURE 5.5 The Conversion Options area in the Color Settings dialog box.

- **Engine.** Generally, the engine is set to Adobe's Color Engine (ACE) for its color conversion algorithms.
- **Intent.** The intent dictates how colors that lie outside the gamut will be treated when converting from RGB to CMYK. If the methods for colorizing, color correction, and color conversion to CMYK are used from this book, Relative Colorimetric or Perceptual is chosen. Experiments with RGB to CMYK color conversion can be done for typical specimens to determine which provides the best rendering for the intent of the image. Perceptual may result in a greater likelihood for preserving the relationship of brightness and darkness values. For graphics, Saturation is chosen. Absolute Colorimetric is generally not used except in specific instances when hard proofing is desired or color matching is absolutely required.
- **Use Black Point Compensation.** When this option is selected (default), the entire dynamic range of the input is converted to the entire dynamic range of the output. Deselect this option when it is important to preserve the relationship of the darkest values to the rest of the image for instances when densities/intensities are measured or when only brightfield images are worked with (when darkest areas are unimportant to preserve).
- **Use Dither.** When converting, gradients are introduced to eliminate artifacts (banding) that result from compressing the dynamic range from a larger space (e.g., RGB) to a smaller space (e.g., CMYK). This option is often deselected because it introduces edge gradients.

- **Advanced Controls.** Unless the user is an expert at color and grayscale conversion, and is familiar with the consequence of changing these settings, these options are deselected.

Standard Procedure

■ **Note:** *When black limits are set, the darkest areas will appear grayish on LCD monitors, even when monitors are calibrated. In almost all outputs, these dark areas will appear darker than shown onscreen.*

A standard procedure for setting contrast and brightness for images uses the Color Sampler tool to place samplers on the brightest and darkest significant areas of the image. Then significant areas are brightened or darkened using Levels or Curves to fit these areas within a dynamic range of tonal values, narrower than the 8-bit range, with specific white and black limits. By setting white and black limits, scientists can be confident that darker and lighter values will reproduce in publications, in posters, for projections, on the Web, and in documents used for grant submission and reports.

1. Output levels and the Color Sampler tool

When making contrast and color adjustments to images, the brightest and darkest significant values in the features of the image or background areas are used as references to determine the white and black limits. Throughout this book, sampling points are placed on the whitest and blackest references in the image *before* Levels or Curves are used. The Color Sampler tool is generally set to a Sample Size of 5 by 5 Average, so that values from 25 pixels surrounding the click point are averaged to determine the intensity/density value.

2. Finding black and white reference points

Normally, reference points are found visually. The eye is very good at finding the darkest and brightest parts of the image. Generally, a featureless background level exists in scientific images. The background area can be used as follows:

- For back-illuminated brightfield images (e.g., on a microscope), use the background (featureless white) area of the image for the sampling point.
- For darkfield images, use the background (featureless black) area of the image for the sampling point.

- Front-illuminated brightfield images and critical applications may create a more difficult situation for visual determination of reference points. The following method can be used to find these areas in the image:

  While using Levels, hold down the Alt/Option key and move the white input triangle to the left until white regions appear: These are the brightest areas. Move the black input triangle to the right until black regions appear: These are the darkest parts of the image. Make a mental note of these areas, and then place the sampling points on these locations in the image.

■ **Note:** *Using the white and black input triangles in Levels to find the brightest and darkest areas in an image can also be used to determine which features clip.*

3. Setting white and black output levels

Once sampling points are placed on respective parts of the image, while the Info palette is open to track changes in numeric values, the white and black triangles are moved to the left and right, respectively. Brightfield images taken by electron microscopy tend to be narrow in dynamic range and low in contrast, and so the Input sliders are used. Darkfield images, on the other hand, usually encompass the full dynamic range, and so the Output sliders are used to narrow the dynamic range. The sliders are adjusted to the dynamic range limits of printing presses in North America according to generic SWOP standards. This dynamic range limit applies fairly uniformly to almost every other output, so it is the generic target. **Table 5.2** contains the generic limits. Post these limits at every workbench where Photoshop is used.

TABLE 5.2 **Black and White Limits for Images**

WHITE LIMIT RGB VALUE	BLACK LIMIT RGB VALUE	WHITE LIMIT K VALUE	BLACK LIMIT K VALUE
240	20	6%	93%

For color images, three readouts are displayed in the Info palette: one for red, one for green, and one for blue. The brightest of the three channels resulting in the maximum value is used to determine the white limit. The darkest of the three channels resulting in the minimum value is used for the black limit.

Practical examples for setting contrast, brightness, and the white and black limits on brightfield and darkfield images are described as follows:

- **Brightfield.** A Transmission Electron Microscope (TEM) micrograph shows Input Levels adjustments used to expand the grayscale values of an image. The Color Sampler tool was used to place samplers (**Figure 5.6A**) on the darkest significant value (#1) and in a bright background portion of the image (#2). In the Levels dialog box, the black triangle was moved to the right until the value of sampler #1 became 20, the target black limit. The white triangle was moved to the left until sampler #2 reached approximately 240, the target white limit (**Figure 5.6C** and **D**). Note the contrast difference between the uncorrected image and the corrected image (**Figure 5.6B**).

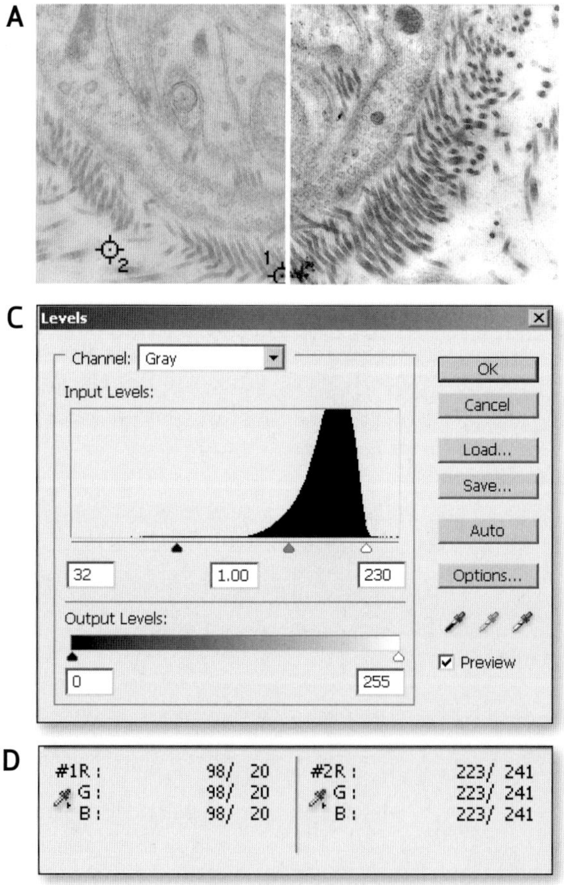

FIGURE 5.6 The standard procedure for setting brightness, contrast, and black and white limits on a brightfield image.

- **Darkfield.** The same target values of 240 for the significant white limit and 20 for the significant black (background) apply to the next example, only the original image exceeds the dynamic range, which is typical of darkfield images (**Figure 5.7A**). For this image, the white output slider is moved to the left until a value of 240 is the readout for #1 (white limit), and the black output slider is moved to the right until the readout of the black limit (#2) is slightly more than the target value of 20 (**Figure 5.7C** and **D**). Note the difference in brightest region of the image (under Color Sampler #1), which shows little detail in the original image, but reveals a fair amount of detail after the adjustment (**Figure 5.7B**).

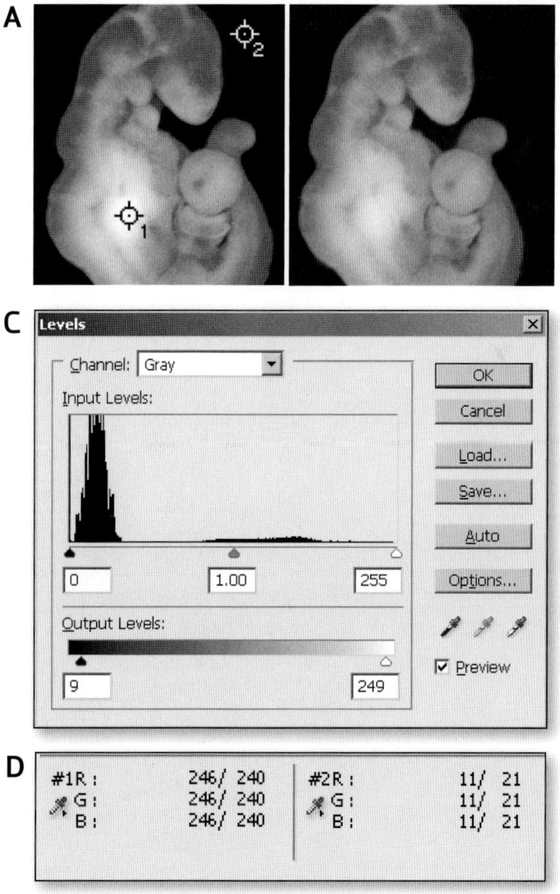

FIGURE 5.7 Standard procedure for setting brightness, contrast, and black and white limits on a darkfield image.

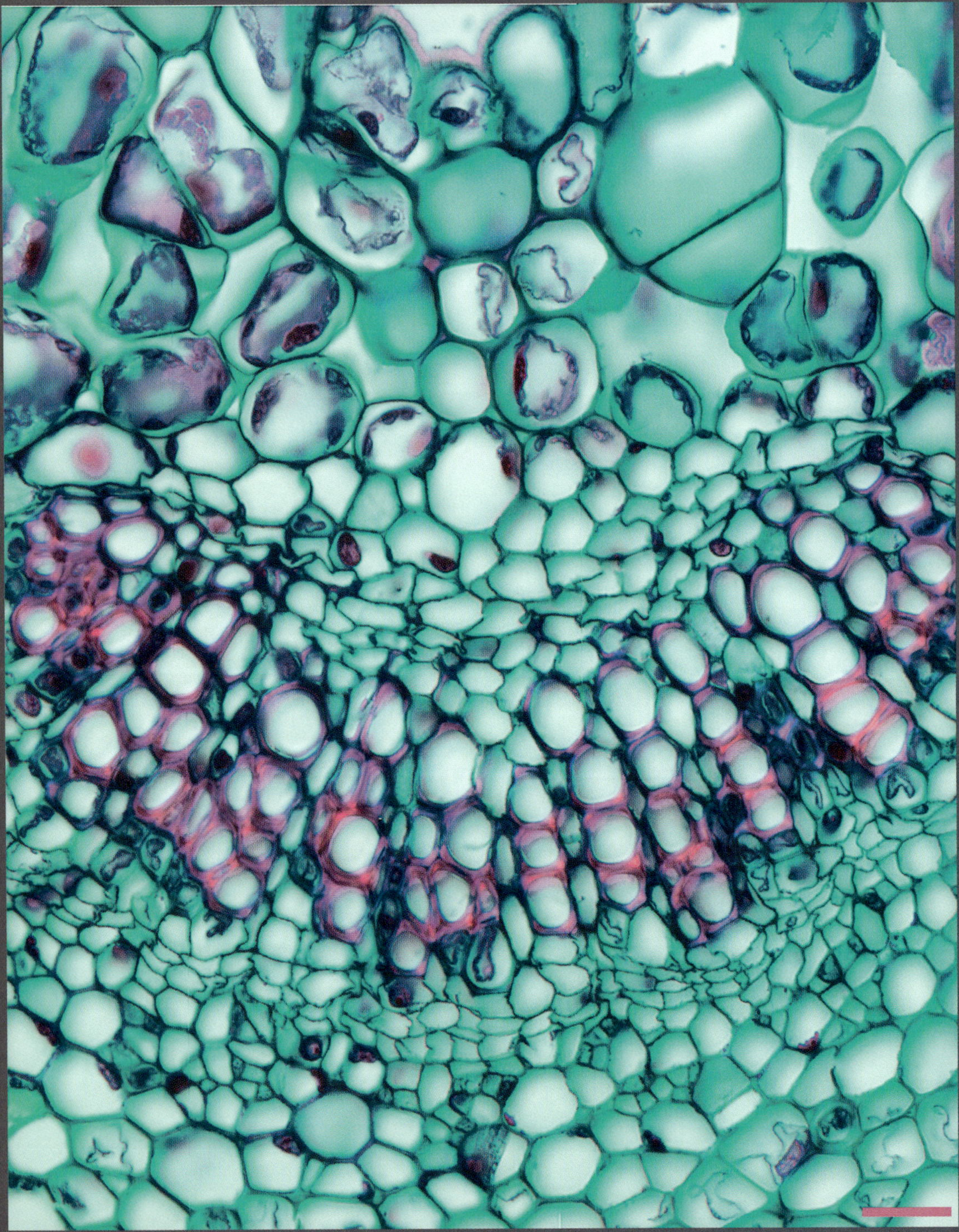

CHAPTER 6

Opening Images and Initial Steps

OPENING AN IMAGE IN PHOTOSHOP can require a few decisions. Because an image contains visual data, like any kind of scientific data, a consistent protocol is necessary. Each workgroup can decide on a protocol so that images are opened in a similar manner.

Certain decisions can have future consequences: If, for example, methods are put in place to ensure that changes are documented and preserved, then a record is available. Also, if nondestructive techniques are implemented, the likelihood of unintentional ethical violations is diminished.

The introduction of ways to open more than one image to make image stacks with layers unlocks new possibilities in Photoshop CS3 Extended—and requires more decisions:

- Images can be opened so that the entire stack is blended into a single image using statistical formulas.
- Multiple images can be opened for image stitching (photomerging), so that a single image can be made from high-magnification images of small areas (fields).
- Video frames from AVI (Audio Video Interleave), MOV (QuickTime movie file extension), and other video-formatted files can be opened and made into image stacks.

After images are opened, several precorrection steps may need to be taken. Foremost among these is mode changes, either from a low to a high bit-depth or from one mode (grayscale or color) to another. Many images then require cropping and straightening. Correction for uneven

Privet leaf (*Ligustrum vulgare*) cross section using Differential Interference Contrast (DIC) illumination and brightfield, acquired on a Zeiss Axioplan 2 microscope using a 20x lens (N.A. 0.8). A Spot 1 camera and SPOT Advanced, version 4.1 software (Diagnostic Instruments, Sterling Heights, MI) were used for acquisition. Several images were combined (photomerged) and final stitched image was color balanced, sharpened, and conformed to printing press, reproducible colors in Photoshop CS3 Extended (Adobe Systems Incorporated, San Jose, CA). Scale bar = 110 microns.

● **More:** *For information on cropping and straightening images, see the document "Photoshop Tools and Functions," which can be downloaded from www.peachpit.com/scientificimaging.*

illumination is common, because many scientific images are prone to uneven illumination. Additionally, the introduction of noise into images frequently obscures details, which is most common when specimens have been imaged in low light.

Special correction methods are used for those images that are loosely called "problem images." Among these problematic images are those in which tonal values are clipped and edges are aliased.

Image Correction Flowchart

As a guide for this and the following two chapters, **Table 6.1** outlines the typical order of steps when correcting and conforming images to outputs. When these steps are followed in order, repetition of steps is avoided and loss of visual data is minimized.

Opening Images

Preserving the original image and retaining a record of the steps that have been taken to correct images are both important. Adobe has implemented safeguards over time to make it more difficult to erase the original image and to keep the correction steps as a record (to reapply edits later if necessary). The first step toward this end was the introduction of the Background layer, which was locked (by default) to limit editing, forcing the user to duplicate that layer. Later, additions were made to create adjustment layers that alter the appearance of an image without touching the original image data. In a greater effort to make image data indestructible, Smart Objects were introduced in CS3 so that filters could be applied to the image nondestructively. Also, Smart Objects prevent the use of certain tools in the toolbox that are used for local changes. These include the Spot Healing Brush, Clone Stamp, and Burn/Dodge tools.

How a lab or workgroup proceeds depends on decisions made mutually or by the manager: No mutually agreed-upon method has been universally accepted or mandated by scientific journals or other scientific organizations as of this writing. If a workgroup wants to ensure that local changes using specific tools from the toolbox are not attempted, the use of Smart Objects would be the best choice (though any intentional effort to insert visual data can always be done with enough expertise).

TABLE 6.1 Flowchart for Image Corrections and Conformance to Output Devices

DARKFIELD (FLUORESCENCE, CONFOCAL)	BRIGHTFIELD, GRAYSCALE (EM, BLOTS)	BRIGHTFIELD, COLOR (HISTOLOGY, ENVIRONMENTAL)
Open, Open As	Open, Open As	Open, Open As
Bit depth	Bit depth	Bit depth
Open unscaled 12-bit in 16-bit format	Open unscaled 12-bit in 16-bit format	Open unscaled 12-bit in 16-bit format
Open in Adobe Camera Raw		Open in Adobe Camera Raw
Frame averaging	Frame averaging	Frame averaging
High dynamic range rendering	High dynamic range rendering	High dynamic range rendering
Opening multiple images merged to single image	Opening multiple images merged to single image	Opening multiple images merged to single image
Opening multiple frames from stack for layers	Opening multiple frames from stack for layers	Opening multiple frames from stack for layers
Mode: Indexed Color to RGB Color	Mode: Indexed Color to RGB Color	Mode: Indexed Color to RGB Color
Flatfield correct	Flatfield correct	Flatfield correct
Crop and Straighten	Crop and Straighten	Crop and Straighten
Problem images: Low contrast or dim, clipped dynamic range	Problem images: Low contrast or dim, reduced or clipped dynamic range	
Noise reduction	Noise reduction	
Color correct: decolorize (color to grayscale); recolorize with reproducible colors		Color and dynamic range correct Color noise reduction Color fringing correction Color to grayscale
Brightness matching	Histogram and background level matching	Color matching
Grayscale to color: Pseudocolor	Grayscale to color: Pseudocolor Add color tone	
Scale bar/Color bars	Scale bar/Color bars	Scale bar
Saving, archiving, organizing	Saving, archiving, organizing	Saving, archiving, organizing
Gamma	Gamma	Gamma
Include in figure/Image Size	Include in figure/Image Size	Include in figure/Image Size
Convert to CMYK		Convert to CMYK
Sharpen	Sharpen	Sharpen
Save	Save	Save

In this book, the method used when opening an image is to duplicate the original image, close it, duplicate the Background layer, and then duplicate the layer whenever an adjustment or filter is applied. Additionally, if the image is 8-bit, it is increased to 16-bit for editing for additional "headroom" (more about increasing bit depth is found in the "Duplicate Image" section later in this chapter). Also, a History Log is set up for each imaging session.

Bridge Database Application (CS2 and CS3)

Images can be opened from the Adobe Bridge application (File > Browse) and viewed as thumbnails. When a thumbnail is selected, a larger preview appears. Bridge is a separate application that "bridges" the various Adobe products that are included with the Adobe Creative Suite. Thus, each Adobe software program in the suite uses the same window for browsing files.

■ **Note:** *You can access a Batch Rename tool in the File browser in the Photoshop CS version by selecting File > Automate > Batch Rename.*

Of the many features available in Bridge, the Batch Rename function is of particular importance when you need to rename nonsequentially numbered files with sequential numbering (CS2 and CS3 versions only). In the Bridge application choose Tools > Batch Rename.

Smart Object or Duplicate Image

When opening images, these options are available:

- Open as Smart Object (CS3 only)
- Open and duplicate image to edit (legacy versions)

SMART OBJECTS

In recent versions of Photoshop, it is possible to protect image data from being edited by converting it into a Smart Object. All editing operations performed on Smart Objects do not change the original image data, but are applied as separate layers which can be edited further or deleted. For that reason, opening images as Smart Objects is an important technique for performing nondestructive editing.

Most editing tools cannot be used directly on a Smart Object; rather, each edit must occur on a layer above the object, such as fill or adjustment layers. Additionally, any filters applied to the Smart Object are also saved as editable additions to the Smart Object.

For a lab supervisor, the use of Smart Objects ensures that all changes to an image are visible in the Layers palette and the local tools cannot be used. Ethical treatment of images is ensured as long as the edited file is saved with layers intact and a History Log records the session: Even Smart Objects can be outsmarted.

DUPLICATE IMAGE

Images can also be opened and then duplicated. The original image can then be closed so that all editing is done on a copy of the original. This ensures that the original retains raw image information but does not prevent the use of local tools or force the use of layers for making adjustments to brightness, contrast, or gamma.

As an additional step when opening an image, the Background layer can be duplicated. This keeps the Background layer untouched so that the original image can always be viewed and retained.

More: *Register your copy of this book at www.peachpit.com/scientificimaging in order to download the supplement, "Tools and Functions in Photoshop."*

Every 8-bit image is converted to 16 bits to minimize the loss of data when filtering or making adjustments due to rounding errors: Because 8-bit images work with only 255 possible brightness values per channel, when images are altered, the possibility for rounding errors is greater than with 16-bit images. For 16-bit images, 65,536 grayscale values are possible (but in Photoshop, the possibility of rounding errors is calculated on half the possible grayscale values, as described in the supplement, "Tools and Functions in Photoshop").

Note: *In pre-CS versions of Photoshop, retaining a bit depth of 8 bits allowed for a greater selection of correction tools and functionality. Post-CS versions provide the full amount of correction tools for 16-bit images. Thus, for pre-CS versions, the only option may be to retain the file at 8 bits for editing.*

When corrections and conformance changes are made and the image is ready for output, the image is reset to 8-bit. Special considerations for bit-depth changes only need to be made with 12-bit images that are saved as 16-bit but contain only 0–4095 grayscale or color values (see "Dark or All Black Images" later in this chapter).

Here are the steps for opening images, including a step to ensure that a History Log is recorded when editing.

To open images using the duplicate image method:

1. Open the image (File > Open) and then duplicate the image (Image > Duplicate). Close the original image (File > Close).
2. Duplicate the Background layer by selecting Layer > Duplicate Layer.
3. Select Image > Mode > 16-Bits/Channel to increase the image's bit depth (CS versions).
4. Create a History Log (CS versions) by selecting Edit > Preferences > General (Windows), or Photoshop > Preferences > General (Macintosh) and selecting the History Log checkbox.
5. Optional: To make sure that color settings are appropriate to the image, check the Color Settings by selecting Edit > Color Settings.

More: *To automate the process of duplicating the image, duplicating the Background layer, increasing bit depth, and setting up a History Log, along with other considerations, download an automated action at www.peachpit.com/scientificimaging.*

Trouble Opening Files

Many believe that Photoshop is the most likely program to open *all* image files because it is the premiere program for image correction and conformance to outputs, but this is not necessarily true, especially for TIFF formatted files. While TIFF is a widely used format and is nearly universally recognized, some additions and variations in its structure can prevent TIFF files from opening correctly (or at all) in Photoshop.

CS3 has provided a much needed advance to identify a TIFF series made for a stack of images by auto-recognizing a sequentially numbered series. However, a single TIFF file that is composed of a subset of images will not be recognized by Photoshop. When these TIFF stacks are opened, only the topmost image from the subset of images is recognized and displayed. More about image stacks can be found in the section "Image Stacks for Blending or Layering" later in this chapter.

Image stacks, along with other problematic files, can often be opened in ImageJ, a free scientific software program available from the National Institutes of Health (NIH; http://rsbweb.nih.gov/ij/download.html). After problematic files are opened in ImageJ, they can then be saved in a different format so they can be recognized in Photoshop. Proprietary file formats (such as the .oib file from Olympus) can be opened in ImageJ with additional plug-ins. For an expansive collection of image format plug-ins for ImageJ, visit the University of Wisconsin Web site at www.openmicroscopy.org/index.html.

When files don't open in ImageJ, a Google search can reveal several programs made specifically for opening odd formats. Check out these other programs before giving up.

When files open and the images are scrambled into parts, it is likely that the file was corrupted when transferred over the network, when writing to a removable disk, or, rarely, when writing to the hard drive of the computer on which the image was acquired. So, many imaging labs discourage saving files directly to removable disks and networked drives: It is best to save a file to a hard drive, and then transfer it to the network or to removable drives.

Before giving up in an attempt to open an image in Photoshop or when the file *does* open but it is nearly all black (when it was formerly well exposed in the image acquisition software), try using the methods in the following sections.

OPEN AS

Before deciding that a file won't open in Photoshop, use the Open As command in case the file was saved with an incorrect extension. That can happen on a Windows derived file when it is named using one extension (such as the filename plus .tif), but it is really in another format (such as JPEG).

It can also happen when no extension is provided and a Macintosh or Windows computer cannot recognize the file format. Keep in mind that the warning for an image unable to open might display illogical text, like "Can't Parse the JPEG file."

In either case, the file format can be specified when using Open As:

- On Windows, select File > Open As and decide on the likely file format.
- On Macintosh computers, select File > Open and choose the file format from the Format menu.

■ **Note:** *Determining the correct file format may become a trial and error operation.*

DARK OR ALL BLACK IMAGES

When 16-bit images do open correctly in Photoshop and they appear all black or dark overall—but didn't look that way when you acquired the image in a scientific acquisition program—the likely reason is that you saved the image in a 16-bit format (such as a 16-bit TIFF file), and the 16-bit file contained only a 12-bit tonal range (0–4095 tonal values). The problem lies in how the 16-bit format is *created* in the scientific acquisition program.

■ **Note:** *Another explanation for all black or dark images in Photoshop might be that monitors were set up differently, and dramatically so, when acquiring the image and then viewing it later on another screen. Of course, a control in a fluorescent labeling experiment would also be expected to appear dark.*

Two possible ways to create a 16-bit file format from 12 bits in scientific acquisition software follow:

- The file can be created as a 16-bit image, but the file retains only 12 bits (0–4095 gray levels) of visual data, leaving four "empty" bits with no values.
- The file can be created as a 16-bit image, but the 12-bit file is converted from 12-bit to 16-bit (0–65,535 gray levels).

But when the file is opened in Photoshop, it is treated as follows:

- If it is a 16-bit file and only 12 bits of information are included (with four empty bits), the 12 bits are retained at 4095 values inside a 16-bit nomenclature.
- If it is a 12-bit file that has been converted to 16 bits, the 16-bit file is opened with adjusted values.

Of the two possibilities, the first produces a dark image in Photoshop when it had formerly appeared bright in the image acquisition software. Because the 12-bit file is created with four empty bits of information that would have included 16 times more gray levels, it appears dark since much of the data consists of zeros. Thus, the image will show a small spike in the histogram composing only 1/16th (or less) of the entire horizontal range.

■ **Note:** *In CS3 Extended the values in the image can be measured by selecting an area and choosing Analysis > Record Measurements. Here the measurement somewhat reflects the actual data because the data shown is a result of 15-bit math calculations: Measured values will be at half the real values and are shown in the Measurement Log under Gray Value (Mean).*

In this case, the histogram is confusing: The *measured* values found by placing the cursor in the histogram show numeric values along the 8-bit scale (0–255) at values no greater than 16. But the *visual* display of the histogram correctly shows values at 1/16th the total. The latter is correct, the former is not.

To convert 16-bit images with a limit of 4095 grayscale values, follow these steps:

1. Open a file with a duplicated Background or a Smart Object layer.
2. Select Image > Adjustments > Levels. Type 16 into the white level input slider box (**Figure 6.1**, left). All gray or color values that compose the image (**Figure 6.1**, center) will be multiplied by 16, resulting in a brightened image (**Figure 6.1**, right).

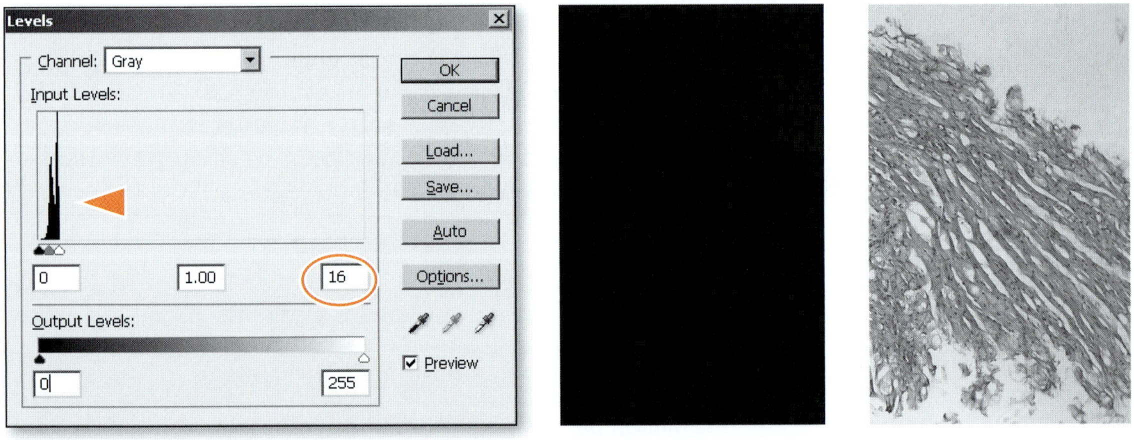

FIGURE 6.1 The Levels dialog box with the image's compressed histogram (left) and the image before and after increasing the brightness (center and right).

■ **Note:** *After entering values, the image may appear posterized (with discernible bands of gray or color ranges). The image should appear correct when applying Levels. If not, click the cache icon in the Histogram palette: If the cache readout in the Histogram palette is greater than 1, Photoshop is displaying a stored low-resolution image.*

3. Optional: Flatten the image to incorporate changes into the Smart Object or copied image. This step eliminates a record of changes made to the image in the Photoshop file (if the History Log is activated, however, there will be a text log). Select Layer > Flatten Image or select Flatten Image from the Layers palette menu.

If flatfield and background images were saved from the same session using the same camera, redistribute the brightness values in

■ **Note:** *Make the 12-bit image adjustment steps into an action and a droplet (File > Automate > Create Droplet), especially if the steps are used frequently.*

these images using step 2. Flatfield and background images can then be used to correct the image for uneven illumination and noise (see "Uneven Illumination Correction" and "Noise Reduction" later in this chapter).

Opening Images in Adobe Camera Raw

▶ **Warning:** *The gamma in Adobe Camera Raw is automatically set to values greater than 1. To preserve the gamma in an image from a digital SLR cameras, use the camera's software to save the image as a TIFF with linear gamma intact, and avoid using Adobe Camera Raw altogether. Or change the RGB editing space in Color Settings to CIE 1931.*

Images saved in the camera raw formats designed specifically for professional consumer cameras are opened with a plug-in called Adobe Camera Raw, which is available only in CS versions of Photoshop. TIFF or JPEG files can also be opened in Adobe Camera Raw to take advantage of functions only available in this program:

1. Use Open As or the Browse window. In the Open As dialog box specify Camera Raw for the file type. In the Browse window right-click/Control-click and select Open in Camera Raw. The Camera Raw dialog box appears (**Figure 6.2**).

● **More:** *Go to www.peachpit.com/scientificimaging to download the CIE 1931 editing space.*

■ **Note:** *JPEG files and TIFF files saved with the default settings in camera software (versus in Adobe Camera Raw), also save at gamma values greater than 1.*

2. Make sure the settings shown at the bottom of the dialog box are the ones you want (Figure 6.2). Click the underlined text to open the Workflow Options dialog box and change from the default settings of 8-bit to 16-bit and from sRGB to the ProPhoto or Adobe RGB (or CIE 1931) color space. Once these specifications are changed, Photoshop retains these settings until they are changed again.

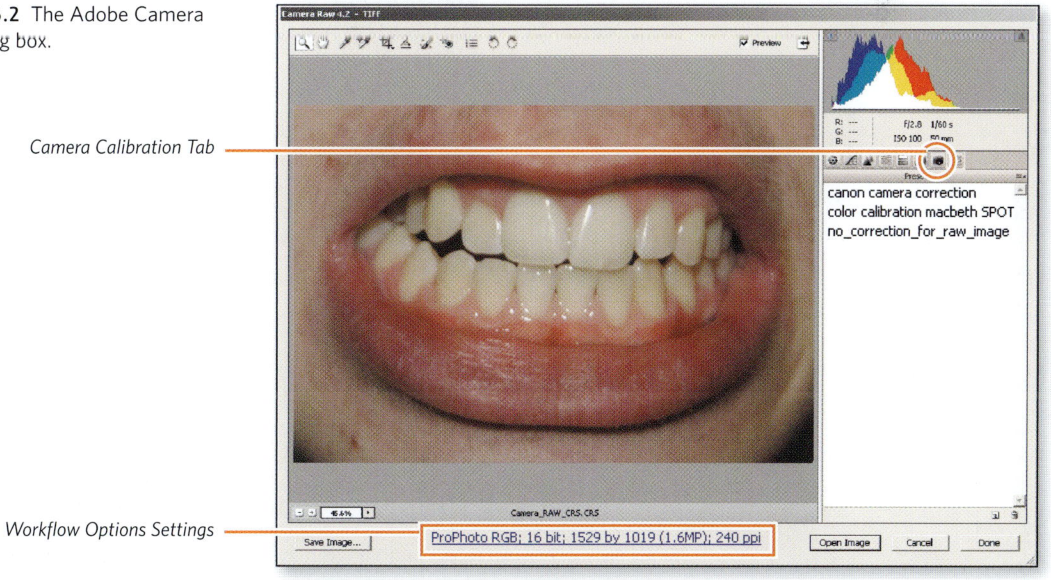

FIGURE 6.2 The Adobe Camera Raw dialog box.

3. To open images consistently, either modify the Workflow Options settings so that no changes are made to the image unless you are applying a calibration by clicking each icon and returning all values to 0 or to the lowest settings, or return all settings to those that match the settings you used to make a representative image (normally done at the first session in a study that occurs over time).
4. Click the calibration (Figure 6.2) icon and set the desired calibration if the image acquisition device has been calibrated.
5. Be sure to click Open Image, not Done. Done simply records the changes to the adjustments but doesn't open the image in Photoshop for further editing.

Opening Multiple Images to Blend into a Single Image

Multiple images can be opened to obtain a single image when several images have been saved for any of the following intents:

- As a way to remove noise (frame averaging)
- As a way to create an image from more than one image to expand the dynamic range (high dynamic range [HDR] image)

FRAME AVERAGING TO REDUCE NOISE

More than one image of a noisy scene or specimen needs to be taken for the noise removal to be effective, as long as the noise is random. More than one image can be averaged to reduce random noise.

To frame average multiple images in CS3 Extended:

1. Select File > Scripts > Statistics.
2. If the images you want to average are already open, click Add Open Files. Otherwise, click Browse and navigate to the folder where the image files are stored. Select the images you want to include and click Open.
3. Choose Mean from the Choose Stack Mode menu and click OK.

■ **Note:** *In the Image Statistics dialog box the images can be automatically aligned by selecting Attempt to Automatically Align Source Images.*

In legacy versions of Photoshop with layer functions, noise reduction is accomplished by layering (**Figure 6.3**, left). Images are placed as layers in a single Photoshop document, and then the Opacity of each layer is changed according to the following formula:

$$\text{Layer Opacity} = 100 \times 1/(L + 1)$$

where L represents the layer's position in the stack (the layer immediately above the Background is 1, the layer above that is 2, etc.).

To frame average multiple images in legacy versions:

1. Open all images that will be averaged.
2. Choose one image as the background on which other images will layered (**Figure 6.3**, center).
3. Choose the Move tool, holding down the Shift key to center images, and then drag the images into the file containing the background image.
4. In the Layers palette, set the opacity for each layer according to the preceding Layer Opacity formula.

■ **Note:** *When the Marquee tool is chosen, hold down Ctrl/Command to temporarily switch to the Move tool.*

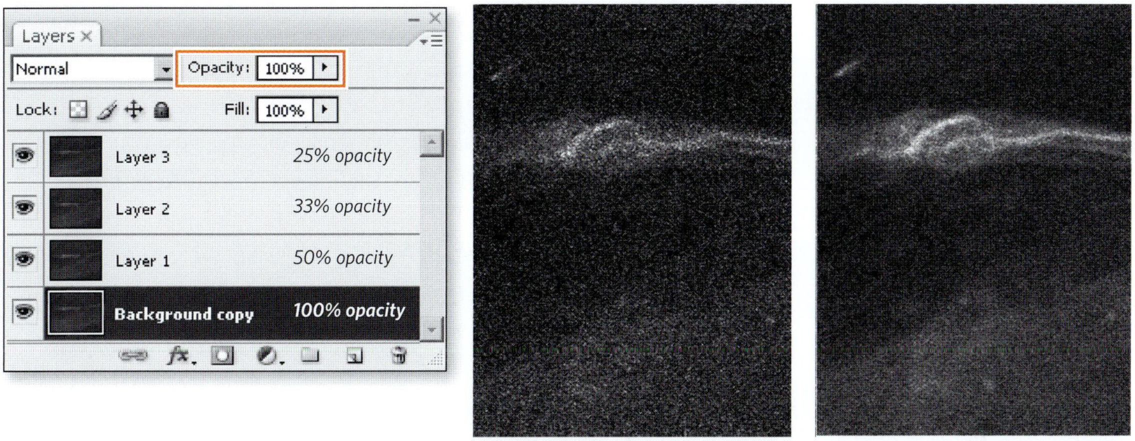

FIGURE 6.3 The Layers palette and Opacity percentages applied to each layer. An image from a single layer is shown (center) next to a layered image (right).

5. Flatten layers (Layers > Flatten Image) to make a single, noise corrected image (**Figure 6.3**, right).

■ **Note:** *A cut and paste method that can be made into an action to automate steps can be used instead of using the Move tool. Choose Select > Select All (Ctrl/Command+A), and then choose Edit > Cut or Copy. Choose File > Close (Ctrl/Command+W) to close the image. Paste the image on the background image, and it automatically becomes a layer.*

CREATING AN HDR IMAGE (CS2 AND CS3 ONLY)

Creating an HDR image from several images at different exposures requires the following steps:

1. Select File > Automate > Merge to HDR. Click Add Open Files or Browse to navigate to image files on your hard drive.

   If the exposure files cannot be read from the metadata saved with the image, Photoshop provides you with the option of manually setting the exposure time. Manually entered exposure times do not necessarily have to match the original exposures so much as they need to be separated at the same multiples. Ideally, a minimum of three images should be taken at the normal exposure (determined by a camera or metered reading), and additional images at half the normal exposure (for capturing brightest features) and two times the normal exposure (for darker features). This translates into choosing shutter speeds that are doubled and halved from the normal exposure (**Figure 6.4**, left).

2. After you enter the exposures manually (when necessary), and click OK, the Merge to HDR dialog box opens, allowing you to set the white point. This setting does *not* affect the image, only the display of the image. The range of values from a 32-bit image cannot be adequately displayed within the gamut of a monitor, so this white point setting is included to aid in visualizing. Click OK and a 32-bit file will be made.
3. Place Color Sampler points on the darkest and brightest significant values, and the appropriate background areas.
4. Select Image > Mode and choose 16-Bits/Channel. In the HDR Conversion dialog box, set the gamma to 1 to retain the

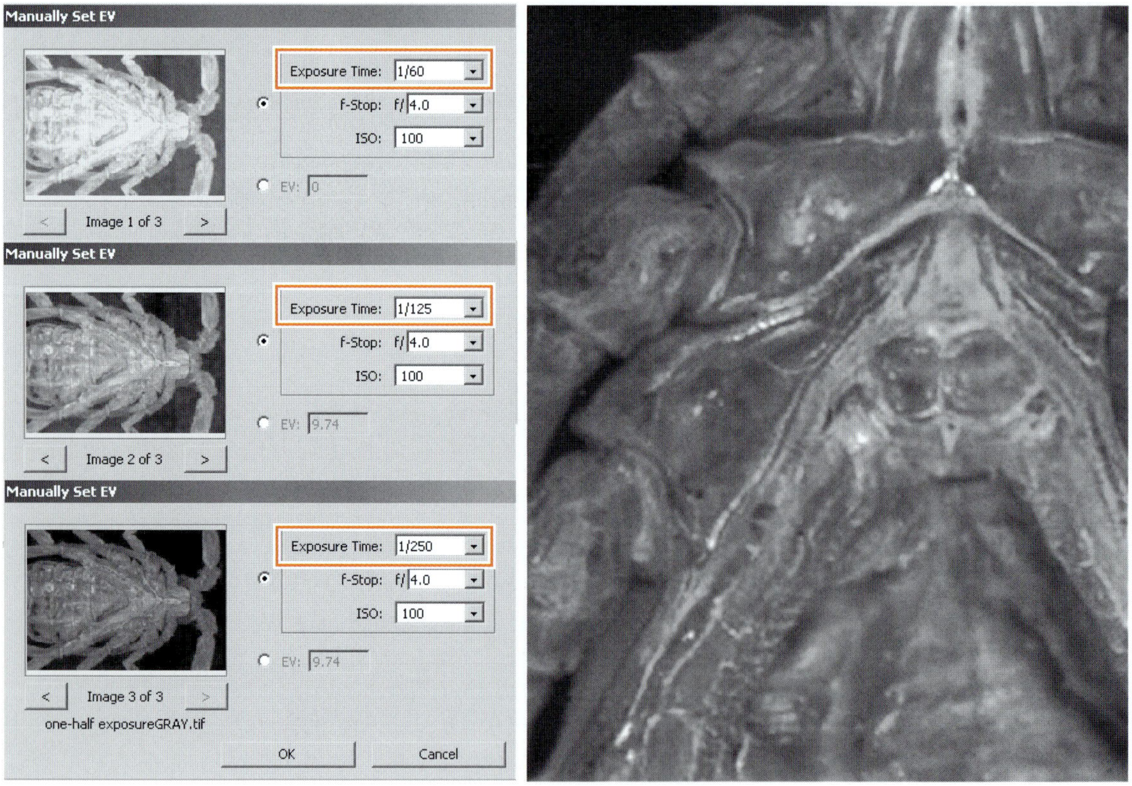

FIGURE 6.4 Manual settings for exposure times (left) and the final HDR image (right).

relationship of tones and adjust the exposure until black and white limits are achieved according to the black and white limits table in Chapter 5 (**Table 5.2**). Click OK.

5. Select Image > Adjustments > Levels, or add a Levels adjustment layer to fine-tune the adjustment (**Figure 6.4**, right).

Image Stacks for Blending or Layering

Single files that contain a subset of images (image stacks containing optical sections) cannot be opened with Photoshop while retaining their optical sections as layers unless the files are in the DICOM format. However, two workarounds exist for opening these files. One is to make the image stack into a video animation. The other has already been mentioned: Divide the image stack into its component image files (called an "image sequence") using scientific software such as ImageJ and put images into layers (remake the image stack) using Photoshop.

For video animations, the images can simply be opened in Photoshop, as long as the format is AVI, MOV, or MPEG, and as long as QuickTime recognizes the file. The AVI format is preferred, because files can often be saved as uncompressed, thus retaining visual data. Note that all formats save in 8-bits/channel only.

To create videos in scientific software, use acquisition software for the instrumentation and find a means to save files as videos, either by using Save As or by selecting File > Export. Save or Export to the following formats (if available): AVI (Windows), MPEG, or MOV (Windows and Macintosh). If the choice is available, save files as AVI uncompressed: MPEG compresses files and MOV is likely to compress them. Lossy compression groups pixels together so that image information is lost.

Deciding on whether to save image stacks in video formats or as image sequences may depend on the limitations of video files:

- Video files can only be opened in 8-bit mode.
- Video files may be compressed.

If neither of these limitations presents obstacles, researchers may decide that video files are more convenient and far less unwieldy than dealing with the number of individual images produced when separating image stacks.

After image stacks are made into recognizable files, a useful layer function called Auto-Align, which is new to Photoshop CS3, can be used. Sections on each layer can be spatially aligned to each other based on their edges or fiduciary marks by using the Auto-Align tool. See the "Multiple Images to Layers" section that follows.

When layering is not desired, and only a blended image is wanted from multiple images, see the "Image Statistics Method" section for the most efficient method, though the "Multiple Images to Layers Method" can be used to accomplish blending as well.

● **More:** *Alternatives to layering image stacks are provided at www.peachpit.com/scientificimaging.*

When the Auto-Align function is not necessary, a layered image is not wanted for blending purposes, and individual image files have been made (versus video), consider the amount of time taken in Photoshop to complete tasks when images are in layers: This can far exceed the amount of time necessary to automate corrections to numerous files within folders using actions and the Batch command.

MULTIPLE IMAGES TO LAYERS (CS3 EXTENDED)

Here is the method for opening video files or image sequences to make images into layers or to blend to a single image:

■ **Note:** *If files are not recognized as an image sequence, a layered image file can be made by selecting File > Scripts > Load Files into Stack. In step 2, the layers can be made into animation frames by selecting Make Frames from Layers from the Animation palette drop-down menu.*

1. For a video file, open the video file by selecting File > Open. The Layers palette shows a single layer, and the layer's thumbnail is marked with a filmstrip icon.

   For an image sequence (**Figure 6.5**), in the Open dialog box, click the first image in the series, and then select the Image Sequence check box. A second dialog box appears: Leave the default frame rate as is. This only opens all images when their filenames contain a sequential series of numbers.

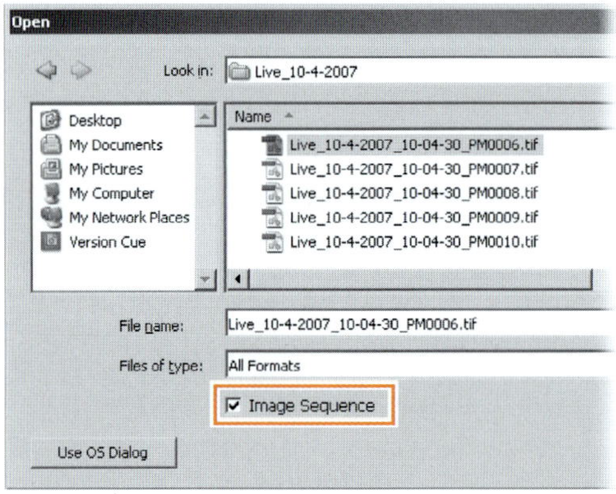

FIGURE 6.5 The Open dialog box showing the Image Sequence check box in CS3.

2. Open the Animation palette by selecting Window > Animation (**Figure 6.6**, top).

3. Use the Animation palette to view the image stack. Drag the current time indicator to view each plane (frame) one by one (**Figure 6.6**, bottom).

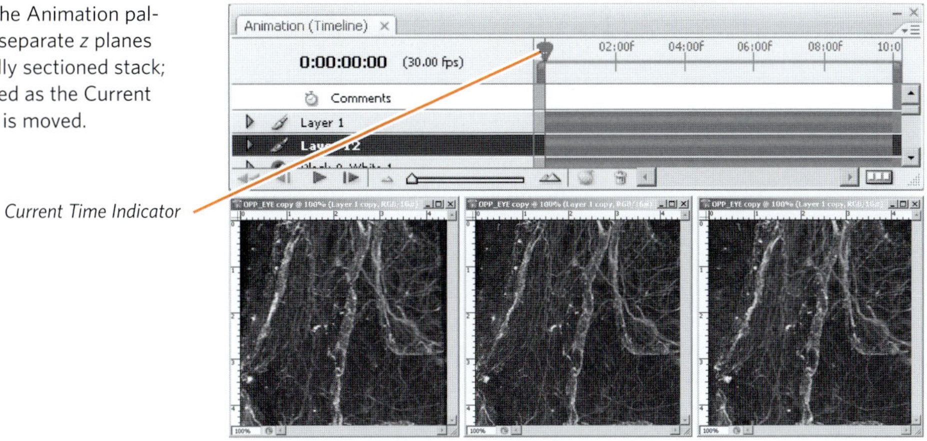

FIGURE 6.6 The Animation palette and three separate *z* planes from an optically sectioned stack; each is displayed as the Current Time Indicator is moved.

4. To create layers from each frame, from the Animation palette menu, choose Flatten Frames into Layers.

   You can select Edit > Auto-Align to align layers to each other. Choose normal when aligning specimen edges or fiduciary features. This function can take a long time to complete.

   Filters can only be applied one by one to each layer.

● **More:** *To apply a filter to all layers in CS3, download and use the Filter All Visible Layers script from www.peachpit.com/scientificimaging.*

To blend all layers into a single image, use the following steps:

1. Choose Select > All Layers and convert to a Smart Object by selecting Layer > Smart Objects > Convert to Smart Object.
2. Choose any of the options available for merging a stack by selecting Layer > Smart Objects > Stack Mode.

IMAGE STATISTICS METHOD (CS3 EXTENDED)

To use an image sequence for blending into a single image:

1. Select File > Script > Statistics to open the image sequence using the Statistics script.
2. In the Image Statistics dialog box, from the Choose Stack Mode menu choose one of these common statistical methods: Maximum, Mean, Median, Minimum, or Summation. Your choice will depend on the nature of the image:
   - For confocal stacks the Maximum (brightest) tonal value is generally desired from the brightest features in each *z* plane.
   - Image stacks from adjacent brightfield sections may include dark stains: In that instance, choose Minimum.

- When tonal values have been clipped in one or more *z* planes, a Mean or Median setting creates a projection in which it is likely that those values will remain within the dynamic range of pixel values. You can also use Median to eliminate random objects that appear frame to frame in front of a constant feature. A Mean will average from several images to reduce noise.
- For dim images, use Summation to add to pixel values from each plane.

MULTIPLE IMAGES TO LAYERS (PRE-CS3 EXTENDED)

Here are ways in which multiple images can be made into layers in pre-CS3 Extended versions of Photoshop:

- In CS versions of Photoshop in which the script function exists, you can make image sequences into layers by selecting File > Scripts > Load Files into Stack.
- For Photoshop 6 and 7 versions, as long as files are contained within a single folder, you can open them easily using Adobe ImageReady, the companion program to Photoshop. In ImageReady, import files into an animation sequence by selecting File > Import > Folder as Frames.

  In the Animation palette, you can view images frame by frame, and the layered file is available by selecting File > Jump To > Adobe Photoshop.

Note: *Opening the images as layers can also be accomplished in CS3 (File > Scripts > Load File into Stack), but the interface when doing so does not mimic software typically available with instruments that create image stacks. Usually, images within a stack can be scrolled through to look at each, which can't be done when the image stack is in layers.*

Opening Multiple Images for Photomerging (Photostitching)

Several high-magnification fields of a large area can be "stitched" together using Photomerge in CS3. The ability for Photoshop to automatically line up images depends on well-defined landmarks in images. Thus, images composed of primarily uniform white or black areas are not likely to be lined up. Because uniform images are often included as part of small fields, the use of photomerge is best done by allowing Photoshop to line up as many images as possible, and then manually lining up those images Photoshop cannot line up automatically. The method for photomerging with manual intervention is as follows:

1. Select File > Automate > Photomerge to open the Photomerge dialog box.
2. Choose Interactive Layout from the Layout area.

3. In the Source Files area, click the Browse button to find the desired images. Select the images you want to include.

   If you want to match the images by brightness and contrast levels, select Blend Images Together.

4. After Photoshop attempts to align as many images as possible automatically (which can take a few minutes), a second Photomerge dialog box opens. Images Photoshop was unable to align appear in the Lightbox above the composition. Drag these images, one by one, and move them roughly into position, and then click OK.

5. Each image resides in its own layer and can still be repositioned, if necessary. Otherwise, select Layer > Flatten Image to flatten the image.

Precorrection Changes

In Photoshop, the mode of the image refers to its makeup. Modes are set along channels that compose the image. Indexed color, RGB Color, CMYK, and Grayscale have been discussed; other color modes are described as follows:

- **Bitmap.** In Bitmap color mode, each pixel is either pure black or pure white. When a continuous tone image is converted to Bitmap mode, the gradations of brightness are represented by patterns of dots in a process called "dithering." The dot frequency, shape, and style of dithering roughly mimics what might be seen when the image is printed. The word bitmap is confusing: It also refers to the fact that an image is composed of pixels as opposed to vectors.
- **Duotone.** This mode is dual-tinted with a black ink and a colored ink, like a sepia-toned photographic print. Duotones are sometimes tinted with more than two inks, which are called tritones or quadtones.
- **L*a*b* Color.** The colors in this mode approximate human vision, as opposed to RGB colors (used for devices that reproduce color by transmitted light) and CMYK (used for devices that reproduce color by reflected light; printing presses and dye sublimation printers). Colors are defined by three channels: Luminance (perceived lightness differences), and opposing colors of the A and B channels. In this system, colors were defined by an international commission (International Commission on Illumination or Commission Internationale d'Eclairage [CIE]) by showing swatches of colors to a number of the participants to determine when one closely related

■ **Note:** *The asterisks between the letters in the acronym L*a*b* distinguish the CIE L*a*b* colors from those determined from a different method earlier in history, also called Lab but without the asterisks.*

color could be distinguished from another. Colors that were perceptually distinguishable were then defined and numbered.

- **Multichannel.** This image mode differs in that it supports more than three or four channels. It is useful for averaging together more than three separate colors.
- **32 bits per channel.** This mode was introduced in CS2 for blending multiple captures of an image taken at different exposures. This is done to accommodate scenes or specimens that exceed the dynamic range of the imaging device. Two or more images are required: one exposed for the brightest portions of the scene and at least one more exposed for the midrange and darkest portions. The 32-bit image is referred to as a High Dynamic Range (HDR) rendering.
- **Color Table.** When a grayscale image is saved as Indexed Color, a color table can then be used to apply colors to the varying grayscale levels in the image, from black to white. This provides a means for pseudocoloring images.

Images can be changed from one mode to another, though some loss of visual data may result, which is visible when mode changes are repeatedly made (though not as likely to be visible in 16-bit). Thus, few mode changes are usually made to prevent grayscale and color pixel values from being duplicated to neighboring values due to rounding errors.

Indexed Color (to RGB Color)

Indexed Color images are used frequently in science for 8-bit images, especially with images of fluorescently labeled specimens. Indexed Color is convenient because the images can be identified by the emissions wavelength color. These are, in essence, grayscale images that are colorized red, green, blue, and so on with 256 shades of a single hue substituted for corresponding grayscale values. In other words, the color values are mapped to grayscale values along the lines of a Look Up Table (LUT). Thus, a dark red, for example, will replace a grayscale value at the same level of darkness.

Indexed Color images require a change to RGB Color first to take advantage of certain functionality in Photoshop, even when the ultimate desire is for a grayscale image. The use of many tools is limited for Indexed Color images, so this mode change is necessary. To change the mode from Indexed color to RGB Color, select Image > Mode > RGB Color.

Uneven Illumination Correction

Images that are derived by shining a light on what are essentially two-dimensional objects, such as microscope slides, generally need uneven illumination correction, especially at low magnification. Imaging devices or magnification tubes may also introduce vignetting (darkening at corners with a spotlit appearance) in every image, no matter how evenly illuminated. Three means for correcting uneven illumination are presented in this section.

The correction method depends on the availability of a flatfield image or on the nature of the image:

- For standard brightfield and darkfield images in which a separate flatfield image was saved, use the steps outlined in "Uneven Illumination Correction Using a Flatfield Image."
- For images in which a flatfield image was not saved, use the steps in "Uneven Illumination Correction Using the Image."
- For images that are vignetted so that the bright spot is centered, use the steps in "Photoshop's Vignette Correction."
- For images that contain large areas of uniform pixel values, such as phase contrast, differential interference contrast (DIC), and images sparsely populated by features, use the steps in "Uneven Illumination Correction Using the High Pass Filter." This filter can be used to correct uneven illumination on grayscale images only.

UNEVEN ILLUMINATION CORRECTION USING A FLATFIELD IMAGE

When a flatfield image was saved from an imaging session (**Figure 6.7A**), the following method is used to divide the flatfield image into specimen images to correct for uneven illumination.

1. Select the Color Sampler tool and choose 5 by 5 Average from the Sample Size menu on the options bar. Place color samplers on two or more points in a specimen image (**Figure 6.7B**) that should provide approximately the same pixel readout if the image was evenly illuminated. Move the eyedropper over the areas that appear bright to the eye, while watching the readout on the Info palette, and place another color sampler in the brightest area of the image.
2. On the flatfield image, increase the brightness (if necessary) using the Brightness slider in the Brightness/Contrast dialog box (Image > Adjustments > Brightness/Contrast) until the brightest point is at slightly less than the bit-depth limit (255 for 8-bit).

■ **Note:** *In CS3, be sure to select the Legacy check box.*

3. Hold down Shift and use the Move tool to drag the flatfield image over the image of the specimen; or select all, copy, and paste. This will put the flatfield image on a layer above the specimen image.
4. Invert the flatfield image layer by selecting Image > Adjustments > Invert (**Figure 6.7C**).

   The flatfield layer should be pure gray. If not, desaturate the flatfield image by selecting Image > Adjustments > Desaturate.
5. In the Layers palette, choose Hard Light from the Blend Mode menu (**Figure 6.7D**).
6. Adjust opacity to 50%, or until the color samplers are at or near the same reading (depending on your confidence at having chosen similarly bright sampling points for the specimen image in step 1).
7. Flatten the image (Layers > Flatten or choose Flatten Image from the drop-down menu in the Layers palette) to complete flatfield correction.
8. The image will be darker than it was when the process began. Move the sampling points to the whitest, significant area and to the approximate darkest part of the image (**Figure 6.7E**). Using Levels (**Figure 6.7F**), set the black and white limits (see the section "Standard Procedure" in Chapter 5).

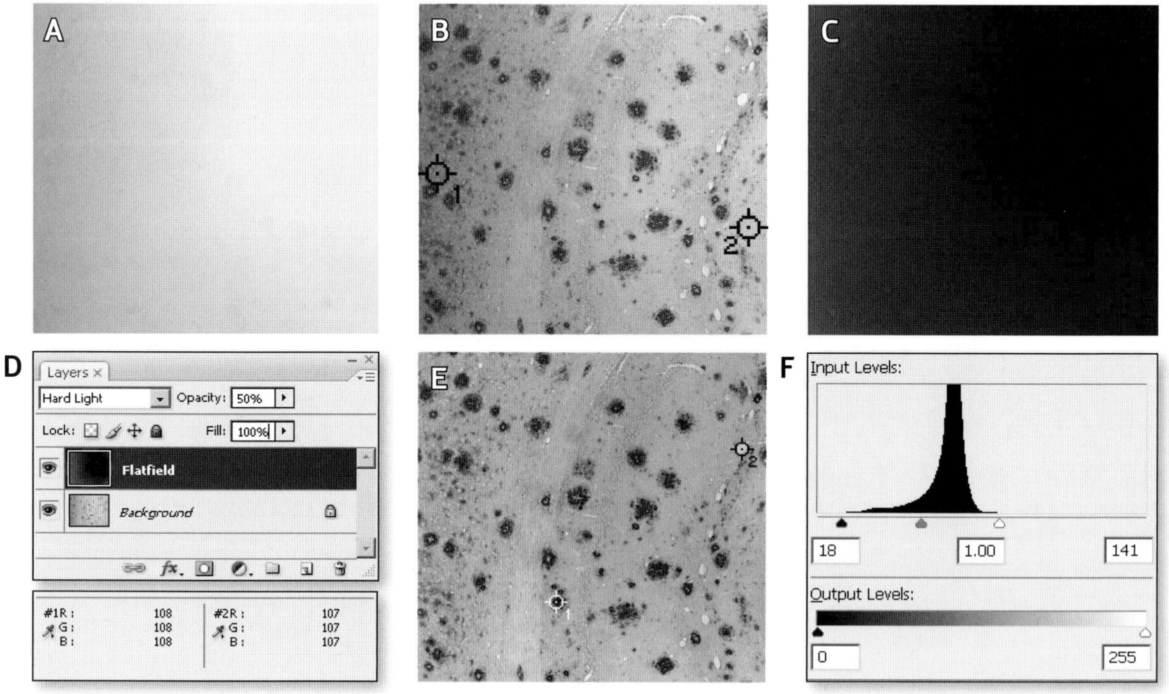

FIGURE 6.7 Flatfield correction using a saved flatfield image.

FIGURE 6.8 The original image (top) and the Gaussian-blurred and inverted layer (center) with the flatfield corrected image (bottom).

UNEVEN ILLUMINATION CORRECTION USING THE IMAGE

When a flatfield image hasn't been saved, and the uneven illumination is not centered in a vignette pattern, the only choice is to use the actual image as a means to correct uneven illumination. Sometimes this is the best choice because agglomerations of bright, fluorescently labeled features can create a cumulative brightness that exceeds the brightness of singular features that are isolated. In this instance, the specimen contributes to uneven illumination, not the light source alone. To use a duplicate of the image to create the uneven illumination pattern, follow these steps:

1. On the image you want to correct, place Color Sampler points on two (or more) areas in the image that should provide approximately the same pixel readout (**Figure 6.8**, top). Be sure to set sampling to 5 by 5 Average.
2. Select Layer > Duplicate Layer and click OK.
3. Select the top layer, if it's not selected already. Select Filter > Blur > Gaussian Blur. In the Gaussian Blur dialog box, set the blur to above 100 (the accuracy is not often important). It will likely take some time for the computer to complete the blur.

   For images with greater degrees of uneven illumination, set the blur amount to the point at which features lose details and are unidentifiable, but no more than that.
4. Invert the top layer (Image > Adjustments > Invert) so that it is a negative image when compared to the specimen (**Figure 6.8**, center). If the image is in color, desaturate it now (Image > Adjustments > Desaturate), or use the color to aid in color correction, especially when the image is unevenly illuminated. This step can be done after the next step, if color is adversely affected (as evaluated by eye).
5. Choose Hard Light from the Blend Mode menu and adjust the Opacity slider to 50%, or adjust the slider until the sampling points are at or near the same reading (depending on your confidence at having chosen sampling points in similarly bright areas). The image may become less contrasty and flat looking overall, which you can adjust in the following steps.
6. Flatten the image (Layers > Flatten or choose Flatten Image from the drop-down menu in the Layers palette) to complete the flatfield correction.
7. Set white and black limits as in step 8 of "Uneven Illumination Correction Using a Flatfield Image" to create a contrast and brightness corrected image (**Figure 6.8**, bottom).

PHOTOSHOP'S VIGNETTE CORRECTION (CS2 AND CS3)

If the uneven illumination is fairly centered with a bright spot in the middle and darkening at the edges of the image (a phenomenon known as "vignetting") use the Lens Correction filter (in Photoshop CS2 and later) as a remedy. The filter allows for adjusting both the brightness of the correction and the diameter of the area affected.

1. Include color samplers at the center and at incremental points to the edge of the image in areas that should be at the same tonal value.
2. Select Filter > Distort > Lens Correction to open the Lens Correction dialog box.
3. In the Lens Correction dialog box, adjust the Vignette slider until the color sampler readouts are either the same value or nearly the same. Adjust the Midpoint slider, if necessary, to determine the amount of the correction both by eye and by examining the readouts for similar values.

UNEVEN ILLUMINATION CORRECTION USING THE HIGH PASS FILTER

The High Pass filter, as mentioned earlier, is used for images in which large areas of similar tones exist, such as DIC images, phase contrast, and possibly electrophoretic samples (for the latter, be sure to report the use of the High Pass filter when publishing). It is an edge detection filter that also introduces a uniform background tone. Follow these steps to use this method:

1. Set color samplers on the brightest and darkest parts of the image (**Figure 6.9**, left).
2. Select Filter > Other > High Pass.
3. Set the High Pass filter to an amount that creates an evenly lit background that does not appear to deteriorate the tonal values of important features (**Figure 6.9**, center). The value of the Radius for the filter depends on the image. Adjust the Radius amount so that the color sampler readouts are nearly identical, but taking care that important features don't lose contrast (**Figure 6.9**, right).
4. Set white and black limits in the Levels dialog box by selecting Image > Adjustments > Layers or by adding a Levels adjustment layer. For phase and DIC images, the background is not black; rather, it is a midtone: The value is set visually to provide the greatest contrast for the features.

■ **Note:** *Because the gray background in Figure 6.9 isn't meant to be white, the Levels adjustment was used to set the white limit (read from the bright edges of cells) with the black limit (background value) at about 119.*

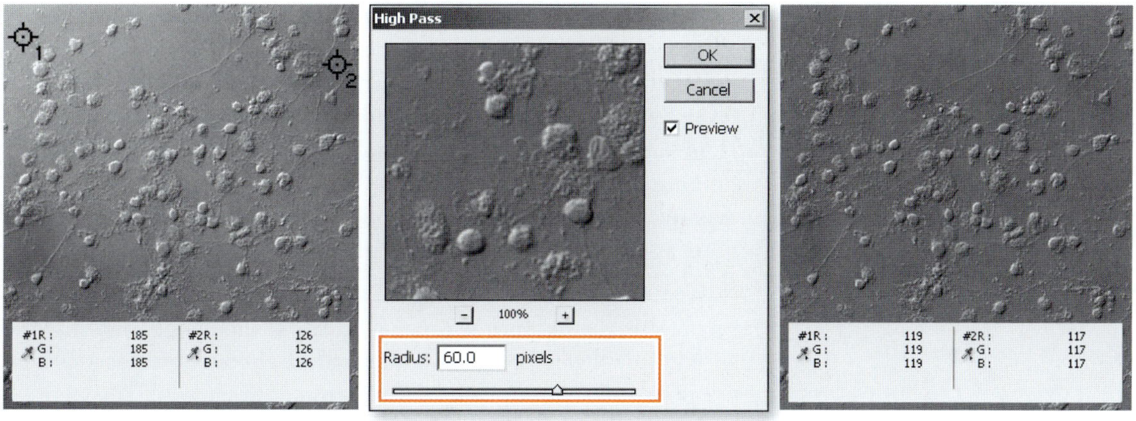

FIGURE 6.9 A DIC image is shown (left) with color samplers added. The High Pass filter is used (center) to create an image that contains a uniform background (right).

Problem Images

If images are light overall with little contrast, or are overly dim, contain features that are too dark while other features are in an expected brightness range, or contain features that are clipped or aliased, they are referred to broadly as problem images.

Each has its own correction method to make it appear as close as possible to that of the specimen while keeping the darkest and brightest significant values within the dynamic range of most outputs. Efforts should also be made to avoid gamma correction, though this may be necessary when details are important to see in dark features when all other brightness levels are within the expected range. It is best to acquire the image again with more than one exposure so that the image can be opened as an HDR image. If those specimens are unavailable, gamma correction is the only option. Gamma correction should be mentioned in the Methods portion of a manuscript.

LOW CONTRAST IMAGES

Low contrast images fall into the category of being lighter overall, and they contain features difficult to differentiate from the background. Use Levels to adjust contrast and brightness:

1. Place color samplers on the image (**Figure 6.10A**) for the darkest significant feature (or background, if darkfield) and the brightest significant feature (or background, if back-illuminated brightfield).

2. Use Levels (Image > Adjustments > Levels or add a Levels adjustment layer) while paying attention to the change in numeric values of the readouts from the color samplers on the Info palette. Adjust white and black input sliders until black and white limits from Table 5.2 in Chapter 5 are achieved (**Figure 6.10B**). For noisy images, it is difficult to know whether the sampling point is averaging noise with the background; set these images by eye, not quite approaching the limit for either the white or black level.

The histogram will show empty pixel values when it is stretched (Figure 6.10B, histogram): This is inevitable. If the image contains noise, additional values will fill in during noise reduction steps. Otherwise, the stretching is a result of the nature of the original image in which a small number of pixel values may exist in the specimen.

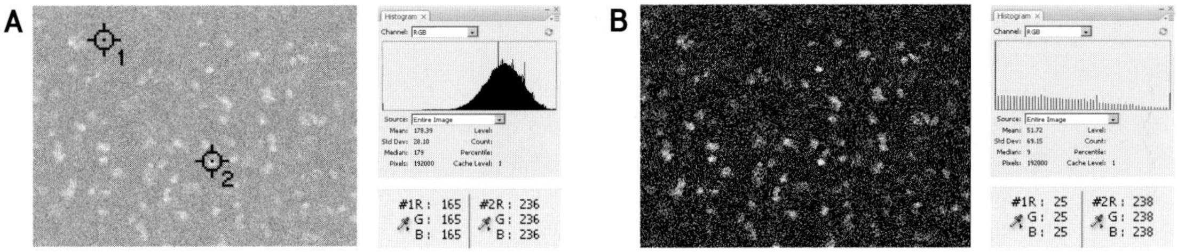

FIGURE 6.10 An example of correcting a low-contrast image. Note the color sampler readouts from the bottom portion of the Info palette for before (**A**) and after (**B**) images.

CLIPPED IMAGES

Typical problems with clipped values include the following: In darkfield images with a fluorescent labeling, nearly every white value is featureless; in back-illuminated brightfield images, the background level is pure white.

Details in clipped values in images cannot be restored, unless those values exist in another channel or optical plane in the following circumstances:

- A percentage of the image information has "bled" into another channel, such as when a primarily red image transfers pixel values to the green or blue channels. This can happen with RGB cameras and resultant RGB Color images. To see whether the image data might exist on another channel, choose Split Channels from the Channels palette menu.

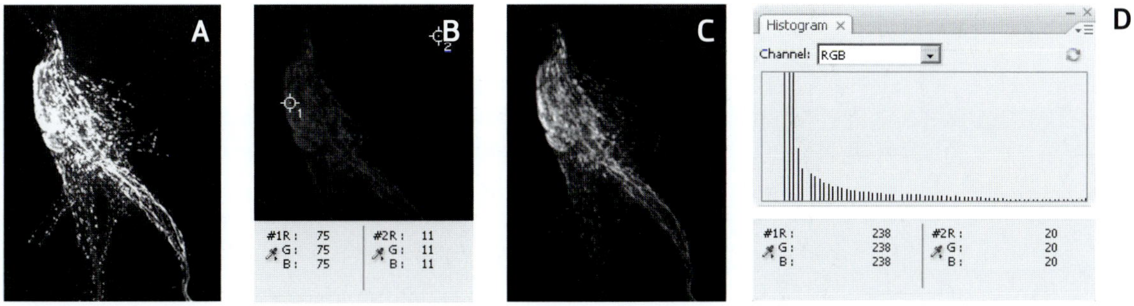

FIGURE 6.11 An example of a clipped image when using Maximum for projecting an image stack (**A**) and a contrast and brightness corrected Mean-projected image (**C**) with Info palette readouts.

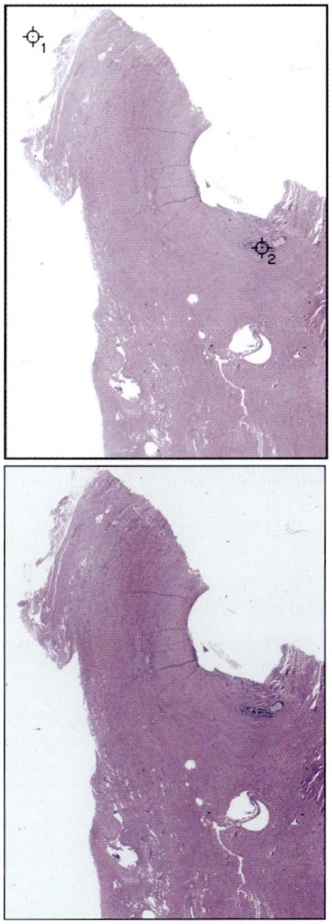

FIGURE 6.12 On the top, an image with clipped background white values. On the bottom, the same image after white and black values have been set within white and black limits.

- The image is a part of an image stack. Rather than choose Maximum for the formula (**Figure 6.11A**) when merging (or projecting) several images into one, choose Average or Mean. The resulting averaged image is dim (**Figure 6.11B**). Color samplers are placed on the significant brightest and darkest parts of the image, and then Levels is used to set sliders to white and black limits using the readout in the Info palette (**Figure 6.11C** and **D**).

When details in clipped images cannot be found in another channel or via a stack, images are modified so that tonal values are within white and black limits (**Figure 6.12**).

GRAPHIC IMAGES

After mentioning black (value of 20) and white (value of 240) limits for images numerous times, one exception exists when those limits are at 0 for black and 255 for white in the 8-bit range. The pure black and pure white limits are for graphic images, such as line drawings, graphs, and charts. When graphic images are scanned as grayscale or color so that fine detail is preserved, the resulting grayish whites and blacks need to be made pure black and white. Use this method:

1. Place color samplers on a black feature and on a white feature that is darkest gray.
2. Using Levels (Image > Adjustments > Levels or add a Levels adjustment layer), move the black input slider to the right until black values read out as 0 in the Info palette, and move the white input slider to the left until white areas read out as 255.

ALIASED IMAGES

Images that contain jagged (pixilated) edges can be smoothed. The method includes increasing the number of pixels that make up the image before the correction is applied. The increase in pixels then provides more pixels upon which to "spread out" the edges.

1. Increase the number of pixels that make up the image by resampling. Use the Image Size dialog box (Image > Image Size) according to the directions provided in "Resample for Output (Image Size)" in Chapter 8. Resample to increase the image at least 200 percent or to a minimum of approximately 1500 pixels in width and height. If the image is resampled too much, excessive blurring will result.
2. Generally, pixilated features are seen against a uniformly white, gray, or black background. The easiest way to select feature edges is to click on the background area of the image with the Magic Wand tool. Set the Tolerance for the Magic Wand tool in the options bar. The higher the setting, the greater the area that will be selected.
3. When you click on the background area in the image, contiguous areas are selected. However, some noncontiguous background areas might be surrounded by features and will not be included. Incorporate any unselected background by choosing Select > Similar.
4. When aliased features are surrounded by the selection, make a border at the selection (Select > Modify > Border) so that the border includes all the aliased edges. Type in a value of 2–10 pixels, understanding that you can repeat this step until you've determined the correct value.
5. Smooth the border with the Median filter (Filter > Noise > Median). Choose a Radius value that smooths the edge and retains sharpness by eye.

   If the border you chose was too narrow or large, undo this step and repeat step 4 with a different border value.

Noise Reduction

Several options are available for reducing the level of noise in an image that may result from long exposures, high voltages in a photomultiplier tube, post-amplification of signal, and high ISO settings, among other contributions. The most effective noise reduction method was covered earlier in this chapter: Select File > Automate > Statistics and use a Mean stack mode to reduce noise while maintaining image information.

To image more than one frame assumes a static object and a static camera. In real-time imaging of moving objects or when objects fade rapidly, noise can be inevitable.

When additional images were not frame averaged at acquisition or when additional images of the same specimen were not taken, other methods are available for noise reduction in Photoshop. Among them is the use of the Gaussian and Median filters, as well as several other filtering options.

The noise filter used depends on both the nature of the noise and whether or not feature borders need to be retained. The Median, Dust & Scratches, and Reduce Noise filters (depending on settings) retain borders, which are of critical importance when subsequently measuring areas of features. Noise filters, however, can create patterns in the image when the strength of the noise removal is too great.

When it is not important to maintain feature areas and borders can expand or contract, blurring filters can be used. The most precise tool is the Gaussian Blur filter. Smart Blur (limited to 8-bit depth images) and Surface Blur limit blurring to the darker regions of the image by using the Threshold tool, which may be useful for brightfield images but is largely useless for darkfield images.

Third-party solutions are recommended for reducing noise when multiple images are made with the same system, because profiles for noise from imaging systems can be created and then applied to the images. This software is relatively inexpensive, and noise reduction is generally greater than what can be attained in Photoshop and in the most commonly used scientific quantification software. Two of these applications include Neat Image (www.neatimage.com) and Noise Ninja (www.picturecode.com).

For color images, see the noise reduction steps outlined in "Color Noise" in Chapter 7.

HOT PIXELS REMOVAL METHODS

Bright pixels that result from heat at long exposures (called hot pixels) can be eliminated with the hot pixels removal method for both grayscale and color images, or through background subtraction when a background image is saved.

If a background image was saved:

1. Open the background image and the image of the specimen (the image taken at the same exposure with no lights on). Be sure the specimen image window is active (click in the bar at the top of the specimen image).

2. Subtract the background image from the image of the specimen by selecting Image > Apply Image.
3. Select the background image for the Source.
4. For Blending, choose Subtract from the drop-down menu. Click OK.

If no background image exists:

1. Open the image and duplicate the Background layer.
2. Eliminate hot pixels by selecting Filter > Noise > Dust & Scratches (**Figure 6.13**, left). For brightfield images, invert them first; darkfield images can be left as is.
3. Select a Radius of 1.
4. Move the Threshold slider to the left while visually inspecting the image (**Figure 6.13**, center, top). If necessary, adjust the slider until it appears that the hot pixels have been removed (**Figure 6.13**, center, bottom). When using the Threshold slider, the brightest pixels are at or near 255 on the 8-bit scale and darker pixels are at values less than 255. Click OK when you're satisfied.

   In most instances, hot pixels have a value of 255 and no threshold adjustment is necessary. In other images, you might have to lower the Threshold to find both hot- and near-hot pixels.

As an optional step, because pixel values are often reduced to zero, you can average values by changing the Opacity of the duplicated layer. A setting of 70% or less averages to a mid-gray value (**Figure 6.13**, right).

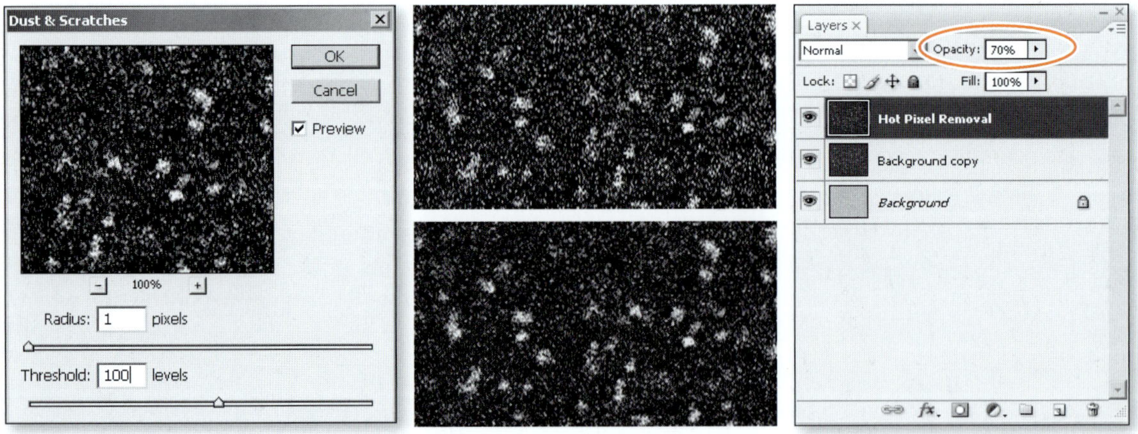

FIGURE 6.13 The hot pixels removal method, using the Dust & Scratches filter.

DUST AND SPECKS

Dust and specks on a specimen, which are common with electrophoretic samples, can be reduced or eliminated with the Dust & Scratches filter (read the author guidelines to see if this filter can be used). The tonal range to which the filter is applied can be set using a Threshold (cutoff) slider. Here are the steps for removing dust and specks:

1. Open the image, convert it to 16-bit, and duplicate the Background layer (**Figure 6.14**, top left).
2. Invert the image to avoid correcting the brighter areas, such as the substrate (background), by selecting Image > Adjustments > Invert or pressing Ctrl/Command+I. The darkest features become whiter and the brighter features become darker (**Figure 6.14**, bottom left).
3. Use the Dust & Scratches filter (Filter > Noise > Dust & Scratches) to reduce or eliminate dust, specks, and scratches. Adjust the Radius to overcorrect the layered image (make it more blurry than desired).
4. Set the Threshold to limit noise correction to within the tonal range of dust and specks (**Figure 6.14**, center).
5. Invert the image again to return the image to the original grayscale values.
6. Move the Opacity slider to interactively fine-tune the level of correction. Adjust the slider so that dust is barely visible to keep the filter effects at a minimum (**Figure 6.14**, right top and bottom).

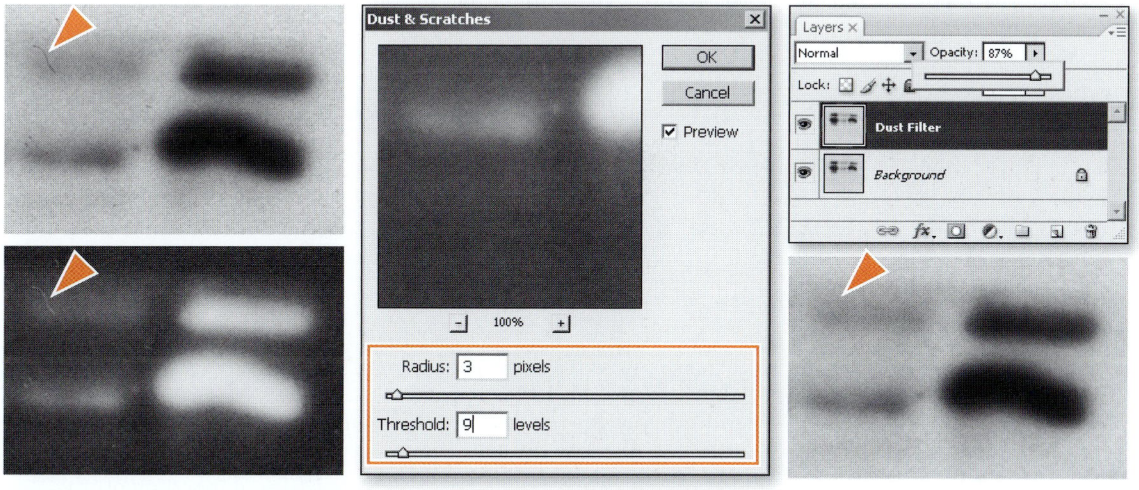

FIGURE 6.14 Images of lanes from an electrophoretic gel show dust (left) and dust removal (right).

LOW NOISE, GRAYSCALE

Varying levels of noise in grayscale images can be reduced by using the Reduce Noise filter or by using the Median and potentially the Gaussian filters in earlier Photoshop versions. In the steps that follow, the Reduce Noise filter is used, but the Median filter can be used in earlier versions of Photoshop:

1. Open the image, convert the image to 16-bits, and duplicate the Background layer.
2. Select Filter > Noise > Reduce Noise (**Figure 6.15**, left).
3. In the Reduce Noise dialog box, balance Strength and Preserve Details iteratively. Set Strength (which affects luminance noise only) to 10, the maximum and increase Preserve Details to visually determine when filtering no longer averages neighboring pixel values to pool or posterize areas of the image (**Figure 6.15**, bottom right). Preserve Details retains edges and image details.

   If the version of Photoshop that you use does not include the Reduce Noise filter, use the Median filter. If the strength is too high and the image is overblurred, reduce the effect by adjusting the Opacity slider on the noise-reduced layer.

■ **Note:** *Do not sharpen in the Reduce Noise dialog box. More advanced sharpening techniques are described in the "Sharpening" section in Chapter 7.*

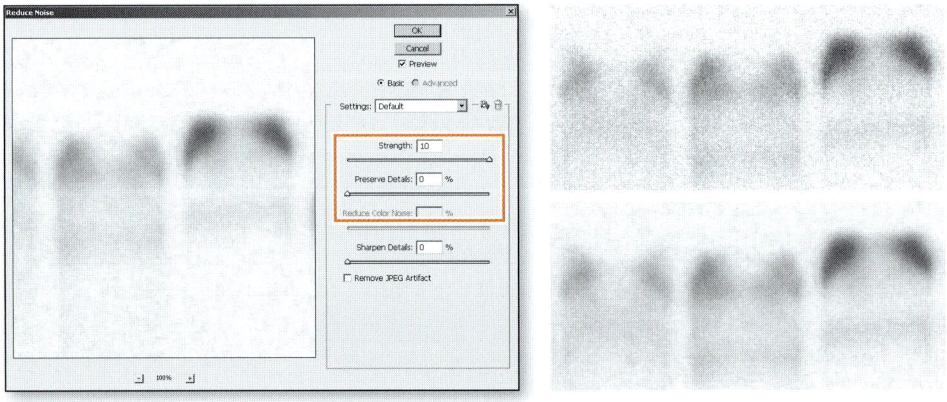

FIGURE 6.15 The top-right image shows the image before noise reduction; the bottom image shows it after noise reduction. Some blurring artifacts (banding) may appear.

HIGH NOISE, GRAYSCALE

High noise images require repeated applications of noise reduction and blurring, along with gamma adjustments to make widely varying tones uniform. The strength of noise reduction varies, depending on the image. Steps to reduce excessive noise may include the following:

1. Open the image, and convert it to 16-bit (**Figure 6.16A**).
2. If a layer already exists from the process of removing hot pixels and that layer wasn't flattened so that all editing steps were retained, make sure it is selected and press Ctrl/Command+Shift+Alt/Option+E to merge all visible layers into a new layer.

   If it is not important to retain the layer, flatten the layers (Layer > Flatten Image) and duplicate a new layer for the remaining steps (Layer > Duplicate Layer or choose Duplicate Layer from the Layers palette menu).
3. Use the Reduce Noise filter (CS2, CS3) or Average Median method (pre-CS2) to reduce noise as described for low noise, grayscale images. With noisy images, Preserve Details is left at or near zero (**Figure 6.16B**).
4. The image may either contain a visible background pattern or noise may still be unacceptable. To further reduce noise, duplicate the existing layer.
5. Apply a Gaussian filter (Filter > Blur > Gaussian Blur) at a greater blur than desired to the duplicated layer. Blur to remove noise but retain some detail (**Figure 6.16C**).
6. Adjust the opacity of the layer to reduce patterns or noise while preserving as much detail as possible. For fine control over opacity, use the Custom Blending options in the Layer Style dialog box, which you open by double-clicking below the name of the layer on the Layers palette. In the Blend If area, drag the white This Layer slider to the left. This prevents the lighter pixels in your blurred layer from blending with the layer below (**Figure 6.16D**). Set the level visually. Click the layer on and off using the eye icon to determine if the level of correction is too great or not enough.
7. If noise is still too great, press Ctrl/Command+Shift+Alt/Option+E to merge all visible layers into a new layer.
8. Using Curves (Image > Adjustments > Curves or a Curves adjustment layer), determine the tonal range in which the noise resides by clicking and holding the mouse button while moving the Eyedropper tool over the noisy areas on the image (the Eyedropper tool appears when the Curves dialog box is open).
9. Flatten the slope of the curve by clicking to place three points above the maximum pixel value in the noisy areas along the base of the line to make it horizontal. Add three more points along the rest of the curve to help it stick to its original diagonal trace. This will make all pixel tones uniform at or below the horizontal line (**Figure 6.16E** and **F**).

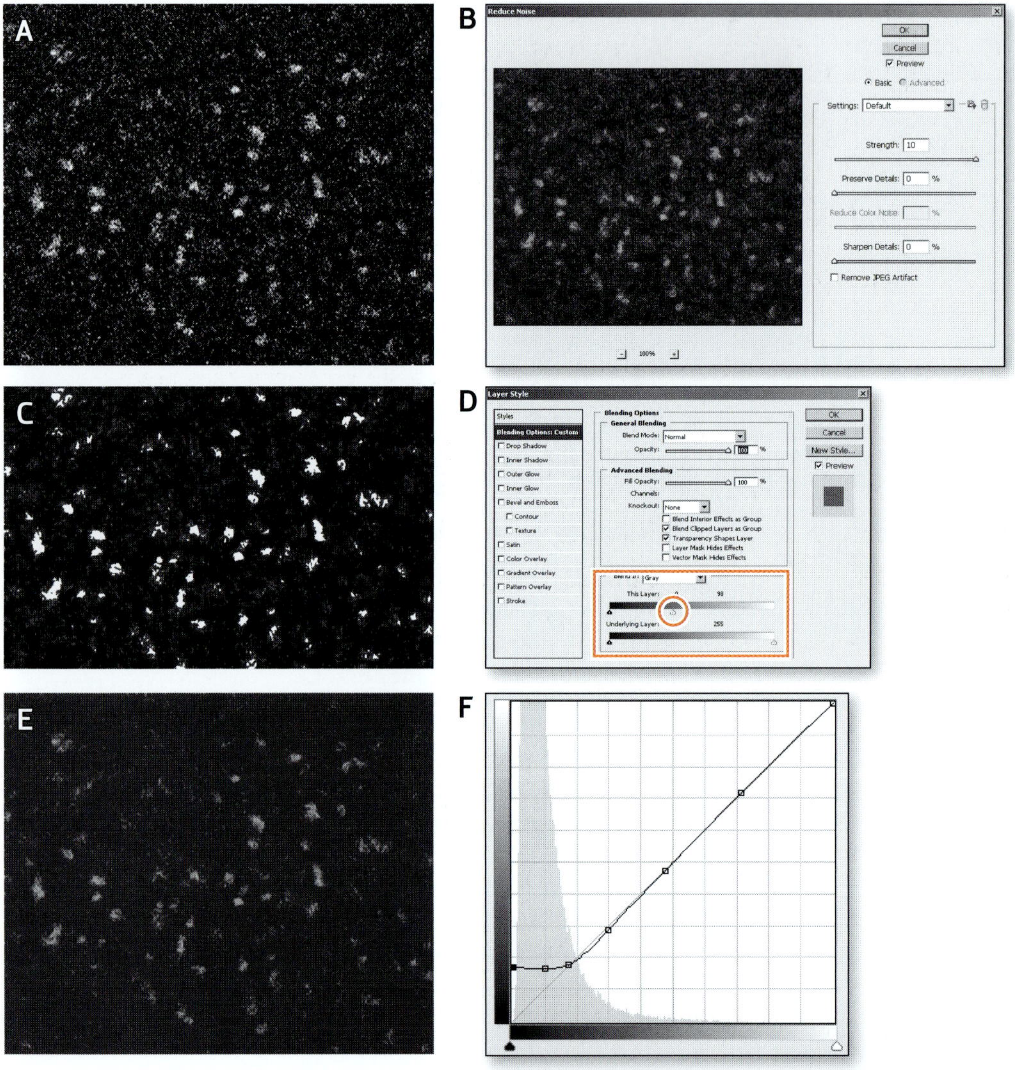

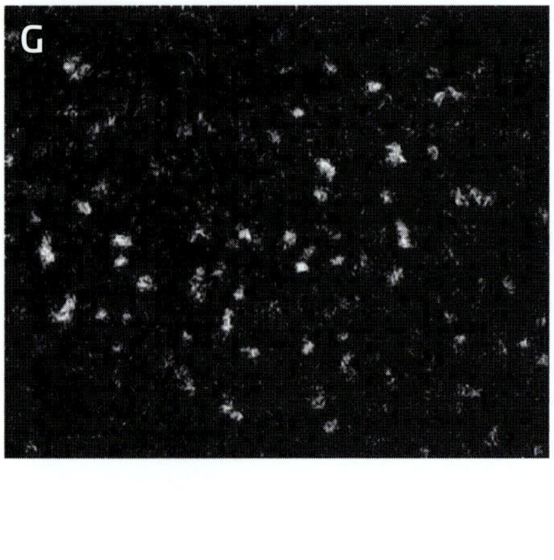

FIGURE 6.16 A high noise image (**A**) with noise level reduced by the Reduce Noise filter (**B**), noise level modified (**C**, **D**), and then further reduced using Curves (**E**, **F**) for a nearly noise-free result (**G**).

■ **Note:** *With repeated use of the noise and blurring filters, contrast levels are reduced and edges are not retained. When the image is representative and when areas are not being measured, noise reduction can be deemed appropriate. Noise reduction and blurring may also be appropriate when noise interferes with OD/I measurements because of the wide standard deviation of pixel values.*

10. Brightness of pixel values may decrease. Increase brightness using Levels according to the "Standard Procedure" section in Chapter 5 (**Figure 6.16G**).

DE-INTERLACING FOR VIDEO

Video cameras capture half the height of images for every image (field) recorded. These are sequentially captured by reading out odd and even rows of microdetectors on chips (digital video cameras). Two fields are combined with even and odd rows ("interlaced") to make the frames that create videos. When the odd and even rows are offset from each other, creating edges with a sawtooth appearance, the interlacing becomes a source of noise. The interlacing then needs to be corrected to eliminate the sawtooth appearance. Here's how it's done:

1. Select Filter > Video > De-Interlace.
2. Choose options in the De-Interlace dialog box to eliminate odd or even fields, or to create new fields by duplication or interpolation.

   Generally, you'll keep the default settings, but you can try different settings until the image is optimally corrected as evaluated by eye.

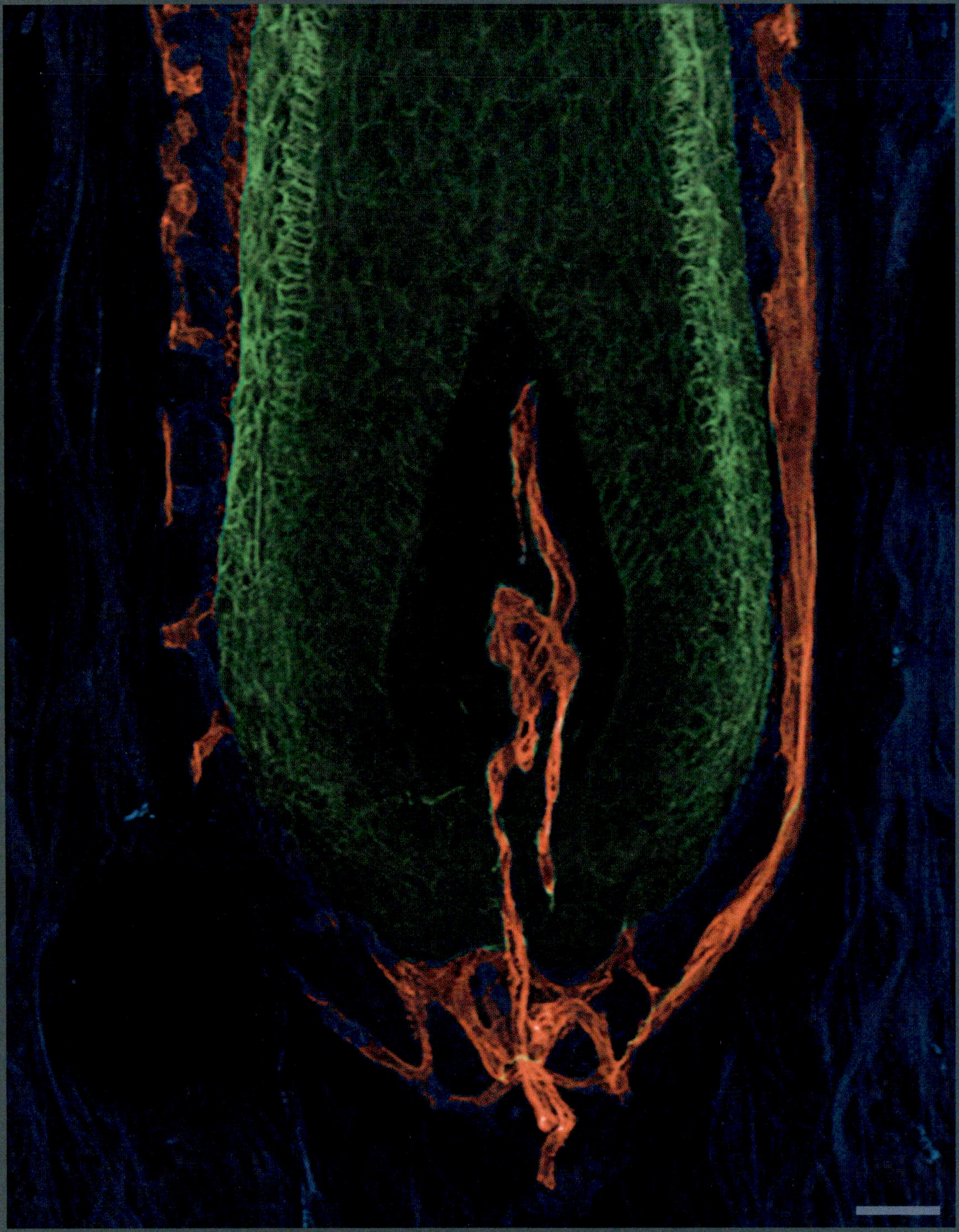

CHAPTER 7

Color Corrections and Final Steps

AFTER CORRECTING IMAGES for uneven illumination, cropping and straightening as needed, and reducing noise, further corrections may be necessary. This chapter describes the steps that may be needed to make color corrections for brightfield and darkfield images. Also included are steps for pseudocoloring and posterizing grayscale images, grayscale toning, sharpening, and making final adjustments to gamma, if necessary.

The term color correction is used broadly in this chapter. It refers to the following:

- **Brightfield color correction.** Returning colors to those that best represent the specimen or scene.
- **Darkfield color correction.** Converting existing colors from Look Up Tables (LUTs) and single-colored labels (such as in fluorescence imaging) to those colors that reproduce to various outputs with original brightness and contrast levels.
- **Color to grayscale conversion and grayscale to color.** Converting from color to grayscale may be necessary when publishing, or grayscale is converted to color when colorizing.
- **Grayscale to pseudocolor.** Differences in tonal values are often pseudocolored as an aid in visualization.
- **Grayscale color toning.** Adding a color tone to better represent the original appearance of the medium used to reproduce the specimen (e.g., x-ray films, black and white photographs, etc.).

Image of human hair follicle (green) and vasculature (orange), acquired on a BioRad 1024 in LaserSharp 3.1 software (BioRad, Inc., Hercules, CA) on an Olympus AX-70 microscope. A 60x , N.A. 1.4 apochromatic lens was used at a zoom of 1. A krypton-argon laser excited FITC, CY3 and CY5 at 488 nm, 568 nm and 647 nm respectively, through bandpass emissions filters: 520/32, 580/30 and 647/32nm respectively. Image was colorized in Photoshop CS3 Extended, converted to CMYK mode, resampled for enlargement, and sharpened with the Unsharp Mask filter. Scale bar = 60 microns. (Courtesy of Marna Ericson, PhD)

More: *For information on adding scale bars to images and saving and organizing image files, see www.peachpit.com/scientificimaging.*

In addition to color changes and alterations, grayscale tones can be reduced so that a limited range of tonal values are displayed. This can be accomplished by posterization.

Brightfield Color Corrections and RGB Color to CMYK

As far as brightfield color images are concerned, much has already been stated about the incorrect interpretation of color from specimens and scenes (see "Accurate Representation of Visual Data" in Chapter 1). Even under the most ideal conditions—when cameras are white balanced and lighting conditions are constant—colors shift toward inaccurate interpretations of scenes and specimens. Color interpretation can only be trusted when experiments are done to validate color consistency and accuracy over time against an external standard. In addition, the greatest likelihood of accuracy is achieved by using a stabilized flash unit as the light source.

Precise Color Correction

Note: *When readouts in the Info palette show one or two point differences along the RGB, 8-bit scale to indicate a disproportionate change after color correction, those differences are attributable to rounding errors.*

Several means for color correction (or balancing) are available in Photoshop and in Adobe Camera Raw (ACR), including functions for auto-balancing color. Not all of these functions produce equally proportional changes to every red, green, and blue tonal value in an image, which can lead to imprecise colors. The aim in this section is to present color correction steps that keep color values proportional (precise) across all tonal ranges: Methods shown in this section affect the red, green, and blue channels equally (incrementally from the darkest to the brightest value) in relation to their brightness level.

When color correction is done, the result is also an expansion or compression of the dynamic range to black and white limits, which is indicated in "Standard Procedure" in Chapter 5. Thus, contrast and brightness corrections do not necessarily have to be done after colors are corrected. The remaining changes in brightness levels may only be gamma changes for publication output.

Reference Areas

To make color corrections on more of an objective basis (some component is usually visual and therefore subjective), a reference of some kind is used in relevant images. The reference can be any of the following:

- **Internal reference.** A grayish-white reference (called a white reference) or gray area anywhere in the image.

- **External reference.** A neutral gray card or other reference object placed in the image with the specimen or taken by itself under the same conditions at the same session.
- **Reference image.** An image that contains accurate colors of the specimen and is used for correcting inaccurately interpreted colors in another image (color matching). The reference image may also be deemed a standard, whether or not colors are accurate, so that matched images are uniform in appearance.

When using white or gray references for color corrections, single or averaged pixels are adjusted to equalize the values of red, green, and blue. The percentages by which those values were changed to make them equal are then applied in incremental percentages to all other pixel values in the image, keeping changes proportional (as stated earlier).

When using a reference image, the pixel values from a reference point (the color doesn't matter) are recorded. Those same values are then changed for a similar color on a related image. Again, the percentage change is applied to all other colors in the related image incrementally and proportionately.

Methods for color correction using reference areas are discussed later in the sections "White or Gray Eyedropper Method" (using internal or external references) and "Color Matching to a Reference Image."

When no references can be located in the image and no external reference was used, or when one part of the image is corrected but other parts are not, manual methods can be applied. Methods for manually correcting images are covered in the "Manual or Auto Color Corrections: Other Methods" section.

Hue and Saturation

After color corrections are made, some colors may yet be too bright—sometimes glaringly bright (especially when viewed on a CRT monitor). These bright, saturated colors are often mistaken as incorrect colors, and Photoshop tools are mistakenly used to change the colors. Generally, these colors are not *incorrect* but are too saturated, so they must be desaturated to correct the color.

Desaturation will also conform images to a printing press when colors are limited to the CMYK gamut. This will make the image "CMYK ready," which also limits the gamut and consequently provides the best image to use for other outputs.

Learn more in "Reduce Saturation, Change Hue, and Make Image CMYK Ready" later in this chapter.

Color Noise

Noise that is particular to color images is referred to as color noise. This includes the introduction of color differences along edges due to chromatic aberration, an optical problem caused by differential focusing of the red, green, and blue components of light and consequent spatial offset. This kind of noise is referred to as "color fringing."

Longer exposures (more than 1/2 second or so), higher ISO settings (International Standards Organization, which used to be referred to as ASA for film and relates to its sensitivity to light) above 400, and higher gain levels all add to noise. Overall graininess of the image can be a consequence but can be corrected using methods described in "Noise Reduction" in Chapter 6. But the kind of noise that is specific to color images—another consequence—involves the blotching of discrete colors, especially in darker areas.

Color noise corrections can be found later in this chapter in the section "Noise Reduction: Color Fringing and Color Noise."

White or Gray Eyedropper Method

Most images can be corrected by finding an area in the image that is nearly white, grayish-white, or gray. That is especially true of brightfield images acquired via a microscope. It is followed by using the Hue/Saturation dialog box, if necessary (see "Reduce Saturation, Change Hue, and Make Image CMYK Ready" later in this chapter).

This method works by resetting unequal red, green, and blue tonal values in white or gray areas to those that are equal (though rounding errors can lead to one-point differences). The percentage change for each red, green, and blue channel is then applied to all pixels in the image incrementally, with the greatest change to brighter values and incrementally less as the values darken.

The use of the White or Gray Eyedropper method simultaneously sets black and white limits for publication (when those values have been set in Levels). Contrast and brightness levels can be changed later, as a possible additional step, when applying gamma corrections (discussed later in this chapter).

To use the White or Gray Eyedropper method:

1. Open an image (as a Smart Object or duplicate [Image > Duplicate]), duplicate the Background layer (Layer > Duplicate Layer), and convert the image to 16-bit (Image > Mode > 16-bits/Channel).

● **More:** *For detailed instructions on using the Levels dialog box, download the supplement "Tools and Functions in Photoshop" from www.peachpit.com/scientificimaging.*

2. Select the Eyedropper tool and choose a Sample Size of 5 x 5 Average.
3. Open the Levels dialog box by selecting Image > Adjustments > Levels or create a Levels adjustment layer (Layer > New Adjustment Layer > Levels). Make sure the white eyedropper is set to 240 for each channel, and that the black eyedropper is set to 20 (see the downloadable supplement "Tools and Functions in Photoshop").
4. Select the white eyedropper in Levels (**Figure 7.1**, left) when the specimen is back illuminated and the light source is part of the picture (as in a brightfield microscope specimen).

   Select the gray eyedropper when the light source is not a part of the image (when front or side illuminated) or when an external reference card has been included with the image.
5. Use the following protocol, depending on the nature of the image:
   - **For a back-illuminated specimen:** Click on a nearly white part of the image: Look for a grayer white versus a pure white, which is often found closer to the edge of the specimen. Click on more than one point to visually determine a correct balance if the first click doesn't produce a satisfying color correction, which is more likely to occur when white areas have a color cast. The center image in Figure 7.1 shows an area chosen for the white eyedropper, and the image on the right shows the corrected image.

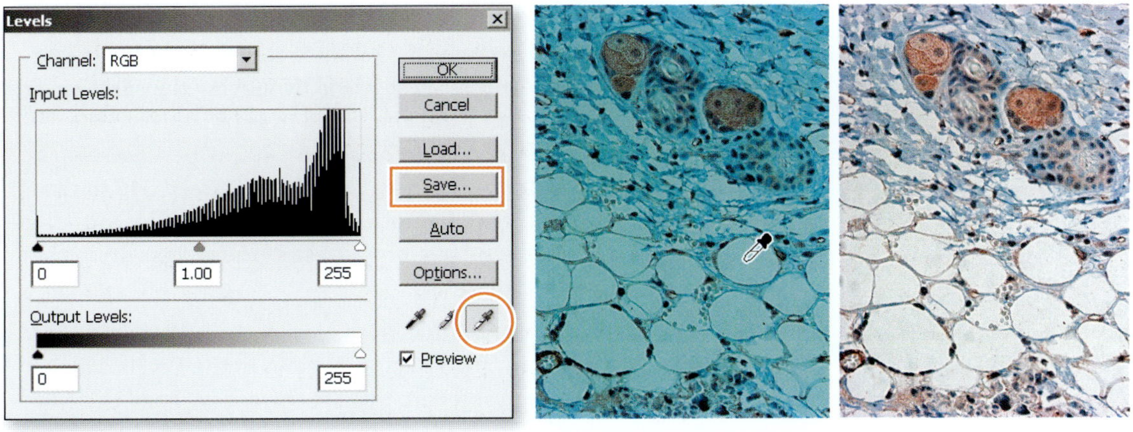

FIGURE 7.1 Location of the white eyedropper in the Levels dialog box (left), the uncorrected image (center), and the color-corrected image (right).

- **For a front-illuminated specimen:** It is preferable to click on a gray area of the image. This may be difficult to find unless an external reference was included in the image. Generally, some portion of the image has an area that is gray.

When choosing an area in which to click, slight changes in color may be confusing: It is difficult to know exactly which color correction is right. Without a calibration target, no "right" setting can be found. It is best to use an average: In some instances the image will be brighter, in others darker. Pick the mid-range correction.

The Histogram palette can sometimes be used to determine whether colors are correct: When the color curves do not overlap, the image is not color-corrected (**Figure 7.2**, left); when color curves overlap, the color is correct (**Figure 7.2**, right). Note, however, that single-colored images, when corrected, will not show overlapped curves.

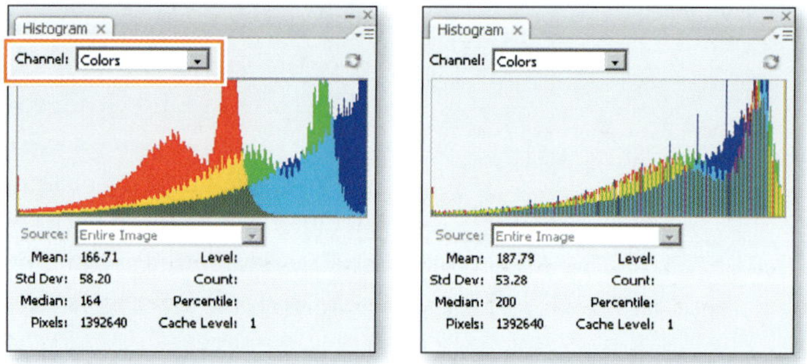

FIGURE 7.2 Red, green, and blue peaks are shown from left to right in the Histogram palette after choosing Colors from the Channel menu.

When colors are correct in one part of the image but incorrect in others, choose a correction that retains color tones in the brightest areas. This correction is best found by moving the cursor over the brightest portions of the image and reading values in the Info palette. Values should not be above 240 (RGB values, 8-bit) on average in the brightest areas. Values that exceed 240 in the brightest area indicate that another click point must be chosen in the image to keep the values for the rest of the image within the dynamic range of outputs.

6. Save the Levels setting so that the same correction can be applied to other images from that imaging session. In the Levels dialog box, click Save. Name and date the .alv correction. Load this file when correcting other images.
7. Determine the next step in the color correction process:
   - If the image contains bright, saturated colors, use the Hue/Saturation dialog box.

- If Hue/Saturation corrections are attempted and colors are not saturated and are still incorrect, use the methods described in the sections "Color Matching to a Reference Image" and "Manual or Auto Color Corrections: Other Methods."
- If optimal CMYK ready colors are desired, check the gamut (step 4 in the section "Reduce Saturation, Change Hue, and Make Image CMYK Ready"). If colors are covered in gray (gamut exceeded), use Hue and Saturation corrections.
- If color noise is visible, follow the steps for noise correction.
- If no noise is present and colors are optimal, correct related images using the saved Levels .alv file.
- If a white or gray eyedropper is used and only inaccurate colors are created, use the methods described in the next two sections: "Color Matching to a Reference Image" and "Manual or Auto Color Corrections: Other Methods."

Color Matching to a Reference Image

Colors can be matched to a reference image that represents the ideal colors for specimens or scenes. The reference image can be any of the following:

- **Permanent.** A "gold standard," color-corrected image stored on a computer as a reference to which all images are matched.
- **Temporal.** An image that is color-corrected during a single session to which all other related images from that session are matched.

■ **Note:** *When a Levels correction is applied to other images during a session (step 4 in the "White or Gray Eyedropper Method" section), colors are also matched, but only to a "reference correction." Either the reference correction method or the color matching method can be used for related images during a single imaging session.*

The first, or most accurate, image in a longitudinal study contains values within the dynamic range of the detector to which other images are compared in terms of color and possibly brightness. It is assumed that this image is color balanced.

The permanent and temporal images are representative images, and should not to be confused with images from a colorimetric longitudinal study in which color values are not altered. The intent of the image determines the color correction method used:

- Use the Automated Match Color to Reference method for representative images.
- Use the Manual Match Color to Reference method for representative images when a gray or white reference cannot be found with the eyedropper method; or use when the Automated Match Color to Reference method doesn't match colors appropriately.

- Use the Manual Match Color to Reference method with an internal (less optimal) or external reference (optimal) for longitudinal studies in which colors are compared.

■ **Note:** *The Match Color function works well with certain types of images, but it will not work with all images. The appearances of two images that are color matched must be within a close range with background areas that are not discolored.*

AUTOMATED MATCH COLOR TO REFERENCE METHOD

The colors from one image can be matched to another using the Match Color dialog box in Photoshop. When this command is used, time is saved: Histogram levels match each other, making colors, contrast levels, and brightnesses similar for comparison and uniformity.

The Match Color command can be used as well for matching contrasts and brightnesses of grayscale images (see "Histogram and Linear Histogram Matching" in Chapter 9).

Here are the steps for automatic color matching to a reference image:

1. Open the reference image and the image that requires color matching (make sure the latter is the active image). Both should be flatfield-corrected.
2. Open the Match Color dialog box (Image > Adjustments > Color Match). Choose the reference image as the Source (**Figure 7.3A**, and as inset in **B**). If the image matches the original by eye, as shown in the image adjacent to the Source setting (circled), or if it is close, click OK.

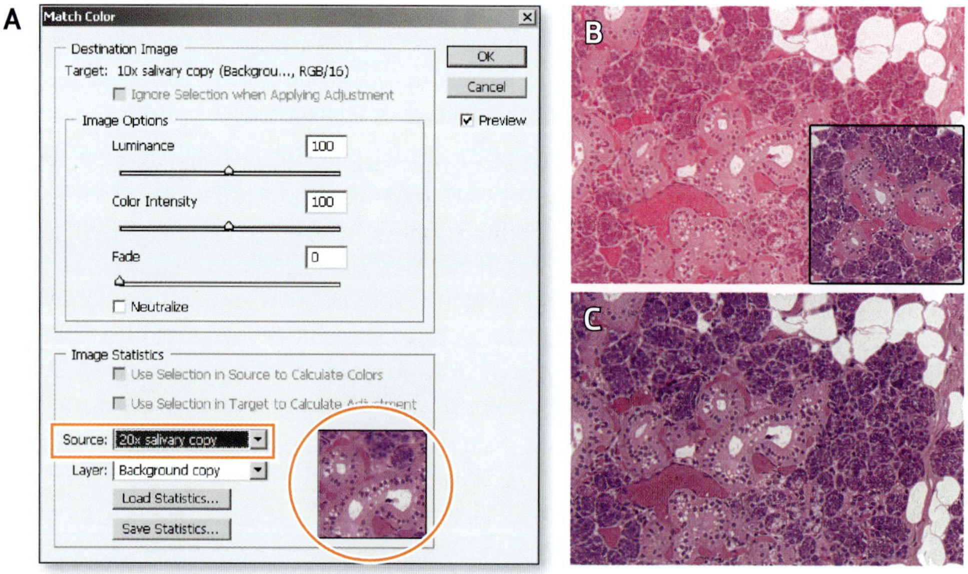

FIGURE 7.3 The Match Color dialog box (**A**); the image to be matched (**B**) and the matched image (**C**).

3. If desired, place color samplers in similar areas of both images to confirm on an objective basis that the match was accomplished. Expect some deviation of numeric values of up to about 10 because similar features can be difficult to find in two different images.

MANUAL MATCH COLOR TO REFERENCE METHOD

Colors of a feature in a reference image can be matched to the same feature in another image (internal reference). Or, as a better solution, if an external reference was acquired, it can be used for matching colors of two different images. Even when external references are used, images will likely appear different when taken under different light sources. The hues might be correct, but the darkness will vary, making it appear as though the colors don't match. When color comparisons are made over time, light sources, such as daylight and indoor lighting conditions, should not be mixed (**Figure 7.4**).

FIGURE 7.4 A daylight image (left) is balanced against an image taken under tungsten light (right). Greens are matched, but backgrounds are not.

If you are using an internal reference, follow these steps:

1. Open the first image—the image that is color-corrected and used as a reference (**Figure 7.5A**).
2. Open the image to be matched (**Figure 7.5B**). Place a sampling point on the part of the reference image that can be used for matching (Figure 7.5A, inset, sampling point 1) and on the image to be matched (Figure 7.5B, sampling point 2). Write down the R, G, and B values for the reference image (sampling point 1).

   The same part of both images may be hard to locate. Attempt to match the reference image sampling point values so that the matched image contains at least one red, green, or blue value that is a close match (or identical). The numeric readout in the Info palette will show R, G, and B values (as long as the palette options are set to display RGB Color values). Sampling markers can be moved by clicking inside the marker area and dragging.
3. While looking at the Info palette readout for sampling point 2, using Curves or Levels (Image > Adjustments > Levels or create a

Levels adjustment layer: Layer > New Adjustment Layer > Levels) adjust the input (**Figure 7.5C** and **D**, arrows) or output values by selecting red, green, and blue channels, one by one, until color sampling values from the second image match the reference image sampling values (**Figure 7.5E**). If the sampling positions are a close match, all the colors will match closely (**Figure 7.5F**).

FIGURE 7.5 Images of matched specimens using internal references from a longitudinal series. The green channel is not adjusted because its reference value is the same as the matched image.

4. When colors don't appear similar visually, the procedure can be repeated, moving the position of the sampling point in the second image to a point that matches more closely, or by choosing another position for the reference image.

If you are using an external reference, such as a neutral gray card, follow these steps:

1. Place a color sampler set to 5 by 5 Average or greater on the part of the image that is occupied by an external reference (e.g., neutral gray card) or on an image of the external reference taken at an imaging session (e.g., session one). Write down the RGB values from the gray card color sampler.
2. Place a color sampler on the external reference included with the image that is to be matched or on an image of the external reference taken at the same session. Try to find a part of the gray reference that is identical to what was chosen for the external reference in the first session. Some variation of tone may occur across the expanse of the gray reference area.
3. Using Curves or Levels, adjust the input or output values for each channel, one by one, so that the R, G, and B sampling values of the matched image are the same as the values that have been written down from session one. Adjust the input in Levels to increase brightness or darkness levels; adjust the output to decrease those values.
4. If this method is used for a single session (temporal), save the adjustments to apply them to all images taken within the same session. Open images one by one, open Levels or Curves, and load the saved adjustment into the Levels or Curves dialog box for related images.

Images should now contain colors that are matched. The colors may be off slightly, but that should be considered part of a standard deviation from session to session.

Manual or Auto Color Corrections: Other Methods

A suitable gray or white area may not be found in the specimen or in the background areas around the specimen (the whites may be clipped because of improper acquisition). Or color may be variable within the specimen from the center to the outside edges as a result of uneven illumination or specimen anomalies. It is assumed at this point that flatfield correction has been done (see "Uneven Illumination Correction" in Chapter 6). If flatfield correction has not been done on an unevenly lit image, perform this step first before proceeding with the following steps.

COLOR CORRECT THE WHOLE IMAGE

Attempt to first color correct the image by using the Auto button in Levels. If that doesn't color balance the image, try to find a reference image from a publication or the Web for manual matching according to the Manual Color Matching method described earlier, using an internal reference. When an image cannot be found (or none are suitable) for images with a full range of colors (versus those that are composed of a single color), the following steps can be taken:

1. Reduce the saturation of the offending colors using the Hue/Saturation dialog box, if they are overly bright.
2. Set black and white limits: Set the brightest significant white or background area to 240 in the R, G, and B 8-bit scale; set the darkest significant black to 20.
3. Adjust each channel in Levels to align color peaks in the histogram when the image is composed of red, green, and blue combinations of colors. Move the top-right slider to the left to increase input values (done most often), and move the bottom-right slider to the left to decrease output values (done less often).

   Increase input or decrease output values for each channel in Levels, one by one, to view the effect on the image. One of the channels will likely affect the image more than the others. Adjust this channel first to a visually acceptable level. Then adjust the remaining two channels to line up color peaks in the histogram with the first channel, either by increasing input or decreasing output values.

■ **Note:** *Histograms for each channel can provide adjustment clues. You can move the white slider for each channel to the left end of respective histograms and then evaluate the effect visually. If one color predominates, such as green, choose that color from the Channel menu and move the slider until that color is diminished.*

You may need to repeat this process more than once to fine-tune the image.

COLOR CORRECT PART OF THE IMAGE: SELECTION STEPS

When parts of the image are not the correct color, start by correcting the background areas of an image first. Then select the problem areas using Color Range or the Magic Wand tool. Selecting parts of the image constitutes local adjustments—generally prohibited in author guidelines for publications—but it is the only means available. The method should be described briefly in publications by mentioning that background areas were color matched.

Color Range selects broad areas within an image. This technique is tried first because it can be most efficient. Also, the selection can be saved and can be included as part of an action. When Color Range includes unwanted areas, use the Magic Wand tool to select areas instead.

To begin making a selection:

1. Duplicate the Background layer or the layer above the background.
2. From the Blend Mode menu, choose Color to place only the color portion of the image on this layer: The luminance of the image is unchanged.
3. Select the desired area with either Color Range or the Magic Wand tool.

Color Range. Choose Select > Color Range to select desired problem areas of the image.

1. In the Color Range dialog box, select the leftmost eyedropper, then set the Fuzziness slider to 0. Click within a problem area of the image. This selects a single starting point in that area, not likely to be visible in the Color Range dialog box display.
2. Select other parts of the image you want to include with the first eyedropper click point. Use the middle, plus (+) eyedropper tool and click on additional points surrounding the first point. Click as many points as possible. As the selected area grows, it is represented by a white area in the Color Range dialog box. Use the minus (–) eyedropper to remove areas from the selection.
3. Once the white area comprises a bit less than 50% of the desired area, adjust the Fuzziness slider to create a larger area but not so large that it includes more than the discolored portion of the background area (**Figure 7.6**).

   Increasing the Fuzziness value changes the selection edge from a sharp boundary to an opacity gradient—it becomes "fuzzy," in other words.

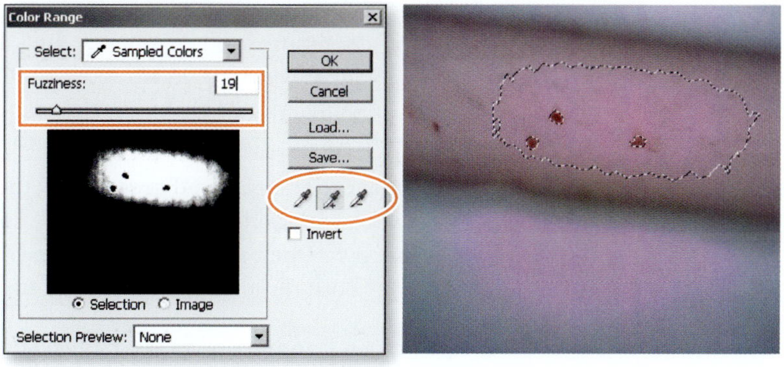

FIGURE 7.6 The Color Range dialog box (left) and the resulting selection covering the desired area of the image (right).

4. Click Save to save the Color Range selection as an .axt file and apply it to other images taken during the same session and then name and date the image.

Magic Wand tool. If a well-defined border exists, the Magic Wand tool is useful.

1. Select the Magic Wand tool and click the first point. All contiguous pixels of the same color (depending on the Tolerance setting) are selected (**Figure 7.7A**). The first click point rarely selects the entire desired area—it creates a selection that includes a handful of pixels.
2. To expand the selection, increase the Tolerance value in the options bar and click again until the selection occupies a small area.
3. Hold down the Shift key and continue to click areas adjacent to the first click (**Figure 7.7B**). The selection grows to include more area.
4. Shift-click several more points until the desired area is encompassed by the selection (**Figure 7.7C**).

Modify a selection. Once you've created a selection, you can then modify it.

- **Use the Lasso tool.** Deselect areas that were included in the selection by using the Lasso tool with the Alt/Option key held down. Drag around unwanted selections.
- **Feather the selection.** Choose Select > Feather (or Select > Modify > Feather) to soften the sharp selection edge (like the Fuzziness slider in Color Range) and then expand or contract the selection (Select > Modify > Expand or Contract).
- **Use Refine Edge.** Available only in CS3, the Refine Edge command (Select > Refine Edge) command combines several selection modification tools in one dialog box (**Figure 7.7D**). Areas and edges are graphically shown as changes are made (**Figure 7.7E**).

Preserve the selected area. Copy the selected portion of the image to its own layer by choosing Edit > Copy, and then Edit > Paste. This preserves the part of the specimen that is being worked on to its own layer both for documentation and for editing later on, if necessary.

COLOR CORRECT PART OF THE IMAGE: CORRECTION STEPS

Once appropriate areas of the image are selected, they are then color corrected. If the selected area is background, and if the background should be uniformly gray, the colors are made neutral. If colors are incorrect in specimen areas, then they are desaturated or matched to a correct color area found in another part of the image.

Correct background areas as follows:

1. Select the background area using methods presented in the previous section. For uniform background areas, return all colors to neutral (the same Red, Green, and Blue values). This is easily done by desaturating the background (Image > Adjustments > Desaturate) (**Figure 7.8**).

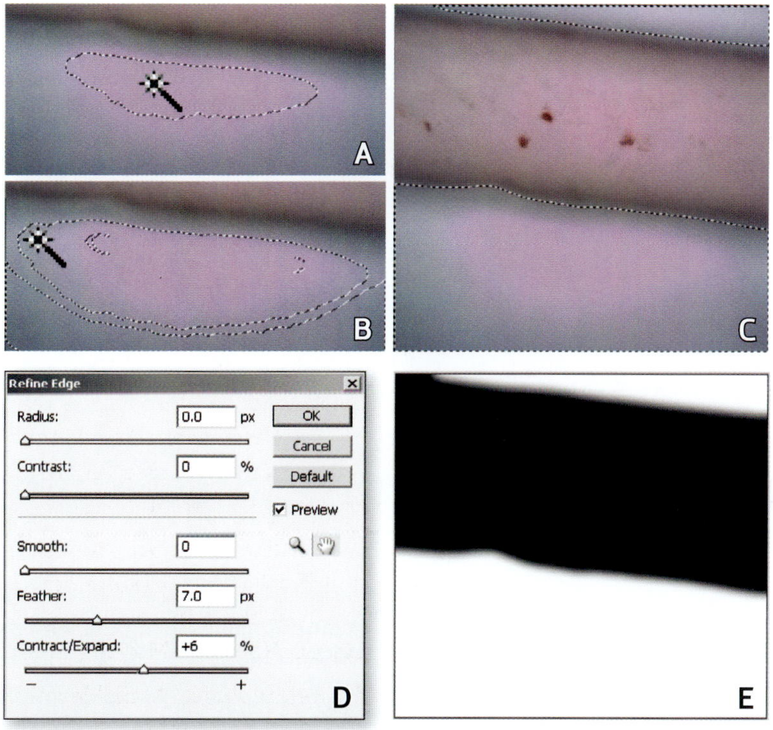

FIGURE 7.7 The Magic Wand tool and the resulting selections (**A–C**); the Refine Edge dialog box with a graphic display of the selection and edge fuzziness (**D**, **E**).

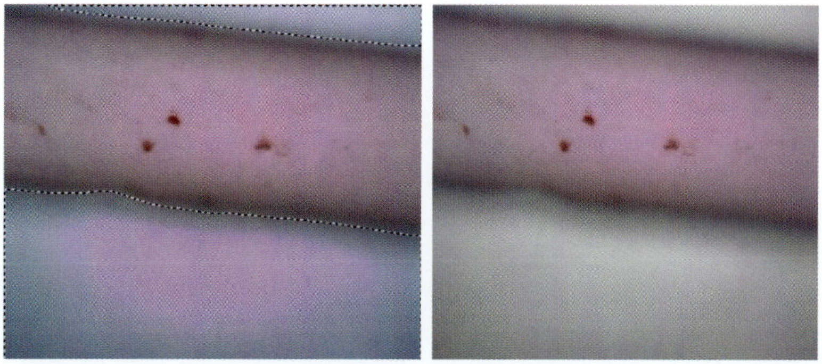

FIGURE 7.8 The selected background area (left); the background correction after desaturating (right).

For incorrect colors within specimen areas, correct as follows:

1. Select the area of the image where offending colors exist. Reduce the saturation of the offending color by selecting Image > Adjustments > Hue/Saturation. Choose the appropriate colors from the Edit menu. Move the Saturation slider to the left until the area is reduced in saturation (see the following section for more information).

2. If reducing the saturation of the offending color doesn't provide a visually pleasing result, adjust the colors. Select the Color Sampler tool (5 by 5 Average) and place a sampler in a representative part of the selected problem area (**Figure 7.9A**, sampler 1). Place a sampler on an area that is color-correct (Figure 7.9A, sampler 2), whether that area is on the same image or on a different image.

   If you've made a selection and its boundary obscures features in your image, press Ctrl/Command+H (View > Show > Selection Edges) to make the selection edges invisible (the selection is still active, but it is no longer displayed).

▶ **Warning:** *It's easy to forget that a selection is still active when it's hidden: Be sure to press Ctrl/Command+H again to reveal a selection, or cancel a selection by pressing Ctrl/Command+D (Select > Deselect).*

3. Open Levels or Curves. Using the R, G, B values from the sampler in the corrected area shown in the Info palette, adjust each channel, one by one, to match those R, G, B values (Figure 7.9A, Curves adjustments and Info palette readout). Look at the values in the Info palette while making your adjustments.

   - **Curves.** Select channels one by one and adjust curves from the top to match color values shown for sampler 1, the correct color.

   - **Levels.** Select channels one by one and adjust the input or output values using the white sliders. Match the R, G, B values from the sampler in the corrected area.

   The colors may appear to be different than the correct values, but continue with the step until the RGB values of color sampler 1 are the same as those for color sampler 2.

4. Change the opacity of the layer set to Color blending mode until the adjusted colors blend visually into the true colors at the center (**Figure 7.9B**). To be sure that the border between the center and edges is transparent, it is best to set the Opacity to a value 1% or 2% lower than what is seen to be correct by eye (**Figure 7.9C**).

5. Cancel the selection (Select > Deselect or press Ctrl/Command+D).

6. Make another selection for smaller areas if the colors are not yet corrected throughout and repeat the color matching process.

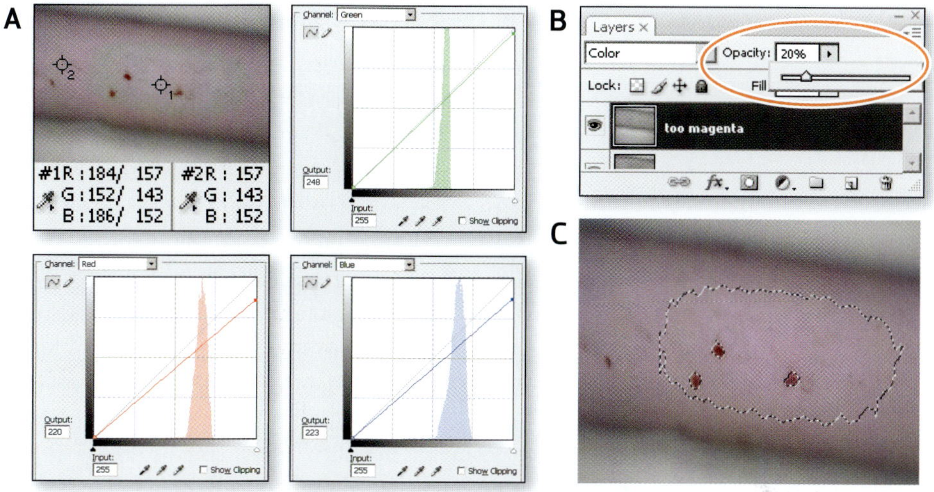

FIGURE 7.9 Color sampler placement, Curves adjustments, and the Info palette readout (**A**); Layers palette showing the Opacity slider (**B**); and the final, corrected image (**C**).

Reduce Saturation, Change Hue, and Make Image CMYK Ready

After color correction, when one or more colors do not match colors in the specimen or scene, it is likely that they are not incorrect in terms of their hue, but of saturation. Saturated colors are pure, neon colors that require some gray to be introduced to lessen their intensity.

Thus far in this book, only RGB and CMYK colors have been described in detail as components of light and pigments, respectively. But not only can the components of color be divided along the lines of their primaries, but also by other means. Color can be divided into useful components along the lines of its hue (what color it is), saturation (how pure or how much gray is introduced into the hue), and lightness (how dark or bright). This means of dividing color provides a robust means for affecting one component without affecting the others. For example, the hue can change without affecting either the saturation or the lightness.

To alter these color components, the Hue/Saturation dialog box can be used. It is sometimes used to alter the hue but is most often used to reduce saturation, because oversaturation is more commonly encountered in scientific imaging.

Follow these steps to reduce the saturation of offending colors:

1. If desired, duplicate the image (Image > Duplicate). Place the saturated image next to the duplicate so that you can view and compare both.
2. Select Image > Adjustments > Hue/Saturation (or add a Hue/Saturation adjustment layer). From the Edit menu choose the offending color (**Figure 7.10A** and **B**).

   Using the bottom slider, expand the range of colors that will be included in the correction. In Figure 7.10A the range of reds is expanded to include magenta and orange. Be sure to drag within the lighter gray segments of the slider (Figure 7.10A, arrow); otherwise, the lighter gray segment of the slider itself will expand or contract in width, increasing or decreasing the rate of fall-off between affected and non-affected colors. This eliminates a sharp delineation between colors.

▶ **Warning:** *To be accurate, the monitor must be calibrated and viewing be done in darkness.*

3. Reduce the saturation of the color by moving the Saturation slider to the left so that the hue becomes more gray (**Figure 7.10C**). This is done visually to arrive at a visually acceptable level (**Figure 7.10D**). The hue at that point may appear incorrect: Make adjustments to the hue to see visually correct colors.
4. To check the Saturation value that you chose against an objective reference, use the Gamut Warning overlay and/or view the Proof Colors (View > Gamut Warning or View > Proof Colors). It is best to memorize the keyboard commands so that the Gamut Warning or Proof Colors changes can be turned on and off (toggled): Press Ctrl/Command+Shift+ Y for Gamut Warning or Ctrl/Command+Y for Proof Colors.

   Gamut Warning provides a gray overlay to show which colors will not reproduce to a printing press (**Figure 7.10E**): Proof Colors displays an approximation of how the image will look in CMYK for viewing purposes only. It is useful to use the Gamut Warning overlay to see which colors are irreproducible and use the Proof Colors to determine the extent of the details that may be lost when the offending color is not adequately desaturated. The ideal situation is when the colors can remain vibrant without losing much brightness when you view them as a CMYK Proof Color. You can choose higher to lower Saturation values iteratively and test these colors against the Proof Colors.

Set Saturation values so that the gray overlay is removed in all but the darkest areas, because a loss of detail in these areas cannot be perceived by eye. This setting will make the image CMYK ready.

5. If you are making a CMYK image, change the mode to CMYK Color (Image > Mode > CMYK Color). Once the image is CMYK Color, open the Hue/Saturation dialog box and increase the saturation value slightly to restore the original brightness while carefully observing for a loss of detail.

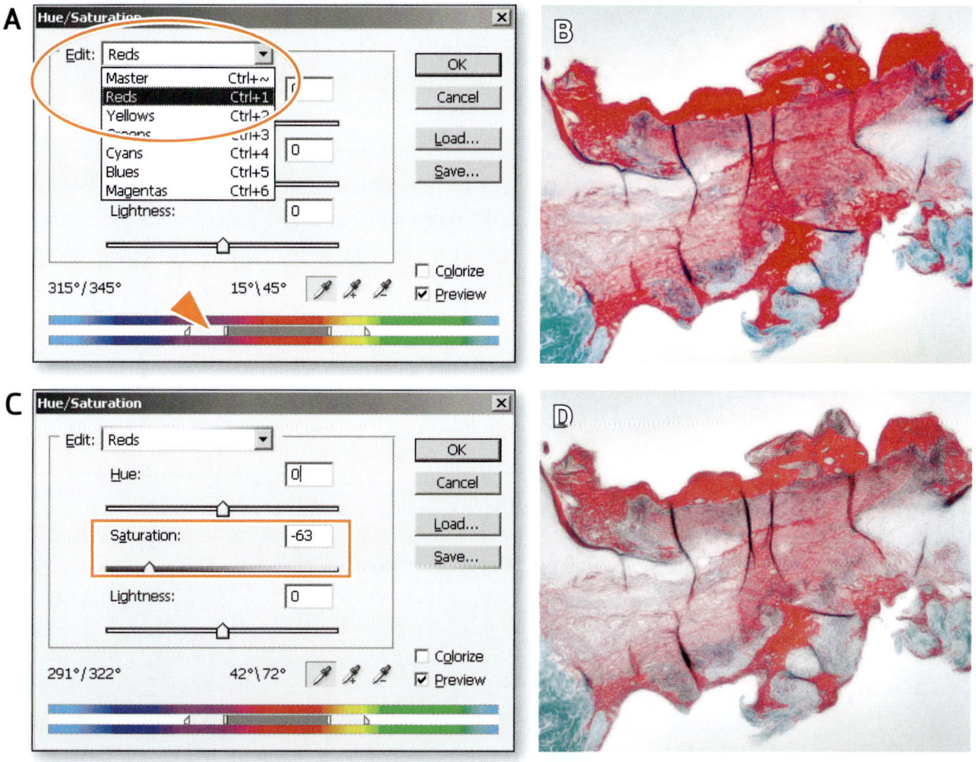

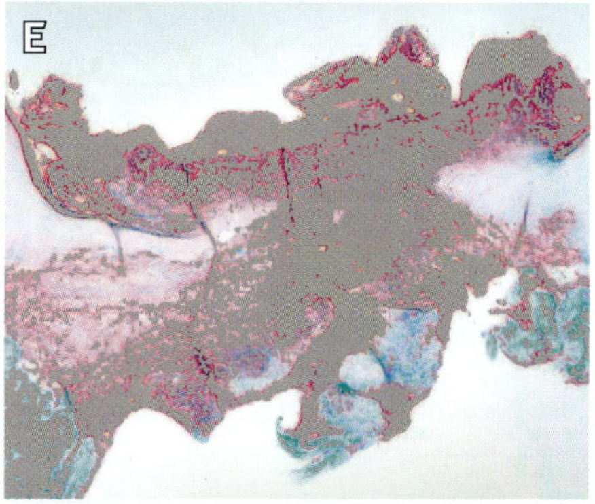

FIGURE 7.10 The Hue/Saturation dialog box and the saturation correction in the red range. The Gamut warning overlay (**E**).

6. When you are satisfied with a saturation level, save this correction so that you can apply it to other images taken at the same session. Click Save, and then name and date the .ahu file. Load this file when correcting other images, or drag the adjustment layer onto subsequent images from the same session.

Noise Reduction: Color Fringing and Color Noise

Color noise can occur as false color at the edges of features as a result of chromatic aberration (color fringing), or as spots or patterns of false color that are a result of long exposures and high ISO settings (among other contributions). Both kinds of noise can be removed using the steps that follow:

1. Duplicate the Background layer (Layer > Duplicate Layer). While this layer is selected, choose Color from the Blend Mode menu. The final image will get all of its color information from this layer, but the luminance information in the original layer will be preserved.

■ **Note:** *Purple or red fringing at the edges of an image can also be removed in the Adobe Camera Raw plug-in.*

2. Choose Filter > Noise > Reduce Noise. In the Reduce Noise dialog box increase Reduce Color Noise (**Figure 7.11**, left) until miscoloring at the edges of the features is removed (**Figure 7.11**, right). This will also blend blobs of color in featureless areas.

This process may need to be repeated for problem images. Note that every noise correction introduces blurring.

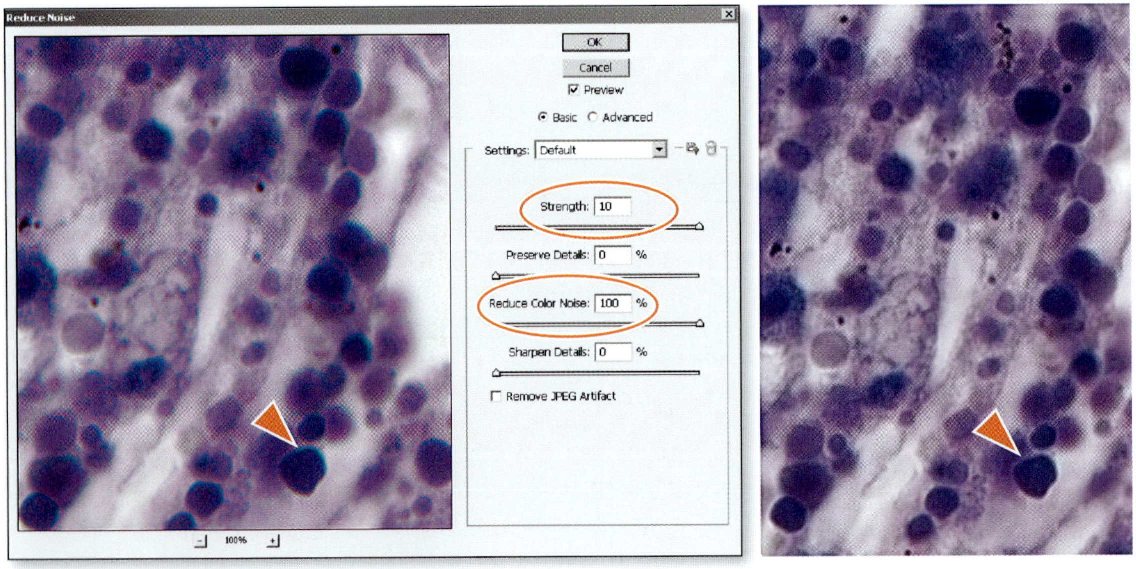

FIGURE 7.11 Images showing color fringing correction.

Brightfield: Color to Grayscale

Converting a color image into grayscale is frequently accomplished through a simple mode change. However, this is not always the best way to differentiate portions of the color image and translate them into grayscale. The simple mode change emphasizes the green channel with little contribution from the red and blue channels, making this method unsuitable for many scientific specimens.

Brightfield images often contain features of interest that are of greatest importance to the research that is done (**Figure 7.12A**, arrow). When images are converted to grayscale from color, it is important to draw attention to these features. To convert RGB Color into grayscale, the red, green, and blue channels that make up the color image are individually adjusted.

In some instances, the rendering of grayscale from color may require inversing the values to show the features. Also, it may be more important to reduce the background than it is to brighten or darken important features. Thus, the first goal is to reduce the background and the second to amplify the important features.

Two functions are available in Photoshop for creating a grayscale image from brightfield color: Black and White Adjustment (CS3 only) and Channel Mixer (earlier versions). Here are the steps for using these features.

To convert color to grayscale using the Black and White Adjustment (CS3 only):

1. Choose Image > Adjustments > Black and White (**Figure 7.12B**). The Black and White dialog box opens.
2. Eliminate the default settings by entering 0 into all the percentage fields.
3. Increase the percentage of each color to visualize its effect on the image. When it is clear which parts of the image are affected by respective colors, decrease/increase those that provide the gray values of interest while maintaining contrast in relevant areas (**Figure 7.12C**). Click OK.

To convert color to grayscale using the Channel Mixer (pre-CS3):

1. Choose Image > Adjustments > Channel Mixer. The Channel Mixer dialog box appears.
2. Select the Monochrome check box at the bottom (**Figure 7.12D**).

FIGURE 7.12 Converting color to grayscale using the Black and White dialog box (**A**, **B**, and **C**) and Channel Mixer dialog box (**A**, **D**, and **E**).

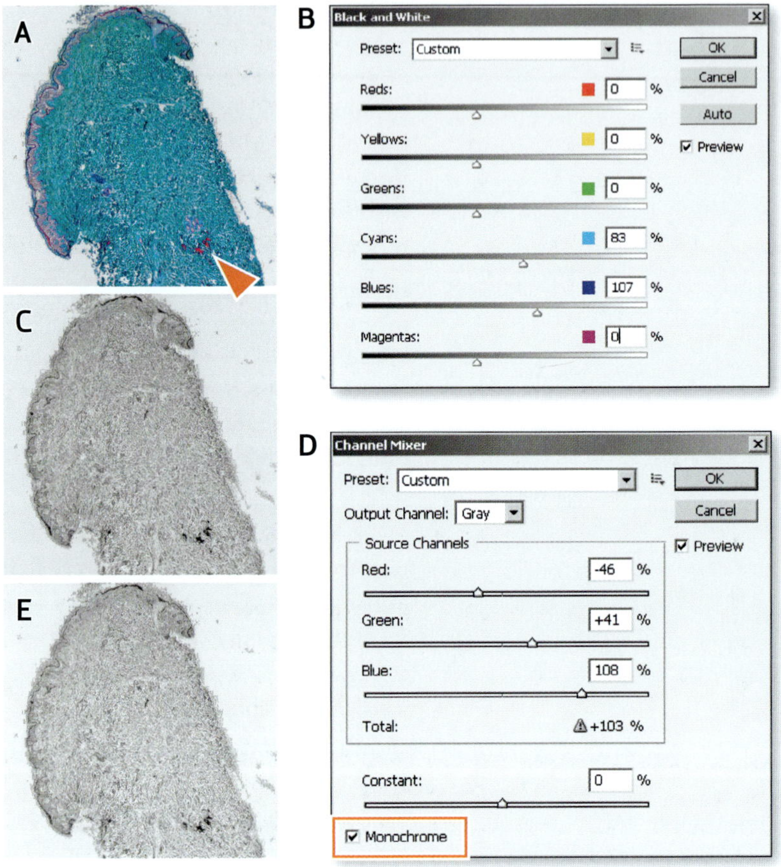

3. Set each color range to 0%, and then increase each to see how the color affects the grayscale interpretation. Increase/decrease values of the colors that best show relevant details in the grayscale image (**Figure 7.12E**).

Single Color, Darkfield Images

Pure colors used in fluorescence imaging do not reproduce with equally perceived brightness and tonal levels, even when pixel readouts show the same brightness values. On a computer display showing the pure-colored primaries, green-colorized images appear brightest to human eyes, reds appear slightly darker, and blues relatively dark. On a printing press, the same phenomenon is true, though green can reproduce darker than red, depending on the image.

Whether for viewing on a computer screen or for use in publication, to attain colors at equal brightness levels, colors need to either be altered or changed entirely (this is especially important for revealing visual details to those who are color blind). This involves making the correct color choices for fluorescent images, because the color can be arbitrarily assigned (when color images are acquired versus grayscale). Those choices can be made when choosing a color LUT (e.g., on a confocal instrument), or the image can be made into grayscale (decolorized) and then colorized to the preferred colors. Existing colors can be altered to colors that contain perceptually equal brightnesses.

Even when the brightest colors are chosen for darkfield images, the images are still corrected for color and tone to reveal detail—especially in the darker areas—and to match brightness levels among the colors used. These steps are described in the next section "Setting Black and White Limits and Brightness Matching."

For additional darkfield fluorescent color steps, refer to the following sections:

- **"Single Color Image to Grayscale."** Use this method when images need to be decolorized to change the color used or when grayscale images are needed instead of color (e.g., for quantification purposes or publication).
- **"Colorize Grayscale Images."** Use this method to colorize or recolorize grayscale images in single colors. If changing original colors, convert images to grayscale images first, and then recolorize or use the following method (Change Existing Colors) for red, green, and blue colors.
- **"Change Existing Colors."** Use this method to quickly change the predominately used red, green, and blue colors to nearly equal perceptual brightnesses on a computer screen (or for laptop projection). This can be done as a substitute method for decolorizing and then colorizing.
- **"Show Colocalization/Coexistence."** Single-color images of the same specimen can be placed in separate layers and blending modes can be used to combine colors. In so doing, places where colors blend demonstrate biological activity from two or more differently labeled features at the same location.
- **"Make Images CMYK Ready."** Images can be prepared for CMYK conversion to publication images so that details are not lost and color intensity is retained (for all but certain blue and magenta-red ranges).

● **More:** *Actions for colorizing and decolorizing can be downloaded from the Peachpit Web site at www.peachpit.com/scientificimaging.*

- **"Colorizing, Decolorizing Actions."** The number of steps in this method is time consuming, so a final description is included for making automated actions for recolorizing up to 12 colors.

▶ **Warning:** *For all steps it is critical to set black and white limits, and it is far more critical for the black end. Also, the Color Settings work space is set to sRGB for viewing the pure colors used in fluorescence (see "Color Settings" in Chapter 5). The Rendering Intent is set to Perceptual. Otherwise, colors will be displayed incorrectly, color relationships will be altered, and methods will not work.*

Setting Black and White Limits and Brightness Matching

Black and white limits are set to conform the dynamic range to the output destinations. These limits can be narrower for darkfield images than those set for brightfield images, especially for publication output.

■ **Note:** *If the images are destined for fluorescent intensity measurements, the brightness values are left as is.*

Brightness levels from discrete fluorophores are matched to identical levels if not already done when acquiring the image (unless images are of controls). This is done to compensate for varying sensitivities of detectors and varying quantum yields of fluorescent probes.

To set black and white limits:

1. Place a color sampler on the brightest significant part of the image (**Figure 7.13A**, sampler 1). When it is difficult to locate the brightest part, open Levels (Image > Adjustments > Levels or press Ctrl/Command+L) and hold down the Alt/Option key while moving the white Input slider to the left. The first areas of the image that appear as white on the image are the brightest. Cancel out of the Levels dialog box once these areas are found.
2. Place another sampling point on the black background where no specimen detail exists (Figure 7.13A, sampler 2).
3. Choose Layer > Duplicate or add a Levels adjustment layer.
4. With the Levels dialog box open, keep an eye on the Info palette readouts from the color samplers and move the output (or input) white slider (**Figure 7.13B**) until the readout for sampler 1 shows a maximum RGB, 8-bit value of 240 (**Figure 7.13C**). Move the black output (or input) slider until the sampling readout shows a value of 20–30 for the background.

   When a value higher than our default (20) is chosen so that the background becomes lighter (less black), dim details hidden in black regions are easier to see, not so much on an LCD computer screen as in laptop projection and other outputs. The black level is especially crucial for conversion to CMYK: Higher values will result in the retention of color and details in darker areas when reproduced (**Figure 7.13D**).

A brightness value of 240 may not be absolutely ideal for every output. Its value should be at or near 240 for laptop projection to retain details in the brightest areas, but images inserted into PowerPoint may darken overall. In tandem, the values may become darker than desired (though the appearance of values in the whitest areas should be evaluated on a laptop projection screen) and these may need to be brightened in PowerPoint.

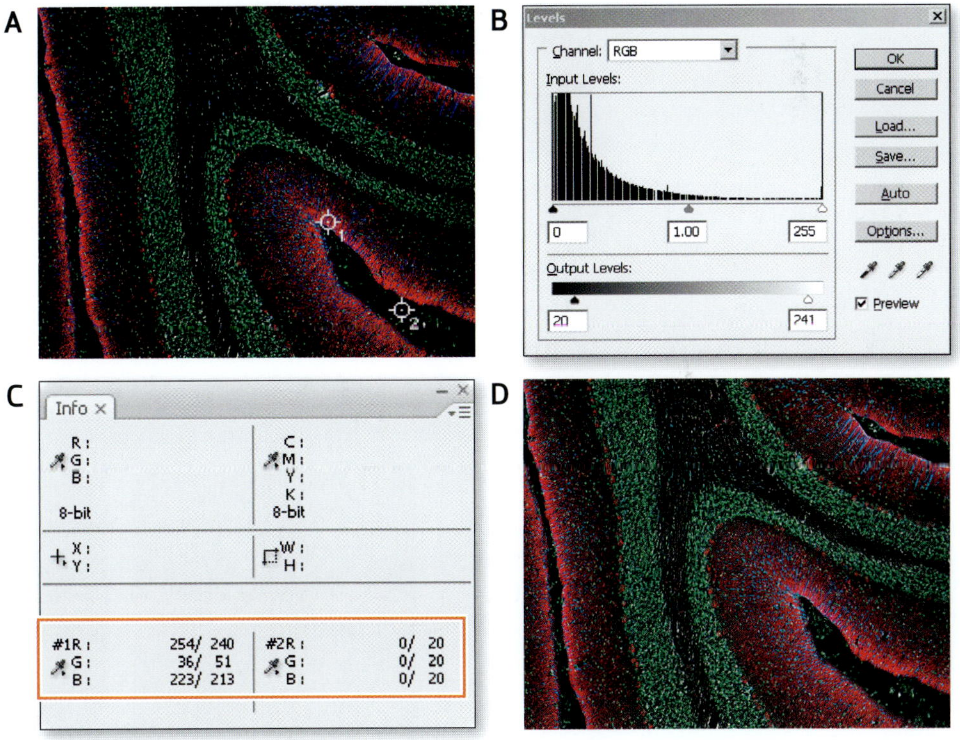

FIGURE 7.13 Setting black and white limits for darkfield images.

For any output, sharpening steps will restore and improve the original appearance, so that the representation becomes more accurate. Images are best judged for tonal range and brightness after sharpening. For information on sharpening methods, see the "Sharpening" section later in this chapter.

After a reference image is chosen (the brightest image of a series) and black and white levels are set, related images are matched to it.

To match brightness levels:

1. Place a color sampler on the brightest significant point in the image you want to match to the reference image.
2. Use Levels to adjust brightness so that the readout from the color sampler matches the reference image (see "Dialog Boxes for Menu Functions" in the downloadable supplement "Tools and Functions in Photoshop").
3. Set the black limit to a value that is the same as the reference image.

Single Color Image to Grayscale

When only a single color is used for an image, such as when a single fluorescent label is used on a specimen, follow these steps to make color images into grayscale. By following these steps, brightness levels are preserved.

1. If the image is an Indexed Color image, convert it to RGB Color by choosing Image > Mode > RGB Color.
2. Make the RGB Color image into a grayscale image (Image > Adjustments > Channel Mixer).
3. In the Channel Mixer dialog box, select the Monochrome check box (**Figure 7.14**, left).

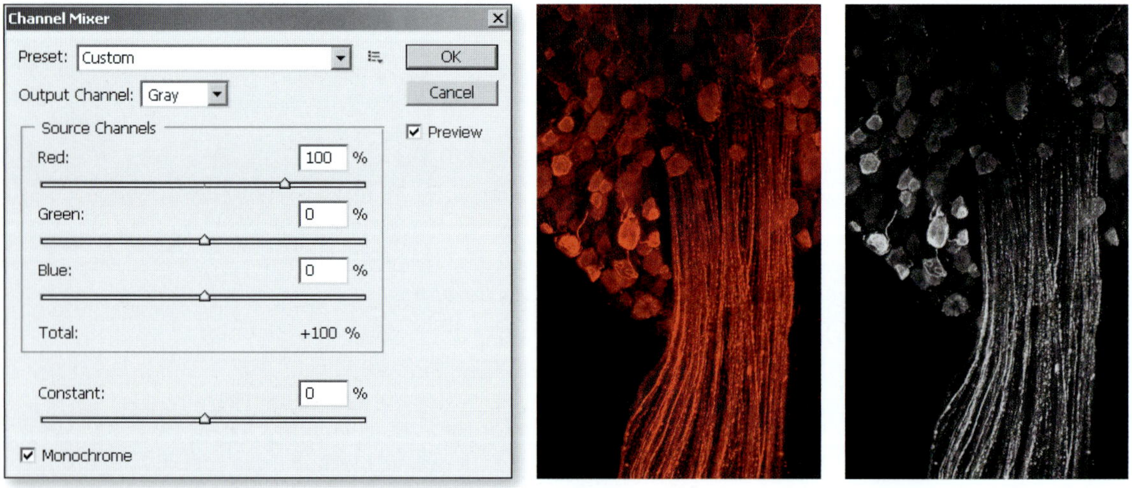

FIGURE 7.14 The Channel Mixer dialog box shown with a color image (center) and the consequent grayscale image (right) with tonal range preserved.

4. Enter values from the chart in **Table 7.1** according to the color of the image (**Figure 7.14** center and right). For example, if the image is colorized green, enter 100% for the green channel along with 0% for the red and blue channels.

TABLE 7.1 **Channel Mixer Percentages Based On Color of Darkfield Image**

	PERCENT RED	PERCENT GREEN	PERCENT BLUE
Magenta	100	0	0
Violet	0	0	100
Blue	0	0	100
Cyan	0	0	100
Green	0	100	0
Yellow	0	100	0
Orange	100	0	0
Red	100	0	0

Colorize Grayscale Images

More than one approach can be taken to colorize grayscale images. Often, colorizing is done by selecting Colorize in the Hue/Saturation dialog box. The Hue slider is adjusted until the relevant color is found, and then the Lightness slider is adjusted to add color to the brightest values, simultaneously darkening the image overall.

To retain pure colors, this colorizing method reduces the overall brightness of fluorescence for display and outputs (but the method *can* work when the colors chosen are not pure).

To retain the original tonal values and a greater dynamic range (even after setting black and white limits), apply this method using Levels to obtain 12 different colors by colorizing:

1. For a grayscale image (or a grayscale image saved as Indexed Color), change the mode of the image to RGB Color.
2. In the Levels dialog box (Image > Adjustments > Levels), choose each channel in turn from the Channel menu and adjust the white output slider (**Figure 7.15**, left) to obtain the desired colors (**Figure 7.15**, right). Colors are made according to **Table 7.2**.

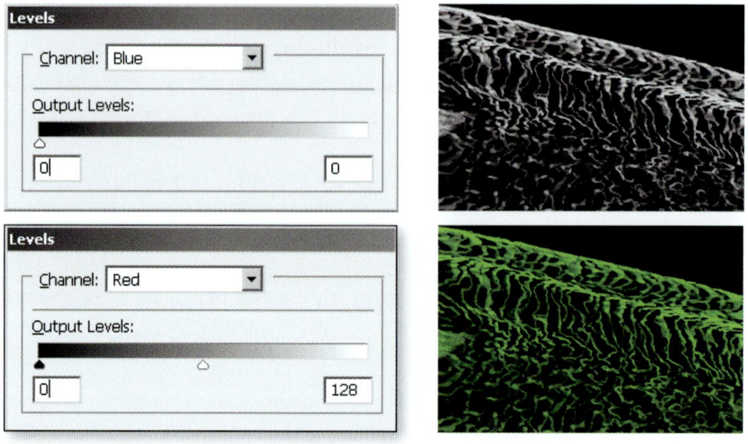

FIGURE 7.15 To obtain green-yellow, the output values in the Levels dialog box were left as is for the Green channel (at 255), adjusted to 0 for the Blue channel, and 128 for the Red channel (left panels). Right panels show the grayscale image and the colorized result.

TABLE 7.2 **Grayscale Colorizing for Darkfield Images**

	RED CHANNEL OUTPUT	GREEN CHANNEL OUTPUT	BLUE CHANNEL OUTPUT
Violet	128	0	255
Blue	0	0	255
Blue-Cyan	0	128	255
Cyan	0	255	255
Green-Cyan	0	255	128
Green	0	255	0
Green-Yellow	128	255	0
Yellow	255	255	0
Orange	255	128	0
Red	255	0	0
Red-Magenta	255	0	128
Magenta	255	0	255

Change Existing Colors

If existing images contain red, green, and blue colors, and they cannot be separated into grayscale components—or a more expedient means is desired—the red, green, and blue values can be altered somewhat to make them perceptually equal. To accomplish this, the hues are shifted in the Hue/Saturation dialog box.

Here are the values for obtaining far more reproducible colors than available through LUTs:

1. Choose Image > Adjustments > Hue/Saturation to open the Hue/Saturation dialog box.
2. From the Edit menu, choose the appropriate color and adjust the Hue as follows:
   - **Blues.** Set Hue to -32 to add green and make the blue more cyan.
   - **Greens.** Set Hue to -32 to add yellow and make green more green-yellow.
   - **Reds.** Set Hue to +20 to add yellow to the red to shift it toward orange.

■ **Note:** *The Hue values provided will likely reproduce closer to what was intended in the first place, even after shifting hues.*

Show Colocalization/Coexistence

Two or more differently labeled and colored features on the same specimen can be blended to show colocalization/coexistence. These are placed on layers and then blended using Screen mode as follows:

1. Open one of the images that will be used for showing colocalization as the background image upon which other images will be stacked. Typically, this is the green colored image, but it can be any color. Be sure to duplicate the image and close the original to be certain it is not overwritten (Image > Duplicate).
2. Open the next single-color image, and then drag the image onto the first image using the Move tool while holding down the Shift key. Close the second image.
3. Open any additional images and drag them onto the first image so that each single-color image is in a layer.
4. Change the blending mode of each layer to Screen. Screen combines values of each layer pixel by pixel and these lighten each other, similarly to two slides being projected onto a screen from two different projectors.

After completing the steps, some colors will still not have the same perceptual brightness as other colors, so the blending of colors doesn't always appear correct. For example, on a computer screen, green appears bright, red appears darker, and blue darker yet, so the red and blue layers of the image recede while the green overpowers the image. It can be argued that perceptually darker colors are legitimately made brighter through the use of Levels or Curves adjustment tools layer by layer (or, to prevent clipping, the opposite is done: brighter colors are darkened), so additional tonal adjustments can be a final step. However, what is frequently done as a final step—often seen in publication—is an overadjustment to the layers so that color values are clipped and all details in the features are lost. To make colocalization/coexistence absolutely clear, use the method in the section "Measuring Colocalization/Coexistence in Photoshop" in Chapter 10.

Make Images CMYK Ready

In a sense, RGB to CMYK conversion is like an hourglass operation where dynamic range is narrowed before it is expanded. Before conversion, the appearance of the image, especially on LCD screens, will be washed out with visually undesirable grayish-black backgrounds. After the image is converted to CMYK, the color intensities can be restored and black levels made darker in background regions. Details can be revealed through sharpening.

■ **Note:** *Color reproduction is specimen specific: Specimens with expanses of featureless areas will always appear brighter when reproduced. Also, the brightness depends on the perceptual capacity for that color and the reflection of light off the page (best viewed in window light or under a 5000-degree Kelvin lamp).*

Not all colors respond similarly, however, when printed. When colors can be chosen to represent features that are a part of a specimen, brighter colors are reserved for those features that are small, narrow, or at a tonal value close to the background. Darker and mid-range colors can be chosen for features that occupy wider spatial expanses. **Figure 7.16** shows a color reproduction for 12 colors using a specific specimen (pollen grain) with detail in the bright and dim regions.

As demonstrated in Figure 7.16, the relative ranking of color brightness and discrimination of detail is listed here:

- **Brighter Colors.** Green-Yellow, Yellow, and Orange.
- **Mid-range.** Red, Green, and Cyan.
- **Mid-dim.** Magenta, Red-Magenta, Green-Cyan.
- **Dim.** Blue, Blue-Cyan.

STEPS TO MAKE IMAGES CMYK READY

The steps for creating reproducible and publishable colors follow. Be sure that Color Settings is set to an sRGB work space:

1. Determine which colors and tonal ranges will not reproduce accurately to CMYK by activating the color gamut overlay. Press Ctrl/Command+Shift+Y or select View > Gamut Warning (**Figure 7.17A**, page 196).

   A gray overlay will cover all or some of the colors in the image: Start by placing a color sampler on the featureless background area of the image (**Figure 7.17B**, left).

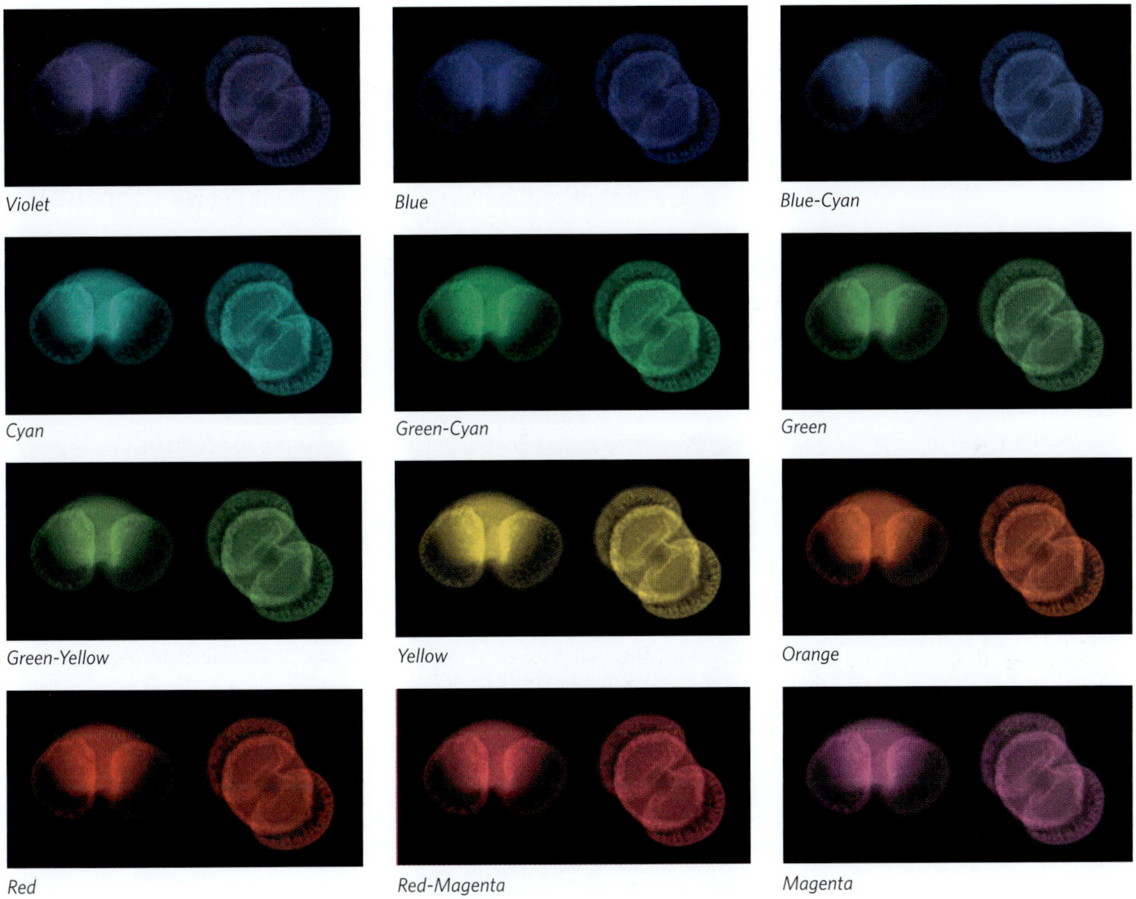

FIGURE 7.16 Twelve hues made into CMYK from saturated colors.

2. Choose Image > Adjustments > Levels and use the black output slider to decrease the darkness of the blacks (**Figure 7.17B**, right). While moving the slider and looking at the sampling point readout in the Info palette, check to make sure that the background black is at but not greater than an RGB, 8-bit value of a maximum of 30 for the red, green, or blue values in the Info palette (this value is usually adequate for reducing some of the gamut overlay, depending on the color). Click OK.

3. Reduce the saturation of the color by adjusting the Saturation slider in the Hue/Saturation dialog box (see "Dialog Boxes for Menu Functions" in the downloadable supplement "Tools and Functions in Photoshop" for more information about

Hue/Saturation). Reduce the saturation until all the gray overlay disappears, or increase the saturation until some gray appears and then back off until it disappears (**Figure 7.17C**). Click OK.

4. Turn off the Gamut Warning (Ctrl/Command+Shift+ Y) and convert the image to CMYK mode (Image > Mode > CMYK Color). The image will appear dimmer than the original (**Figure 7.17D**, left).

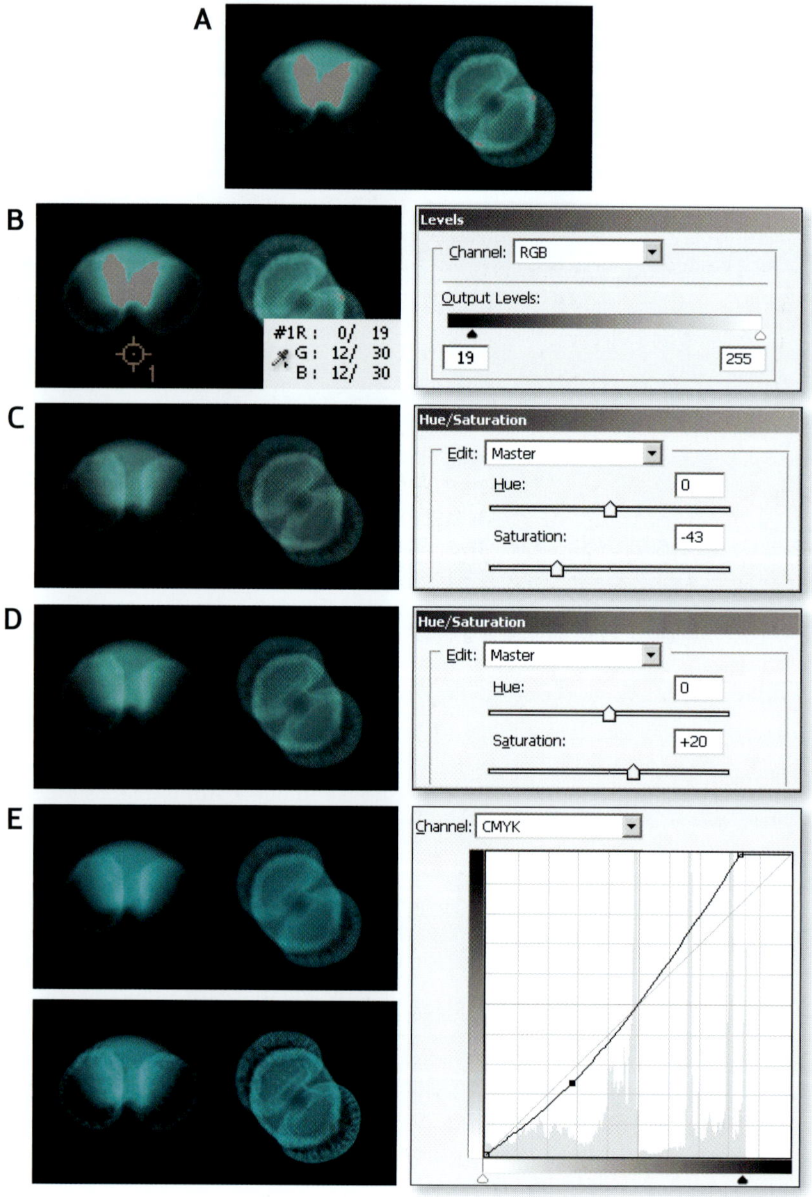

FIGURE 7.17 Images and cropped dialog boxes showing a series of steps when converting saturated color images to CMYK while preserving the details.

● **More:** *Check the book's companion Web site at www.peachpit.com/scientificimaging for any updates to the colorizing tables in this chapter.*

5. Open the Hue/Saturation dialog box again and set saturation values according to the suggested maximum values in **Table 7.3** (**Figure 7.17D,** right). Set values in the Saturation column while Master is chosen from the Edit menu. Then choose Cyan from the Edit menu before adjusting the %Cyan value, etc. These are not hard and fast values: For positive saturation values, saturation amounts are increased as much as possible without obscuring details. For negative saturation values, saturation amounts are decreased until the image overall appears brighter to the eye.

6. After setting the Hue and Saturation, use the Curves tool to darken the background. This increases the perception of brightness of the foreground (**Figure 7.17E**, left top) along with subsequent sharpening (**Figure 7.17E**, left bottom). Choose Image > Adjustments > Curves and choose Black from the Channel menu (**Figure 7.17E**, right). Bend the line in the darker regions to increase the darkness to greater than 93%–100% or so, but rely on the visual appearance of the image as well: Carefully observe for loss of details in the specimen.

   You can increase the ability to adjust colors within limited ranges by placing three dots on the adjustment line to retain all the values above or below the affected tonal range. Determine where the tonal ranges occur along the line in the image by placing the cursor over different parts of the image and clicking: A circle indicates where the tones at the click point occur along the line.

TABLE 7.3 Setting CMYK Saturation and Channel Values

	SATURATION	% CYAN	% MAGENTA	% YELLOW
Violet	-20			
Blue	-10			
Blue-Cyan	-10			
Cyan	+20			
Green-Cyan	+40			
Green	+60			
Green-Yellow	0			
Yellow	+5	Decrease to 0%		
Orange	0			
Red	-15			
Red-Magenta	-20	Decrease to 0%		Increase to 50% of Magenta value
Magenta	-10	Decrease to 0%		

■ **Note:** *At this point the gamma may be altered for improved perception of darker or brighter ranges of values. A gamma change may have to be reported, depending on the publication's requirements.*

FINAL STEPS: SHARPEN THE IMAGE AND CHANGE GAMMA

As final steps, sharpen the image, either by using Unsharp Mask or the High Pass method. See information about sharpening later in this chapter. Sharpening can be regarded as a correction step that must be reported in certain publications. The point of sharpening for darkfield images is to reveal details that would otherwise be hidden, making the image a more representative specimen closer to the original image.

Colorizing, Decolorizing Actions

● **More:** *Actions can also be downloaded from the book's companion Web site at www.peachpit.com/scientificimaging.*

The number of steps for decolorizing and colorizing can take a great deal of time. So the entire series of steps can be made into an action and then into a droplet that can be placed on the Desktop: Steps only need to be practiced once, and then recorded as an action once the steps are understood. All files with the appropriate colors can then be dragged into the droplets on the Desktop, and Photoshop will open and complete the tasks.

When making the action, be sure to create a stop to alert the user to place color samplers on the brightest significant part of the specimen and the background before running the action. If the user has forgotten to do so, the action can be stopped, samplers can be added, and then the action can be run again.

Before using Levels or Curves to set black and white limits, be sure to include another stop to let users know what they are doing. Then make the step in which Levels will be used interactive. When the user completes setting the limits by referring to sampler readouts in the Info palette, and then clicks OK, the action will continue.

Colorizing values are entered without the need for user intervention because they are fixed values.

Additionally, the sharpening step can be included with user interaction and a stop to describe that step.

Be sure to provide a Save As step at the end. This can be included by selecting the Insert Menu Item command from the Actions palette menu. When the Insert Menu Item dialog box appears, use the mouse to select File > Save As. Then click OK in the Insert Menu Item dialog box. This step will be interactive without having to set the interactivity manually.

Test the action with a random image. If everything works, create a droplet (File > Automate > Create Droplet). Place the droplet on the Desktop if desired.

Grayscale to Color: Pseudocolor and Colorizing

Grayscale images can be made into pseudocolored images to better show levels of optical intensity or density, or to draw attention to what is difficult to see. Often, phenomena that result in a subtle change in optical intensities or densities also affect a narrow range of pixel values. These are impossible to observe until that range is colorized with various hues. For images of this nature, the grayscale image is colorized along a color table, or the tonal values are made into a graphic display in which ranges of grayscale values are grouped or binned together. These are either pseudocolored or posterized.

Pseudocolored Images Along a Color Table

The following steps will convert an image into one that contains 256 grayscale values, and then will assign each grayscale value a color:

● **More:** *Download the grayscale bar from the book's companion Web site at www.peachpit.com/scientificimaging.*

1. Download a 0–255 grayscale bar to use as a reference if a color bar wasn't created along with the image in the scientific acquisition program you used. This grayscale bar will be colorized in the remaining steps at the same pseudocolor values as the image.
2. Open the image to be pseudocolored, and then using the Move tool, drag the color bar (which isn't in color at all but is at this point a grayscale gradient) into the image and place it along the bottom. You can also select the bar (Select > All), then copy and paste it into the image. Extra room can be made for the color bar image by enlarging the canvas (Image > Canvas Size). Add to the Height.

   If the color bar is too large (or small) in dimension, expand or contract it by dragging a corner with the Transform tool (Edit > Transform > Scale) while holding down the Shift key to keep proportions intact.

■ **Note:** *If a dialog box appears, keep the default values and click OK. Layers will have to be flattened.*

3. Change the Mode to Indexed Color (Image > Mode > Indexed Color). This may not be straightforward: If the image is 16-bits/channel, it will have to be converted to 8-bits/channel before it can be converted to Indexed Color. If it is a grayscale image that is in RGB Color, convert it first to grayscale and then to Indexed Color.
4. Choose Image > Mode > Color Table.
5. In the Color Table dialog box, choose Spectrum from the Table menu to show conventional colors along the visible wavelengths (violet to red) to indicate dark to brighter values (**Figure 7.18A** and **B**). Other color tables can be chosen as well.

If colors need to be reassigned (remapped) to existing pixel ranges, you can modify the colors in the color table. All modifications to the colors in the image will be reflected in the color bar as a reference to show what was done.

6. To reassign colors, click and drag on the colors shown in the color table that are to be changed (**Figure 7.18C**, left, top). If you are uncertain about the range, place sampling points on the parts of the image where colors are to be changed at the brightest and darkest parts within that range. Check the readout in the Info palette. Pixel brightness values correlate to the 256 colors in the table from top to bottom and left to right.
7. After clicking and dragging, a dialog box appears and prompts you for the first color (not shown in Figure 7.18). Choose the color from the color picker or from the Color Libraries. A second dialog box prompts you for the final color. The increments in between are created automatically (**Figure 7.18C**, bottom and **D**).
8. Return the image to RGB Color so that the full range of Photoshop functions and tools can be used on the image.

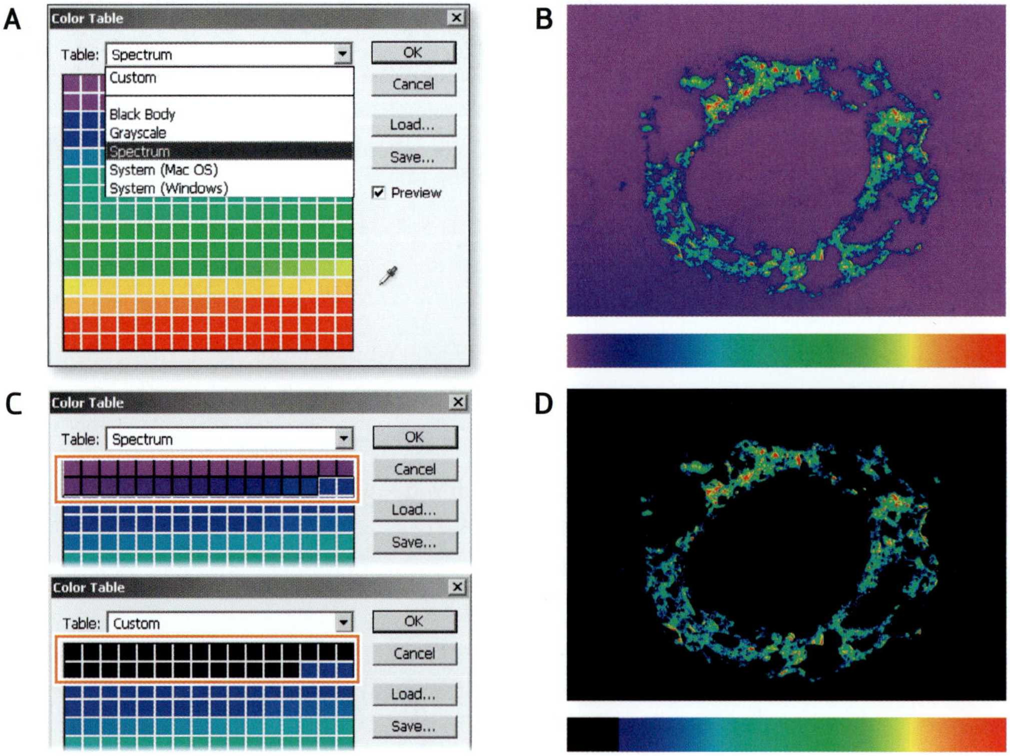

FIGURE 7.18 Creating and editing pseudocolored images.

Posterizing

Grayscale or color images can be made into "islands" of color or grayscale with the Posterize command (**Figure 7.19**). When using this command, the image must be in RGB Color or in Grayscale mode. The color bar isn't needed for this function, though it can provide a means for determining ranges of grayscale values that are affected. This function requires only one interactive step: To posterize, select Image > Adjustments > Posterize. Iteratively change the numeric value to a point at which pertinent visual information is best revealed.

More on posterization can be found in "Using Color Range and Posterize" in Chapter 9.

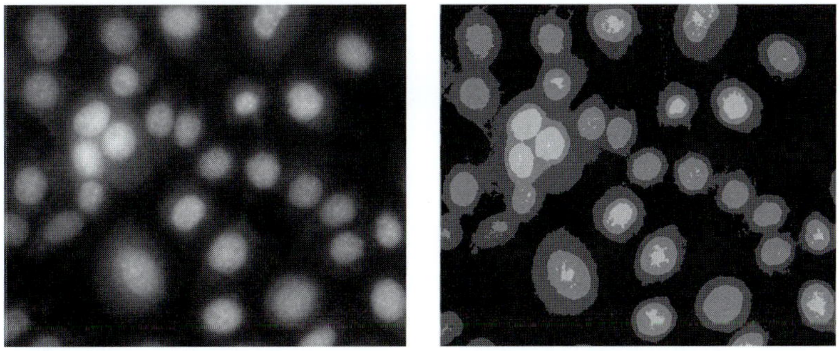

FIGURE 7.19 The original image (left); the image posterized at a value of 9 (right).

Grayscale Toning

As mentioned earlier, grayscale images can be colored to conform them to the expected tones for each profession. Often, that tone is shifted toward blue, but depending on the specialty, it may also be shifted toward other colors. The color blue, perceptually, increases contrast.

Color toning can be done more than one way. The method for toning in this book follows earlier methods that avoid changes in gamma. Gamma changes are done as a separate step. Grayscale images are first converted to Duotone mode, which is only available for 8-bit images. The images must then be saved as RGB Color for use with most outputs or as CMYK Color images for publication.

Here are the steps for color toning:

1. Convert the image from grayscale to Duotone mode (Image > Mode > Duotone). If the image is a higher bit depth, convert it to 8-bits/channel first (Image > Mode > 8-bits/channel).

2. The Duotone Options dialog box appears: Choose Duotone from the Type menu (**Figure 7.20A**).
3. Change the ink type by double-clicking the Ink 2 color box on the left. A second dialog box appears. Choose Pantone Solid Coated from the Book menu.
4. Using the bottom and top arrows on the color bar, choose a color from the list. In **Figure 7.20B,** Blue 072C is chosen.
5. Place color samplers on the darkest significant area (or background, if darkfield) and on the brightest significant area (or foreground, if brightfield). Adjust the white and black limits with Levels. Set the darkest black to an 8-bit, RGB value of 20 and the brightest significant value to 240 by using the input or output sliders (see "Standard Procedure" in Chapter 5).

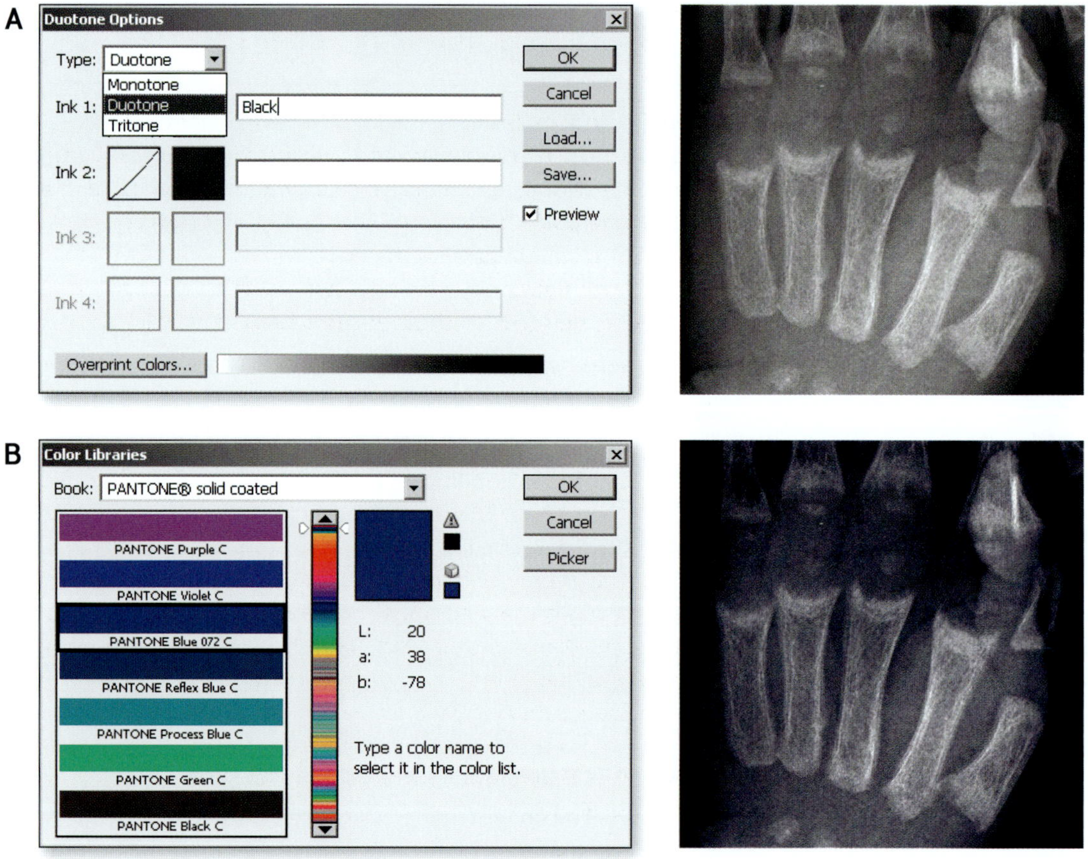

FIGURE 7.20 The method for color toning a grayscale image.

Sharpening

The use of a sharpening filter is usually delayed until the end of the correction process. But sharpening doesn't necessarily have to occur at the end: When problem images are out of focus and critical details cannot be separated, it can be appropriate to make sharpening corrections on a Smart Object or separate layer as an earlier step, often before Levels corrections are made. Darker and brighter tones can exceed the black and white limits when images are sharpened.

Some publications require that sharpening be reported when it is performed on images. It is a curious requirement, for nearly all published images appear as better representations after sharpening. As an added benefit, inks are not as likely to bleed into each other when ranges of tonal values are isolated—a result of sharpening. Also, small details are revealed, thus presenting to the viewer all the visual information versus leaving that information obscured when the image is slightly blurred.

However, edge artifacts can be enhanced or introduced after sharpening, in particular with backlit, brightfield images. Thus, when sharpening is done on an image, caution must be taken so that these artifacts are not introduced and consequently misinterpreted. It is assumed that those performing digital imaging corrections are also familiar with light scattering artifacts as a result of improper microscopy techniques (e.g., when Koehler illumination is not applied).

Sharpening is approached with specific requirements for output based on the type of image and inherent pixel resolution. Brightfield images on the whole do not require a great degree of sharpening to reveal detail (versus noise), but darkfield images generally require greater degrees of sharpening.

The methods discussed in the next two sections produce edge sharpening through the use of incremental darkening at edge borders; its extent (spatially) depends on a chosen value. In the photographic profession, when this kind of sharpening was performed using film, that edge border effect created what was called "acutance." Acutance was a reference to that slight darkening at the edges of features and was more enhanced when feature edges contained greater contrast against the background. Features with uniform tonal ranges remained largely unaffected.

The following two sharpening methods—Unsharp Mask and High Pass—create edge separation much like acutance. The choice of one method or the other is determined through trial and error.

▶ **Warning:** *Sharpening is not recommended for the following purposes: 3D reconstructions, quantification, and OD/I measurements.*

The level of sharpening varies with the intent:

- For publication it is recommended that the Radius for the Unsharp Mask sharpening method be set at or between 2.5 and 3.0.
- For projection in particular and for other outputs, higher levels of sharpening are recommended to ensure that relevant features are prominent.

Unsharp Mask Sharpening Method

When using the Unsharp Mask sharpening method, the edge border takes on a spatial width related to the Radius value. A Radius amount up to 3.0 leads to improved sharpening: Radius amounts that exceed 3.0 lead to increased sharpening but can also lead to a reduction in detail, depending on the nature of the image.

1. Select Layer > Duplicate Layer to make a new layer for sharpening.
2. For brightfield, color only, change the new layer's blending mode to Luminosity so that color artifacts are not introduced when sharpening. Sharpening effects will be applied only to the grayscale component of the image, not to the color components.
3. Choose Filter > Sharpen > Unsharp Mask (**Figure 7.21**, left).
4. In the Unsharp Mask dialog box, set the Radius first. Start with a width of 1.5. Then increase the Amount until the image appears correct visually: If the image is over sharpened, it takes on a graphic appearance.

   Experiment by increasing the Radius in increments of 1 to larger values and at the same time decreasing the Amount. For darkfield images, you can set the Radius to amounts exceeding 3.0 and then visually determine the effect by inspecting how effectively brighter objects separate from the background (**Figure 7.21**, center and right insets). Brightfield images are often left at a Radius of 1.5 to 3.0, depending on the effect. Again, too much sharpening can introduce artificial edge effects.

   You can also choose a smaller amount for the Unsharp Mask and repeat the filtering several times (Ctrl/Command+F) to avoid artifacts. As a result, rounding errors are less prevalent.

5. (Optional) Double-click the sharpened layer in the Layers palette to open the Layer Style dialog box. In the Blending Options area, use the Blend-If options to limit sharpening to specific tonal ranges. Often, the darkest and brightest parts of the image do not require sharpening.

■ **Note:** *The recommendations for the Radius setting differ from other experts' recommendations: They recommend keeping the Radius below 2.5. Scientific images are made to show differences among features, so higher Radius values are often necessary.*

FIGURE 7.21 The Unsharp Mask dialog box (left) with before (center) and after (right) effects.

Using the This Layer slider, decrease the white slider until the brightest portions of the image are not sharpened. By decreasing the slider dramatically to view the effect, and then increasing it slowly, you can find this point more easily. Often, it is just below 240.

Increase the black slider to eliminate sharpening on the darkest parts of the image, and then decrease the slider to find the point at which the darkest parts of the image are not sharpened. Again, this is done visually.

6. Reduce the Opacity slider, if desired, when the sharpening strength is too great.

High Pass Sharpening Method

The High Pass Sharpening Method relies on the High Pass filter to detect edges. The width and darkness of the edges are adjusted interactively by setting the Radius amount.

1. Select Layer > Duplicate Layer to make a new layer for the High Pass filter.
2. Select Filter > Other > High Pass to display the High Pass filter dialog box.
3. The Radius setting depends entirely on the nature of the image. Start at 0 and move the slider to the right until the edges appear. Continue until darkness at the edges increases. At some point details will become visible. Create an image in which edges are well

defined but image information is absent (**Figure 7.22A** and **B**). That point is variable, but for most images it is between 2.5 and 6. The greater the radius, the greater the sharpening. Click OK.

4. In the Layers palette, choose Hard Light from the Blend Mode menu.
5. Double-click on the layer to which you applied the High Pass filter. Follow the directions in step 5 in the Unsharp Mask Sharpening method (**Figure 7.22C** and **D**).

A B C D

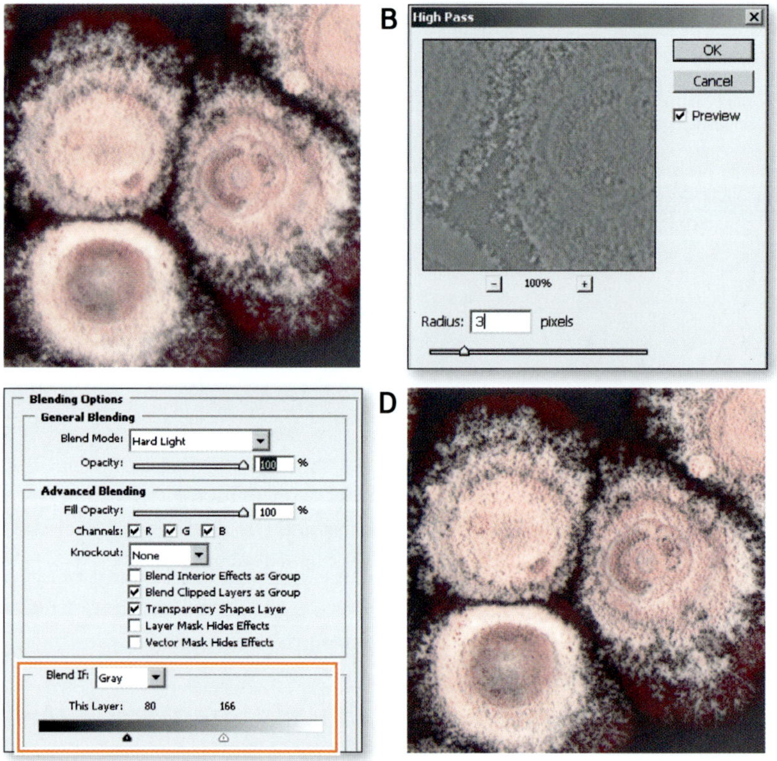

FIGURE 7.22 The original image (**A**) and the appearance of edges after using the High Pass filter (**B**). Blending options are altered (**C**) to reduce background noise (**D**).

Gamma

A change in the relationship of tonal values is necessary for optimal reproduction when the output is for publication. The most recommended change is a brightening of darker values and a greater tonal separation of the brighter values. Another is to brighten the image overall. The gamma changes that are made depend entirely on the nature of the image. The method used for changing the gamma is visually determined via a calibrated monitor.

The reason it is necessary to change gamma for press reproduction lies in a mismatch between the 8-bit scale used in digital photography and the optical density scale used for press reproduction. To fit the tonal range to the press, the relationship of tonal values must be altered.

■ **Note:** *The best means for showing and resolving relevant features would be to make a high-definition rendering from three separate exposures, as described in "Creating an HDR Image (CS2 and CS3 Only)" in Chapter 6.*

Gamma may also be changed when relevant features are too dark. To adequately discriminate these features, they are brightened without affecting other tonal values.

Changes to the gamma can occur at an earlier step, usually after black and white limits are set. A gamma correction is ideal for adjusting tonal brightness and darkness of midtones without substantially affecting the white and black limits. It is generally performed at the end of the processing steps, because it likely requires a change only for publication, reports, and grants, but not for monitor display, animation, 3D, and laptop projection. For the latter outputs, changes in gamma are often unnecessary, but each person must judge whether or not gamma changes should be done on his or her images.

Any changes in gamma are reported. This is important not only to be in compliance with ethical considerations, but as a practical matter: Publications increasingly spot-check images with software designed to find gamma changes, among other post-processing alterations. Gamma changes are not applied to those images on which OD/I measurements are done or to any image in which darkness or brightness of features is mentioned in the manuscript.

Here are ways in which gamma can be changed to improve the quality of press reproduction or to darken or brighten specific tonal ranges so that important features are revealed.

To change gamma for contrast:

1. Select Image > Adjustments > Curves (**Figure 7.23A**) or use a Curves adjustment layer (Layer > New Adjustment Layer > Curves).
2. Adjust the image so that the darker values below the midpoint are darker, and the brighter values above the midpoint are brighter. In general, adjust on a visual level so that changes are more subtle versus dramatic (**Figure 7.23B**).

To change gamma for brightening overall:

1. Open Curves (as in the previous step 1).
2. Place a point near the top of the line and drag the line upward (**Figure 7.23C**).

To change gamma for brightening dark areas:

1. Open Curves.
2. Place a point on the Curves line near the center to anchor the upper part of the curve, and place another point near the bottom and drag upward to brighten the darker regions of the image (**Figure 7.23D**).

   When determining where specific areas of the image occur along the line, while the Curves dialog box is open, drag with the cursor (it becomes an Eyedropper tool) across the image. An open circle moves along the Curves line to show the location at which these tones occur. Place a point on the line within this location and bend the line from that point.

   When bending the line, undesired tones may also be affected. To limit the correction to a narrow range of tones, place three points above or below that range along the line, as mentioned in "Noise Reduction" in Chapter 6.

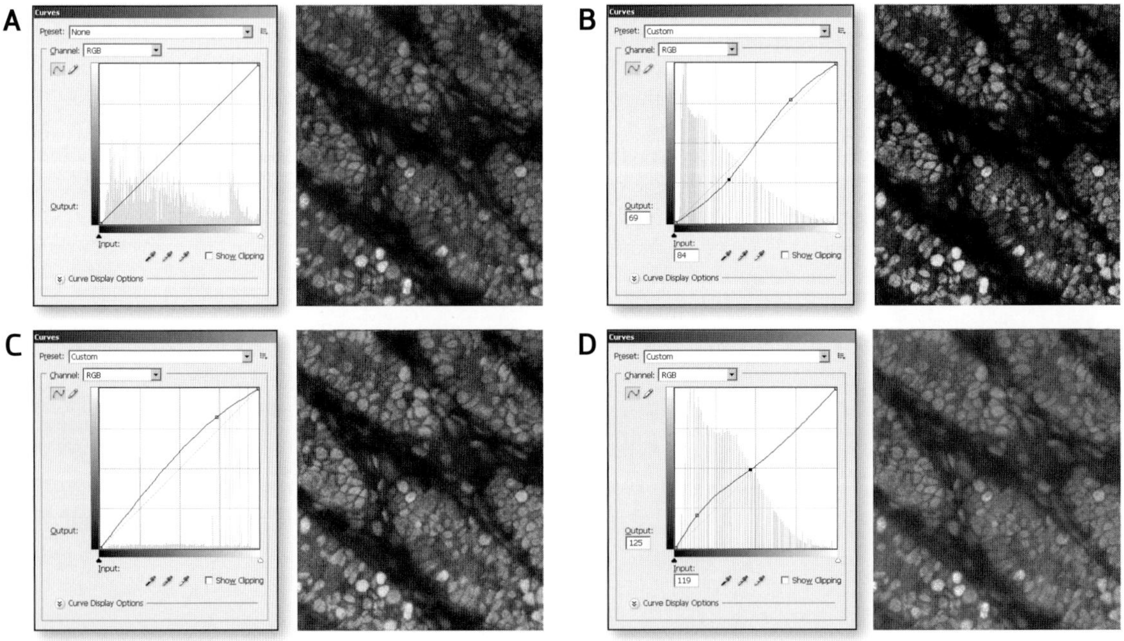

FIGURE 7.23 Changes in gamma using the Curves dialog box and the associated changes in the image's tonal range; the original image (**A**).

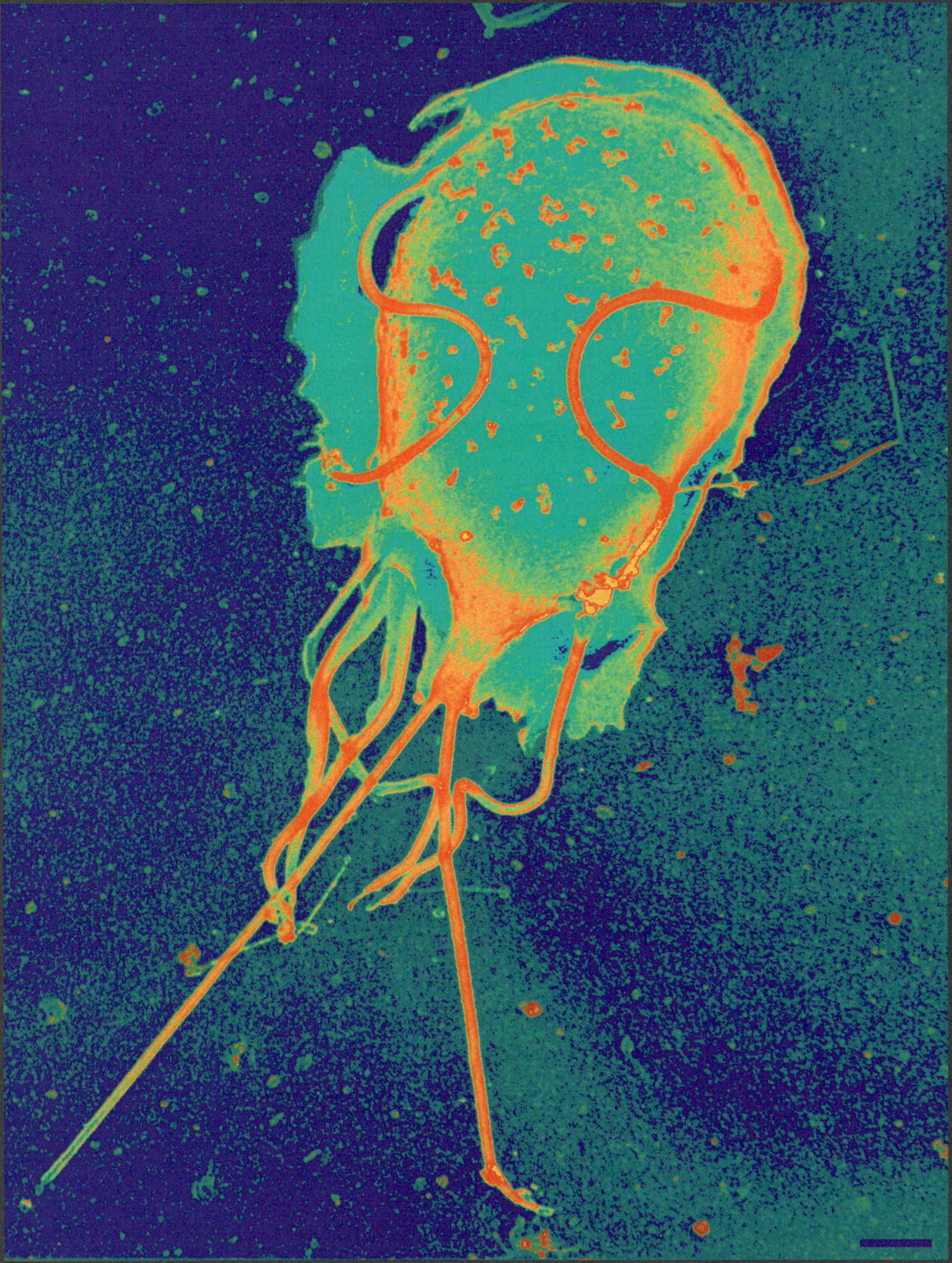

CHAPTER 8

Making Figures/Plates and Conforming to Outputs

THE FINAL DESTINATION for a representative image is for a figure that is used in posters, prints, laptop presentations, electronic documents, a publication, or a Web page. These outputs serve not only as a means to present visual data, but also as a way to convey information about those who performed the research: High-quality images communicate "high-quality" workgroups. If the images appear with suboptimal quality, that communicates something about the group that performed the research as well.

Thus, it is critical to retain or increase pixel resolutions of images that make up figures. This is accomplished in one of two ways:

- Resample images that make up figures at publication resolutions (300–600 ppi) to bring them up to "gold standards." These figures can then be resampled again, when necessary, for appropriate outputs.
- Keep figures at original resolutions, and then resample for relevant outputs.

The use of one or the other method often depends on the kind of specimen and the way in which it was acquired. Electrophoretic samples and low-resolution images can be resampled to publication resolutions so that lettering and symbols are at adequate pixel resolutions. Images from high-resolution cameras are best retained at original resolutions,

Dorsal surface of *Giardia* trophozoite indirectly immunolabeled for cyst wall antigen using 15 nm colloidal gold (yellow-orange spots). Image psuedocolored and prepared for CMYK reproduction in Adobe Photoshop CS3 Extended (Adobe Systems Incorporated, San Jose, CA). Scale bar = 1 micron. *Photo from the late Stanely Erlansen, Ph.D.*

even when file sizes are large, to reduce the number of times images are resampled.

By using these methods and then using correct practices when producing outputs, superb figures will communicate a clear message about your workgroup.

Making a Figure or Plate

The two methods for laying out a figure are called the Retain Resolution Method (for retaining original resolutions of images) and the Publication Resolution Method (for resampling images to publication resolutions). For either method, layout can be accomplished by using automated or manual steps, depending on the nature of the images and the version of Photoshop:

- Manual methods are used when images are mixed with vector graphics and are at varying pixel resolutions.
- Manual methods may have to be used for either the Retain Resolution Method or the Publication Resolution Method when using pre-CS versions of Photoshop.
- Automation for the Retain Resolution Method is used when all images are at identical pixel resolutions.

However, the method that is chosen can also be based on the working habits of the individual:

- If it is easiest to determine cropping and arrangement of images when all images are placed on a page, the Publication Resolution Method is ideal.
- If it makes more sense to predetermine the arrangement of images, the Retain Resolution Method is more appropriate.

After a method is chosen and steps are taken to lay out a figure, additional steps may be necessary. These include the following:

- Performing further image alignment, including lining up lanes for electrophoretic samples.
- Matching image backgrounds if it wasn't done earlier. Image matching generally requires an optical density match of background areas. Color matching is done with individual images in earlier steps (see Chapter 7, "Color Corrections and Final Steps").
- Adding lettering, symbols, and insets. For specimens in the area of molecular biology, these additions require lettering at angles, tic marks, and symbols to indicate groupings of data.

When the figure is completed, two possible additional steps may be needed but are *not* described in this chapter—changing the bit depth and CMYK conversion:

- Bit depths must be changed to 8 bits (grayscale) or 8-bits/channel (color) when they are saved for those outputs that require it. When working on the figure, bit depth is kept at 16-bits/channel in CS versions of Photoshop.
- CMYK conversion can be done after all images are assembled, or the CMYK conversion can have occurred in an earlier step (see Chapter 7 for color conversion to CMYK). Figures and stand-alone images do not have to be converted to CMYK when that step is taken by the publisher, but it is highly encouraged in this book.

To begin the figure assembly process, the two layout methods are described in the following sections.

Retain Resolution Method for Figures: Automated

● **More:** *A script specifically made to retain resolutions for figures can be downloaded from www.quickphotoshop.com.*

Use the Retain Resolution Method whenever possible so that intrinsic pixel resolutions of images are retained (although for most publications the resolution will need to be changed to varying output resolutions, depending on the publisher's requirements). This method is used most of the time because images for figures generally come from the same source at identical pixel resolutions, and when automated, it simplifies layout.

1. Place all image files that are included in a single figure within a folder. Give the folder an appropriate name.
2. Automate figure production by choosing File > Automate > Contact Sheet II (**Figure 8.1**, next page).
3. In the dialog box, click Browse to navigate to the folder containing the images.
4. In the Document area, choose Pixels from the Units menu. Set the Width and Height to a multiple of a single image plus an additional 20 pixels for the border. For example, if you want two images side by side, multiply the width of the first image (in pixels) by 2 and then add 20 pixels (or another user-determined amount).

   In this instance, the Resolution setting is not used, so any numeric value is ignored.
5. Choose an appropriate setting from the Mode menu.

■ **Note:** *If the pixel dimensions of a single image are unknown, click Cancel in the Contact Sheet II dialog box, open an image that makes up the figure, and then select Image > Image Size to see how many pixels compose the image in height and width.*

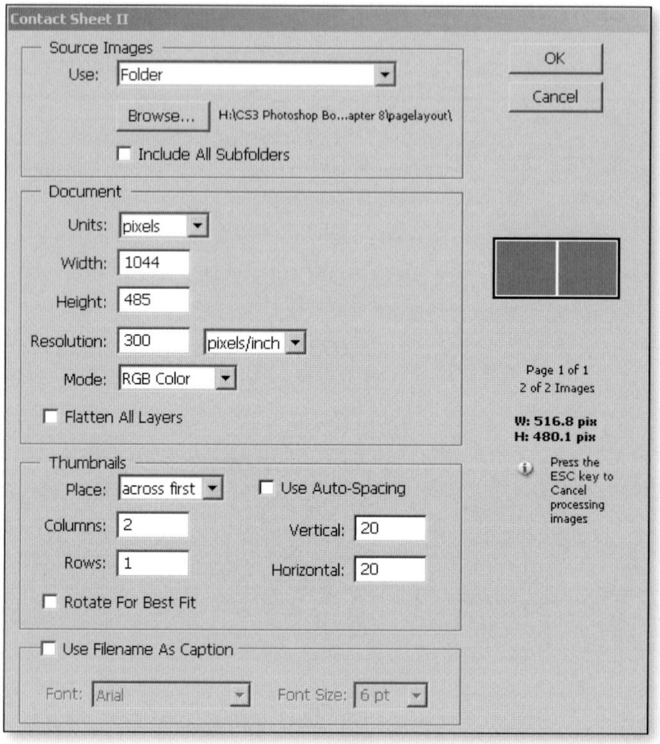

FIGURE 8.1 The Contact Sheet II dialog box.

6. In the Thumbnails area, deselect Use Auto-Spacing and enter 20 for the Horizontal and/or Vertical value (or a user-determined value).
7. Enter values in the Columns and Rows fields.
8. Deselect Use Filename as Caption to prevent filenames from appearing below each image.
9. Click OK. A compound figure will be assembled.

   Double-check image resolutions by choosing Show > Document Dimensions from the status menu at the bottom of the image window.

   If the resolution is incorrect, the wrong values were entered in the Contact Sheet II dialog box. Use a calculator to determine the correct values, or iteratively add to values until the correct resolution results.
10. Proceed to the section "Add Lettering to Figures" later in this chapter.

Retain Resolution Method: Manual

Earlier versions of Photoshop do not provide a means to deselect Auto-Spacing in the Contact Sheet II dialog box, resulting in unpredictable resolutions. More times than not, the resolutions are slightly resampled to larger or smaller dimensions. Also, the automated method does not preserve layers (though this is often unimportant because the layers should have been saved with the individual images that make up the figure). In either case, a manual method needs to be used.

1. Open the first image to be included in a figure and decide whether other images will be added below or beside the first one.
2. Make sure the background is pure white before adding extra space to accommodate additional images for the figure. Press D to reset foreground and background colors to their defaults (black and white).
3. Open the Canvas Size dialog box (Image > Canvas Size) to add extra white space to the first image (**Figure 8.2**, left).
4. Change the Width and Height units to Pixels.
5. Multiply the number of pixels by the number of images you want to add in each direction (e.g., if you want to add a second image below the first, multiply the Height value by 2). Add an additional 20 pixels for the space in between the images.
6. Click the square in the Anchor grid to show which part of the new canvas will be occupied by the existing image. Click OK.
7. Press Ctrl/Command+minus (–) to zoom out and see the entire canvas with the additional white space (**Figure 8.2**, center).
8. If the first image is grayscale and additional images are in color, change the mode to RGB Color by choosing Image > Mode > RGB Color.
9. Using the Move tool, drag images one by one to the existing document (**Figure 8.2**, right).

   Before dragging layered images into the document, the layers must be linked. Select the top layer in each image, then Shift-click the bottom layer to select all layers. Click the Link Layers button (its icon is a chain) at the bottom of the Layers palette. Then drag the layered image into the document.

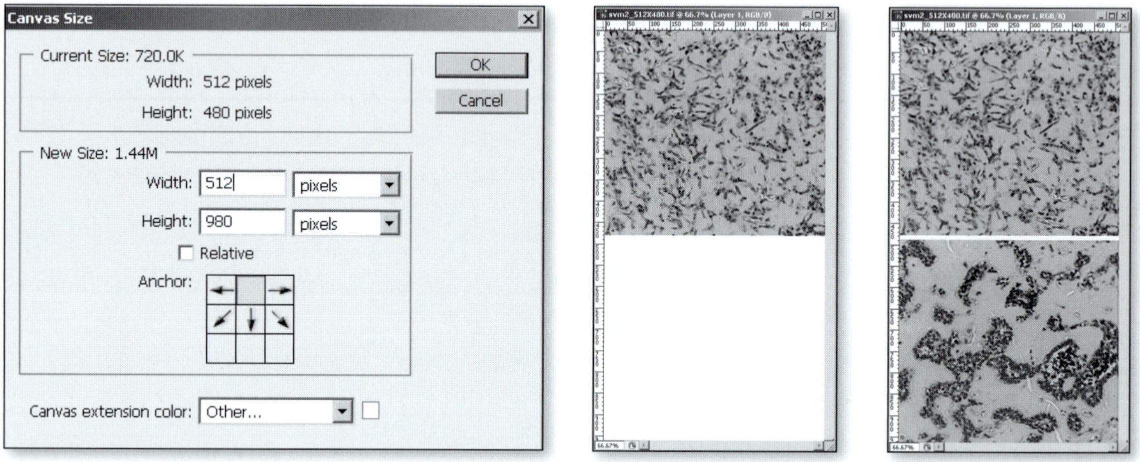

FIGURE 8.2 Canvas Size dialog box (left) with additional white space added to the image (center) and an additional image placed (right).

To reduce the clutter of too many layers, organize layers in groups:

1. Select layers you want to group.
2. Press Ctrl/Command+G to collect the selected layers into a group, which is indicated by a folder. Give this group a name, if desired. To view individual layers in the group, click the triangle to the left of the folder icon.
3. Proceed to the section "Aligning Images" for the remainder of the steps.

Publication Resolution Method: Automated

■ **Note:** *Aliasing artifacts are created when vector graphics are included with the image as opposed to keeping vectors separate from the image. These artifacts are avoided when graphic elements are created in programs like Illustrator or when images are saved with vector layers to PDF. Publications are increasingly accepting Illustrator files but have not yet fully embraced PDF file submission for publication.*

The Publication Resolution Method guarantees enough pixel resolution to adequately resolve lettering and symbols. Resolution, in this instance, is a function of image dimensions when producing output. For publication and poster presentations, the images often need to be enlarged to dimensions that reveal aliasing artifacts along lines, lettering, and other symbols. For that reason, images at resolutions less than 800 or so pixels in either dimension are often upsampled when composing more than 1/4 to 1/2 page dimensions to prevent pixilation of nonaliased vectors.

To ensure that images are at an adequate resolution to prevent the pixilated appearance of graphics and images, a blank page is created at publication resolutions (300 ppi or higher). Images and graphics are then placed on this empty page to make a figure.

1. Place all images for a figure in one folder and give the folder an appropriate name.
2. Follow the procedure described in the section "Retain Resolution Method for Figures: Automated" except for the following changes.
3. Choose Mm or Inches for Units instead of Pixels.
4. Set the Width and Height to 7.5 x 10 inches (190 x 254 mm) as the default dimensions for the image. This size provides a standard "printed area" of a U.S. page and is conveniently the same dimensions as a PowerPoint slide.

   These Height and Width dimensions can be used as a starting point, and then the figure can be resampled to fit any output without significant loss of visual data.

   However, to avoid resampling more than once (when images are placed on the page, they are likely resampled once), set the dimensions according to specific requirements:

   - If the figure is intended for publication, the effective dimensions of the entire figure are based on one or two column widths (unless the figure is intended for the cover). These dimensions are found by referring to the author guidelines for the respective publication.
   - If the figure is intended for electronic submission, the maximum dimensions for a single figure can be found by consulting with the respective agency's rules.
5. Set the resolution to a generic target output resolution that is at or higher than most required output resolutions: 300 ppi. That resolution setting, while higher than necessary for inkjet and laserjet printers, preserves anti-aliased edges on lettering. It can also be the resolution used for electronic submission, as long as the file size is JPEG compressed adequately to fit the file size requirements of the respective publisher, grants agency, or recipient.

■ Note: *If the figure is intended for an inkjet printer, including a poster printer (also an inkjet), the resolution is set to 200, even when advertised resolutions for the printer are much higher. To date, the inherent resolutions of printers, regardless of the diameter of sprayed dots of ink when using inkjets, lie between 150 and 200 dots per inch. A value of 200 is used to preserve sharp, nonpixilated edges of lettering.*

Or set the (output) resolution of the page according to the required resolutions for the output by the publisher. If the figure is destined for another output, such as a poster printer, set a publication resolution and resample later to change the resolution of the figure to conform it to the other output. See the section "Resample for Output (Image Size)" later in this chapter.

Publication Resolution Method: Manual

When you are unsure about cropping or sizes of images before making a figure, often it is best to assemble all the images on a blank page. This is especially true when working with electrophoretic samples. This method provides a way to manually lay out a figure.

1. Create a new file (File > New) to serve as a template (**Figure 8.3**, left). For the Width, Height, and Resolution settings, refer to step 5 in the section "Publication Resolution Method: Automated"; or set at a nominal resolution of 300 ppi when lettering is not included, and 600 ppi when lettering, symbols, and numbering are included.
2. Add the first image to the new file (template) according to the description in step 9 of "Retain Resolution Method: Manual."
3. Once the first image is added to the page, you will likely need to rescale the image to a height and width that is as large as possible but that will also accommodate the remaining images with borders and white area for text. Determine the width and height of the first image by calculating how many images will fit across and down within the maximum dimension limits for the entire figure, leaving room for at least a 10–20 pixel border (or more) between images/graphics. Alternatively, approximate the dimensions by eye.
4. Rescale the image using the Transform command (Edit > Transform > Scale) (**Figure 8.3**, right). Hold down Shift (to scale proportionally) and drag from the corners (the cursor will change to a double arrow). If the corners are not visible, zoom out (Ctrl/Command+minus [-]), and then enlarge the image window until the Transform rectangle is visible. To accept the new size, double-click within the Transform rectangle or press Enter.

■ **Note:** *As in the procedure for incremental resampling using the Image Size command (see "Resample for Output (Image Size)" later in this chapter), so, too, can rescaling be done by degrees. Rescale by 10% increments by looking at the Info palette to determine the percentage. Between increments, press Enter to accept the Transform.*

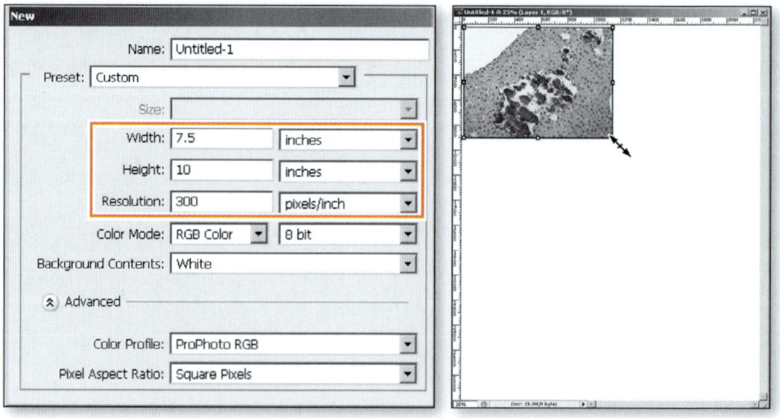

FIGURE 8.3 The New dialog box (left) and the Transform box with a double-arrow cursor.

5. Once the first image is rescaled on the page, additional images will need to be added and then rescaled to match the first image (and, if applicable, subsequent images). Then the images or graphics will need to be aligned with each other.

ALIGNING IMAGES

When using manual methods for making figures, once images are on a page or canvas (and, if necessary, rescaled to match each other) they are moved into rows and columns with a border between images.

1. Choose View > Show > Grid to place a grid over the image (**Figure 8.4**). The grid spacing has been set to 20 pixels to match the image's border. Select Preferences > Guides, Grid, Slices and Count and set Gridline Every to 20 pixels with 1 subdivision.

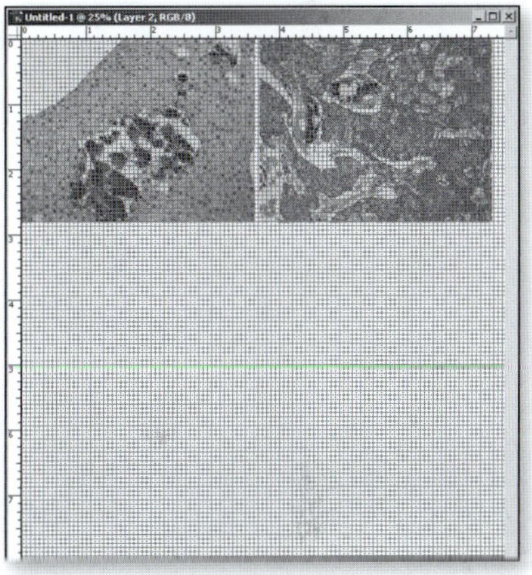

FIGURE 8.4 A grid overlay shown with two aligned images.

2. Align images using the Move tool and gridlines as a visual aid. The image, if not in layers, will snap to the gridline (make sure that View > Snap is checked).

   Because gridlines may not line up with all image borders, it can be difficult to know if one image is separated from another by exactly 20 pixels (or another user-chosen border dimension). To attain a separation of images by 20 pixels (or user-defined distances), place the image that is to be aligned so that the borders touch. Hold down the Shift key and use the arrow key to move the nonaligned image away from the aligned image. Each time the arrow key is pressed, the image moves 10 pixels: Press the arrow key twice and the images are separated by 20 pixels.

3. When images are aligned, crop the image by choosing Image > Trim to delete all but the image area.

▶ **Tip:** *A guide can be dragged from either ruler into the document as an alignment aid.*

LINING UP LANES IN ELECTROPHORETIC SAMPLES

Perfect alignment of lanes isn't always possible because lanes come from different samples and because some substrates (such as SDS-PAGE gels) warp, stretch, and "smile" (become bowed). Alignment is possible by using guides and the Transform command:

1. Using the Move tool, drag the first image of the desired set of lanes from the original image (create a selection with the Marquee tool and include some excess area) onto the template as described earlier in "Publication Resolution Method: Manual."
2. If the grid is visible, hide it. Instead, drag guides from the rulers instead to use as alignment aids (if rulers are not visible, choose View > Rulers). Place the guides by eye so that they pass through the centers of the lanes (**Figure 8.5A**). Determine an average center when aligning a bowed set of lanes across from each other horizontally.
3. Drag the image to be matched onto the template and line up the centers of these lanes with the guides (**Figure 8.5B**).

   If the image is warped so that the lanes do not line up, start by lining up the first lanes on the left to align. (Line up the top lanes when lanes are next to each other.) Then stretch the layer

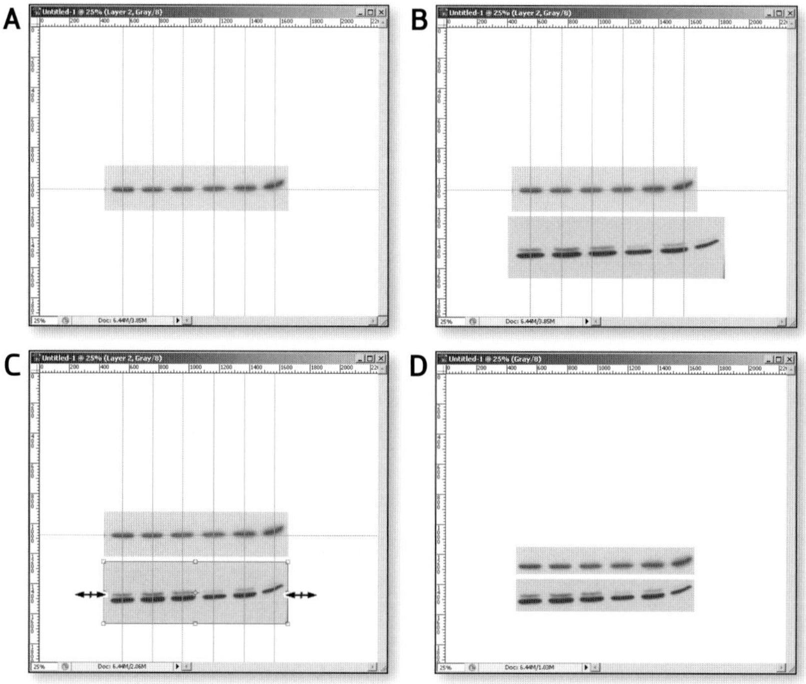

FIGURE 8.5 An electrophoretic sample is shown as an example of using guides and scaling to align images.

containing the bowed lanes in the horizontal or vertical direction with the Transform command (Edit > Transform > Scale) (**Figure 8.5C**). Do not, in this instance, hold down the Shift key to keep scaling proportional: Scaling, in this case, is done to stretch or shrink the image along a single axis.

4. Using the edges of the first image to guide you, trim off excess area from the second image: Select the first image, hold down the Shift key and move the selection down over the second image. Inverse the selection, and press the Delete key (if this doesn't work, the correct layer isn't selected). The final images will be aligned with identical image areas (**Figure 8.5D**).

Matching Backgrounds of Images

As mentioned earlier, the optical density of backgrounds are matched so that they are uniform. If black and white limits were set as described in earlier chapters, this step should be unnecessary. Colors, at this point, should also contain matched backgrounds, assuming earlier steps have been followed.

If, however, no changes have been made to the images, such as what might be true with electrophoretic samples, backgrounds may have to be matched. Subtle changes in backgrounds can also appear even after correction and matching steps have been followed.

Here is a method for matching the optical density of backgrounds:

1. Use the Color Sampler tool to place a color sampler in the background of each image. A maximum of four samplers can be placed in each image. Using the menu in the options bar, be sure to choose a Sample Size of Five by Five Average pixels or greater.
2. The black limit of a black background is 20 (in an 8-bit RGB image), and the white limit of a white background is 240 for publication. These two values are appropriate "set points" to use in the next step.

   For gels the background is a light gray, so the set point is closer to 227 (RGB Color) or 12% (Grayscale). Alternatively, the set point can be determined by measuring the background of an image that appears to be a good match to the original sample.
3. Using Levels, slide the black or white input slider to make the background value darker or brighter; or use the black or white output sliders to reduce darkness and brightness. Adjust the sliders until the readout from the color sampler in the Info palette matches the set point.

Add Lettering to Figures

● **More:** *Download the free supplement "Tools and Functions in Photoshop" from the book's companion Web site at www.peachpit.com/scientificimaging.*

To choose fonts, font sizes, and other lettering-related features, select Window > Character. Some features of the Type tool are described in the downloadable supplement, "Tools and Functions in Photoshop."

The typeface for lettering must be easy to read when reduced in size, so sans serif fonts are preferred. Helvetica and Arial are the most commonly used and requested ones. Courier is requested and preferred as a font for numbers, because all number characters are the same width (monospaced) and align vertically when arranged in columns.

Letters are capitalized unless the convention of a field of study prefers lowercase letters.

Lettering is sometimes placed in a box inside the image, inset from the image edge. It is often placed in a corner where no relevant detail exists in all images unless, by convention, it is placed in a specific corner, depending on the field of study.

Here are the procedures for adding lettering:

■ **Note:** *The font color can be changed in the Character palette for existing text by first selecting the text and then clicking the Text Color box to open the Color Picker.*

1. Choose a font color by changing the foreground color. Press D to set the foreground color to black, and the background color to white. Press X to reverse these colors.

   Click the Foreground Color box to choose a hue. However, publications generally discourage the use of anything but black or white.

2. Choose a font from the Character palette: Helvetica (Macintosh), Arial (Windows), or Courier. To start, set the font size between 12–24 points.

3. Make sure you've selected the top layer in the Layers palette. Otherwise, lettering may be hidden below an image layer.

■ **Note:** *If a specific point size for the font is requested by a publisher, the assumption is that the image is at a specific resolution. When using a method for layout that retains variable resolutions, the font size is also variable. Check the font size of that publication by looking at published figures. Estimate font sizes by eye based on published images.*

4. Choose the Type tool and click within the image where you want to place the text. Type the letter desired (**Figure 8.6**, top).

   If the lettering is too small (so small it can't be seen) or too large, highlight the letter and choose a different font size from the Character palette. The final font size should be readable when the image is zoomed out to the approximate dimensions when printed.

5. Move the lettering into place and allow for some image area on all sides of the letter. To do this, move the cursor away from the text until it turns into the Move tool , and then drag the lettering into place.

6. Drag guides from the rulers to mark the letter's position in both the horizontal and vertical axes. This will aid in aligning other letters (**Figure 8.6**, bottom).

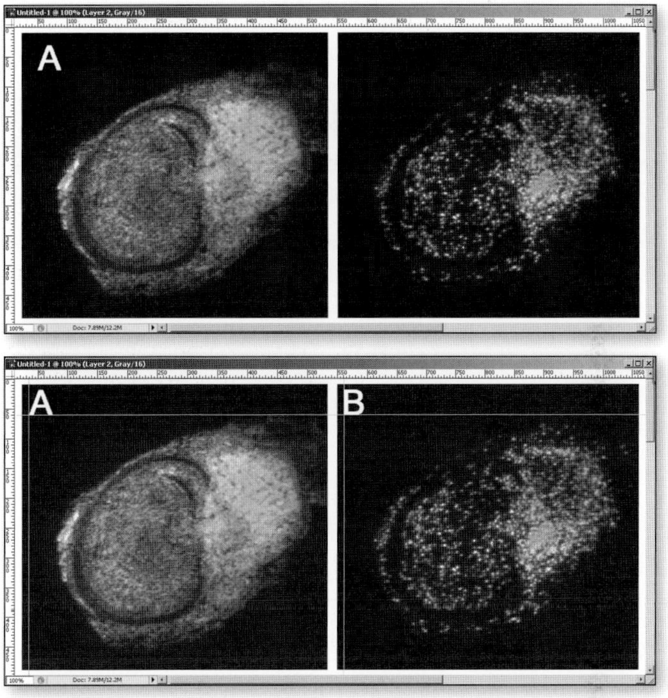

FIGURE 8.6 Using guides as an aid to the alignment of lettering.

7. Click the Commit button (√) on the options bar to complete work on the text and to ensure that the next time the Type tool is selected the text will be placed on a separate layer.

8. Click the Type tool again and repeat steps 5, 6, and 7, lining up each additional letter along the guides. If guides aren't useful for aligning lettering consistently along the vertical and horizontal axes, perform the same technique as when aligning images: Click on the Move tool after the letter is typed, move the lettering to the edge of the image, hold down the Shift key, and use the arrow keys to move the letter 10 pixels. Or, if you are having problems aligning the letters with the guides, use the arrow keys to move the letters by single-pixel increments.

AUGMENTING LETTERING TO MAKE IT VISIBLE

Letters against a background that is both dark and bright can be difficult to read (**Figure 8.7**, left). Or conventions in areas of study may require that boxes be placed behind letters to make them obvious. In either situation, lettering is augmented. Lettering can be bordered with a contrasting color (stroked) or a box can be created, duplicated, and placed behind each letter.

To add a stroke to lettering:

1. Select the text layer in the Layers palette. Choose Layer > Layer Style > Stroke.
2. In the Layer Style dialog box double-click the Color swatch to choose a contrasting color (black if the lettering is white; white if the lettering is black).
3. Adjust the Size slider to increase or decrease the width of the stroke. Zoom in to see the effect on the lettering. Generally, a stroke of 3 is adequate (**Figure 8.7**, right).

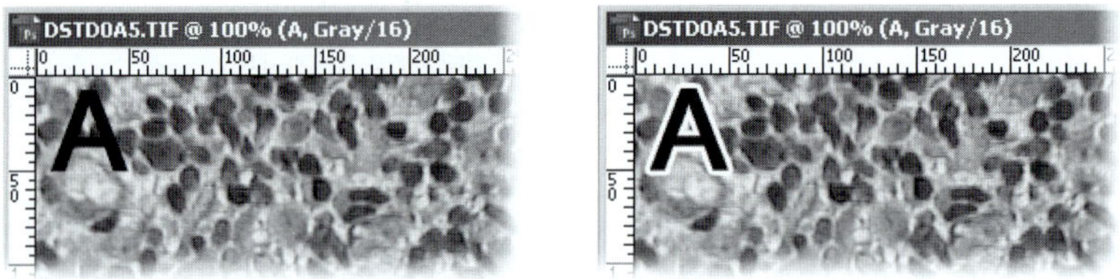

FIGURE 8.7 A single letter with the Stroke Layer effect applied (right).

■ **Note:** *Be sure that layers containing boxes are beneath the layers containing the text they frame.*

To add a box behind lettering:

1. Click on the layer below the bottom text layer. Choose Layer > New > Layer to add a new layer.
2. Choose a contrasting color for the foreground.
3. Using the Rectangle tool, draw a box at the desired size using the grid as a guide.
4. Drag guides to mark the position of the box. This will aid in lining up remaining boxes.
5. Duplicate the layer (Layer > Duplicate Layer) as many times as needed to match the number of text layers.
6. Click the Move tool in the toolbox and move the boxes into place behind the lettering layer by layer using the grid and guides as alignment aids.

Aligning Text, Numbering, and Symbols

Identification of data is required for genomic, proteomic, electrophoretic, and other samples in which experimental results are in columns and rows. Text, numbers, and symbols used for identification of data is often done in a program designed for that purpose, such as Illustrator. However, for convenience, labeling can be done in Photoshop. The challenge is aligning text with columns and rows. Three typical challenges are presented: text at angles, tic marks (dashes), and brackets.

LETTERING AT ANGLES

For CS versions of Photoshop:

1. Choose the Line tool.
2. Click the Paths button in the options bar. This is the middle button in the set of three at the leftmost end of the options bar.
3. Draw a line at 45 degrees in the desired position. To tilt the line to 45 degrees, hold down the Shift key while drawing.
4. Choose a foreground color.
5. Choose the Type tool. Carefully position the Type tool cursor over the line. When the Type cursor changes so that a wavy line appears through the center, click at that position. Zooming in will help you see the change in the cursor.
6. Type the text (**Figure 8.8**, left), and then reposition the text if necessary.
7. If the text is not the right size, change the size in the Character palette (View > Character). Make sure the font is Helvetica or Arial for text and Courier for numbers (or Symbol font for Greek lettering).

For pre-CS versions of Photoshop:

1. Drag guides from the rulers into the image area through the center of the data arranged in columns as an alignment aid (choose View > Ruler if the ruler isn't visible).
2. Create a line at an angle. See steps 1–3 for CS versions of Photoshop.
3. Choose a foreground color.
4. Using the Type tool, click at the top of the line and drag to the bottom of the line to create a rectangular outline. Type in lines of text to identify data using a rough spacing estimate between the lines (**Figure 8.8**, right).
5. If the text is not the right size, change the size in the Character palette (View > Character). Make sure the font is Helvetica or Arial for text and Courier for numbers (or Symbol font for Greek lettering).

FIGURE 8.8 Type set at a 45-degree angle when using CS versions (left) and pre-CS versions of Photoshop (right).

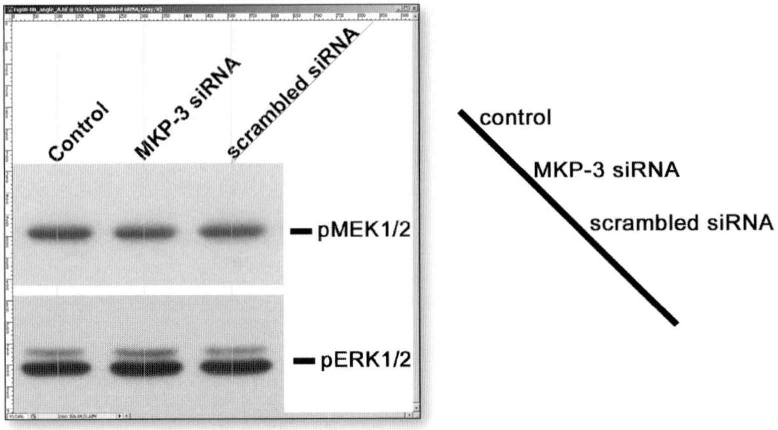

6. Use the spacebar to move text for each line to the edge of the angled line.
7. When done, move the Type tool to the corner of the outline until its cursor turns into a curved arrow. While holding down the Shift key, rotate the text until it is parallel with the horizontal axis of the image. Move the Type tool cursor away from the outline until the cursor becomes the Move tool, and then drag the lettering into place.
8. Expand the distance between the lines of text by changing the line spacing until the lines of text match the distances of the columns. If the lines of text do not match up on the horizontal axis, change the kerning by clicking at the beginning of the line. You can enter higher and lower values manually.
9. When the text is complete, press Enter. In the Layers palette, select the layer of the angled line and delete the layer (Layer > Delete Layer).

TIC MARKS

Tic or dash marks are used with text and numbers, most often as location indicators along images of electrophoretic samples. Here's how to create and align tic marks:

1. Choose a foreground color for the tic marks. Choose the Line tool. Create a short tic mark at the first position.
2. Set the Weight (thickness) of the line in the options bar. Start with a weight of 10 and draw a short line with the Shift key held down. If the tic mark appears to thin or too thick, select Edit > Undo, set the Weight to a different amount, and then redraw the line.

3. Make more than one tic mark of the same size by duplicating the layer in the Layers palette to match the number of tic marks needed (**Figure 8.9**, left). Or, use copy and paste to create the number of tic marks needed.

4. Select the tic mark layers, choose the Move tool, and Shift-drag the tic marks into place, one by one (**Figure 8.9**, right). Holding down the Shift key constrains its movement along the vertical or horizontal axis.

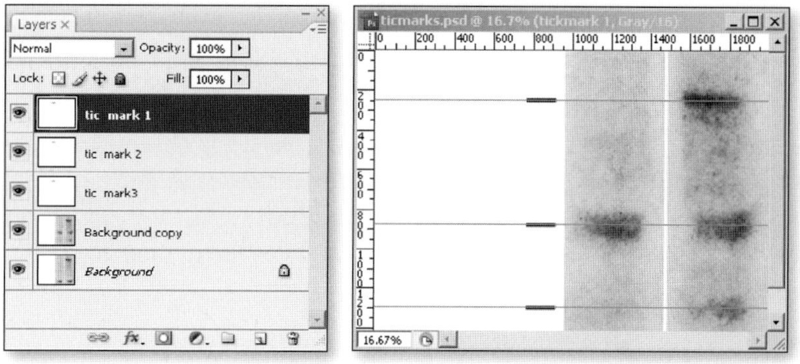

FIGURE 8.9 The Layers palette shows the tic mark layers (left) along with the image to which marks have been included (right; additional white space added to allow for lettering).

BRACKETS FOR TEXT AND NUMBERS

Brackets are made above, below, or alongside text or numbering to indicate a grouping of data. Because bracketed data can extend over several lines of text, the Line tool is used to create brackets rather than the [or] key on the keyboard.

1. Choose a foreground color, and then choose the Line tool. Set the Weight (thickness) of the Line tool as in step 2 in "Tic Marks." While holding down the Shift key, draw a line to the length that includes relevant data entries.

2. Draw orthogonal lines at either end of the first line: To make the lines start and end at the desired length, drag guides from the rulers. Set the first guide along the length of the drawn line. Set the second guide at the desired length of the orthogonal lines. When drawing the orthogonal lines with the Shift key held down, the lines will automatically start and stop at the guidelines.

Flattening Text and Line Layers into Single Layers

The number of layers created by adding text and lines can clutter the Layers palette. To reduce the number to a manageable amount, layers can be merged into a single layer. By doing so, the lettering will no longer be in vectors (lettering is not scalable and can appear blurred when enlarged), but 300 dpi or greater resolution images are rarely enlarged to the degree in which lettering is compromised.

To merge all text or line layers into a single layer:

1. Click the eye icons in the Layers palette to hide all but the text or line layers (eye icons disappear).
2. From the Layers palette menu, choose Merge Visible.

Symbols, Shapes, and Arrows

● **More:** *For a collection of arrowheads, open arrowheads, asterisks, and other symbols, download the Symbols.psd layered file from www.peachpit.com/scientificimaging.*

The addition of symbols (including arrows) and shapes aids in drawing attention to the relevant parts of the image. While Photoshop does not have symbols commonly used in science, the essential symbols can be made.

The creation of arrows, circles, and boxes is discussed here with an additional method provided for open boxes and circles that is easy to do in Photoshop.

To create arrows:

1. Set the foreground to the desired color.
2. Choose the Line tool. In the options bar, select the Weight (thickness) of the arrow by starting with a weight of 10 points (this can be changed later). Adjacent to the Weight box, click the down arrow to reveal the Arrowheads options (**Figure 8.10**).

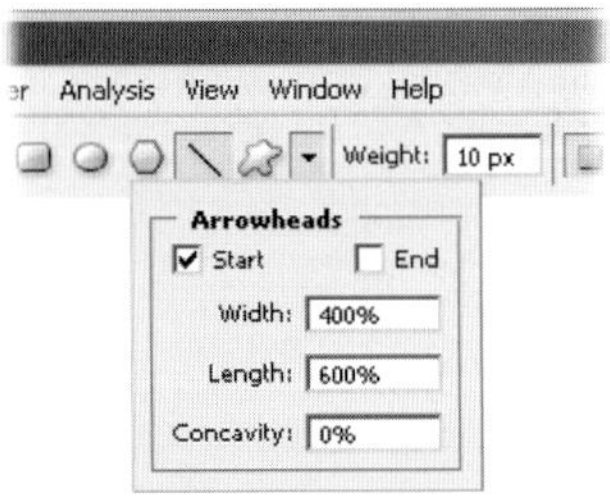

FIGURE 8.10 Arrowheads options.

3. Select the Start or End check box depending on where the arrowhead should be on the line.
4. Select a Width and Length for the arrowhead. Suggested values are 400% for the Width and 600% for the Length.
5. Draw an arrow at the desired position on the image. Hold down the Shift key while drawing the arrow to constrain the angles to 45-degree increments.
6. If the arrow is drawn over bright and dark areas of the image (making the arrow difficult to see), stroke the edge of the arrow (see "Augmenting Lettering to Make It Visible" earlier in this chapter).
7. Duplicate the arrow layer to create more arrows at the same length and angle. To do so choose Layer > Duplicate Layer for as many arrows as desired. With the Move tool, drag each arrow to its desired position.

To create open circles and boxes:

1. Drag guides into the document window to define the edges of the open circle or box.
2. Choose Layer > New > Layer to create a new layer.
3. Choose the Pencil tool.
4. In the options bar, click the brush thumbnail to open the Brush Preset Picker, and choose a Master Diameter for a round, hard-edged brush tip (**Figure 8.11**, top left). The diameter is greater than one pixel for publication purposes and generally between 3 and 15, depending on the pixel resolution of the image.

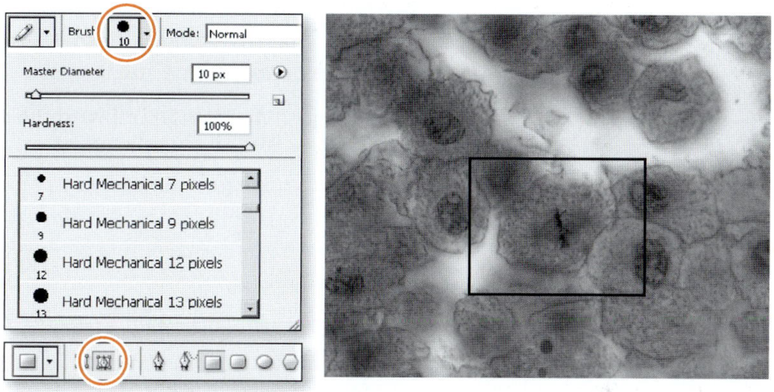

FIGURE 8.11 Top left: The Brush tool options bar, showing the Brush Preset Picker (circled); bottom left: the Shape tool options bar, showing the Paths button (circled). The box is shown on the image (right).

5. Choose the Rectangle or Ellipse tool. Click the Paths button in the options bar (**Figure 8.11**, bottom left).
6. Draw a rectangle or ellipse at the desired size. To draw a square or circle, hold down the Shift key while drawing.
7. Right-click/Control-click inside the shape and choose Stroke Path.

   The Stroke Path dialog box appears. Choose Pencil from the menu.
8. If the diameter of the stroke is too wide or narrow, choose Edit > Undo, change the diameter of the Brush, and choose the Stroke Path command again (**Figure 8.11**, right).

An easy method for creating open circles and boxes follows:

1. Select Layer > New > Layer to create a new layer.
2. Click the Marquee tool and choose the rectangle or ellipse shape. Draw a selection at the desired size. To draw a square or circle, hold down the Shift key while drawing.

■ **Note:** *The "easy method" for creating open circles and boxes does not create a scalable, vector layer.*

3. Select Edit > Stroke to stroke the selection. In the Stroke dialog box, choose the Width (diameter) of the line that will be traced along the selection (generally at 3 pixels or greater) and the color.
4. Undo the stroke if the diameter of the stroke is too wide or narrow (Edit > Undo), and repeat step 3 with a new stroke width.

Working with Graphs

Graphs, drawings, and, possibly tables (graphics) may require additional work. Most often, additional steps include:

- Changing colors within bars that make up a bar graph or inserting textures.
- Adding and eliminating text, lines, and symbols.

Bar graphs may contain unprintable colors, or entire graphs may have to be converted to grayscale for publication requirements. In the former instance printer-friendly colors can be created in Photoshop, and in the latter instance textures or solid tones of white-to-black can replace existing bars when graphing programs cannot be easily used for that purpose.

Adding text was described earlier in this chapter. But the elimination of text can also be done in Photoshop by drawing a selection around relevant elements, and then pressing the Delete key or filling the selection with white (select Edit > Fill and then choose white from the Use drop-down menu). The Eraser tool can also be used to remove text.

● **More:** *Additions to bars in graphs can be done via methods that can be found at www.peachpit.com/scientificimaging.*

It is assumed that the white backgrounds of graphics are 100% white (at 255 on the 8-bit scale) and 0% black (see "Problem Images" in Chapter 6). Check these values against readouts in the Info palette to be sure.

Image Insets

Parts of the image may contain details that are best viewed at a high magnification. Insets are used for this purpose (**Figure 8.12**). They are placed at the corners of images as larger fields of view. To create insets, follow these steps:

1. Make a marquee selection around the desired area. To make this easier, place guides around that part of the image and draw the selection within the guides.

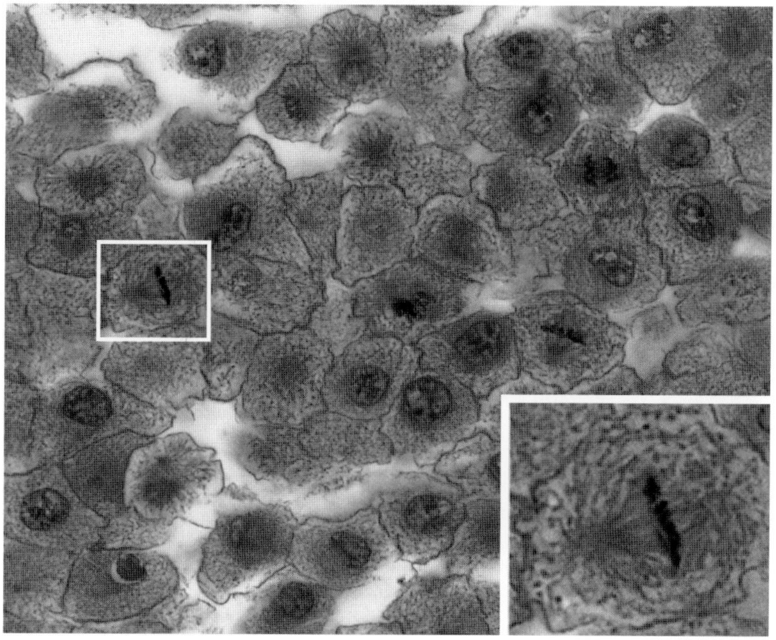

FIGURE 8.12 An image with an inset at a high magnification to show details.

2. Copy the selected area (Edit > Copy) and paste (Edit > Paste) it to make an new inset layer above the existing layer.
3. Select the Background layer and choose Layer > Duplicate Layer and click OK . On this layer choose Select > Reselect and stroke the selection to indicate the part of the image from which the inset was taken (see the steps to create open circles and boxes in the section "Symbols, Shapes, and Arrows" for a description).
4. Select the inset layer in the Layers palette. Choose the Move tool and drag the inset to an empty or irrelevant corner of the larger field of view image. Line up the outer edges.
5. Using the Transform command (Edit > Transform > Scale), enlarge the inset layer to the desired magnification. Hold down the Shift key when rescaling to retain the proportions. If you rescale the image from the corner farthest from the edge, the inset will be enlarged and the outer edges will remain aligned. Enlarge the image until the inset interferes with relevant features in the larger view image below it.

   If the inset does not adequately magnify salient features, undo the inset steps and repeat the steps using a smaller initial selection.
6. Stroke the edge of the inset layer (Layer > Layer Style > Stroke), choosing white for the color and Outside for the Position.

Resample for Output (Image Size)

After figures or stand-alone images have gone through correction and conformance steps, some additional steps may be required before they are ready for each kind of output. The pixel dimensions and output *resolution* (pixels per inch or millimeters) of the image or figure may or may not need to be increased or decreased, depending on its destination.

▶ **Warning:** *Avoid resampling and resharpening until an image is part of a figure. This eliminates potential loss of visual data in the event that either (or both) of these alterations occur more than once. When images are stand-alone figures, they are sharpened, gamma-altered, and appropriately resampled (or not).*

■ **Note:** *Dots are clearly seen when using a magnifying glass to examine publications and laser printer outputs: Inkjets, in particular, overlap dots to make them indistinguishable.*

■ **Note:** *Resolution settings for images placed in Illustrator follow the recommendations provided in Table 8.1.*

The unit of measurement for output resolution is in pixels per a spatial unit because the assumption is that the output will be hard copy. The unit of measurement may also be indicated as *dots* per inch. This is a convention used in the printing industry because pixels from a digital image are resampled into individual dots, the element that makes up an image on paper. More than twice the number of pixels is required to create the dots, because the current limit of dots on a printed page is 150 dpi.

Table 8.1 indicates generic, target settings when using the Publication Resolution Method for output. The recommended settings keep resolutions at a level in which embedded lettering remains sharp and unpixilated (embedded lettering isn't retained as vectors). Figures created using that method can be resampled again according to the settings in Table 8.1. The output resolutions in this table also include all other figures and stand-alone images. A small number of publishers require that resolution settings remain at inherent resolutions: Check the author guidelines for publication requirements.

TABLE 8.1 Output Resolution Settings

PUBLICATION: IMAGES ONLY	PUBLICATION: IMAGES AND TEXT	PUBLICATION: GRAPHICS	POSTER PRINTERS	INKJET/ LASERJET	DYE SUBLIMATION, PHOTOGRAPHIC PRINTERS	MICROSOFT, ACROBAT	VIDEO, WEB
300–500 ppi: Check guidelines	600 ppi	1200 ppi	If resampling, 200 ppi: Set dimensions	Don't resample: Change dimensions only	Manufacturer recommendations	200 ppi, set dimensions and compress file	Set number of pixels in *x* and *y*

The instances in which resampling is not required may appear counterintuitive in the case of inkjet printers, which are advertised at much higher resolutions. As mentioned earlier, the true resolution of these printers is approximately 200 dpi. If a figure is at a low resolution and is enlarged more than two times to fit on a poster, resampling may produce better results. With newer, high-resolution cameras, that is not often the case.

Ultimately, the aim is to avoid resampling whenever possible because it may introduce blurring. Steps can be taken when resampling is necessary to reduce blurring and retain as much visual information as possible: The extent of the change in pixel resolution (whether increasing the number of pixels or decreasing them) can be done in increments. Neighboring pixels are then averaged with greater accuracy.

Also, the algorithms used for resampling can be carefully selected in the command used: Image > Image Size. The correct selection will optimize the quality:

- Choose Bicubic Smoother for upsampling.
- Choose Bicubic Sharper for downsampling.
- Choose Nearest Neighbor for graphics.

Here are the steps for resampling an image on an incremental basis:

1. Mathematically determine the percentage increase or decrease in the image size by dividing one dimension (width or height in pixels) into the desired dimension. To find the desired pixel dimension, choose Image > Image Size, enter values for the output, and determine the increase or decrease in pixels in *x* and *y*. If the image size increases by more than 10 percent, resample the image by that percentage.
2. In the Pixel Dimensions area of the Image Size dialog box, choose Percent from the menu. Enter a 10 percent difference (e.g., to increase the image size, enter 110 percent, as in **Figure 8.13**; to decrease the image size, enter 90 percent).
3. Repeat this process until the resampling amount is less than 10 percent. Change the Pixel Dimensions units to Pixels and enter the final values for the last iteration of resampling.

■ **Note:** *A script for resampling by 10 percent increments is available for download from www.quickphotoshop.com.*

Generic resolutions for specific outputs are indicated in Table 8.1. Specific resolutions can be found in author guidelines for publications or obtained from manufacturers' recommendations.

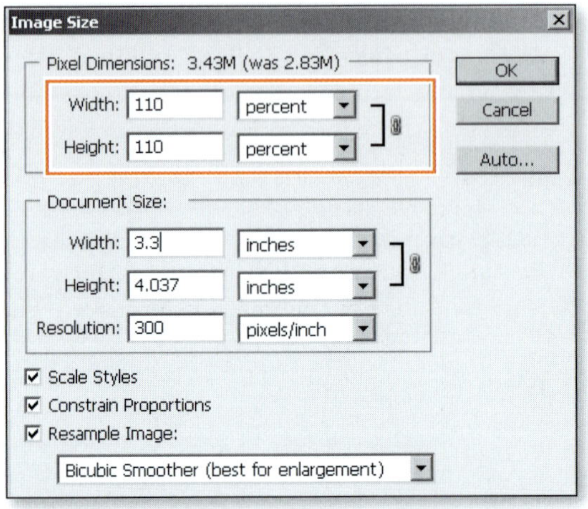

FIGURE 8.13 The Image Size dialog box: resampling by incremental percentages.

Resampling to resolutions indicated (e.g., 300 dpi) by page layout programs like Illustrator and PowerPoint (when used as a layout program for poster production) is done after all the images are laid out at the desired dimensions. Once those dimensions are known and the layout is finalized, resampling is done to fit the indicated dimensions. Until then, a duplicate image is used for placement and scaling purposes.

Sharpening, Gamma, CMYK Color, and Saving Figures

Remaining steps for figures can include sharpening, gamma adjustment, a change in mode to CMYK Color, and saving the final, optimized figure. All the methods for each of the corrections were discussed in Chapters 6 and 7. Figure corrections can be applied to images on each layer, or the layers that contain images can be flattened into a single layer. The gamma and sharpening corrections can then be applied to the single layer. CMYK conversion includes all layers.

● **More:** *For information on saving and archiving images in PSD or TIFF format (which applies also to figures) download the free document, "Scale Bars and Options for Input and Output" from www.peachpit.com/scientificimaging.*

Figures and stand-alone images are likely to be saved in one of three compressed formats: JPEG, PNG, and Adobe PDF. A fourth choice is given by publishers for saving as EPS (Encapsulated PostScript) files at full resolution. Each is discussed here:

- **JPEG, PNG.** Saving as a JPEG or PNG for Microsoft products is crucial for smooth operation of the software: Files with a large file size that are saved as TIFF files can overload the capacity of the software. To avoid lossy compression, save figures and images as PNG files. These can be inserted into Word, PowerPoint, and

Publisher documents, and have the added benefit of displaying similarly on different monitors when used with these programs.

▶ **Warning:** *The operative word is "inserted" when describing how images are included not just in Microsoft products, but in any software. Do not cut/copy and paste. This will likely result in a low-resolution image when copied and pasted between different software manufacturers.*

Saving as PNG is straightforward. A prompt concerning whether or not the image is interlaced (parts of the image appear when opening on a Web site before the entire image) is the only additional step. Unless the destination is for the Web, choose None. When saving as a JPEG, use the following procedure:

1. Select File > Save As. Choose JPEG from the Format menu. The JPEG Options dialog box appears.
2. Set the Quality to Maximum (12). This will result in the least compression, resulting in an image indistinguishable from the original to the eye. If the file size is still too large, reduce the quality as much as possible without introducing artifacts into the image.

- **PDF.** For PDF files, figures can be included with a document or submitted as separate, stand-alone files; or PDF files can be created after images have been included in a document. For stand-alone images, follow the requirements for file size limitations, if any. For stand-alone PDF files, JPEG compression is used. Use the same Save As procedure as that for JPEG, described earlier. In Photoshop, stand-alone PDF files are saved as Photoshop PDF files.
- **EPS.** EPS files are typically created from drawing programs to preserve vectors or when graphics are made into PDF files and then saved in the EPS format. If, however, a Photoshop file contains a significant amount of text and shape material, and layers are preserved as vector layers (versus having been rasterized), the image is best saved as EPS. This format preserves vectors, and as a result, text retains its sharp edges. Use the Save As option in the File menu. The EPS format does not compress the image.

Output

After the images are optimized and figures are completed, the digital images are ready for output devices and other software programs. The focus throughout the previous chapters has been primarily toward publication, because it is the output that requires the highest resolution and quality. However, before publishing—or when the final aim is a report (electronic document)—several other outputs can be used: Images and figures are often printed to get an idea of how they will appear, posters are made for meetings before publication, laptop presentations are made, and electronic documents are produced. For those images that compose a video animation, a format and CODEC (compression/decompression utility) is determined.

● **More:** *For information about preparing documents for onscreen uses such as projection, video animation, and Web publishing, download "Scale Bars and Options for Input and Output" from www.peachpit.com/scientificimaging.*

Each output has specific requirements not only for images, but for color management, the treatment of fonts, and other special considerations. Outputs are divided into six categories: inkjet printing (including poster printing), laser printing, laptop projection, electronic documents, video animations and Web pages.

Inkjet Printing

Inkjet printing is divided into two categories:

- Poster printing using either PowerPoint or Illustrator for layout
- Making an image on paper to provide examples or representations of images, or making a *proof*: a way to get a good idea of how images will appear when they are published.

POSTER PRINTING FROM POWERPOINT

Although PowerPoint wasn't exactly intended for poster layout and production, it is often used. PowerPoint is accepted by agencies that provide poster printing services, but color matching may be more of a challenge because this program was never intended to take control of colors used when printing. Also, the colors that are viewed on the monitor in PowerPoint are limited, so the intensity of the "real" colors are only viewed correctly when they are within that limited range (with the exception of pure blue to blue-violet hues, which are all difficult hues to reproduce at viewed intensities on a monitor). In PowerPoint, as well as in colorized darkfield images, saturated colors are the rule, not the exception.

Gradients for backgrounds can also present challenges when creating a poster. Gradients require far more of an inkjet printer's internal memory than do solid colors, which can affect the reproduction of images. When memory runs thin, images can become pixilated, leading to the conclusion that it must be the resolution of the images causing the pixilation. This problem can be confirmed by printing the image separately from the poster.

■ **Note:** *The setting of 72 dpi is a legacy screen resolution, and its designation is an alert to inform users of a low resolution: In the context of images derived from digital cameras, 72 dpi is essentially a meaningless designation because the important quantity when speaking of resolution is the number of pixels in x and y, not the output resolution of 72 dpi.*

The problem of resolution is often lamented when creating posters. Most of the problems are also the result of copying and pasting from one manufacturer's program to another or of saving files as TIFFs or JPEGs at low resolutions, often at a default setting of 72 dpi (see the accompanying note). The instructions provided in Chapter 4, "Getting the Best Input," overcome the problems of low resolution and associated pixilation with charts, tables, graphs, and so on.

Fonts can also present problems when the fonts chosen were not TrueType fonts (a digital font description developed by Apple Computer so that representations of the font can be seen on the computer screen while vector qualities are communicated to devices). It is best to limit font styles only to TrueType; otherwise, bullets can change to other symbols along with other inexplicable font replacements when printed. It is also best to limit fonts for figure captions to Arial or Helvetica, numbers used in tables to Courier, and body text to Times New Roman or another TrueType serif font.

Here are some tips when using PowerPoint to create posters:

- **Colors and background gradients.** Use nonsaturated colors to match colors more closely to the monitor. Expect that blue range colors will reproduce darker than what appears onscreen. Do not use gradients for backgrounds.
- **Fonts.** If nonstandard fonts are used, change to TrueType by selecting Format > Replace Fonts. From the Replace menu select each font you need to replace with a TrueType font (designated by a double T icon in Windows).
- **Saving.** Choose File > Save As and embed all fonts into the document, so that the computer on which the poster is printed (or projected) does not need to search for each font when displaying and printing. In the Save As dialog box, choose Embed TrueType Fonts from the Tools menu.
- **Page Size (File > Page Setup).** The page size for the document is limited, at this writing, to 56 inches. When either dimension exceeds 56 inches, make the page size at one-half the dimensions and ask the poster printing agency to double the size when printing. This will not result in a perceivable loss of resolution.
- **Image type.** As mentioned earlier, the image type that works most efficiently in PowerPoint is the JPEG (at Maximum resolution settings) or PNG format. Check with the poster printing agency for its requirements in case TIFF and EPS files are required.

POSTER PRINTING FROM ILLUSTRATOR

Illustrator offers several advantages over PowerPoint:

- Colors are managed, thus the likelihood that colors match is greater (except for the blue to blue-violet range, which prints darker).
- High-resolution TIFF and EPS files can be used.
- Exact placement and alignment of images, graphics, and text are easier to accomplish.
- Zooming can be accomplished as in Photoshop without having to use a menu.
- More options are provided for spacing and placement of text.

The learning curve for Illustrator is greater than the short amount of time that users normally set aside to create a poster, so it is wise to start early when deciding to use Illustrator instead of PowerPoint to create posters.

Beginning users generally make a few notable mistakes, both with the text and the means through which images are included in the poster. It is critical that images be included in the correct way, or the computer may slow down due to memory issues, especially when too many images at high resolutions are included. Some important considerations for creating posters in Illustrator are:

- Once a new file is open with desired poster dimensions, *Place* images on the artboard for the poster (File > Place). Do *not* copy and paste or open the image so that it becomes a part of the poster (embedded).
- Enlarge and reduce the dimensions of the images while holding down the Shift key to keep proportions the same in *x* and *y*.
- When images are at the desired dimensions and the layout is complete, resample images in Photoshop to these dimensions using the Image Size dialog box. For printing to posters, the resolutions do not need to be set except when the poster printing agency requires it. Only resolutions at less than 150 dpi after dimensions are set need to be resampled, according to methods described earlier in this chapter.
- Include the images along with the Illustrator file when submitting the poster to the poster printing agency. Because the files were placed, the images on the page are in effect virtual images, and each virtual image serves as a placeholder.

When these considerations are followed when dealing with graphics that have been made into image files using methods provided in Chapter 4, pixilation will not occur unless it is a printer memory issue. As in the suggestions given for PowerPoint, it is best to exclude background gradients when making posters, because they are normally the source of memory problems with the printer.

Other mistakes that are made include the problem with missing or replaced fonts and color reproduction. Here are the solutions for both:

- **Change Text.** Select all blocks of text by holding down the Shift key and clicking with the Selection tool. Create outlines for text by selecting Type > Create Outlines. The text becomes a collection of shapes, making it, in essence, fontless. This eliminates font problems when submitting the poster to a printing agency.
- **Use RGB Color Mode.** Even though the inks used in an inkjet poster printer are cyan, magenta, and yellow (plus black)—the primary colors for pigments—the printer anticipates RGB Color images. While that may seem counterintuitive, inkjet manufacturers know that images on a computer are worked on in RGB Color, so these manufacturers created conversion tables specific to their devices.

The color settings for Illustrator should be the same as those for Photoshop to maintain color consistency and accuracy. Select Edit > Color Settings to access these settings.

PROOF PRINTING

Proofs are often made on an inkjet printer except when dye sublimation or photographic printers are available. These dye sublimation and photographic printers can be used, as well, to see how images will appear when published. Glossy paper is generally required, and the best results are produced by using manufacturer recommended paper stock. The inkjet printer used for this purpose does not necessarily have to be expensive, but a professional model provides more inks and possibly more options.

● **More:** *To determine the true resolution of the printer, download a test document containing periodically spaced dots from www.peachpit.com/scientificimaging. Print these dots at varying output resolutions. The resolution at which the dots print as seen onscreen indicates the correct output resolution.*

Matching the output resolution in pixels per inch to the printer resolution is not absolutely necessary, though a near-imperceptible amount of blurring may be introduced when there is a mismatch. The degree of blurring usually will not be noticed until an image with matched resolution is placed next to one that is mismatched. Another situation will also produce difficulties when image resolution in pixels per inch is not the same as inkjet resolution: Arrays of periodically spaced dots will print with larger and smaller dots, or dots that are missed entirely.

How an image is printed depends on the version of Photoshop being used. Earlier versions do not provide the options for printing that are available in CS2 and CS3. Printing options are described here for earlier versions of Photoshop as well as for CS2 and CS3.

Legacy versions of Photoshop. If steps presented in this book have been followed, especially in regard to oversaturated colors, calibrated monitors can provide colors that are a fairly close match to the print (when the print is viewed under industry standard lighting at 5000K). When images do not match closely, taking into account that blue to blue-violet ranges print darker than on the screen, use the ICM (Windows) or ColorSync (Mac OS) setting on the inkjet printer as an alternative method for earlier versions of Photoshop.

The ICM or ColorSync method allows the computer to manage colors with the input and output profiles managed by the printer driver. This setting may produce a closer match than using the automated printer management settings (default settings versus custom settings).

CS2 and CS3. The best means for color matching the print to the monitor is to have Photoshop manage the colors. Accurate color matching is achieved when both the monitor and printer have been profiled. Monitor profiling was discussed in Chapter 5. Printer profiling is different from monitor profiling in the following ways:

- Profiles for printers are made for each kind of paper stock, so more than one can exist (though, for efficiency, only a glossy or semi-gloss stock needs to be profiled for standard proofs).
- Profiles need to be made only once for a specific printer/paper combination.
- Profiling tools are more expensive for printers, so profiles can be done by third-party agencies to save on expenses.

Note that printer profiles provided by the manufacturer will not result in accurate colors. Just like monitors, printer to printer variability exists, even when they are the same brand. Instructions for creating profiles for a printer can be found by contacting third-party agencies (search for "printer profiling" on the Web) or included with purchased densitometers for this purpose. Color swatches are printed, and the results are read from a densitometer for profiling. When printing the swatches, all color management is turned off in the Print dialog box, all automatic features are disabled, and the correct paper type is selected.

Once a printer profile is made for a specific paper, there are separate procedures for providing an ideal example of how the image should look and for creating images that resemble press-created pages. Printed images to accompany manuscripts are sent to publishers whenever they are requested. Send the *document* when CMYK conversion will be done by the publisher; send the *proof* when CMYK conversion has already been done.

To print an example of the way the image *should* appear in publication (representative image) as opposed to *how* it will appear (proof):

1. Select File > Print.
2. In the Print dialog box, choose a printer. From the menu at the top of the right side of the dialog box, choose Color Management.
3. In the Print area, select Document.
4. From the Color Handling menu, choose Photoshop Manages Colors.
5. For the Printer Profile, choose the profile that was created for the printer with the specific paper stock (if more than one stock was profiled).
6. Select the Rendering Intent to match the RGB Working space used when working on the image and click Print.

To print a proof of the way the image will appear when published (**Figure 8.14**):

1. Follow steps 1 and 2 in the previous procedure.
2. In the Print area select Proof.

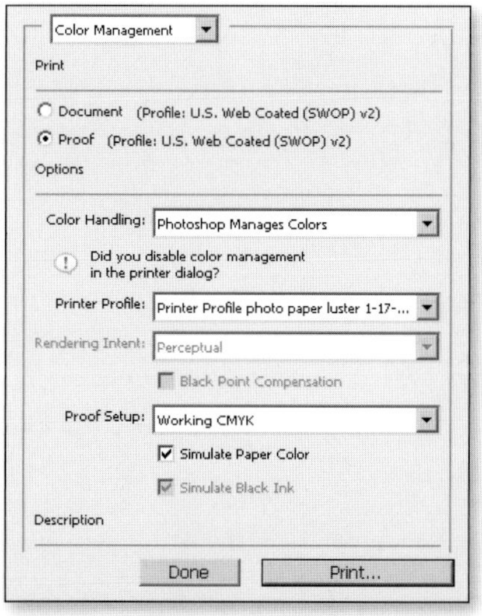

FIGURE 8.14 The right side of the Print dialog box in Photoshop, with Color Management chosen from the top menu. The selected options will produce a proof.

3. For the Printer Profile, choose the profile that was created for the printer with the specific paper stock (if more than one stock was profiled).
4. For the Proof Setup, choose Working CMYK (or if another setup space was created, choose the appropriate space).
5. Select Simulate Paper Color and click Print.

■ **Note:** *The proof showing how an image will appear when published is still an approximation insofar as published images are composed of discrete dots and proofs of blended dots. When Simulate Paper Color is selected, a slightly grayed background color results, mimicking the off-white of coated paper when published.*

After clicking the Print button at the end of either procedure, the Print dialog box closes, and a setup dialog box specific to your hardware opens. Select Properties, Advanced, or Options (the exact command varies from one manufacturer to another) to turn off color management in the printer driver (**Figure 8.15**). Also, select the profiled paper type.

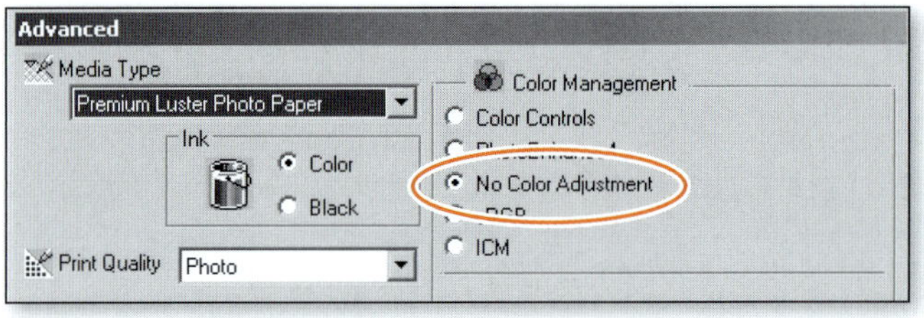

FIGURE 8.15 Choosing No Color Adjustment in the printer's Advanced options.

Laser Printing

Fortunately, with the growing demand for electronic submission, the days of printing mounds of paper from laser printers is fast coming to a close. However, in some instances, laser printers are still used for printing documents with images.

Because most laser printers use discrete dots for printing, resolution and dynamic range suffer. Increasing the resolution of images by upsampling will not necessarily result in improved resolution of detail, because the bottleneck is in the use of dots.

A more frequent problem when using software (mostly Word) for laser printing is in the use of overly compressed JPEG images. Small details are lost when images suffer lossy compression, so when compressing images in Photoshop to the JPEG format for use in Word or PowerPoint, choose the highest quality compression (Maximum, or a setting of 12). As in PowerPoint, do not copy and paste images into Word, because they will likely be downsampled.

The dynamic range of laser printers is typically narrower than that of inkjets. Thus, it is important to keep images within narrow black and white limits. Color images cannot contain out of gamut colors, or they will not reproduce as they appear on a monitor.

Here are some ways to solve laser printing dilemmas when printing images:

- When printing stand-alone images (images not incorporated into the body of the text), print from Acrobat instead of Photoshop: Save Photoshop files as Photoshop PDF files, open them in Acrobat, and then print. Unless the screen frequency of the printer is set to 999 (as high as possible), images will contain fuzzy edges around features.
- Do not use highly compressed JPEG images: Instead, compress them as nonlossy PNG files before inserting them into Word.
- Set colors so that they are CMYK safe. Make sure the gamut of any one color does not exceed the CMYK gamut. Then sharpen images to reveal important details.

■ **Note:** *When inserting images into Word, the size of the image as well as its placement can be controlled by using a Text box. Create a Text box first (Insert > Text Box) and then insert the image into the Text box (Insert > Picture > From File). The image can then be enlarged or reduced to the size of the text box. The image will "float" above the text until the box is formatted (Format > Text Box > Layout).*

Electronic Documents

"Electronic documents" strictly refers to any documents that can be transferred electronically. But in this section, the most universal format is discussed: Adobe PDF. While this format can be confounding because content is not easily edited, it is especially useful for the following attributes: small file size, compatibility across platforms, ability to include and read data fields, and retention of fonts and formatting.

The first attribute is often taken advantage of when including PDF documents as part of a Web page. When documents are saved to the PDF format at default settings, images that are part of the document are compressed so that file sizes are small and, consequently, download time is shortened. But creating PDF files at default settings with compressed images can also be frustrating when full resolution and quality is desired. For that reason, documents are converted to PDF with the tools that come with the full version of the Acrobat program (not the free Adobe Reader). Alternatively, third-party Acrobat conversion software can be downloaded to create PDF files, but the freeware versions often perform poorly when images are included with text.

TO ACROBAT FROM MICROSOFT WORD

For most users, documents begin as Microsoft Word files. Several steps are important before creating a document that is destined for conversion to a PDF file. These steps can be taken after a document is created, but many formatting and font decisions are made in Word based on the printer that will be used. If the document is finished, save the document, apply the following steps, and then determine if formatting or fonts have changed. If so, they will need to be corrected while in Word before converting the document to PDF. Here are the steps for Windows (**Figure 8.16**). Only steps 1, 2, and 5 apply to Macintosh computers:

1. Set up the Adobe PDF printer as the default printer by choosing Start > Settings > Printer and Faxes (Windows XP); or choose System Preferences from the Apple menu, and then choose Print & Fax (Mac OS).

2. Right-click on Adobe PDF and choose Set as Default from the drop-down menu (Windows XP). From the Default Printer menu, choose Adobe PDF (Mac OS).

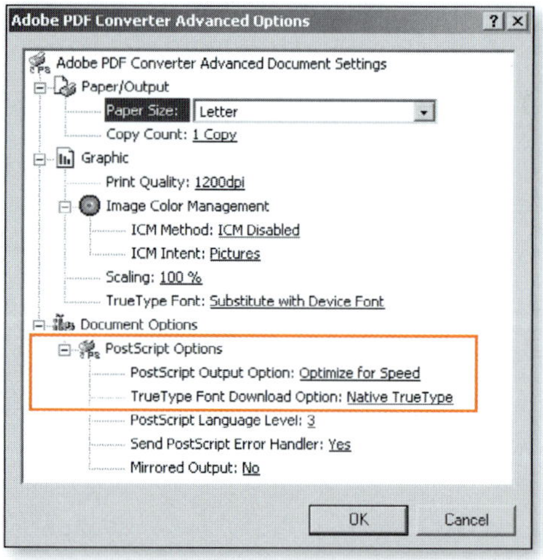

FIGURE 8.16 An example of the Adobe PDF Converter Advanced Options dialog box.

3. Configure the Adobe PostScript printer driver for TrueType Font preservation by choosing Start > Settings > Printer and Faxes (Windows XP).

4. Right-click on Adobe PDF and choose Properties from the menu. Click the General tab, click Printing Preferences, click the Layout tab, and then click Advanced. Click the plus sign next to PostScript Options: Select the TrueType Font Download Option and choose Native TrueType from the drop-down menu (Windows XP).

5. Acrobat conversion uses printing options that are set in the Print dialog box. Select File > Print. Choose Options (in Mac OS choose Microsoft Word from the menu beneath the Presets menu and

click Word Options) and deselect Reverse Print Order (if selected). Select other desired options (if the document contains line graphics, select Drawing Objects).

If the page size is nonstandard (e.g., not letter sized), in the Print dialog box click Properties (Windows only). On the Paper/Quality tab, click Advanced and choose Custom from the drop-down menu of the Page Size menu item. Enter the height and width values.

Once printing options are set up in Word, formatting and fonts are far more likely to convert seamlessly from the .doc file to PDF format. To be sure that images appear with as much resolution as possible in a PDF file created from a Word document, treat images as follows:

- When inserting images into Word via a text box (see the note in the "Laser Printing" section), be sure the images are set at 200 dpi or higher to ensure that they appear smooth. Microsoft applies anti-aliasing to images at resolutions less than 200 dpi, but Acrobat will only anti-alias images at 200 dpi and higher.

  To create a 200 dpi resolution in Photoshop, in the Image Size dialog box (Image > Image Size), deselect Resample and type in 200 pixels per inch for Resolution. Ignore the height and width settings. Click OK.

  This will not change the inherent resolution of the image, but the image will be interpreted as 200 dpi and subsequently smoothed when converted to the Acrobat PDF format.

- To draw attention to details, it is often best to use sharpening methods versus changes to darkness or brightness.

The conversion from a .doc format to PDF only requires default settings when the output is for the Web: But grant applications, reports and the like often require that images retain as much resolution as possible. When the full version of Acrobat is loaded, several options for conversion are available, either by printing to Acrobat or through Adobe PDF menu items (Acrobat 7 and later). The latter provides more options for color management and inclusion of hyperlinks, graphics, styles, bookmarks, and embedded tags.

To preserve details and image resolution, use the following settings when converting to a PDF file, depending on whether Adobe PDF is chosen from the Word menu or the PDF is created through the Print main menu item (File > Print):

- **Acrobat 7 and 8.** In Adobe PDF on the Word menu, choose Change Conversion Settings. Choose Press Quality or High Quality Print from the Conversion menu.

- **Print to Acrobat.** In the Print dialog box, click Properties (Windows) or PDF Options (Mac OS X), click the Default and from the menu choose either Press Quality or High Quality Print.

Problems with conversion to PDF can arise as a result of charts, graphs, and tables. Complex charts, graphs, and tables can become scrambled. Rather than keeping them as vector files, instead save graphics from their originating programs as high-quality JPEG or PNG image files using techniques described in Chapter 4.

When limitations exist for the file size—often allotted by granting agencies—and these are exceeded (after having made the PDF file and checking its size), the most likely contribution is from images. These can be compressed so that limitations are not exceeded. The section that follows, "To Acrobat from Photoshop," provides ways to compress PDF image files, but the easiest way to reduce file size follows.

▶ **Warning:** *Last-minute editing can be accomplished by creating fields in Acrobat into which text is added. These fields significantly add to the file size. Remove these fields from the PDF file, and instead add text in the program used to create the original document.*

If the file size does not meet the specified limits, resample the images to 200 dpi in Word by right-clicking on the image and choosing Format Picture. Click the Compress button and select the desired attributes. Color and grayscale images are JPEG compressed to a mid-range quality: Some compression artifacts can be seen when zoomed in, but they will not be visible at magnifications used for reading documents.

TO ACROBAT FROM PHOTOSHOP

When images are included as appendices as stand-alone images, they are saved directly as Photoshop PDF files at the highest quality levels of JPEG compression. If file size limits are required for the PDF document, compression quality is set so that, combined with all other images, total file size will not exceed maximum limitations. This is normally an iterative process where file sizes are saved at various resolutions until the file size requirement is satisfied. All images are derived from a single, full-resolution file: JPEG compressed files are *not* used for further compression, because the JPEG file will become more degraded.

After Photoshop PDF files are created, these PDF files can be added to an existing PDF file in the full version of Acrobat by selecting Document > Insert Pages. In the Insert Pages dialog box, browse to select the files to insert. A second dialog box will appear so that you can select in what order the new files will appear in the existing PDF document.

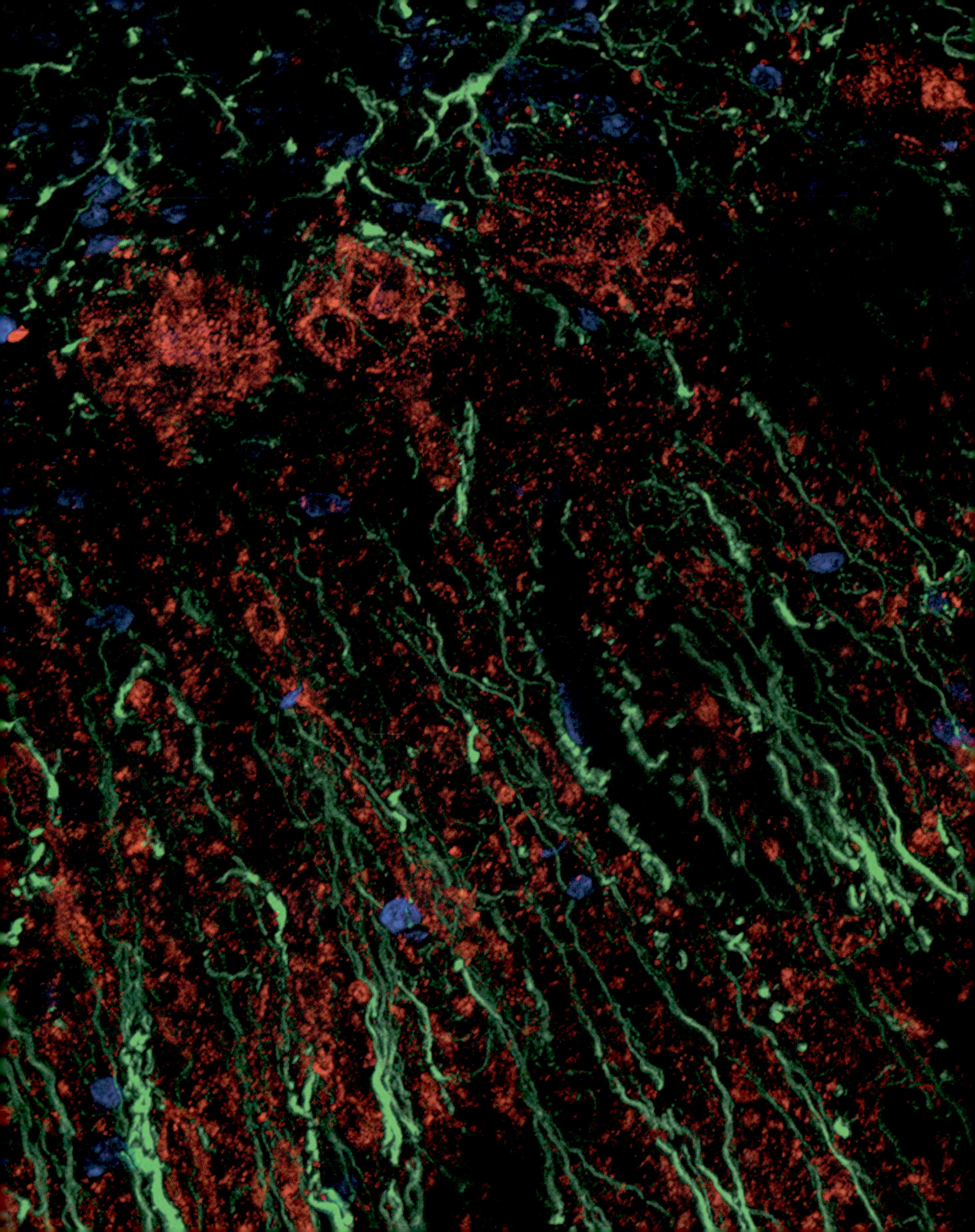

PART 3

Segmenting and Quantification

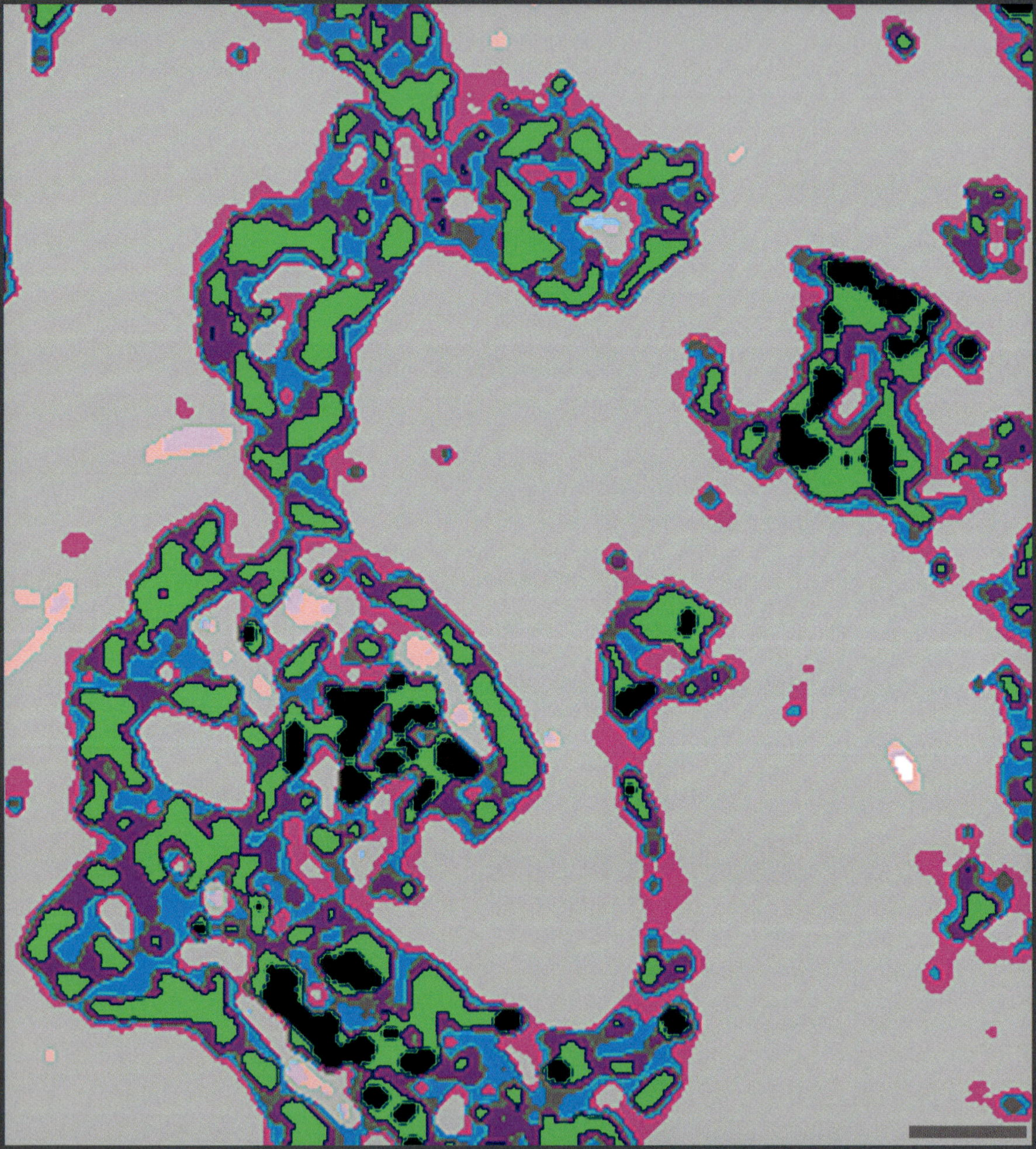

CHAPTER 9

Separating Relevant Features from the Background

Colorized image of variously stained cells in murine lung. Image was posterized, blurred, and colorized in Photoshop CS3 Extended (Adobe Systems Incorporated, San Jose, CA). Scale bar = 220 microns.

OF ALL THE POWERFUL TOOLS in Photoshop, the most unrecognized are those that can be used to separate relevant features from the background (segmenting). These tools can operate far more effectively than those included with more expensive scientific software. As an added benefit, few of these tools need to be used to garner results unattainable in other software programs.

Once relevant features are separated, they can be measured, either with measurement tools available in CS3 Extended or for area, colorimetric, and OD/I data in earlier versions of Photoshop. Alternatively, segmented images can be analyzed in other software packages when data analysis is unavailable in Photoshop.

The methods used for segmenting create images that can be measured so that two or more conditions can be compared. None of the methods are intended to provide absolutely exact measurements: Rather, the methods provide a consistent means for obtaining statistically accurate results when derived from a number of measured images. It is up to each researcher to validate the resultant numbers, and then to report standard deviation.

The segmenting methods also reduce user intervention and potential bias. At some point the researcher must make a decision, but the decision only needs to be made once. Thereafter, the decision is applied consistently to the related images.

For every image of specimens, it is crucial that the following applies:

- **Flatfield correction.** Segmentation simply does not work unless specimens are evenly illuminated.
- **JPEG images.** Highly compressed images will not provide accurate results: Minimally compressed images absent of JPEG artifacts can be used.
- **Positively identified features.** Features must be unquestionably identifiable.

Segment Images with Photoshop or Use Stereology?

Before discussing methods for segmenting images, some comments need to be made about measurement approaches. Photoshop can be included in two approaches: stereology and computer-aided image measurement. The approach depends on the nature of the specimen, though image analysis may be used for nearly all specimens (unless a journal favors stereology).

Both stereology and computer-aided measurement as means for deriving data from images are mentioned because stereology requires specific approaches to sectioning three-dimensional volumes. *How* images are measured must be decided before sections are cut. Once decided, the probes can be generated in Photoshop, or images can be segmented for image analysis.

Stereology

Stereology is an unbiased statistical method used for determining counts, lengths, and areas (for volumes). It requires segmentation by eye: So-called stereologic probes (periodically spaced lines, circles, crosshairs, or boxes) are placed over the image, and a limited number of features are marked that intersect with the probe or exist within a box. That number is often less than ten, which virtually eliminates human counting or identification error.

● **More:** *For information on using Photoshop to create stereologic probes, visit www.peachpit.com/scientificimaging.*

One advantage of stereology is that measurements of three-dimensional structures can be derived from two-dimensional sections (slices from the sample), but only when specific procedures are followed. Another advantage is that it relies on a relatively small number of measured areas within sections to derive accurate estimates, making stereology potentially more efficient than computer-aided image measurement.

An additional advantage is that stereologic methods overcome two common errors:

- **Errors introduced when measuring features that are at different *x*, *y* dimensions.** For example, when counting two cell types that are at different sizes, the larger size will be overcounted when it's part of a larger volume.
- **Errors related to tissue sectioning.** The top and bottom of tissue sections can include cells that are pulled out by the knife edge; these areas are avoided in stereologic protocol.

■ **Note:** *Stereology books are written with arcane titles for methods. For the most part, when measuring areas to obtain volumes and when counting through several optical sections (versus physical sections), look for two methods: Cavalerie and the Optical Fractionation methods, respectively.*

When counts, lengths, and areas/volumes of features are needed within a three-dimensional structure and sections are used for measurement, the stereology method should be considered. More information about stereology can be found in several books, such as the clearly written introductory book *Principles and Practices of Unbiased Stereology: An Introduction for Bioscientists* (Johns Hopkins University Press, 2002) by Peter Mouton.

Computer-Aided Image Measurement

Computer-aided image measurement via segmented images is best suited for those measurements not available through stereologic methods or for specimens that are not a part of a three-dimensional structure, such as a single layer (monolayer) of cells.

Images used for figures in this chapter are in some instances better suited for stereologic measurement, but computer-aided measurement is used instead so that Photoshop segmentation methods can be shown.

Mixing Both Methods

Stereologic approaches can be mixed with computer-aided analysis. Rather than measure all features in a single image, an unbiased, statistical approach can be taken: As in stereology, the image can be divided into smaller parts, in this case by using a grid. Then certain parts of the grid can be measured, as long as they are consistently measured in all related images. If a particular part of the grid is measured (e.g., the top-right grid) and the specimen is compromised (e.g., a large artifact, the tissue is folded over, etc.), a consistent rule can be followed to determine where to measure: For example, the next grid to the right without the artifact is measured. As long as the rule is consistently followed, the measurements are unbiased.

In the end, the dimensions of each area (field) measured are not most important. In biological research, if possible, it's always most important to have enough animals (n) to overcome biological diversity (n = 7); of next importance is the number of sections; and of least importance is the number of areas (fields) measured.

Manual Measurement

Manual measurements without using stereological techniques can be a cause for concern. Though many studies using manual methods are corroborated, the potential for error is far greater than when using either computer-aided techniques or stereology. Problems inevitably arise when different researchers identify features in different ways. Some researchers will include all features in their measurements: partial, whole, and out-of-focus features. Others will make determinations about which are counted. In combination, the standard deviation can be wide. That kind of variability as a result of manual counting is overcome through computer-aided image analysis and stereology.

Computer-Aided Measurement: Procedure for Segmenting Images

Because of image variability, steps in a segmenting procedure vary. Sometimes steps are eliminated, and sometimes steps are repeated more than once. Frequently, several Photoshop functions and techniques are tried, and then perhaps out of order, and the procedure most successful at separating relevant features from the background is applied. User experimentation is encouraged.

The overall approach is to try a method to separate relevant features from background on an image, and test the image with the Threshold function to see how well relevant features are separated. The Threshold function will binarize features of interest. If binarized features of interest separate from surrounding areas (background), use that method: If not, try other method and test with the Threshold function again until you are successful.

Once the image is binarized, the resulting graphic image makes it easy to see the following:

- The borders of features
- The features that are selected versus background
- The unwanted background areas that are also selected

The binarized image also makes it easy to store a graphic representation on a layer so that binarized features can be compared with the original image. The stored image provides, as well, a record of the method and how it was applied to each image. Finally, the binarized image is easily selected for measurement in Photoshop or other scientific quantification programs.

● **More:** *To aid in determining how segmentation is done, additional sample images are provided at www.peachpit.com/scientificimaging.*

For the majority of images, the typical procedure follows the steps in **Table 9.1**.

Features may need to be modified before or after the image is binarized for the following reasons:

- Features need to be grouped or joined together when evaluating clustering or agglomeration.
- Feature borders may be difficult to distinguish, or features contained within a discrete structure subdivide into several parts, so an averaged feature needs to be created.

TABLE 9.1 Computer-Aided Segmenting Approaches

OD/I IMAGES	SINGLE-LABEL, COLOR OR GRAYSCALE	MULTIPLE LABELS, COLOR
Reduce noise	Reduce noise	Reduce noise
Correct uneven illumination using flatfield image	Correct uneven illumination	Correct uneven illumination
Duplicate to layer	Duplicate to layer	Separate channels or by hue
High Pass filter or posterize	Sharpen with High Pass filter	Choose channel with segmented features
Blur or reduce noise	Find feature edge, or High Pass filter, or posterize	Duplicate to layer
Binarize layer	Blur or reduce noise	Blur or reduce noise
Select features and inverse for background only	Binarize layer	Binarize layer
Fill background with black, features with white		
Change layer mode		

- Small artifacts and partial features that intersect with the border of the image need to be eliminated.
- Areas that surround or neighbor features need to be selected.

After the features of a single (representative) image are segmented, modified, and readied for measurement, related images are tested using the same procedure. One of two methods can be used with related images:

- Related images can be segmented by setting the binarizing value (set in the Threshold dialog box) or filtering values for each image at varying amounts, depending on sample-to-sample differences.
- Related images from a session or experimental group can be made similar in tonal distribution, so that each image can be binarized at the same level, thus eliminating user intervention and potential subjectivity. This process is referred to in this book as equalizing histograms.

The means for modifying segmented features or for equalizing histograms are presented in **Table 9.2**.

■ **Note:** *Certain images do not lend themselves to segmentation. These include images created through specialized microscope illumination techniques, such as phase, DIC, and Nomarski.*

The steps contained in Table 9.1 and Table 9.2 are combined in a typical segmenting procedure. Apply specific steps to each image depending on the nature or intent of the image as shown in Table 9.1 and depending on other needs as outlined in Table 9.2. More details about each table entry are discussed in the sections that follow.

Some feature attributes must not be altered, depending on what is being measured. Except when grouping features together and eliminating small features, the following descriptions of steps and tools provide the means to retain feature attributes.

TABLE 9.2 **Modifying Segmented Features and Equalizing Histograms**

GROUPING TOGETHER OR AVERAGING FEATURES	ISOLATING/ELIMINATING FEATURES	EQUALIZING HISTOGRAMS
Blurring/Maximum/Minimum (before binarizing)	Blurring/Maximum/Minimum (before binarizing)	Match Color tool (histogram fitting to single image)
Expand (dilate) selection of features to select neighboring features	Contract (erode) selection of features to eliminate smaller features and separate features that touch	Equalize tool (histogram fitting to full tonal range)
Smooth selection of features	Eliminate features intersecting with edge of field	Linear histogram equalization (histogram fitting to brightness level)

Check Image for Corrections Needed

Before starting the segmentation steps, examine the representative image. Foremost in the examination is to check for uneven illumination and noise levels (including color noise). This can be accomplished either by visually checking the image (**Figure 9.1**, left) or by using Levels or Threshold to binarize the image (**Figure 9.1**, right). When looking for color inaccuracies, a visual examination is often adequate. If colors are visibly incorrect, make color corrections by using the methods described in Chapter 7, "Color Corrections and Final Steps."

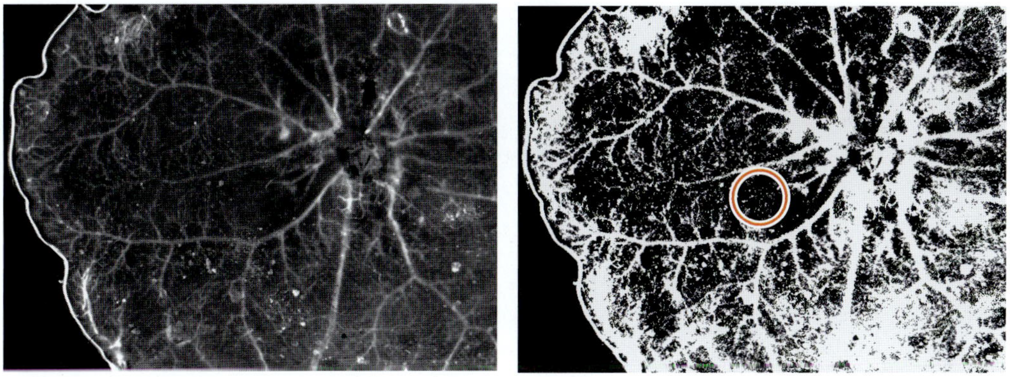

FIGURE 9.1 Examining an image using a Threshold method. The image on the right shows uneven illumination and noise (circled).

■ **Note:** *These instructions are for images in Grayscale mode. In RGB Color images, Alt/Option-dragging the input sliders shows clipping as areas of intense color.*

To check for uneven illumination and noise using Levels:

1. Select Image > Adjustments > Levels to open the Levels dialog box.
2. Hold down the Alt/Option key and move the white input slider to the left for darkfield images or move the black input slider to the right for brightfield images.
3. Look for the introduction of black (for brightfield images) or white (for darkfield) as you move the slider. If all features (darkfield) or the background (brightfield) become covered in black or white simultaneously or within 10 input values (read in the Levels dialog box) as the slider is moved, the image is likely a good candidate for segmentation.

   Look for small, discrete particles that appear as white or black (Figure 9.1 right, circled). Also look for crescent shapes around cells to indicate color fringing or nonspecific collections of particles. If these appear, the image needs to be corrected for noise (see "Noise Reduction" in Chapter 6).

4. If relevant features are covered in black or white in greater than 10 values (Figure 9.1, right), it is best to correct the image for uneven illumination according to the section "Uneven Illumination Correction Using the Image" in Chapter 6.

   If relevant features occur along bright and dark "spots," sharpen the image using the following method.

HIGH PASS FILTERING FOR SCATTERED BRIGHT AREAS

Anomalies in the background can cause randomly occurring bright areas (**Figure 9.2**, left). In that instance, a High Pass correction for scattered bright areas is used. This method increases the brightness of relevant features by sharpening the image so that these areas are brighter than surrounding features. In so doing, all features brighter than a cutoff tonal value will be selected when using Threshold.

1. Duplicate the original image to a layer (Layer > Duplicate Layer).
2. Set the layer blending mode to Hard Light, but do not adjust the opacity.
3. Apply the High Pass filter to the layer (Filter > Other > High Pass). In the High Pass dialog box, adjust the High Pass slider until you reach a point when bright areas appear darker while the rest of the image looks uniformly filtered. Alternatively, look at the features of interest and move the slider until they appear brighter than the surrounding areas. Once satisfied, click OK. Don't forget to write down the Radius value shown in the dialog box in case this step has to be repeated and as a way of keeping a record of the steps.
4. Select Layer > Merge > Down to merge layers.

Because the image is sharpened (**Figure 9.2**, right), a noise reduction filter should be applied after merging layers.

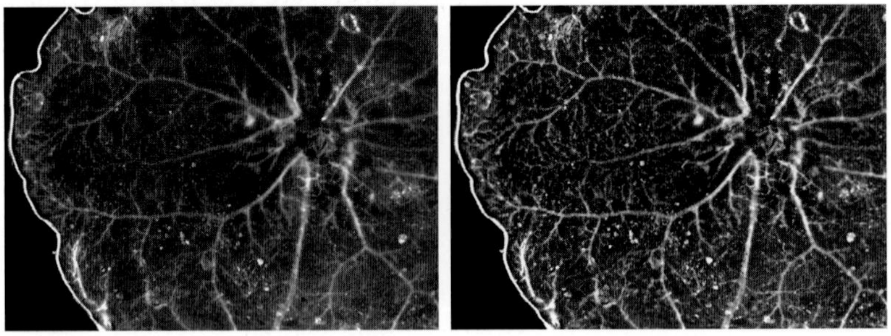

FIGURE 9.2 The image on the left contains bright and dark areas; features of interest are brightened in the image on the right.

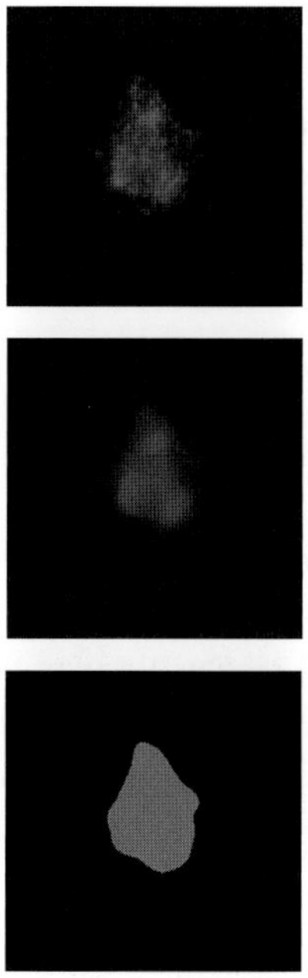

FIGURE 9.3 Averaging borders of an image using the Median filter. A binarized image (bottom) was colorized gray.

Group Together or Average Features

When grouping together or averaging features (**Figure 9.3**, top) before binarizing, generally some form of blurring or noise reduction is used. Among the possible filters that are used, the Median filter is preferred because it does not shrink or enlarge features (**Figure 9.3**, center). However, the Gaussian Blur and Reduce Noise filters can also be used, depending on the degree of blurring needed. The Gaussian Blur filter blurs while enlarging feature borders, and the Reduce Noise filter produces a finer blurring.

Use any of these filters iteratively at varying settings for the best results. The Median and Reduce Noise filters are found in the Noise menu (Filter > Noise), and the Gaussian Blur filter is in the Blur menu (Filter > Blur).

For a more aggressive way of grouping features, the Maximum or Minimum filter can be used for agglomerating features, or for removing smaller artifacts or irrelevant features (Filter > Other > Maximum/Minimum). These filters are referred to as grayscale erode filters, because they "erode" small features and expand those that are larger. In this instance, retention of image areas would not be important.

After any of the filters described have been applied, the image can then be binarized (**Figure 9.3**, bottom) by selecting Image > Adjustments > Threshold (see "Binarizing with Threshold" later in this chapter). Or, when binarizing does not adequately separate relevant features from the background, use other methods that follow before thresholding.

Color Images: Finding a Grayscale Channel with the Highest Contrast or Selecting by Color

As mentioned earlier, color images are composed of channels, each in grayscale. Depending on the color of the relevant features, one channel will contain brighter features than other channels, and equally important, darker surrounding areas. Thus, the brighter features can be isolated by thresholding to a pixel value at which only brighter features are binarized. In that way, features of interest are segmented from the background.

For singly colored, darkfield images, the Channel Mixer is used to make the grayscale image (see "Brightfield: Single Color Image to Grayscale" in Chapter 7). For brightfield images and multiple-colored, darkfield images, the correct channel may not be the one that is expected. Surrounding colors can interfere with strong contrast, and several channels from more than one color mode may have to be tried iteratively before the ideal channel is found. Thus, in the following section ("Grayscale Channel with Highest Contrast"), color channels are created in RGB Color, CMYK Color, and Lab Color, and then the channel with the greatest contrast between features of interest and the background is selected.

It may seem counterintuitive to find a grayscale channel when relevant features can be isolated by selecting the color of the relevant dye that stains the specimen. For brightfield images, when more than one color is used to stain the specimen, hues can mix with each other, making identification by color impossible. For example, if a blue peroxidase stain and a brown DAB stain are used, colors of the brown stain can range from a yellow brown at the feature edges to a purple brown where the stains mix. The purple brown can be so close in hue to blue that the blue-stained features can be included when attempting to isolate only the brown.

■ **Note:** *If a color camera was used for acquiring images in which OD/I measurements are desired, the grayscale channel is generally measured. Use the channel with the highest readouts of RGB Color, 8-bit in the Info palette when sampling points are placed on relevant features.*

In instances where the colors are discrete or when a grayscale channel with adequate contrast cannot be found, relevant colors (hues) can be selected by using functions within Photoshop. These include Color Range and Posterize. Choosing hues using Color Range, especially when combined with posterizing, can work well with single-color images, even when backgrounds vary in tonal range.

GRAYSCALE CHANNEL WITH HIGHEST CONTRAST

To find the grayscale channel from an RGB Color image with the greatest tonal separation between features of interest and surrounding areas, perform the following steps:

1. Duplicate the original image (**Figure 9.4A**) three times (Image > Duplicate) and close the original.
2. For one image, change the mode to CMYK Color (Image > Mode > CMYK Color). If the tonal separation is compromised after making the mode change, undo the change (Edit > Undo) and reduce the saturation of the image before changing the mode to CMYK (see "Reduce Saturation, Change Hue, and Make Image CMYK Ready" in Chapter 7).
3. For the other image, change the mode to Lab Color (Image > Mode > Lab Color).

The third image—the duplicate of the original—remains as a RGB Color image.

■ **Note:** *Split Channels is not available if the image contains layers.*

4. For each image, separate the channels (this includes the duplicate, RGB Color image). Open the Channels palette (Window > Channels), and choose Split Channels from the palette menu.

5. One by one, inspect the channel images that show the best separation of stained features from the surrounding area (**Figures 9.4B, C, and D**), and choose the image with the greatest promise for segmenting (Figure 9.4D). Inspect each high-contrast channel by using Threshold (Image > Adjustments > Threshold). Move the Threshold slider until features of interest are binarized (see "Binarizing with Threshold" later in this chapter). Compare channels and use the channel with the best segmentation.

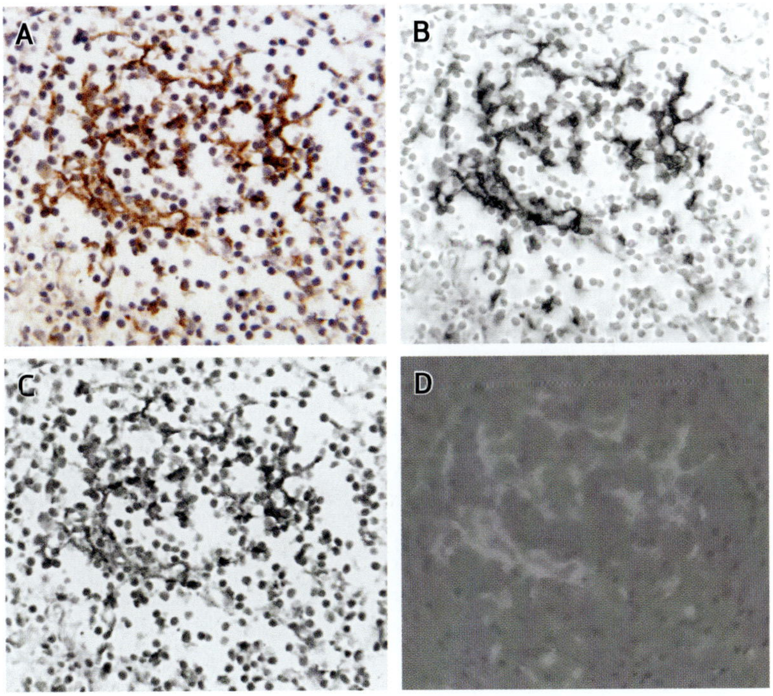

FIGURE 9.4 The original image (**A**); one image derived from the yellow channel of the CMYK Color image (**B**); another from the red channel of the RGB Color image (**C**); and another from the b channel of the Lab Color image (**D**).

If features do not segment as desired, use the following method (Using Color Range and Posterize) on the original RGB Color image or use the most promising grayscale channel and try posterizing (threshold again after posterizing to check efficacy) or using the High Pass filter (see the section later in this chapter, "Applying a High Pass Filter").

USING COLOR RANGE AND POSTERIZE

One function in Photoshop aids in selecting features dyed with discrete colors: Color Range (Select > Color Range). This command not only selects specific colors, but it can select tonal ranges within a single color or tonal ranges in grayscale. Another function—Posterize—reduces the number of color (or grayscale) values by reassigning a large color palette to one that is smaller, which is user-defined by setting the Levels value in the Posterize dialog box (Image > Adjustments > Posterize). After posterizing, colors can be selected by using the Color Range function, or features of interest can be separated from the background by thresholding.

Here is a method for selecting by hue using Color Range and Posterize:

1. Choose Select > Color Range to open the Color Range dialog box. Move the Fuzziness slider to 0. Use the leftmost eyedropper and click on a relevant feature. Then choose the plus (+) eyedropper. Click on as many colors as you want from all the features so that all colors in the features are chosen. The graphic display will update as you click to show the extent of the features chosen. If you increase the Fuzziness value, more area will be selected, but including area in this way creates fuzzy (soft-edged) borders and will possibly include nonstained areas.
2. Save the selection by clicking Save in the Color Range dialog box and then naming the Color Range selection. Click OK, and then visually inspect the image to determine whether or not the selection includes all the relevant features. If it does, you can apply the saved Color Range selection to all the related images.
3. Repeat steps 1 and 2 if the Color Range selection inadequately selects features of interest or if it includes unwanted surrounding features.
4. If it is difficult to select features by color (**Figure 9.5**, left) because colors are similar to the surrounding features or the background, reassign the colors to a smaller palette by selecting Image > Adjustments > Posterize (**Figure 9.5**, center). Set the Posterization Level value by eye: The smaller the value, the fewer colors that are used.
5. Use Color Range to select the features (don't forget to save the Color Range selection) after posterizing (or use Threshold).

When a selection is made—versus using the Threshold function—the image still needs to be binarized. To accomplish that, continue with the following steps:

■ **Note:** *Each image must be evaluated to ensure the inclusion of all features in the selection. When some features are not selected, it is likely that colors in those features—or parts of features—do not contain the same purity as those in the selected features. That impurity, especially if confirmed by readings in the Info palette, may be an argument to ignore impure features.*

1. After the selection is successfully made in Color Range and while the selection is still active, create a new layer (Layer > New Layer).
2. Select Edit > Fill. In the Fill dialog box, select White from the Use menu to fill the selected area with white.
3. Inverse the selection (Select > Inverse), select Edit > Fill, and then select Black from the menu to fill the selected area with black.

   This will create a binary layer for subsequent measurements (**Figure 9.5**, right), keeping this layer separated from the image.

FIGURE 9.5 The original image with an uneven background (left), a posterized image (center), and the result after binarizing (right).

Differentiating the Edges of Features from the Background

■ **Note:** *When features of interest are not sufficiently included or background is also included in the binarized layer, the High Pass filter and, possibly, noise filters will need to be applied before thresholding. When the High Pass filter is used, tones are altered and Color Sampler tool readouts no longer provide information about the outermost edge of features.*

■ **Note:** *Some filters can show the edges (such as a Sobel filter), but even then edges can be uncertain.*

As mentioned earlier, gradients make it difficult to determine where the edges end and the background begins. To determine the outermost edge of features objectively, use the Color Sampler tool. Once the tonal level is found, the Threshold function can be used to create a cutoff between the edge of the feature and the background.

1. Select Layer > Duplicate Layer to duplicate the original image to a layer.
2. Find a feature in the representative image and zoom in on that feature until it fills the screen.
3. Place up to four sampling points at the edge of the feature in various positions (**Figure 9.6A**). It might be useful to choose Point Sample or 3 by 3 Average from the Sample Size menu in the options bar. Determine the average or maximum value from the readouts in the Info palette (**Figure 9.6B**), assuming all sampling points were placed at the edge of the feature. The average or maximum value is then used for the threshold amount when using the Threshold function (**Figure 9.6C**). See "Binarizing with Threshold" later in this chapter.

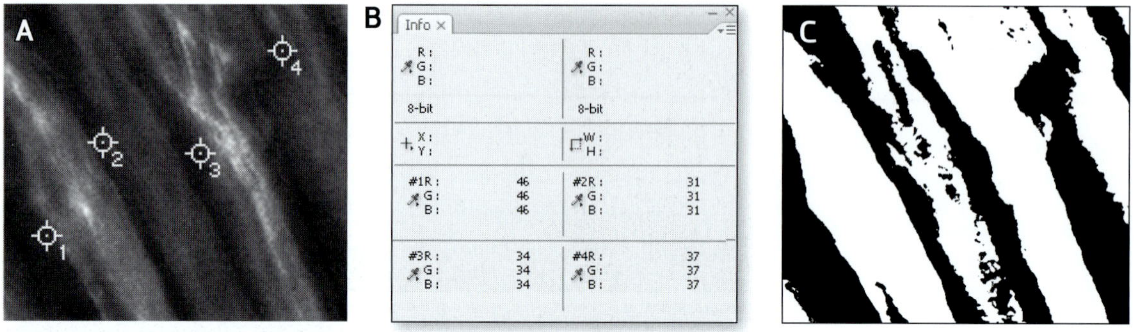

FIGURE 9.6 Sampling points are positioned (left), and the readout values (center) are used to determine the threshold amount for a binarized image (right).

When thresholding, if the use of the maximum or average value for the threshold amount causes an unintentional loss of features or feature edges are expanded beyond the sampling points, choose a cutoff value by eye that appears to include features to their outermost edges.

Applying a High Pass Filter

A High Pass filter is typically applied to images in which thresholding with previous methods produced unsatisfactory results. Even when the High Pass filter has been applied earlier to sharpen and create even illumination on a specimen spotted by bright areas, the High Pass filter is applied again in a different way.

In rare instances, the image can be binarized without applying a High Pass filter: When good results cannot be obtained by using the High Pass filter, try binarizing the image without using the High Pass filter and compare the results. Then choose the method that most accurately separates the relevant features from the background.

1. Duplicate the Background layer (**Figure 9.7A**).
2. Select Filter > Other > High Pass to open the High Pass dialog box. Adjust the Radius slider to a value that causes the features of interest to be brighter in relation to the surrounding area. The level of feature brightness can be misleading: Very bright (**Figure 9.7B**) and moderately bright (**Figure 9.7C**) features may not necessarily segment as well as minimally bright features (**Figure 9.7D**).

■ **Note:** *For RGB Color images, the High Pass filter is often set to 255.*

After the High Pass filter is applied, use the Threshold function to create a binary image. Measurements can then be made from the binary image.

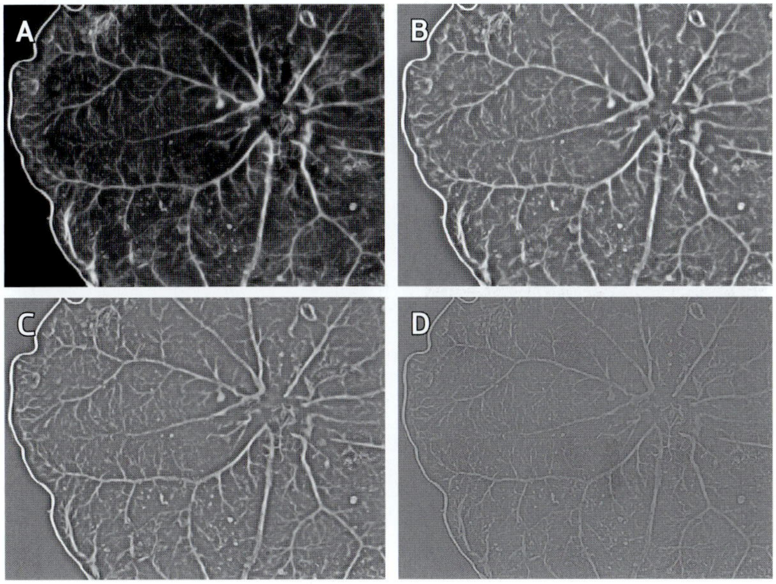

FIGURE 9.7 The original image (**A**) is filtered with the High Pass filter using three different Radius slider amounts (**B**, **C**, and **D**).

Binarizing with Threshold

■ **Note:** *If the binarized images are measured in scientific analysis software, whether features are white or black may make a difference. If so, white and black can be inverted by selecting Image > Adjustments > Invert.*

This binarizing step creates black features and a white background, or vice versa. When measuring in Photoshop, it is then easy to select only the black (or white) features, and the selection step can be incorporated into an automated action. If the image is saved for analysis in a scientific measurement program, the black (or white) areas can be easily measured (after thresholding again) and incorporated into a macro (similar to an action).

1. Set the Opacity of the layer you are thresholding to 50–60% so that the original image on the layer below the duplicated layer is visible. That way you can see the extent of the binarizing while adjusting the Threshold slider (**Figure 9.8**, left).
2. Select Image > Adjustments > Threshold and adjust the slider visually (**Figure 9.8**, center) or by using an average or maximum value derived by measuring edges with the Color Sampler tool. When the Threshold Level is adjusted visually, carefully inspect the edges of features and move the slider until the outermost edges are binarized. Reset the Opacity of the layer to 100%. The Threshold value is set correctly when the features are binarized without including too many artifacts or any unwanted features (**Figure 9.8**, right).

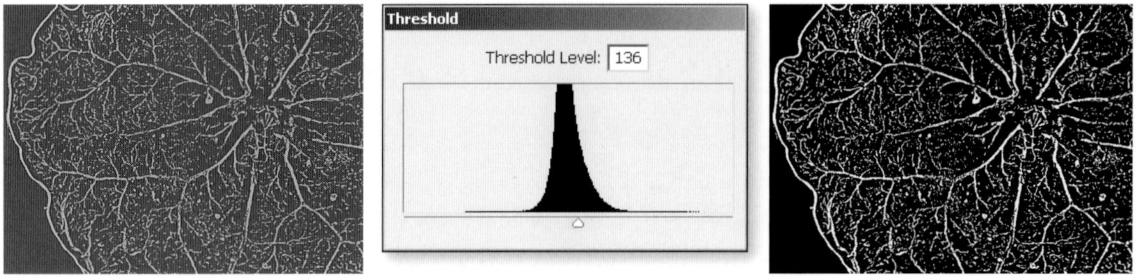

FIGURE 9.8 The layered image (left) is binarized with the Threshold slider (center). The resulting image (right).

Often, the Threshold value can be set at more than one amount within one or two points of each other and "look" correct. Choose a Threshold value, click OK, and then compare the binarized layer with the original below by clicking the eye icon in the Layers palette repeatedly. Zoom in, if necessary. You can undo the results (Edit > Undo) and then repeat this step if necessary.

When thresholding does not include all the relevant features or when too many extraneous areas are included along with the binarized features, consider the following:

- If extraneous objects are included and the extraneous objects are smaller or larger than the relevant features, they can be eliminated by modifying the binarized image.
- If all relevant features are not included, carefully examine the excluded features. If they are out of focus (often appearing lighter than other features), partial features, or fragments, it is appropriate to exclude them.
- If the relevant features that are included appear at a discrete location, such as the center of the image, and excluded features are in another location (or when excluded features are binarized, a discrete area then includes artifacts), the image is unevenly illuminated. Correct the uneven illumination more than once, if necessary, or use the High Pass filter method described earlier.
- If extraneous areas are included and these areas are at the same brightness level as the relevant features—and their appearance isn't due to uneven illumination but rather unevenness in the actual specimen—manual methods will need to be used to select or identify the relevant features.

Modifying a Binarized Image

Modifications to a binarized image can be done for the following reasons:

- To eliminate artifacts (erode) or include neighboring particles (dilate). This includes modifications to separate discrete features that touch each other.
- To eliminate features touching the edge of the image field.
- To make a mask (which can be done for measuring OD/I).
- To select areas surrounding the features.

These modifications are described in the following sections.

ELIMINATE OR INCLUDE BINARIZED FEATURES

■ **Note:** *The erode function can also be used when features touch each other.*

Binarized images may require the elimination of included artifacts or partial features, or the grouping together of small particles or features with larger features. The process is called Erode when small artifacts or features are reduced in area (via Select > Modify > Contract). When relevant features are expanded in an area to include neighboring features (via Select > Modify > Expand), the process is called Dilate.

Often, the two processes are combined: When erode is used, *all* features are reduced in area along with those that are reduced to zero (eliminated). To restore shrunken areas of remaining features, dilation is required. When these two functions are combined, the process is called Open. The opposite process, dilation followed by erosion—used when including neighboring features and then restoring approximate original area—is called Close.

To eliminate artifacts (erode) or include neighboring particles (dilate):

1. Select all binarized features using the Color Range function (Select > Color Range). From the Select menu, choose Shadows or Highlights, depending on the color of the features (**Figure 9.9A**). Click OK.
2. To erode the selection, choose Contract first (**Figure 9.9B**); to dilate, choose Expand first (**Figure 9.9C**). Estimate the expansion/contraction pixel amount. Start with a pixel value of 1–3, click OK, and then determine whether the selection either eliminates small artifacts (erode) or includes neighboring particles (dilate). Click OK.

3. If you are not satisfied with the result, choose Select > Deselect or press Ctrl/Command+D.
4. Start over again, but this time change the Contract or Expand pixel value until you're satisfied.
5. If a setting of 1 eliminates relevant small features along with partial features and artifacts, the image has a low-pixel resolution. Resample the image to double its pixel dimensions by selecting Image > Image Size.

■ **Note:** *Step 5 may have to be done incrementally: see the section "Resample for Output (Image Size)" in Chapter 8.*

6. To Close: After expanding the selection, contract it to return to the original selection and borders with additional, neighboring pixels.

   Select Edit > Fill, and then choose Black or White from the Use menu (**Figure 9.9D**) to fill additional areas created around larger features.
7. To Open: After contracting the selection, expand it by the same amount to return to the original selection and borders for larger features.
8. Inverse the selection (Select > Inverse) and eliminate artifacts by pressing the Delete key (be sure that the background is set correctly in the toolbox because this determines the delete color) or select Edit > Clear (**Figure 9.9E**).

■ **Note:** *Selections can also be smoothed by choosing Select > Modify > Smooth. Choose a pixel amount, click OK, inverse the selection, and then press the Delete key or select Edit > Clear.*

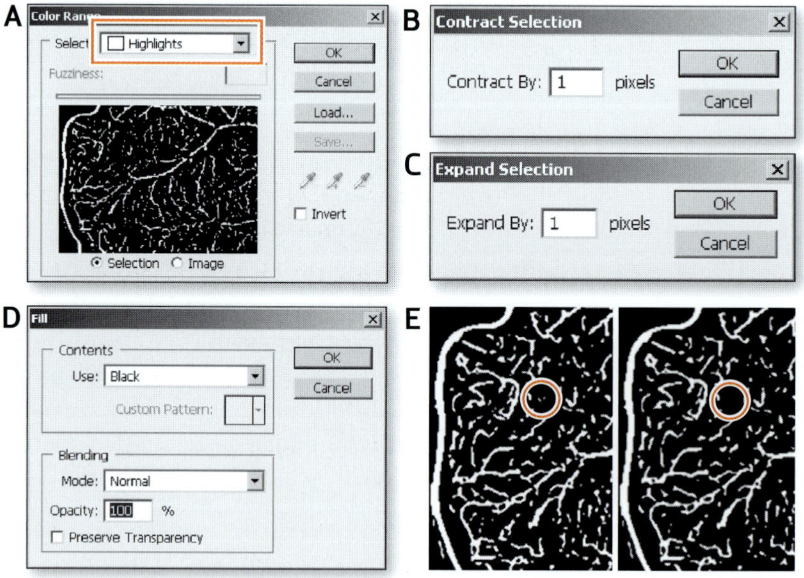

FIGURE 9.9 Dialog boxes used in Erode, Dilate, Open and Close steps; and comparison of images before (**E**, left) and after (**E**, right) Open step.

ELIMINATE FEATURES TOUCHING IMAGE BORDERS

Features that touch image borders are cut off: These are partial features. Because complete features are not visible, you cannot be certain that any of these partial features really compose complete features. Thus, when quantifying, these partial features are not included. Here is a method for eliminating partial features that touch image borders:

1. If necessary, select Image > Mode > RGB Color.
2. Choose Select > All or press Ctrl/Command+A to select the entire image.
3. Create a line along the border by selecting Edit > Stroke. In the Stroke dialog box, choose a Width of 2 pixels (px). Click the color swatch and choose red from the Color Picker. For Location, select Inside. Set Opacity to 100%.
4. In the Color Range dialog box (Select > Color Range) choose Red from the Select menu.
5. Include features that touch edges by "growing" the selection (Select > Grow).
6. Press the Delete key to eliminate features or select Edit > Clear.

CREATING A MASK

A black mask can be created to cover all image areas not included for subsequent quantification. This is especially useful when measuring the mean OD/I of all but what is masked: The tonal separation between the black mask and relevant features makes it easy for you to select relevant features (by using the Color Range function in Photoshop) for OD/I measurement.

The typical way to make a mask in Photoshop is by using an alpha channel. That method is not described here: Instead, the mask is created on a layer.

1. Select the binarized features (if the previous selection is not active) by choosing Select > Color Range. In the Color Range dialog box, choose Shadow or Highlights from the Select menu, depending on the color (black or white) of the binarized features. Click OK.
2. Choose Select > Inverse to select the inverse of the existing selection.
3. Select Layer > New > Layer to make a new layer. Fill the inversed selection with black by selecting Edit > Fill.and choosing Black from the Use menu. If the features are black, inverse the selection again and fill with white.

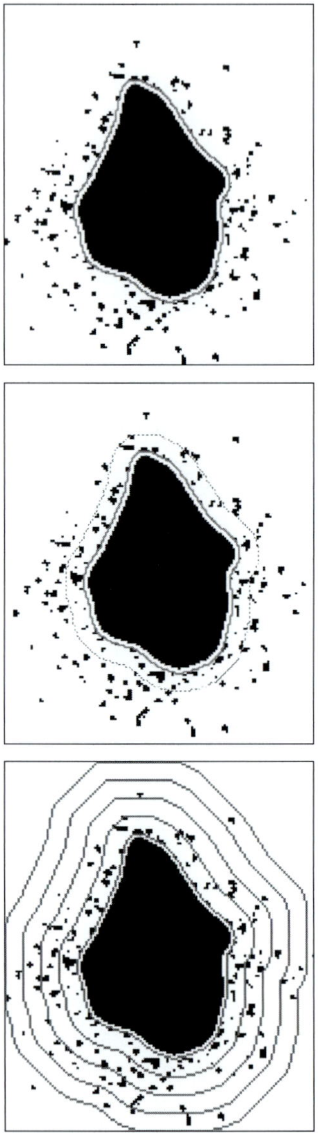

FIGURE 9.10 Selection of bordering particles in incremental orbits.

■ **Note:** *Each expansion of the selection will result in a change in shape less similar to the feature borders due to rounding errors. These shape changes are most noticeable with circular borders.*

4. When measuring in Photoshop, eliminate layers between the mask and the original image by selecting Layer > Delete > Layer. On the mask layer, set Layer mode to Darken. Flatten the image so that features of interest appear surrounded by a black mask.

   When measuring in scientific software, delete all layers except the mask layer and save the mask separately as an image. In scientific software, a region of interest (ROI) will need to be created on the mask image. That ROI will then be transferred to the original image (unless the software contains a mask function). The mask will isolate measurements to only the relevant features.

SELECT AREAS SURROUNDING FEATURES (ORBITS)

Important features can surround other features. Often, these surrounding features are smaller than the features they "orbit." These features can be bounded by orbits to determine where they exist by incremental distances from larger features.

1. Select the binarized features (Select > Color Range) if the selection is not active. In the Color Range dialog box, choose the appropriate color (white or black) from the Select menu.
2. Assuming that smaller features are surrounding a much larger feature, Open the selection by using the methods shown in step 7 of the procedure "Eliminate or Include Binarized Features," earlier.
3. Select Layer > New > Layer to make a new layer.
4. Select Edit > Stroke and choose a Width of 3 pixels and a Color of white. Then select Inside for the Location and click OK. This strokes the first orbit with white on the inside of the active selection to create a border between the partial particles and the larger feature.
5. Open the Stroke dialog box again and change the Width to 1 pixel, the Color to gray, and the Location to Center. Click OK. This creates a ring around the feature (**Figure 9.10**, top).
6. Expand the selection (Select > Modify > Expand) by the desired amount (**Figure 9.10**, center).
7. Stroke this selection. To create several more "orbits" around the features, repeat steps 5 and 6 (**Figure 9.10**, bottom).

When subsequently measuring features within orbits, use the Magic Wand tool and click inside the desired orbit. Then choose the binarized layer to obtain the measurements.

To create an action for measuring features within orbits, on each layer, create different colors for each orbit. Select respective orbits by color using Color Range.

Reference Area

Features make up an area within a larger dimension. That larger dimension can be the structure on which the features exist (e.g., tissue), a smaller number of features among a greater number, or the amount of features within a field of view. In any case, each kind of measurement is some fraction of a larger area called the reference area (**Figure 9.11**, top).

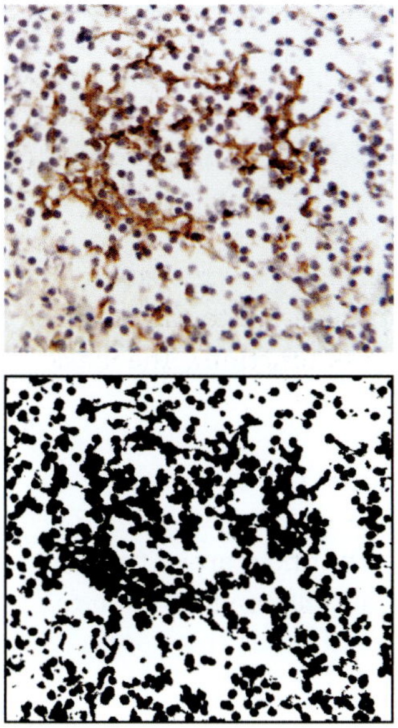

FIGURE 9.11 An image of original tissue sections with features of interest (top) and a binarized reference area (bottom).

▶ **Warning:** *Black or white background (nontissue) areas must not be included, because they are not part of the reference area.*

Thus, the reference area must also be included in any measurement. When the reference area is simply the field of view, no further segmentation needs to be done. Otherwise, the reference area—the total number of features or the tissue or substrate in which relevant features exist—must also be binarized for subsequent measurement (**Figure 9.11**, bottom).

Segmenting the reference area can be done in the same way that you have segmented relevant features. When automating steps via an action, the reference area should be placed on its own layer. Be sure to name the layer for easy identification when creating actions.

Testing Segmentation Procedure with Related Images

Once you have decided on the methods that are necessary for segmenting relevant features on a representative image (and the reference area of that image) and you have created a series of steps for segmenting, the same steps are then applied to a related image from the same experiment. This will confirm that the segmenting steps work identically (or within acceptable deviations) on more than one image. If features are not selected correctly in related images (like they are in the representative image)—for example, if more or less relevant features are selected or feature edges do not extend to the same outer boundaries—the segmenting steps can be changed as follows:

■ **Note:** *If the High Pass method was used as a part of the segmenting steps, variation should have been eliminated: The High Pass filter also matches tonal ranges of images to each other.*

- Apply a different Threshold Level. All segmenting steps contain a thresholding step: A different Threshold Level may need to be applied to related images than to the reference image because of specimen to specimen variation. The threshold step can be user interactive so that the Threshold Level can be changed, depending on the specimen. While this approach is prone to user subjectivity, it can be validated against a reference image.

- **Statistically determine a deviation.** After performing measurements on binarized features (see Chapter 10) from several images for a pilot study, the deviation can be statistically determined and then validated against statistical tests. If the deviation is within acceptable limits, the segmenting steps can be used on all related images.
- **Match images.** The images can be matched to each other (equalized) before using segmentation steps, either by expanding or compressing the grayscale distribution to fit a reference image (histogram matching with Match Color tool) or by matching the median, brightest or darkest value of the grayscale distribution for each image (linear histogram matching).
- **Match images to a target histogram.** The images can be matched to a target histogram before using segmentation steps, which is done with the Equalize function (Image > Adjustments > Equalize) in Photoshop. Generally, for biological images, this approach doesn't produce satisfactory results.

Histogram and Linear Histogram Matching

Histogram matching using a reference image was discussed in "Color Matching to a Reference Image" in Chapter 7 via the Match Color command (Image > Adjustments > Match Color) in Photoshop. This method can also be used on grayscale images after they are mode-changed to RGB Color (Image > Mode > RGB Color). The use of Match Color for equalizing images to a reference image in Photoshop has not, to the author's knowledge, been validated for this purpose through a study. Any use of this function in the segmenting process would require validation against what is known (such as a comparative study of measurements derived from manual methods for selecting features for measurement on several images versus the use of the Match Color function to aid in selecting features for measurement on the same images).

Linear histogram matching is useful when it is clear that grayscale distribution from one image to another has not changed, just the overall brightness or darkness. This is easily determined by looking at histograms. Here is how linear histogram matching is done in Photoshop:

1. Open the image to which others will be matched—the reference image.
   - **Photoshop CS versions.** Select Window > Histogram to open the Histogram palette.
   - **Pre-CS versions.** Select Image > Histogram to open the Histogram window.

● **More:** *Download "Scale Bars and Options for Input and Output" from www.peachpit.com/scientificimaging.*

2. Take a picture of the screen (see "Screen Capture Methods" in "Scale Bars and Options for Input and Output"). The picture of the screen image will contain the histogram display of the reference image (**Figure 9.12A**).
3. Crop the screen image to only the histogram. Position the screen image above or below the Histogram palette.

▶ **Warning:** *For Photoshop CS3, be sure to select the Legacy check box so the Brightness value is added or subtracted equally from all tones in the image (newer methods for determining alterations in tonal range have been introduced in CS3).*

4. Open a related image. Select Image > Adjustments > Brightness/Contrast to adjust the Brightness slider until the "live" histogram shifts along the horizontal axis to align with the reference image histogram display (**Figure 9.12B**). Depending on the image, the median, darkest or brightest values are aligned.
5. Repeat step 4 for all related images.

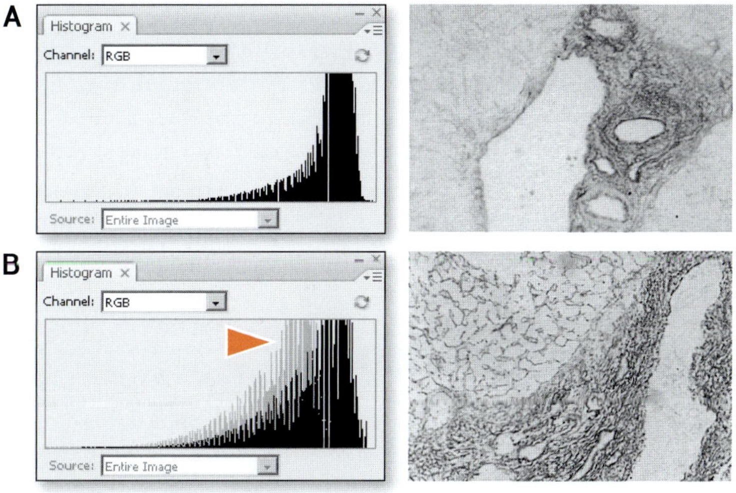

FIGURE 9.12 The reference image histogram (**A**) is used for linear histogram matching of a related image (**B**).

Creating an Action (or Script) to Automate Steps

● **More:** *The supplement "Tools and Functions in Photoshop" is a free download from www.peachpit.com/scientificimaging.*

The number of steps required to create a segmented image can be time consuming. Use the Actions palette to record the segmenting steps according to the directions in the section "Actions Palette" in "Tools and Functions in Photoshop." Some pointers follow:

- **Insert Stop (for comments).** Be as descriptive as possible when making comments via the Insert Stop command, even when creating actions for a single user. As time goes by and more images need to be segmented, reminders will be necessary. Select Insert Stop from the Actions palette menu to type in any informative comments. Be sure to select Allow Continue unless the comment is at the end of an action.

- **Open an image or not.** Decide whether or not to include a step to open images to be segmented. To avoid potential confusion when using the Batch function to apply the action to all images in a directory or when creating a droplet into which images can be dragged, the Open step should not be included (or, for that matter, neither should the Save step). However, in certain instances, such as when opening files from more than one directory (which is necessary for creating merged images of more than one channel), Open steps are helpful. Choose Insert Menu Item from the palette menu, and then choose File > Open to ensure that Photoshop does not look for a specific file: Rather, a user interactive step will be created where the user can specify which file to open.
- **Allow for user interaction.** Consider making the Threshold step interactive, as well as the High Pass and blurring steps. The slider values for each of these functions can be changed when images are inconsistent in contrast and brightness. In the Actions palette, click the Toggle Dialog on/off box next to the relevant step in the Actions palette to make it interactive.
- **Keep actions short.** Don't always attempt to make one long action: Rather, divide steps into a series of actions, especially when segmenting includes both manual and automatic selections.

● **More:** *Visit www.peachpit.com/scientificimaging to see several examples of actions and steps used to segment images.*

Manual Segmentation

When grayscale or color differences cannot be used to separate features of interest from surrounding areas, manual methods can be applied. Consider these situations before taking a particular approach:

- Especially for counts, an efficient approach would be to divide the image field into smaller fields by using a grid, and then consistently count from similar (but randomly chosen) positions on the grid.
- Especially for OD/I measurements, smaller, fixed selections can be created and then placed on pertinent areas of the image. If a consistent approach is used to determine where to place the selections, the approach will be considered repeatable and accurate.

If neither of these situations applies, selections can be created with the Lasso tool, the Magic Wand tool, or the Quick Selection tool (only in CS3) to manually separate features.

Dividing Images with Grids

Individual boxes that are created when using a grid overlay can be used as smaller fields within an image. Features that exist within these boxes can then be counted or measured for other data using segmentation steps or manual selections. The use of smaller fields—and a method for determining which fields to measure—ensures that unbiased methods are used for determining areas to measure, which is especially important when large numbers of features compose images. The following steps describe the process:

1. Select Edit (Windows) or Photoshop (Mac) > Preferences > Guides, Grids and Slices to create a grid with an arbitrary spacing between gridlines or with spacing values that correlate with calibrated units of measurement.

2. Decide on the number of grid boxes needed to cover the reference area: The correct number of individual grid boxes across the reference area depends on the frequency of sampling, which is often decided after a pilot study is done and is then analyzed statistically. It is not as important to measure within a great number of boxes that make up a grid (measurements per field) as it is to measure from a number of samples (measurements per sample).

3. Decide which box positions will be used for measurement. Moving from the top-left box and counting across and down, use a random number generator to determine the starting position, and then choose the remaining boxes by the same number. For example, if a random number generator produced the number 3, measure from the area composed of the third box, and then every third box thereafter.

   If a box does not contain parts of the specimen or compromised tissue, apply the rule about moving forward 1 box until an appropriate area is found. Just make sure this rule is consistently followed, or the approach will not be unbiased.

■ **Note:** *An action can be applied to boxes in a grid as long as a selection is drawn with the Marquee tool to include the area composed of the box.*

Creating Small, Fixed Selections

In some instances, the use of small selections for measurement within features may be deemed most efficient (and accurate) when features do not segment. This can be especially true when measuring features for OD/I: When all but masked features are measured, often too many pixels tones are included in measurements, many of which are close in tone to the baseline (background values). When using smaller areas from which to measure, parts of features are selected versus entire features, potentially leading to more accurate measurements. Fixed selections can be created as follows:

1. Choose one of the Marquee tools:, Rectangle, Ellipse, Single Row or Single Column.
2. In the options bar choose Fixed Size from the Style menu. Enter the desired Width and Height in pixels (px). Dimensions of the fixed size fits within the dimensions of measured features (5–20 pixels).
3. Click on more than one position over relevant features by holding down the Shift key while clicking. Determine the positions to measure on the feature by using a grid (**Figure 9.13**), by using similar spacing along a feature, or by using consistent landmarks in the specimen (e.g., a position adjacent to a landmark).
4. While selections are active, they can be measured in CS3 Extended or by recording values of the Pixels field in the Histogram palette (for pre-CS versions, select Image > Histogram).

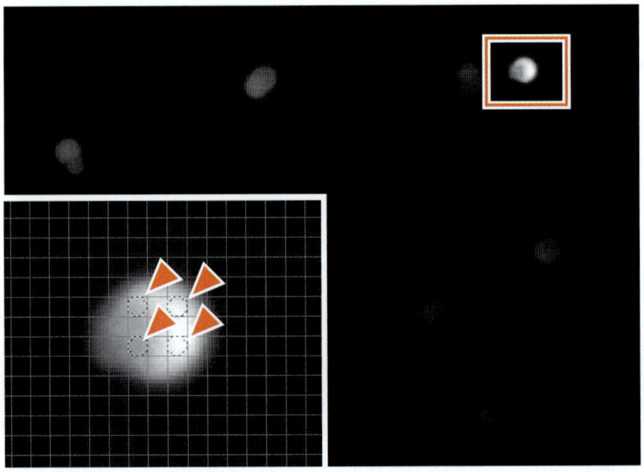

FIGURE 9.13 Grid boxes are used to determine the location of fixed selections.

Manual Selections Using the Lasso or Magic Wand Tools

Note: *To make the selection process less time consuming, use a grid overlay and only select features within chosen boxes (see "Dividing Images with Grids").*

Some images simply cannot be segmented by automated methods as described earlier in the section "Computer-Aided Measurement: Procedure for Segmenting Images." In those instances, images can be selected using various tools in Photoshop.

Note: *The Lasso tool selection method works similarly to another variation of the Lasso tool—the Polygonal Lasso tool—except that the last click does not have to connect to the first (an annoying feature of the Polygonal Lasso tool).*

Here are the tools that can be used, along with some pointers:

- **Lasso tool.** Rather than attempt to click and drag the mouse to outline the relevant feature, click in a position with the Lasso tool, and then hold down the Alt/Option key. Move incrementally around the feature, clicking along the way to create several short, straight lines.
- **Magic Wand tool.** The Magic Wand tool works by selecting contiguous areas until a border is found. The sensitivity of border detection is set by choosing a Tolerance setting in the options bar. A low setting (1–10) limits the extent of the selection; a high setting (11–50) broadens the selection to larger areas. This tool works very well when selecting white or black background areas, and then inverting the selection (Select > Inverse) to include relevant features. However, the Magic Wand tool cannot be included in an action unless the position of the click point is always the same when segmenting from more than one image.
- **Quick Selection tool (CS3).** This tool requires that a brush size be chosen from the options bar. Choose a brush size that is smaller than the widest diameter of the feature. With the brush chosen, repeatedly click or simply drag the brush along the edge of the feature. If more than the edge is chosen, ignore the additional selection and continue (**Figure 9.14**, left). Then hold down the Alt/Option key and repeatedly click or drag along the side of the feature where the extraneous selections were made to eliminate the additional selection and return the selection to the feature borders (**Figure 9.14**, right).

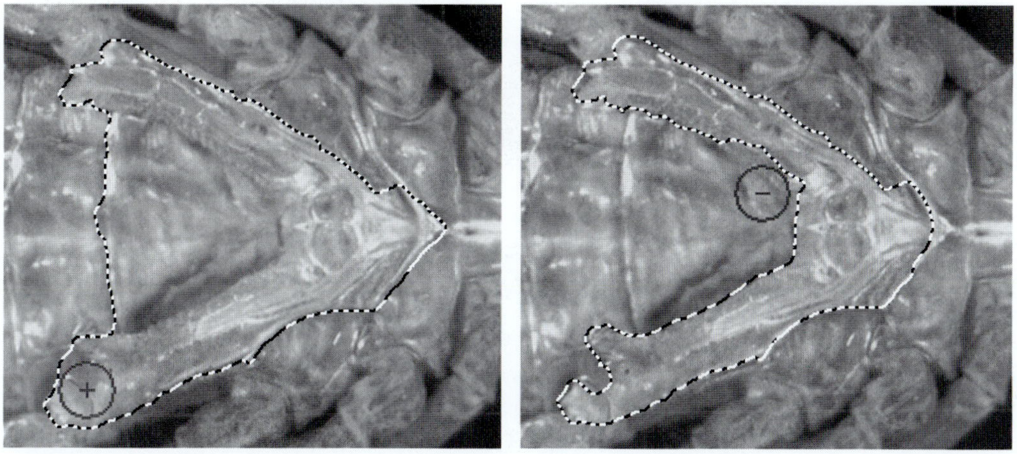

FIGURE 9.14 The Quick Selection tool is used to select a single feature (left) and is then used to eliminate an extraneous selection area (right).

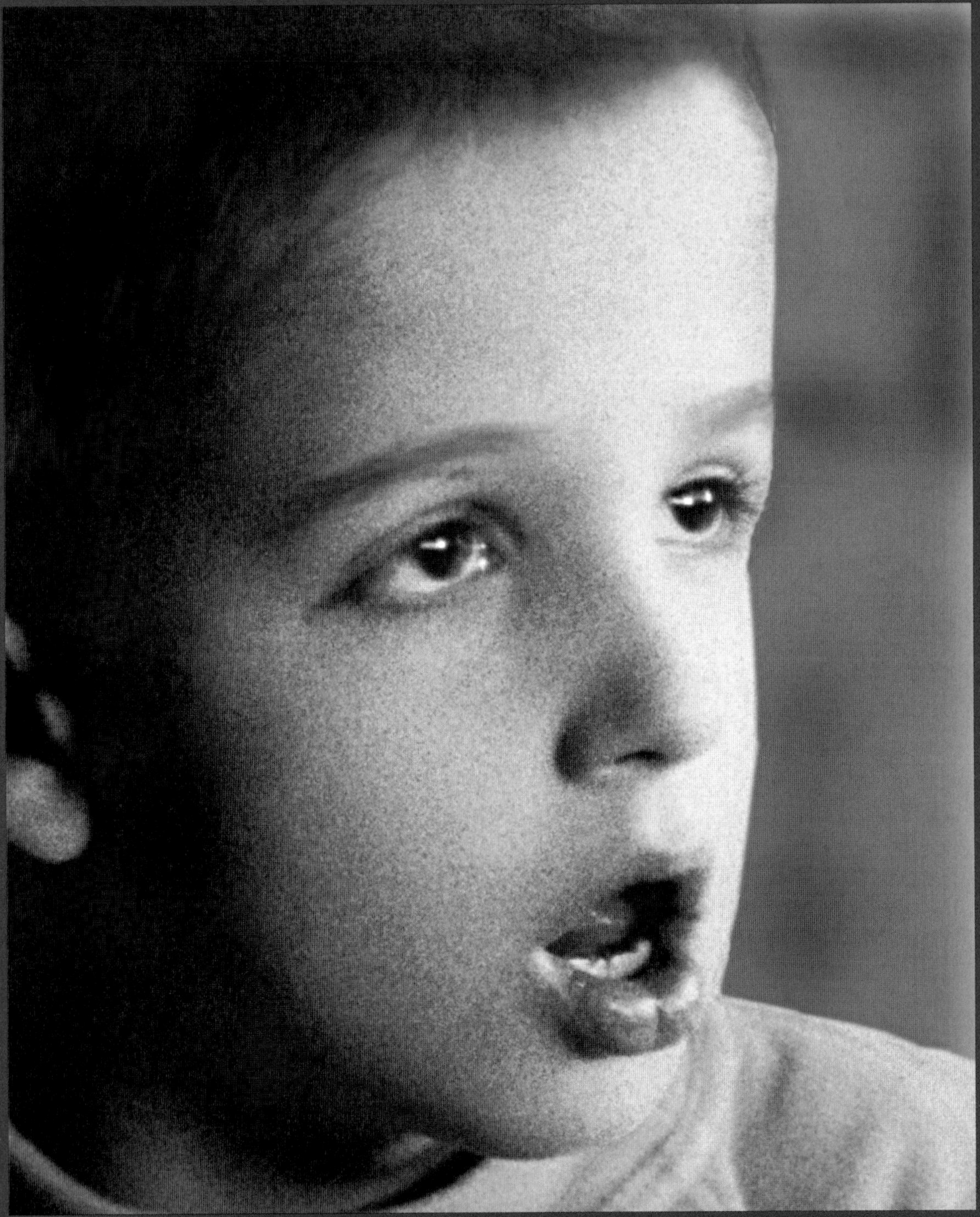

CHAPTER 10

Measuring Images

AFTER IMAGES ARE SEGMENTED, measurement is fairly straightforward, and it occurs via three modalities:

- By selecting relevant features so that each measured feature is surrounded by an animated selection
- By using the Ruler tool and associated measurements found in the Info palette (pre-CS3 Extended) and in both the Info and Measurement Log palettes (when measurements have been recorded in CS3 Extended)
- By using the Count tool (CS3 Extended only)

In pre-CS3 Extended versions of Photoshop, somewhat limited data from selected features can be found in the Histogram palette, which provides area, mean OD/I, standard deviation, and median. Measurements derived from the Ruler tool provide widths and heights, along with lengths and angles, which are all found in the Info palette.

In Photoshop CS3 Extended, however, a greater range of data points from selected areas can be measured, including circularity, length, counts, perimeter, integrated density, height, width, histogram, and several for OD/I. The same data points found in the Info palette are derived from the Ruler tool.

Unlike previous versions of Photoshop in which limited data points needed to be written down and then entered into a data analysis and graphing program, now up to 700 features can be analyzed for data points. These are stored in the Measurement Log palette. The data

Image of 6-year-old child watching TV from a 12-minute series of images, taken on black and white film (Kodak Tri-X 400) and then digitized (Nikon Coolscan LS-2000). Image was modified in Photoshop 7.0 (Adobe Systems Incorporated, San Jose, CA) by darkening edges of the photo, blurring the background, and optimizing the brightness and contrast for publication.

points can be exported to tab delimited text or comma separated values (CSV) files. The files can be opened in a data analysis or spreadsheet program, such as MatLab and Excel.

Thus, Photoshop CS3 Extended has now become a powerful tool for nearly all imaging requirements: Not only can correction and conformance steps be applied to images, but images can also be segmented and analyzed for data crucial to researchers.

Measuring Selected Features

Before any measurements can be made in Photoshop CS3 Extended, the features must be set apart by making a selection. After completing the steps presented in Chapter 9, "Separating Relevant Features from the Background," the result will be one of two possibilities:

- A binarized image or layer
- Selected features manually outlined with the Lasso, Magic Wand, or Quick Selection tools, or with the Color Range function

When the image or layer has been binarized, a selection of the white or black features can be made:

1. Choose Select > Color Range.
2. In the Color Range dialog box, choose Highlights (for white features) or Shadows (for black features) from the Select menu.

After the features are selected, measurements can be made.

Measuring in Photoshop CS3 Extended from Selected Features

● **More:** *Download the bonus chapter "Scale Bars and Options for Input and Output" from www.peachpit.com/scientificimaging.*

■ **Note:** *When no scle is shown, the default is 1 pixel = 1 pixel, which is often referred to in publications as arbitrary units (a.u.).*

Choices for measurement are found in the Analysis menu. These include tools described in the bonus chapter "Scale Bars and Options for Input and Output," such as setting the measurement scale and placing the scale marker. Options are also available for selecting data points (selecting the kind of measurements desired and image attributes) and for recording the data points. Ruler and Count tool menu entries activate the respective tool (in the toolbox) when chosen.

SELECTING DATA POINTS

The kinds of measurements available in Photoshop CS3 Extended include those most commonly reported in scientific literature. For each data point entry, a column of data is produced in the Measurement Log palette, which can then be exported into tab-delimited text or a CSV document. These columns of data can then be opened in a spreadsheet or database program. Data point entries can be selected by choosing Analysis > Select Data Points > Custom.

Each measurement entry in the Select Data Points dialog box is described in the following list.

Options in the Common (image and measurement attributes) area include:

■ **Note:** *Choosing Label does not mean that features will be labeled on the image.*

- **Label.** Selecting this option results in a column of numeric references to features, starting with 1. The number of the feature is determined by its spatial location in the image, starting with the 0 *x* and 0 *y* position (top left) and moving across and down to the bottom right.
- **Date and Time.** This column shows the date and time at which measurements are made.
- **Document.** The name of the image appears in each row of a column.
- **Source.** This option indicates whether the measurements were derived from a selected area of the image or by using the Ruler or Count tools.
- **Scale.** This option uses the entry made in saved presets for the Set Measurement Scale tool (Analysis > Set Measurement Scale). In other words, if you created a scale bar, and then saved and named the scale bar as a "preset," the name you gave the preset appears as an entry. If the name you used was "20 microns = 400 pixels," its name would be informative and useful as a saved data point.
- **Scale Units.** This column uses the unit of measurement indicated when using the Set Measurement Scale tool.
- **Scale Factor.** The entry for Scale Factor indicates how many pixels make up a single unit of measurement (e.g., if 20 microns = 400 pixels, then 1 micron = 5 pixels or 5 pixels/micron: scale factor of 5).

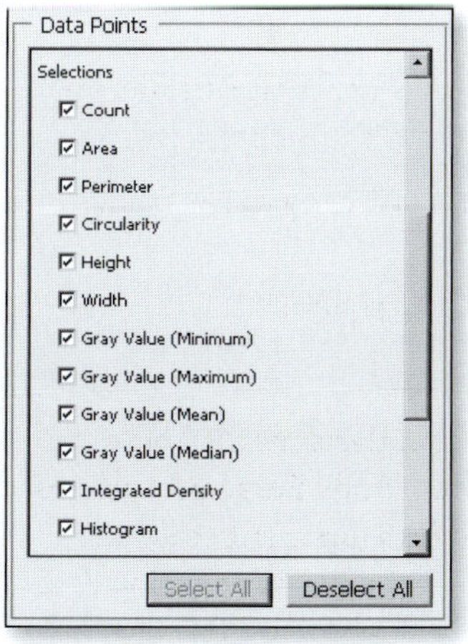

FIGURE 10.1 Selection data points.

Options in the Selections area (**Figure 10.1**) include:

- **Count.** The number of selected features; if a Count tool is used, the number of counted items on the image. If a Ruler tool is used, the count is the number of ruler lines visible (1 or 2).
- **Area.** The area in pixels of each selected feature. This is reported as pixels squared. If the measurement has been calibrated, the area is determined by multiplying pixels by the scale factor and is reported as the unit of measurement squared (e.g., square microns).

- **Perimeter.** The perimeter of the selection.
- **Circularity.** This is a ratio that describes the compactness of a shape. It is equal to 4π X area/perimeter^2. A perfect circle has a numeric value of 1. As circles become increasingly elongated, values approach 0.
- **Height and Width.** These measurements use the horizontal (x) and vertical (y) axes for values. Height is determined by a max y – min y formula: Width by max x – min x. Neither yields a length unless the longest axis of the feature is oriented along the x or y axis.

▶ **Warning:** *For RGB Color images, the gray values are derived from a default grayscale image. In other words, if the image was changed to grayscale using a mode change, the resultant gray values are used for calculations. Because the green channel predominates when converting to the grayscale mode, gray value readings may be flawed.*

- **Gray Values.** Minimum, Maximum, Mean, and Median gray values can be chosen. The measurements are taken from areas within selections. Each value is a measurement of optical densities or intensities in units of measurement determined by the bit depth: 8-bit numeric values range from 0–255 and 16-bit from 0–32,768 (*not* the expected 16-bit range of 0–65,535).
- **Integrated Density.** The sum of the gray values for each pixel within a selection. When selections of features vary in area, the resulting measurement would yield measurements that provide information about both area and optical intensity and density. When areas are kept at a consistent dimension—such as when fixed selections are used on features—optical density or intensity information is measured without the additive introduction of "area" data points.
- **Histogram.** Records the number of pixels at each gray value from 0–255 (on the 8-bit scale only: 16-bit images are converted to 8-bit). Histogram data is saved in the CSV format in the same location as the measurement log file when exported. For multiple selections, one histogram is generated for the total selected areas, and additional histogram files for each selected area.

MAKING AND EXPORTING MEASUREMENTS

To measure features after selections have been made, follow these steps:

1. Select Analyze > Record Measurements, or press Shift+Ctrl/Command+M to record the measurements.

   Measurements appear in the Measurement Log palette (**Figure 10.2**). The first line of measurement is the summary. It includes a count of all the features. Other rows of data are measurements from discrete features, starting with the feature closest to the topmost and leftmost position.

2. In the Measurement Log, click the Export icon to create a tab-delimited file and a CSV file (if you have selected Histogram as a data point).

   To delete your measurements, click the Select All icon, and then click the trash icon.

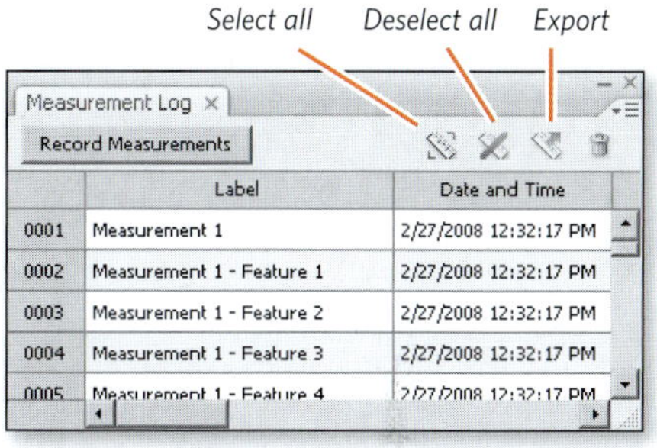

FIGURE 10.2 Measurement Log palette.

TRANSFER SELECTIONS TO RELATED IMAGES

It is possible to apply the same selection to several similar images. Here are the steps:

1. Save the selection (Select > Save Selection) from the original image. In the Save Selection dialog box, you can simply click OK and a generic name will be given to the saved selection or you can name the selection.
2. In the image to which the saved selection is transferred, load the selection (Select > Load Selection). In the Load Selection dialog box, if necessary, choose the saved selection from the Channel menu.

When transferring selections, the following applies:

- Selections cannot be transferred to a another image unless the image dimensions and pixel resolutions are identical.
- A saved selection is stored as an alpha channel. The file containing the additional alpha channel may not open in other software programs.
- To preserve the selection when opting to delete the alpha channel from the original image, save a duplicate image with the alpha channel to preserve the selection.

OPTICAL DENSITY/INTENSITY MEASUREMENTS (OD/I)

As mentioned in Chapter 9, OD/I measurements can be accomplished either by making a selection over entire features or by using multiple fixed selections with an unbiased approach. From the selected features, you can obtain any of the Gray Value measurements in the Measurement Log, or integrated densities.

When measuring OD/I, it is important to think about human visual perception versus automated measurements taken by computer. It is easy to perceive that one feature is brighter or darker than another, but far more difficult to average values together with midtones that are frequently present in measured features (what a computer does). Thus, it is useful to create profiles across features to determine a baseline (where the background begins). That baseline should be above the background and noise levels, and can be set at a high gray level to include only the brightest or darkest values. The measurements then become averaged maximum values and will more closely match what the eye perceives.

Here is a method for creating a line profile in Photoshop CS3 Extended:

1. Choose Analysis > Set Data Points > Custom to select the type of data points you want to measure. If desired, select only Selections: Gray Value (Mean) to eliminate excess data.
2. Choose the Pencil tool (it may be hidden behind the Brush tool). In the options bar, click the Brush Preset Picker and set Hardness to 100% at a pixel diameter of 1.
3. In the Brushes palette (Window > Brushes), click Brush Tip Shape and set Spacing to an amount at which dots first become visible (179%). Make sure Shape Dynamics is turned off. This amount should create dots that are spaced every two pixels.
4. Choose Layer > New > Layer. Click OK to accept the defaults in the New Layer dialog box.
5. Hold down the Shift key and draw across a single, representative feature. It will only be possible to draw along the *x* or *y* axis (**Figure 10.3**, left).
6. Create a selection around the dotted line by holding down the Ctrl/Command key and clicking the layer thumbnail in the Layers palette. Click the eye icon on the dotted line layer to turn it off so you don't take measurements from this layer.
7. Select Analysis > Record Measurements to record the measurements. Export the measurements to a graphing or spreadsheet program.

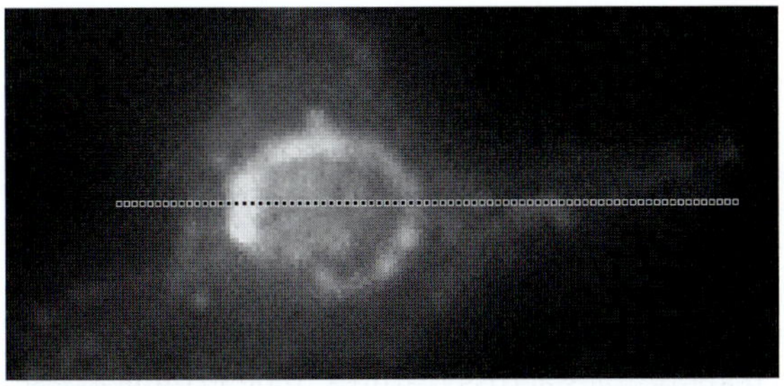

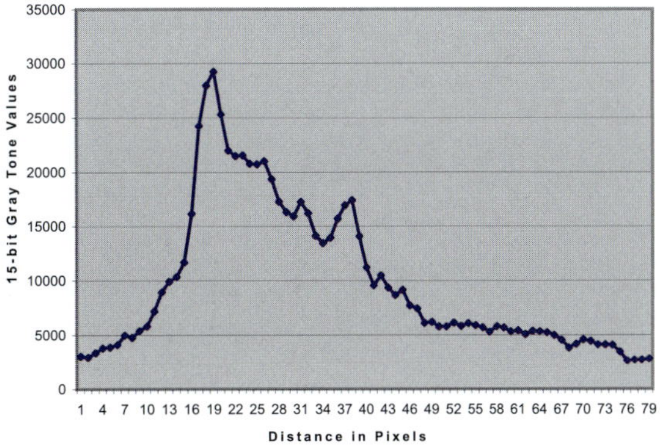

FIGURE 10.3 An image with a dotted line drawn across the features (left) and mean gray level measurements taken at each dot (right).

■ **Note:** *A line plot along the extent of a feature can also be made in a scientific quantification program.*

8. In a graphing program, create a line plot from the Mean Gray Value column (**Figure 10.3**, right). From that plot, you can determine the baseline gray level.

▶ **Warning:** *If measurements are made from specimens that are backlit (light passes through the specimen), the scattering of light is subject to the Beers-Lambert law—light travels logarithmically through a medium based on the density of interfering objects. Thus, all numbers are multiplied by* $\log_{10}$ *and are often multiplied as well by a scaling factor of 100 or 250 for 8-bit images and 1000 for 16-bit images. Gray values from graphs can be found by back calculating.*

MEASURING WITH THE RULER AND COUNT TOOLS

The Ruler tool provides the following data points:

- **Length.** This is the length in the chosen unit of measurement from one end of the Line tool to the other.
- **Angle.** The angle is the orientation of the ruler line in polar coordinates, 0 to ±180 degrees.

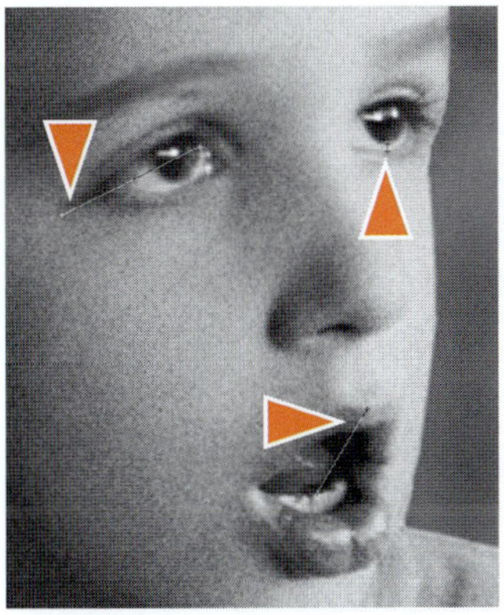

FIGURE 10.4 The Ruler tool is used to measure the lack of jaw and eye movement of a child watching TV over a period of 12 minutes.

The Count tool provides a total (summary) count when you make click points on the image as well as marked positions on the image. A screen shot is necessary to save the counting marks with the image (see "Screen Capture Methods" in the downloadable chapter, "Scale Bars and Options for Input and Output"): The marks cannot be included with the image and saved to a file.

The use of either the Ruler or Count tool involves manual intervention versus automated measurement, thus making these tools less efficient for large numbers of images. However, with a small number of images and a small number of features to count, these tools are useful. They can certainly provide immediate data points for cursory evaluations, and when lengths and angles are needed, the Ruler tool is essential (**Figure 10.4**).

Taking Measurements in Legacy Versions of Photoshop

When measuring in legacy versions of Photoshop, data points can be taken from the Histogram palette (Photoshop CS and later) or in the Histogram dialog box (in pre-CS versions select Image > Histogram) and the Info palette.

● **More:** *Registering this book at www.peachpit.com/scientificimaging allows you to download the free supplement, "Tools and Functions in Photoshop," where you can read more about the Histogram palette.*

For versions of Photoshop in which the Ruler tool is included, the angle and length are displayed in the Info palette, and these measurements can be written down or recorded to a database/spreadsheet program. The histogram measurements that include Mean, Standard Deviation, Median, and Pixels (area) values can also be recorded manually.

▶ **Warning:** *Measurements in the histogram can be inaccurate, depending on whether a low-resolution cache is used or a zoom of less than 100%. Be sure to test measurements at various zoom levels against a known area of a feature.*

Measuring Colocalization/Coexistence in Photoshop

Several methods are available for determining colocalization/coexistence in various software programs. These programs likely include more refined methods for measuring the pixel overlap of the same feature in two or more images.

However, if a feature is labeled positively with a dye—determined by its brightness or darkness relative to the background—it can be considered 100 percent labeled and 100 percent positive. Colocalization/coexistence measurements can then be done in Photoshop.

In that situation, only the background level needs to be determined for all images (see "Differentiating the Edges of Features from the Background" in Chapter 9). Then all gray or color values above the background can be clipped, or saturated, to 100 percent of a desired color through binarizing with the Threshold slider. The images can be compared, and then the overlapping, binarized features can be measured.

Here are the steps for determining overlap using the colors red (for one image) and green (for the other), which when combined create the color yellow:

1. Open one of two images, the image that you will colorize green (**Figure 10.5A**). Find edges or use other methods to segment the image and then threshold. All features of interest will be binarized to white or black.

2. Choose Select > Color Range to select the white or black features, depending on their binarized color.
3. Select Layer > New > Layer. In the New Layer dialog box, click OK.
4. Click the Foreground Color box in the toolbox and choose green (if the image is grayscale, change it to the RGB Color mode first).
5. Select Edit > Fill and choose Foreground Color from the Use menu. The selected areas are filled with green (**Figure 10.5B**).
6. While the selection is active, measure the area of the green-colored features by selecting Analysis > Record Measurements.

   In legacy versions of Photoshop, write down the Pixels value from the Histogram palette (or dialog box).
7. Open the second image, the one that you will colorize red. Repeat steps 1–6, but this time fill the selection in steps 4 and 5 with red instead of green (**Figure 10.5C**).
8. Overlay the red-colorized layer of the red image on the green image by first deselecting the active selections (Select > Deselect). With the Shift key held down use the Move tool and drag the red-colorized image onto the green-colorized image.
9. Select Screen for the layer blending mode from the Blend Mode menu in the Layers palette. This mode will blend an equal amount of each color (**Figure 10.5D**).
10. Choose Select > Color Range and click on a yellow area with the leftmost eyedropper tool to select only the yellow areas.
11. Measure the entire yellow area to determine the extent of colocalization/coexistence by selecting Analysis > Record Measurements.

    In legacy versions of Photoshop, write down the Pixels value in the Histogram palette (or dialog box).

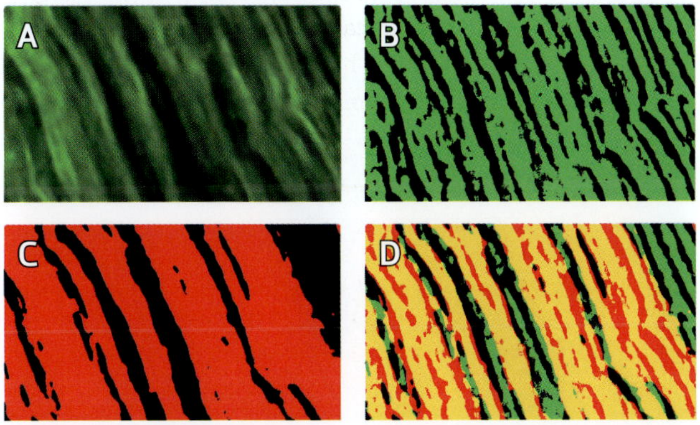

FIGURE 10.5 Panels showing the steps taken when measuring colocalization/coexistence.

The level of colocalization becomes a percentage of either the red- or green-colorized image. Red and green are not the only colors that can be used to determine colocalization of more than two colors: When colors are blended, a discrete third color is created. The third color is then selected in Color Range to measure colocalization/coexistence.

Using a Database/Spreadsheet Program to Distinguish Features

When features cannot be adequately separated by shape or size after binarization, separation can be accomplished in a database or spreadsheet program. To separate features by shape, the data points for circularity can be used. Features can be eliminated when they are elongated—such as when fibers or dust are included with selected features—or eliminated when they are more circular, such as when nonfibrous particles are included with selected features. To separate features by size, features that are smaller or larger than the selected features can be excluded.

Area	Circularity	Fiber Check	Useable
95149	0.037	TRUE	
5934	0.202	TRUE	
4154	0.203	TRUE	
1337036	0.022	FALSE	9115.01
4113578	0.04	FALSE	7648.21
2647170	0.018	FALSE	6895.22
900259	0.022	FALSE	5104.69

FIGURE 10.6 Excel columns showing data included depending on false or true conditions.

Data can be sorted in database programs, and features outside a specific cutoff value can be manually excluded. Or, to automate the procedure, logical IF statements can be included and data can be sorted by whether the data is below or above certain cutoff values (true) or whether data lies within the desired range of values (false). When data points are true, a second IF statement can be used so that data ranked as false is placed in another column to be included in the final measurements (**Figure 10.6**).

Finally, statistical tests can be made, outliers determined (if necessary), and standard deviations found, among other possible measurements. When database and spreadsheet programs are combined with measurements in Photoshop, the final destination for an image—quantification—is accomplished.

Bibliography

Blatner, D., C. Chavez, and B. Fraser. 2008. *Real World Adobe Photoshop CS3,* Berkeley, CA: Peachpit Press.

Fraser, B., C. Murphy, and F. Bunting. 2005. *Real World Color Management,* 2nd Edition. Berkeley, CA: Peachpit Press.

Fraser, B., and J. Schewe. 2008. *Real World Camera Raw with Adobe Photoshop CS3.* Berkeley, CA: Peachpit Press.

Grube, E., U. Gerckens, A. C. Yeung, S. Rowold, N. Kirchhof, J. Sedgewick, J. S. Yadav, and S. Stertzer. 2001. Prevention of distal embolization during coronary angioplasty in saphenous vein grafts and native vessels using porous filter protection. *Circulation* 104(20): 2436-41.

Haase, A. T., K. Henry, M. Zupancic , G. Sedgewick, R. A. Faust, H. Melroe, W. Cavert, K. Gebhard, K. Staskus, Z-Q. Zhang, P. J. Dailey, H. H. Balfour, Jr., A. Erice, and A. S. Perelson. 1996. Quantitative Image Analysis of HIV-1 Infection in Lymphoid Tissue. *Science* 274: 885-1048.

Kelby S., 2008. *The Adobe Photoshop CS3 Book for Digital Photographers.* Berekely, CA: New Riders.

Leong, F. J. W-M., M. Brady, and J. O'D. McGee. 2003. Correction of uneven illumination (vignetting) in digital microscopy images. *Journal of Clinical Pathology* 56(8): 619-621.

Margulis, D., 2007. *Professional Photoshop: The Classic Guide to Color Correction,* 5th Edition. Berkeley, CA: Peachpit Press.

McNamara, G. 2005. Color Balancing Histology Images for Presentations and Publication. *The Journal of Histotechnology* 28(2).

Mouton, P. 2002. *Principles and Practices of Unbiased Stereology: An Introduction for Bioscientists.* Baltimore: Johns Hopkins University Press.

Reilly C., S. Wietgrefe, G. Sedgewick, and A. Haase. 2007. Determination of simian immunodeficiency virus production by infected activated and resting cells. *AIDS* 21(2):163-8.

Rudney, J. D., R. Chen, and G. J. Sedgewick. 2001. Intracellular *Actinobacillus actinomycetemcomitans* and *Porphyromonas gingivalis* in buccal epithelial cells collected from human subjects. *Infect Immun*. 69(4): 2700-2707.

Sedgewick, J. 2008. Considerations When Altering Digital Images. In *Current Protocols Essential Laboratory Techniques,* ed. Sean Gallagher and Emily A. Wiley. New York: Wiley Publishing.

Sedgewick, J. 1997. Cover image, *Science* Vol. 276.

Sedgewick, J. 2003. Photoshop Tutorials: Selecting ROIs from Brightfield Images. *Microscopy Today*. 11(2): 16–20.

Sedgewick, J. (In publication) Post-Processing Confocal Images. In *Confocal Microscopy: Methods and Protocols,* 2nd Edition, ed. Stephen Paddock. Totowa, NJ: Humana Press.

Sedgewick, J. 2002. Resolution Confusion. *Microscopy Today* 9: 18.

Sedgewick, J. 2003. Segmentation Before Quantization By Using Photoshop: Darkfield Images. *Microscopy Today* 11(1): 18–22.

Sedgewick, J. 2003. Use Adobe Acrobat to Keep Original Resolutions and to Make TIFF Files From Any Program. *Microscopy Today*. 10: 16 -18.

Sedgewick, J., and M. Ericson. (unpublished) Using Strobe as Light Source for Scientific Illumination.

Sedgewick, J. 2002. *Quick Photoshop for Research: A Guide to Digital Imaging for Photoshop 4x, 5x, 6x, & 7x.* Kluwer Academic/Plenum Publishers.

Sedgewick, G., Z-Q. Zhang, and N. Pham. 1996. Cover Image, *Science* 274.

Wild, R., S. Ramakrishnan, J. Sedgewick, and A. W. Griffioen. 2000. Quantitative assessment of angiogenesis and tumor vessel architecture by computer-assisted digital image analysis: effects of VEGF-toxin conjugate on tumor microvessel density. *Microvascular Research* 59(3): 368–76.

Yokoyama, Y., G. Sedgewick, and S. Ramakrishnan. 2007. Endostatin binding to ovarian cancer cells inhibits peritoneal attachment and dissemination. *Cancer Research* 67(22): 10813–10822.

Zhang, Z-Q., D. W. Notermans, G. Sedgewick, W. Cavert, S. Wietgrefe, M. Zupancic, K. Gebhard, K. Henry, L. Boies, Z. Chen, M. Jenkins, R. Mills, H. McDade, C. Goodwin, C. M. Schuwirth, S. A. Danner , and A. T. Haase. 1997. Kinetics of CD4+ T Cell Repopulation of Lymphoid Tissues After Treatment of HIV-1 Infection. *Proceedings of the National Academy of Sciences USA* 95(3): 1154-1159.

Web references: See the book's companion Web site at www.peachpit.com/scientificimaging and the author's Web site at www.quickphotoshop.com.

Index

Numbers

A

B

C

D

E

F

I

J

K

L

M

Q

R

S

T

Peachpit

Essential books for the creative community

Visit Peachpit on the Web at www.peachpit.com

- Read the latest articles and download timesaving tipsheets from best-selling authors such as Scott Kelby, Robin Williams, Lynda Weinman, Ted Landau, and more!

- Join the Peachpit Club and save 25% off all your online purchases at peachpit.com every time you shop—plus enjoy free UPS ground shipping within the United States.

- Search through our entire collection of new and upcoming titles by author, ISBN, title, or topic. There's no easier way to find just the book you need.

- Sign up for newsletters offering special Peachpit savings and new book announcements so you're always the first to know about our newest books and killer deals.

- Did you know that Peachpit also publishes books by Apple, New Riders, Adobe Press, Macromedia Press, palmOne Press, and TechTV press? Swing by the Peachpit family section of the site and learn about all our partners and series.

- Got a great idea for a book? Check out our About section to find out how to submit a proposal. You could write our next best-seller!

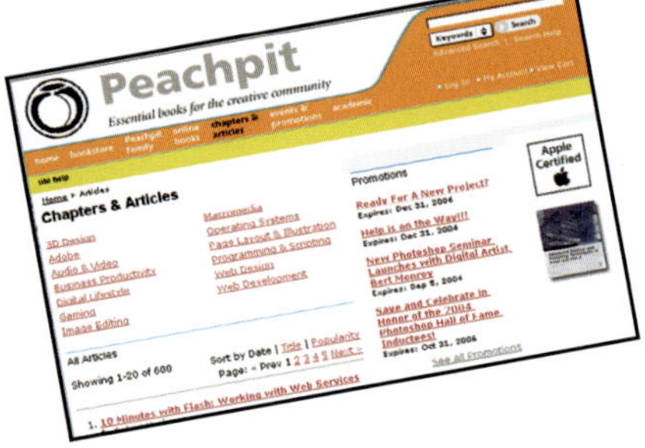

You'll find all this and more at www.peachpit.com. Stop by and take a look today!